Inside Toronto

Inside Toronto

~ Urban Interiors 1880s to 1920s ~

Sally Gibson

Cormorant Books

The publisher gratefully acknowledges the support of the Canada Council for the Arts
and the Ontario Arts Council for its publishing program. We acknowledge the
financial support of the Government of Canada through the Book Publishing
Industry Development Program (BPIDP) for our publishing activities.

Printed and bound in Canada

LIBRARY AND ARCHIVES CANADA CATALOGUING IN PUBLICATION

Gibson, Sarah Duane Satterthwaite, 1946–
Inside Toronto: urban interiors, 1880s to 1920s/Sarah Duane Gibson.

Includes bibliographical references and index.
ISBN 1-896951-95-3
ISBN-13 978-1-896951-95-9

1. Interior decoration — Ontario — Toronto — History — 19th century — Pictorial works.
2. Interior decoration — Ontario — Toronto — History — 20th century — Pictorial works.
3. Toronto (Ont.) — Buildings, structures, etc.—Pictorial works.
4. Toronto (Ont.) — Social conditions. I. Title.

FC3097.37.G42 2006   971.3'54103   C2005-906943-0

Cover design: Angel Guerra/Archetype
Text design: Tannice Goddard/Soul Oasis Networking
Printer: Friesens

CORMORANT BOOKS INC.
215 SPADINA AVENUE, STUDIO 230, TORONTO, ON CANADA M5T 2C7
www.cormorantbooks.com

PERMISSIONS

Grateful acknowledgement is made for permission to reprint from material under copyright
and for permission to use materials held in public and private archives from the following:

City of Toronto Archives

The Law Society of Upper Canada

Dr. Lillian Petroff

Russell Phillips

Sears Canada Inc.

TD Bank Archives

The Women's Art Association of Canada

From Front Street to Queen's Park: The Story of Ontario's Parliament Buildings
by Eric Arthur © 1979, published by McClelland & Stewart Ltd.
Used with permission of the publisher.

The Blind Assassin by Margaret Atwood © 2002, published by McClelland & Stewart Ltd.
Used with permission of the publisher.

Doyle, Lucy. "He Has Served Eleven Governors" In *The Toronto Star Weekly*,
Saturday January 30, 1932. Used with permission of the publisher.

Gompers, Samuel. In *Canada Investigates Industrialism*. Ed. Greg Kealey.
Toronto: University of Toronto Press, 1973. Reprinted with permission.

Roger Hall. *A Century to Celebrate/Un Centenaire à fêter 1893–1992:
The Ontario Legislative Building/L'Édifice de l'Assemblée législative de l'Ontario.*
(Toronto: Dundurn Press, 1993). Published with permission of Dundurn Press.

Mertins, Detlef. "Mountain of Light" In Bureau of Architecture and Urbanism (BAU) in
Toronto Modern: The Exhibition Revisited. Toronto: Coach House Books with Association
for Preservation Technology International, 2002. Used with permission of the author.

Piva, Michael J. *The Condition of the Working Class in Toronto 1900–1921.* Ottawa:
University of Ottawa Press, 1979. Reprinted by permission of the University of Ottawa Press.

Sotiron, Minko. "Robertson, John Ross." *Dictionary of Canadian Biography, Vol. XIV
1911–1920.* Toronto: University of Toronto Press, 1998. Reprinted with permission.

While every effort has been made to contact the rights holders of material reprinted in this
book, if inadvertently material has been used without permission, please contact the publisher.
Permission will be sought and acknowledgement thereof will be printed in future editions.

To my daughters

Meg and Katie

Contents

I

A Little Bit of Light Magic

Photography ... is the sworn witness of everything presented to her view ...

What are her studies ... but facts which are neither the province of art nor description,

but of that *new form of communication* between man and man — neither letter, message,

nor picture — which now happily fills up the space between them?

LADY ELIZABETH EASTLAKE, *PHOTOGRAPHY*, 1857[1]

Photographs contain miniature worlds. They capture ... enrapture ... reveal ... and sometimes conceal what comes to be regarded as "the truth" or "the way it was." Photography, as Lady Eastlake suggests, was, indeed, a new form of communication, and one that had a profound impact on not only the Victorian world, but every era since. Suddenly — or so it seemed — permanent pictures of the natural and built environments could be drawn by sunlight and fixed forever.

Photographs as Historical Records

Transfixed by the magic realism of the new medium — in which there was more detail than the hand could produce or the unaided eye detect — early observers, and their descendants, forgot, ignored, or were unaware of just how much a human construction all photographs are, whether created in 1839 or now. Although recorded by a mechanical device — with its own limitations, requirements, and tendencies — every photograph is the product of human intention. It is influenced by the who, what, where, when, and why of its creation ... as well as its reception.[2] When using photographs as primary sources, as this book does, all these factors must be noted down (wherever possible) and considered. For this reason, the photographs in this book are as carefully identified as knowledge about their creation and use will allow. Each photograph is regarded, at best, as "one way it was," not as a singular or unalterable "truth." And very often, other non-photographic materials

have been investigated to enhance understanding of the miniature worlds contained in the photographs.

For all their distinctiveness, photographs are records like any other. As Lady Eastlake hinted, they can tell us much that cannot be communicated in any other way, just as letters and videos and maps each have their virtues and their limitations. Photographs offer immensely detailed and valuable records of what once appeared before the camera. But they also reflect the people who took them, who posed for them, who purchased them, and who received them. Like other primary sources of information, photographs must be subjected to intense scrutiny. What bias might the photographer — like the cartographer or diary-writer or film-maker — bring to the subject? What personal interest might the photographer, or the subject, or the publisher of the photograph, have in the dissemination of the picture? What was going on while the photograph was being taken? Was something excluded from the record? Was the photograph created to celebrate the sitter or a client institution? Was the photographer trying to produce a commercial product that would sell? And so on. Such questions are important and a healthy scepticism is often required to assess just what might be learned from the object in hand.[5]

Interior Life of a City

Interior photographs are relatively rare, always informative, and often evocative — drawing the viewer further and further into their private and

1.1: *Emily Brown, 1902*
In the absence of diaries, letters or other documentary evidence, reading this photograph depends almost entirely on the contents of the picture, its relationship to other photographs collected by sculptor Merle Foster and presented to the City of Toronto Archives, and a few scraps of information gleaned from such sources as City Directories and Assessment Rolls.[3]

In 1902, when this snapshot was taken, Merle Foster's grandparents, the William Brown family, lived at 1050 Bloor Street West, near Dufferin Street. Here, Merle's aunt, Emily Brown, sits casually by the window, in a thoughtful, even languid, dreamy pose. No flash or artificial light has been used to capture the chiaroscuroed figure. Whether she is holding music (as she was in another photograph), a sketch pad, or something to read is unclear. But she conveys an artistic more than a conventional respectability. The photograph is obviously an amateur snapshot rather than a professional portrait, and was perhaps taken by Ms Brown's sister, Merle Foster's mother, who is seen with her sister in other family snaps, sitting on the front steps of 1050 or riding bicycles along Park Road near Rosedale.

The atmosphere is intimate, casual, and very Victorian, although the date is actually a year after Queen Victoria's death. Ms Brown is surrounded by the accoutrements of a modest, middle-class parlour — upright piano, uncomfortable Victorian ladies chair, potted Kentia palm[4], gold-framed Prince Albertine gentleman, subdued floral wallpaper, and cluttered corner-cabinet decorated with odd knick-knacks. The unusual, if amateurish, hand-tinting reveals that the auburn-haired Ms Brown was wearing a blue, lace-trimmed gown, and suggests that this small, 3.5 by 4.5 inch snapshot was an especially precious family object. The cracks in the picture — one through the central portrait and one along the right-hand edge — support this view. Rather than being thrown out, the damaged picture was kept, and perhaps cherished.
CITY OF TORONTO ARCHIVES: Fonds 1185, Item 29

sometimes mysterious depths. The reasons for their rarity are many — technological, social, and commercial. From a technical perspective, interior photography had to await the developments of more sensitive photographic plates, faster films and shutters, smaller cameras, and the invention of flash photography. From a social perspective, interior photography depended on such factors as the access the photographer had to private realms, whether homes or jails or corner offices. Commercially, professionals photographed what the clients would pay for — studio portraits, business-related scenes, or mass-produced postcards — and left the rest undocumented or to the amateur.

Most books about cities use photographs and other graphic materials as afterthoughts to illustrate the text and perhaps amuse potential readers. Even when photographs — vintage or modern — are integral parts of the book-creating process, most of the images are exterior views that illustrate the city's public face. This, of course, distorts our understanding of Toronto or any other city. For the reasons just mentioned, less than 10% of surviving photographs from the era under study were interiors, and generally only 10 to 15% of those published portray the spaces and places inside buildings where most urban life then, as now, actually took place. It is a measure of Toronto's maturity as an historical subject that the time is ripe to focus on the *interior* parts of the city.

1.3: Consumers' Gas: *An Illuminating Client*, 1913
F. W. Micklethwaite was hired by Consumers' Gas to photograph the
company's products and operations. Here, Micklethwaite looks inside the
gaslit Columbia phonograph plant, where stacks of 78s stand ready to be
hand-stuffed into brown-paper record jackets; flammable containers lie
higgledy-piggledy around the room; and Watson's Confection is perched
atop a pile of records. Obviously, Consumers' Gas was more interested in
its own bright illumination than the record company's cleanliness or
efficiency. For modern viewers, both the lighting — which appears very
uneven and inadequate to a modern eye — and the contents of the usually
off-limits factory are fascinating. Micklethwaite's view camera appears to
have captured ghostly activity during its long time-exposure, but nothing
more was required: photographing workers was not part of his contract.
CITY OF TORONTO ARCHIVES: Fonds 1034, Item 908

Thanks to such pioneering books as Eric Arthur's *No Mean
City* and William Dendy's *Lost Toronto*, we know what many
of Toronto's grander buildings looked like on the outside.
Now we have the intellectual luxury of concentrating on
what they looked like and how they functioned on the inside,
where most people spend much of their lives. This is the
first book to use vintage and contemporary photographs
to investigate the wide-ranging interior life of a single city,
Toronto, which happens to be my chosen home.

Social Spectrum

Most heavily illustrated books about cities concentrate on grandly built
environments, and on the lives of the rich and famous — the movers and shakers,
rather than the moved and shaken. The reasons for this are many and are
explored later. Occasionally, books about the poor and the disenfranchised
have appeared, for example Robert Harney and Harold Troper's exceptional
Immigrants: A Portrait of the Urban Experience, 1890–1930, as it was played
out in Toronto. But the heavily illustrated books seldom tried to cover the social
spectrum, or spectra, not only for the high and mighty, but also the middle and
the lowly. Thanks to luck and good planning, Toronto has a rich photographic
heritage that embraces the working and non-working poor, as well as the
middle- and the upper-class working and non-working wealthy. This book
draws on that heritage, especially the resources of the City of Toronto Archives,
and hopes to encourage others to do the same. There are serious gaps in the
record, but perhaps these will begin to be filled in or at least bridged over.

1.4: *Strachan Avenue Storm Sewer*, Sept. 18, 1913
City photographer Arthur Goss documented the dramatic linking of two tunnels, and some of the men who did the digging. Goss could have photographed the tunnels and the tools alone, but he chose to include three men in their underground site. By candlelight and flashlight, Goss captured the event, showing the men and the almost impossible task these men faced: carving a tunnel out of nearly solid clay, without the help of heavy, earth-moving equipment. The grim darkness "enjoyed" by the workers is evident in the black pit opening behind the top man. The central man holds a candle and looks over the photographer's shoulder; the other two men look directly at the camera ... and across the century at us.
CITY OF TORONTO ARCHIVES: Series 372, Subseries 59, Item 126

Physical Spectrum

People live complex lives, moving through many kinds of spaces in the course of their daily routines. Books about cities, heavily illustrated or not, often focus on a limited social range of people and a limited range of functional spaces — usually on domestic (especially grandly domestic) spaces, and sometimes on a single theme: transportation or courts or public architecture, and so on. This book crosses the social and the physical spectra to discuss domestic life (from homelessness to opulence), working life (factory floor to corner office), commercial life (farmer's market to carriage trade), and public life (city halls to government houses). Not every sphere of life can be tackled in a single book. Transportation, education, and the arts are among the topics referred to but not explored in depth. The organic complexity of urban life is addressed directly by discussion and indirectly by presentation of many diverse images.

Space here is treated as "lived space," not abstract, theoretical spaces, but actual places where real people — paupers or potentates — acted out their daily dramas. Some of the images are devoid of people, but not devoid of life, or potential life. Of particular interest is how people and places interacted — how the physical environment may have shaped human behaviour, and how humans shaped their physical environments. Again, this theme emerges from the images, discussion, and example.

Photography in Toronto

Photography came early to Toronto, as it did to many towns and cities in the New World. In 1839, Frenchman Louis Jacques Mandé Daguerre and Englishman William Henry Fox Talbot announced processes to permanently capture pictures created by sunlight. On April 15th of that year, the *Quebec Gazette* published the first Canadian article about photography, which focussed on Talbot's "sun painting."[6] And on May 3, 1839, Torontonians were first informed of Daguerre's process by an article appearing in *The Patriot*.[7] Itinerant daguerreotypists probably took the first photographs in Toronto. The process was dicey and weather-dependent, since sunlight was necessary for taking the photograph (which took a *long* time), and also for developing the image.

The first known photographers to set up shop in Toronto both did so in July 1840. A Mr. Finch from New York established a studio in the Wellington Building on King Street near Toronto Street. More interesting from a Canadian perspective, Collingwood-born Richard A. Pauling arrived in Toronto via New York City, and opened a studio on the corner of Newgate (now Adelaide) and Upper George Streets.[8] Just how long each lasted is unknown, but turnover was rapid in the early days. Only Eli J. Palmer, who arrived in 1847, established a long-lasting business that survived until the mid-1870s. Given the technical limitations of the process and the commercial demands for personal "likenesses," most daguerreotypes were studio portraits. Very few have survived. Apparently L. W. Dessauer, who worked intermittently in Toronto from 1843 to 1845, took "views of Houses, Streets, Country Seats,"[9] as well as the usual portraits, but none of his work has surfaced. It's highly unlikely that he took any interior photographs other than studio portraits.

Knowledge of the new, wet-plate process first came to Toronto in 1855, spurring the establishment of several important new firms.[10] Among these was Armstrong & Beere, which became Armstrong, Beere & Hime between about 1857 and 1861. The earliest known surviving, non-studio photographs of

View in Museum of the University Toronto C.W.

1.5: *Natural History Museum ca. 1859*
Seen through a stereoscope, Armstrong, Beere & Hime's two small images magically popped into a single, eerily three-dimensional view of the recently opened museum. Created around the time that Darwin's Origin of Species was turning the religio-scientific world on its ear, the University College museum was designed and stuffed (sometimes literally) by Rev. William Hincks. He beat out celebrated zoologist T. H. Huxley for the post of Chair of Natural History at Toronto, despite Darwin's support for Huxley.[15] The University's new museum was what Harvard biologist Stephen Jay Gould would call "a classical Victorian 'cabinet' museum of natural history."[16] In approach, the Victorian natural history museum was very archival: displaying significant items in the glass cases (here designed by architect Frederic Cumberland), and storing as full a range of related items as possible, in wooden drawers under the display. As in other up-to-date Victorian museums, the walls were painted a light colour and light floods in through Cumberland's enormous windows, which were poised to illuminate the display. Incredibly, a single, casually dressed visitor, who had paused long enough to study the contents of a display case, had registered on the plates in the stereographic camera. This museum, along with many Armstrong, Beere & Hime photographs, was destroyed by fire on February 14, 1890.
CITY OF TORONTO ARCHIVES: Series 958, File 109, Image 9

1.6: *Bugle Band,* **1879**
Taken by an unidentified, but obviously professional, Toronto photographer in 1879, this group portrait of the Queen's Own Rifles Bugle Band reveals more than just the faces of the band members. Part of the studio's painted scenery is evident off-centre to the left, and a curtain rod runs across the top of the photograph with a touch of drapery hanging down the right edge. It's unclear why the soldiers — who are holding their poses with admirable military precision — were so casually, even unprofessionally posed. Fortunately, the lackadaisical composition gives modern viewers an unexpected glimpse into a late-Victorian photographic studio.
CITY OF TORONTO ARCHIVES: Series 327, Subseries 3, File 2

stereograph, i.e., a card bearing two, small photographic images of the museum, taken (probably by a single camera with two lenses) about two inches apart. When examined through a stereoscopic viewer, a single, three-dimensional image was (miraculously) seen. Stereographs were immensely popular during the 1850s,[13] and technically able to capture images in reduced light.[14]

Beginning around 1861, the first stereographic craze was overtaken by a new photographic craze: the lust for small, 3.5 x 2.5 inch "cartes-de-visite," which hit Toronto in the early 1860s, lasted until the new *new* thing: 6.5 x 4.5 inch "cabinet cards," which arrived in the late 1860s and survived at least until the end of the century.[17] Most cartes-de-visite and most cabinet cards presented very stylized portraits of people, not places.[18] Given the dominance of portrait photography among commercial photographers, it's worth taking a peek into two studios for a look at an early group portrait and a later individual portrait.

The 1880s brought the dry-plate process, which provided much faster exposures (ten times as fast as the wet plate) and freed photographers from the immediate need for a darkroom; hand-held cameras, which freed photographers

Toronto is a set of 25 exterior views taken by this firm in late 1856 or early 1857. The set was probably bought by the City and submitted as part of its (losing) bid to become the capital of Canada.[11] Made by the new, wet-plate process, these views provide insight into the mid-Victorian city that had put its name forward.

Given this history, it seems only fitting that the oldest known surviving, non-studio *interior* photograph of Toronto was also taken by Armstrong, Beere & Hime: a view of the Museum of the University of Toronto. It was probably created in 1859 or '60,[12] and used a process different from the exterior photo-graphs they took to document the construction of Frederic Cumberland's magnificent University College. The interior photograph was a

1.7: *Unidentified Children's Aid Society Child,* ca. 1892

Both cartes-de-visite and cabinet-card studio portraits followed strict Victorian conventions. Beginning in the 1860s, the drawing-room theme was the most widely used studio set[19] — often with fashionable furniture in the foreground and a painted column in the background. During the 1890s, the Toronto Children's Aid Society took many of its abused, abandoned, or otherwise uncared-for residents to a local photographer for their portraits, some of which appeared in the Society's annual reports. In these circumstances, the use of the drawing-room setting is jarring in the extreme: a one-legged youth, with perfectly combed hair, foppish neck-scarf, and oversized crutch, poses in the studio of an unknown professional photographer. Was this because the Society didn't want to record conditions at its Adelaide Street residence, or because photographing children in a domestic setting was technically extremely difficult or, because the children looked better cared-for in the studio? Whatever the reasons, the juxtaposition of a one-legged CAS child and elegant surroundings is ironic and disturbing.

CITY OF TORONTO ARCHIVES: **Series 542, File 1, Image 251**

1.8: *Toronto Camera Club,* 1906

"Amateurs" — i.e., non-commercial photographers — had long been at the forefront of photography, as inventors and as image-creators.[22] But the age of amateur photography really took off in the 1880s, with the invention of dry-plate photography, and the lightweight, celluloid film camera; and the age of mass photography was born around the turn-of-the-century with the invention and marketing of the Brownie box camera. Examples from each of these groups are found throughout this book.

In the mid-1880s, serious amateurs began forming camera clubs where they could attend lectures, exchange technical information, share darkrooms, organize field trips, display photographs, and generally have a good time. In Toronto, a group of men (it was only men) gathered in the Gents Parlour of the Queen's Hotel on March 17, 1888 to form an Amateur Photographic Association, which became the Toronto Camera Club in 1891. (It took 50 years for the Toronto Club to finally accept women as full, active members.) By 1906, when this photograph was published in *The American Amateur Photographer,* the Toronto Camera Club had taken up residence in its third location at 391 Yonge Street / 2 Gould Street. There, Club members enjoyed three darkrooms (with running water and lead-lined sinks), "modern" enlargers, a "well equipped studio," and a large front room (shown here), which served as club lounge, library, and exhibition space.[23] Among its members were future City photographer, Arthur Goss, who pursued soft-focus Stieglitzian "pictorial" photography in his private photographic life;[24] future City Works Commissioner, R. C. Harris, who hired Goss as City Photographer in 1911; and future City Architect, John J. Woolnough, who published amateur photographs in the short-lived *Massey's Magazine.*[25] Goss caused a ruckus when the Club moved to these new quarters and he covered the walls with selections from Stieglitz's influential photo-magazine, *Camera Work.*[26]

LIBRARY AND ARCHIVES CANADA: **PA-134948**

1.9: *Alfred Pearson's Darkroom, 1927*
This is one of three photographs taken by long-time TTC photographer Alfred Pearson on June 10, 1927 to document his darkroom. In the early years, all photographs were contact prints. A 5 x 7-inch negative created a 5 x 7-inch positive print. An 8 x 10-inch negative created an 8 x 10-inch print. And so on. It was only with the invention of enlargers that larger prints could be produced from fixed-size negatives. Here, Pearson's 1927 enlarger is mounted in one of the walls, pointed horizontally toward a movable frame where the photographic paper would have been set on an easel (removed for the photograph) and exposed. (Modern enlargers move up and down vertically and can be manipulated by a single person standing in one place, a far more efficient and convenient method than the horizontal set-up shown here.) Another photograph in this series shows the "wet side" of Pearson's darkroom, with its "lead lined sink with both hot and cold water service," and enamel-developing trays underneath.
CITY OF TORONTO ARCHIVES: Series 71, Item 4984

from reliance on large, heavy, tripod-dependent cameras (although many continued to use much more cumbersome cameras than are common today); and flashlight, which freed photographers from reliance on natural or non-photographic artificial light. These, and related developments like the evolution of roll-film, better lenses, faster shutters, and the 1901 arrival of the simple, inexpensive, and wildly successful Kodak Brownie camera,[20] radically altered both photography and photographers.

Professional photographers were no longer chained to their studios and the heavy equipment that limited where they could go and whom they could photograph. (Mind you, photographers were a hardy breed, used to dragging darkrooms across country, climbing mountains, and performing other deeds of derring-do to get the photograph they wanted.) On-location photography, photojournalism, casual, nighttime, and interior photography were all set free. Moreover, the ranks of amateurs — both serious "art" photographers and occasional

"happy snappers" — were vastly expanded.[21] The number of interior images taken, and the number of images likely to survive, was hugely increased, causing this book to focus on the post-1880 period.

Darkrooms — the inner sancta of the working photographer — tend to remain secret. For one reason or another — most likely lack of interest and lack of time, rather than desire for secrecy — few photographs of early darkrooms survive.[27] When they do fetch up, they are of particular interest.

Light Effects

Light makes the picture.[28] Many other things obviously are involved. But without adequate light — however defined — no photograph can happen. Equally obvious, the nature of the light has a profound impact on the nature of the photograph. Compare, for example, two photographs taken around 1892 in the same parlour — one during the day using natural light, and one at night using artificial "flashlight." Other elements have changed — most importantly is the inclusion of people in one but not the other. But it is the quality of the light that more than anything changes the quality of the picture.

Flashlight photography came early to Toronto, as it did to other photographic centres, like New York City. Until the German invention of the flashbulb in 1925, photographers were dependent on the "hit-and-miss pyrotechnics" associated with firing off magnesium flash powder,[29] an exciting, but often cumbersome and sometimes dangerous new technique invented in 1887. Perhaps the most famous early use of flashlight was crusading journalist Jacob Riis's photographic forays into the darkest alleys, lowest dives, and most impoverished tenements of New York. In the spring of 1887, Riis scanned his local paper, spotted a four-line announcement of the new German discovery, and emitted such an outcry that he startled his wife. "There it was, the thing I had been looking for all these years," he later wrote. "A way had been discovered ... to take pictures by flashlight. The

1.10: *Dr. James Rea's Parlour by Natural Light, ca. 1892*
The time exposure necessary to take this photograph of physician James Rea's parlour (at 301, now 1265, Dundas Street West) makes the (overexposed) sun-filled windows the centre of attention. It casts elements of the room into light and shadow that help create a sense of depth, highlights some elements (like the picture moulding), and eliminates some details altogether (notably the light-erased oil painting over the sofa).
CITY OF TORONTO ARCHIVES: Fonds 1467, Item 4

1.11: *Dr. James Rea's Parlour by Artificial Light*, ca. 1892
Here is the same room at Dundas and Dovercourt, photographed with flashlight by amateur photographer and professor of Architecture, Dr. Charles Wright. The curtains are literally and metaphorically drawn. No exterior light intrudes. A wrecked ship emerges from the painting on the wall. Leaded glass panes are picked out on the smaller window. People can be, and obviously are included, although even in flashlight, the smallest child is a blur. Many details are flattened — especially the faces and such light-coloured objects as a statue on the mantelpiece. No one looks at the camera, perhaps because of the bright flash expected to explode at any second.
CITY OF TORONTO ARCHIVES: Fonds 1467, Item 1

darkest corner might be photographed that way." Riis instantly purchased a camera and the necessary equipment, learned how to take pictures, and set off on his journey into the slums ... and into documentary photographic history.[30] To grab these pictures, Riis had to carry a 4 x 5 wooden box camera, plates, plate-holders, tripod, magnesium powder, and a frying pan rigged up as a flash pan, into the roughest and sometimes most unfriendly parts of the city. The flash and the camera were not synchronized, so the photographer had to set up the camera, remove the lens cap, quickly ignite the flash powder, replace the cap and, sometimes, race away.[31] Once, Riis exploded the flash into his own face (fortunately he was wearing glasses). Another time he set fire to a tenement room.

The adoption of flashlight photography in Toronto was almost as early, but certainly less dramatic. Probably the earliest example in this book (and perhaps at the City of Toronto Archives) is F. W. Micklethwaite's photograph of his wife, which was taken in the late 1880s and is reproduced in the next chapter. Sometime between late 1888 and November 4, 1889, members of the Toronto Amateur Photographic Association attended a demonstration of "Flash Light Photography" by a representative of the Eastman Dry Plate and Film Company.[32] A decade later, flashlight photography was still cumbersome and potentially dangerous. In January of that year, Dr. A.W. Powell gave a lecture to the Camera Club, in which he described his own favourite flashlight apparatus, which was based on a flowerpot saucer, an alcohol-saturated piece of asbestos, and a clay pipe filled with magnesium powder. At the critical moment, with the camera focussed on its subject, the alcohol was lit, the flame blown across the powder, and the flash ignited. Hardly a precise science.[33] But, precise science or not, flashlight revolutionized photography and made much of this book possible.

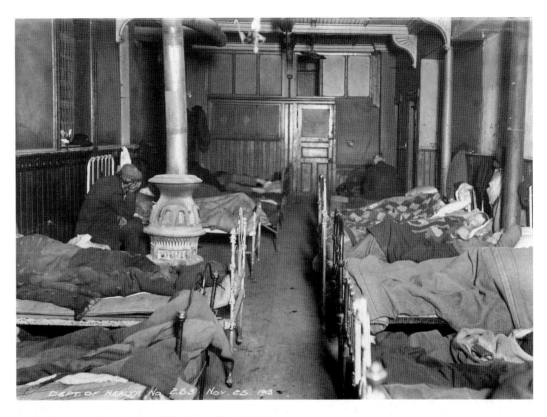

1.12: *A Flash of Victorian Humour*, 1896
Without flashlight, this unexpectedly humourous Victorian photograph by future City Architect John J. Woolnough would have been impossible. Woolnough was a dedicated, and published, amateur photographer who experimented with both flashlight (see also "A Consulting Room (flashlight)" in Chapter 4) and special effects.[34] We often think of Victorians as unremittingly earnest, sober, and humourless. Obviously, this was not always the case, as this photograph, originally captioned "Good Company ... but he has seen better days!" reveals.

1.13: *Dept. of Health No. 253*, Nov. 25, 1913"
Unlike Jacob Riis, City Photographer Arthur Goss was no crusading journalist. He wrote no muckraking articles or books about what he observed in Toronto's slums. He left no written observations about what he photographed or how he felt. He was the consummate, quasi-objective, professional photographer. And yet his clear-eyed, professionally executed photographs often pack as big a wallop as do those of his American predecessor. This photograph, labelled with "just the facts" of who ordered the shot (the City Health Department) and when it was taken (November 25, 1913), takes us into an unidentified men's shelter. The "facts" as arranged by Goss tell their story. A dozen shabbily dressed men are exhausted, even ashamed. (No one looks directly at the camera.) While sympathetic, the photograph is also intrusive. Almost certainly, neither Goss nor his boss, public-health reformer, Dr. Charles Hastings, had asked the men's permission to photograph them. (Some men are looking away, and others are still asleep.) Without flashlight — which bounces off the back wall — this photograph would have been impossible, and we would have a poorer understanding of early twentieth century Toronto.

Toronto 1880s–1920s

Toronto was a very British, North American city — with powerful political, economic, cultural and emotional ties to mother Britain, and increasingly strong economic and social ties to neighbouring Uncle Sam.[35] In 1793, the city had been founded by Lieutenant-Governor John Graves Simcoe, on the edge of Lake Ontario in the North American wilderness, as the military and political capital of a new British province, Upper Canada. During the period under investigation here — roughly the 1880s to the 1920s — the twin features of British birth and North American location continued to exercise strong influences on the rapidly growing capital of the still new, confederated Province of Ontario.

Physically, Toronto looked more like her Great Lakeside, mid-western American neighbours than her British progenitors, but love of Queen and the call of Empire remained strong. The city was influenced by building and architectural trends from south of the border: the City Beautiful (in Union Station), Richardsonian Romanesque (in Queen's Park and City Hall), and the office skyscraper (in Simpson's Department Store and the Dominion Bank). Architectural influences also floated across the Pond: the Garden City (in Spruce Court), and the Arts & Crafts Movement (in Wychwood Park). The mix came to be distinctly Central Canadian. Demographically, Toronto grew dramatically — by immigration, migration, annexation and natural increase — from about 86,000 in 1881, to about 210,000 in 1901, and over 630,000 in 1931. Economically, Toronto emerged first as a regional centre, dominating the Southern Ontario hinterland, and then as a national centre, second only to Montreal in size and importance. The influence of all these factors is felt throughout this book.

Socially, the City remained predominantly British (93% in 1881 and still 85% in 1921[37]), intensely loyal, but more bumptious and socially open than class-obsessed Britain. (This is not to say that Toronto was classless — far from it, as this book makes abundantly clear. But the class system was generally more porous in the New World than the Old.) British aristocrats — such as Lord and Lady Aberdeen, and Lord and Lady Minto — remained in Vice-Regal Rideau Hall and at the pinnacle of Canadian social life.[38] Elsewhere, however, rising through the social ranks was not only possible, but the norm, at least for those of British descent. The Masseys and the masses may have parted ways by the end of the century, but the Masseys — like the Eatons, the Flavelles and many other turn-of-the-century Canadian aristocrats — had made their money in commerce. Daniel Massey had even been a supporter of rebellious William Lyon Mackenzie before returning to his foundry and forging a commercial empire from ploughshares and other agricultural implements. Timothy Eaton had been a small town dry-goods merchant before cobbling together a department store empire. And Joseph Flavelle had been a meat-packing entrepreneur prior to entering the ranks of financial and social distinction. Many Toronto aristocrats were not to-the-manor-born ... but they certainly got nicely used to the manor when they reached it.

The social and physical worlds inhabited by Torontonians depended very much on such factors as class, gender, and ethnicity, each of which is explored, to a greater or lesser extent, throughout this book. Class has emerged as particularly important, partly because Toronto's surviving photographic record reveals many — but certainly not all — aspects of life at the bottom of the social scale, as well as at the top. This is especially true of domestic life, documented so fearlessly by Arthur Goss for the housing study compiled by his boss, Dr. Charles Hastings.

Gender and ethnicity are far less well-documented, both here and in the public record. Many of the photographs in this book show women's lives — and this is important — but very few are by female photographers. Although a substantial number of women did become professional photographers, and/or made their living from photography — somewhere between 5% and 20% according to some researchers[39] — none of their work is found here, because so few photographs by women from this period have survived in public archives.[40] (The struggle for women to be admitted as full members to the Toronto Camera Club underlines just one reason why women are under-represented in the photographic record.) As for ethnicity, nearly all the photographs of identifiably non-British ethnic subjects reproduced here are by photographers of British descent. Arthur Goss could, and did, document the lives of some non-British immigrants living in abject, or relative poverty, but he photographed only subjects deemed important by his civic masters. William James also documented the lives of non-British — as well as British — immigrants, but he was mostly interested in images he thought he could sell to local newspapers. Clearly, only part of the non-British immigrant experience was captured by them, or is reproduced here.

Text and Context

Most non-tourist books about cities use photographs as illustrations for the text, not as primary sources of information for analysis. Sometimes, perhaps more often, the photographs are selected by someone other than the author of the text, and only after the text has been completed. They are adjuncts to, not integral parts of researching and writing the book.

This book emerged first and foremost from the photographs. The text was written to elucidate, analyze, and provide the context for the images. Who is the woman in the photograph? Why were these "slum interiors" photographed? Where was this sewer tunnel being dug? How did the owner of this mansion make his money? What did police officers in 1889 do? What speeches were given in this Parliamentary chamber and what cases were argued in this Court Room? What image was the client trying to project? When did brand-name teas or cash registers or escalators come into existence? When did electric streetcars replace horse-drawn vehicles? Are the people in the photograph willing participants or hostile objects? What can we learn from this photograph?

Sometimes, of course, a deliberate search was made to uncover photographs to "illustrate" points made in the text. For example, the chapter on commercial life began with two memorable images — Christmas Day among

1.14: *Victoria 1819–1901*, January 1901
When Queen Victoria died on January 22, 1901, Toronto was plunged into mourning, as demonstrated by this anonymous photograph taken in Holy Trinity Church near today's Eaton Centre. On the day before the Queen's death, *The Daily Mail and Empire* published a black-edged image of Victoria, calling her "The Greatest Sovereign Who Ever Reigned in Any Country." Such hyperbole may sound comical to modern ears, but was entirely in character for a city and a people who had known no other monarch. "No one under thirty years of age," Jesse Edgar Middleton wrote in 1923, "can understand the effect of Queen Victoria's death on the mental processes of the leaders in civic life and of the public in general."[36] The Victorian invention of photography offers modern viewers a rare opportunity to look directly inside a city in mourning.
ARCHIVES OF ONTARIO: S 18139, Photo: A.R. Ward, 311 Yonge St., Toronto. [January 1901].

the carcasses at a butcher's stall in the St. Lawrence Market and an unidentified, but glitteringly upscale jewellery store. Once the commercial-life theme had been identified, a deliberate effort was exerted to fill in the theme, with the results now found in Chapter 6, *From Farmers' Market to Carriage Trade*. The book-creating process was an interactive one, but it started with the photographs, and places the images at the centre of the analysis.

This book may have emerged primarily from the photographs and the sense that "inside Toronto" was an interesting and unexplored concept, but the material could have been presented in any number of ways. This is only one possibility. Naturally, the result reflects not only the available materials, but also my own values, interests, and experiences. I hope others will find as much pleasure as I have had in exploring these miniature worlds, and using Lady Eastlake's "new form of communication" to understand urban history as it unfolded in one, particular place.

2

From Homelessness to Opulence

The comforts of home are both practical and psychological, essential and elastic.[1]

Everyone needs, but not everyone obtains, shelter, heat, and spaces for food-preparation,

self-care, and sleeping. Virtually everyone wants, but not everyone enjoys, the opportunity to shape

their home place to reflect their own values, tastes, and desires, whether this imprint is in the form of

a family photo, religious icon, ad torn from a magazine, or Old Master painting on the wall.[2]

What is deemed essential varies over time and space. What was once completely unavailable,

or available only in big cities, or only to the rich, is now regarded as basic, such as central heating,

indoor toilets, light at the flick of a switch, or hot water at the twist of a tap.

*D*uring the period covered by this book, the gap between rich and poor was arguably more extreme than at any other period in Canadian history, with the possible exception of now. These disparities were reflected in all aspects of domestic life, from amount of space to quality of space and furnishings. How the differences, and similarities, played out depended on the available public services, domestic technology, building materials, fashion, ethnic experiences, class expectations, gender roles, and so on. Urban indoor plumbing depended on the existence of public water- and sewer-systems, and the availability of water-closet technology. Indoor lighting was provided initially by individual candles and lamps, then on publicly available gas and electricity. Heating evolved from fireplace to stove to furnace. Personal display was the result of personal taste (cheap Millais print or Dufferin Race Track poster), and personal resources (cheap lace curtains or extravagantly swagged draperies; singular family Bible or lavish family Library).

Photographic documentation also varies. Fortunately, Toronto has good records of how the very rich and the very poor lived. The rich, and the commercial photographers on-the-make, ensured that the public rooms of the wealthy were documented: the drawing-rooms, parlours, dining rooms, libraries, conservatories, and front halls were all captured for posterity. The family's bedrooms, bathrooms, dressing rooms, and other private spaces, were less frequently photographed; and servants' spaces were almost completely ignored, especially their own, private rooms. Kitchens and hallways did receive some attention. At the other end of the social spectrum, Toronto's crusading Medical Health Officer, Dr. Charles Hastings, ensured that so-called "slum housing" was photographed, so we have a good selection of materials depicting how the very poor lived during the Progressive Era, from about 1911 to 1918. But relatively little exists from before or after that period.

As for the growing middle class, its domestic spaces are more difficult to illustrate, either because fewer photographs were taken (which may or may not be the case, given the explosion of amateur photography during the period), or because fewer photographs have survived. Most photographers themselves fell into the ranks of the middle-class, and many services provided by companies such as Consumers' Gas were used by the middle class, so some documentation has survived in public archives.[4]

From these various sources, we can observe domestic life across the social spectrum in Toronto, from the unhoused and underhoused, through the modestly housed, to the distinctly overhoused, always bearing in mind that the physical spaces depicted were *lived-in* spaces, not simply pretty or arresting photographs or abstract architectural environments. Real people lived in real places. What might their lives have been like?

Homelessness

Homelessness haunts us still. Ironically, images illustrating homelessness in Victorian and Edwardian Toronto — both on and off the street — look more familiar to viewers at the turn-of-the-millennium than they did ten, twenty or thirty years ago, when sleeping on modern streets was a much less frequent occurrence.[5]

Around the turn of the twentieth century, homelessness was also a sadly common occurrence. *Police Duty Books* from the period are sprinkled with references to "homeless waifs" having spent the night at the police station.[7] Investigative reporters occasionally dared to enter the House of Industry or other unsavoury locales.[8] And in the period before the Great War, roving photojournalist, William James, documented both families and individuals sleeping outside. The clothes and coverings may have changed — no denim, parkas, or sleeping bags covered James's homeless — but the eyes and grim demeanour of his subjects spark a disturbing shock of recognition across the years.[9] (See 2.2.)

Some of these "homeless waifs" undoubtedly ended up under the care of the Children's Aid Society (est. 1846).[10] Other homeless victims might be put up at such institutions as the House of Providence (est. 1855) on Power Street, and the House of Industry (est. 1837) on Elm Street, where conditions for "the deserving poor" (as opposed to the so-called "thriftless and improvident" who might not deserve charitable attention[11]) were harsh, of limited duration, but essential to survival.[12] (See 2.3.)

2.1: *Photographer's Parlour, 1880s*

With the help of a photographic "flashlight," F. W. Micklethwaite photographed his young wife in the family parlour at 40 Jarvis Street, where he also had his business. Based on Mrs. Micklethwaite's dress, with its narrow sleeves, tightly fitted bodice, dark colour and drooping bustle, the photograph was probably taken in the late 1880s.[3] Clearly, the photographer, who ultimately became extremely successful, had not yet moved beyond his lower-middle-class domestic environment, with its kerosene lantern lighting, stove heating, cramped space, unevenly plastered ceiling, and multi-purpose room. Amid the late-Victorian touches of many-patterned papers and parlour piano, are evidences of the photographer's trade. Rather than paintings and knick-knacks, for example, the Micklethwaites have covered every available horizontal and vertical space with photographs — almost exclusively portraits — of all sizes, shapes, and descriptions. A camera-obscura-like box stands on the table near the lace-curtained window, a most unusual piece of furniture in a Victorian parlour.

CITY OF TORONTO ARCHIVES: Series 388, Item 8

2.2: *Front Street Flop House*, ca. 1912

Labelled "10 Cent Lodging House on Front Street," this photograph was taken around 1912 by the City's official photographer, Arthur Goss, to illustrate the connection between poor housing and poor health. Although crusading Medical Health Officer, Dr. Charles Hastings, had some success in driving this point home, and various significant public-health advances were made during his time of reform, the lesson appears to have been lost in more recent years.

Probably located where some of Toronto's most glittering modern architecture now stands, this Front Street "flop house" was occupied by those poor souls who could rustle up the necessary ten cents; a not insignificant price at a time when a substantial, Eden Smith-designed house, in relatively affluent Wychwood Park cost only $6,400 to build.[6] Among the seventeen rumpled cots crammed into this dreary, unfinished room is a single occupant. His jacket and bowler hat hang on a nail across from the uncomfortable bed where he is a tossing-and-turning blur. This is one of the few domestic interiors that displays virtually no personalization of the space. Self-expression, even the posting of an ad, requires an element of stability and a sense of ownership (not necessarily the fact of ownership) — both clearly absent here.

CITY OF TORONTO ARCHIVES: Series 372, Subseries 32, Item 6

2.3: *At Dinner, House of Industry*, 1891

In the 1880s and '90s, no activist photographer prowled the streets of Toronto, documenting conditions among the poor, as Jacob Riis had prowled the streets for his gritty and influential portrayal of New York, *How the Other Half Lives*.[13] But the odd journalist did poke his nose into Toronto's darker corners, sometimes with sympathy, more often with the prejudices so alive in the wider society. Toronto's House of Industry was at Elm Street, where this Dickensian scene was recorded for the *Globe* in January 1891, when Toronto was in the grip of a depression.[14] The House of Industry provided three services during this period: permanent residence for elderly and infirm "inmates" who had no alternative supports; short-term food and lodging to "casuals" who had to work breaking stones, chopping wood or doing other workfare-style tasks, in order to qualify for assistance; and food and fuel to needy families who required "out-door relief" in order to survive at home. The "casuals" shown here were given a bath, a basin of soup with six ounces of bread for dinner, a bench for a bed, and tea with six ounces of bread for breakfast (on Sundays with butter). "But the tramp ought not to complain too much of his treatment at the casual wards," commented the reporter. "In this country he can not regard any system of relief as his inalienable right in the event of his finding himself under the weather."[15]

CITY OF TORONTO ARCHIVES: Series 806, File 3

2.4: *Macedonian Boarding House*, ca. 1912

Most early Macedonian immigrants were young men — either bachelors or recently married and childless — who travelled to "Upper America" (i.e., Canada) to work hard, live frugally, save money, and return home to continue life with their families in their home villages. The first Macedonians reached Toronto in 1902. By 1910, 1090 Macedonians lived in Toronto — 340 bachelors, 754 married men, and only 8 men with families. They congregated in three distinct areas: Eastern Avenue/ Cabbagetown, King/Niagara, and The Junction, where there were large employers, such as the William Davies meat-packing firm near the Don, looking for hard workers. The Macedonian boarding house, like this one on York Street, was a community institution, where the men tended to help one another find jobs and survive in a foreign culture.[23] Ever the consummate documentary photographer, Arthur Goss managed to persuade his standers to come out of their tightly packed rooms ... and stare at his lens. Meanwhile, a heating pipe snakes along the ceiling; battered wainscotting lines the hallway; and decorative wallpaper adds an extra layer to paper-thin walls. The fact that the lodgings were "since improved with modern conveniences" was recorded on the back of the photograph. Just what these "modern conveniences" might have been is unknown.

CITY OF TORONTO ARCHIVES: Series 372, Subseries 32, Item 3

Lodging Houses

By 1911, when Dr. Charles Hastings published his first survey of "slum housing,"[16] the Riisian power of photography to document conditions and mobilize opinion had finally found its way to Toronto.[17] In Toronto's case, however, the social activism came more from the public-health official, Dr. Hastings,[18] than the photographer, Arthur Goss. Unlike his New York predecessor, Jacob Riis, or his American contemporary, Lewis Hine, Goss appears to have remained detached from any social movement to right the wrongs documented. In fact, his private photography suggests that Goss was more interested in artistic, than social issues, for advancing the case of Steiglitzian pictorialism, than social reform. But he was a fine photographer

and applied his considerable photographic skills to every assignment. While not stumping for reform, as Riis and Hine did, Goss did provide the ammunition for reform, and deliberately included images of both the physical environments (whether water-main construction or housing conditions) and the people associated with them. This instinctive humanism reaches out across the years.

In the period before, as well as during, the First World War, Toronto was experiencing one of its many housing crises.[19] Naturally, the crisis was felt most acutely by those at the bottom of the social ladder. Although being completely uninterested in the "immigrant experience"[20] and distressingly inclined to blame "foreigners" in part for their own misfortune — "their ideas of sanitation are not ours"[21] — Dr. Hastings did focus contemporary attention on the plight of two groups: desperately poor, mostly immigrant,

The half-basement, which was used as an
assembly-room, was filled with benches; according to the health department regulations, no
sleepers are supposed to be accommodated in
this space. There were 54 men sleeping on
the benches and on the floor, all without bed
clothes, and every one sleeping or resting fully
dressed. The half basement had six small windows, all of which were found tightly closed.[22]

male roomers; and desperately poor, largely immigrant, home-dwellers. (See
2.4, 2.5.)

Hastings' landmark 1911 report, and the New York Bureau of Municipal
Research's follow-up 1913 report, both cited dismal statistics about lodging-
house crowding. For example, the BMR described a three-storey building
at 59 Frederick Street, where George Brown College now stands. Health
regulations of the day would have permitted 79 lodgers (dreadful overcrowding
by modern standards). The unscrupulous landlord of 1913 managed to stuff
128 lodgers into the space, each paying between five and twenty-five cents
per night:

The BMR, like Hastings before it, argued for a municipal lodging house, but
nothing came of the plea.

The Ward

The following conditions peculiar to great cities are found to be
present [in Toronto] to a lamentable extent: rear houses, dark rooms,
tenement houses,[25] houses unfit for habitation, inadequate water supply,

2.6: *Mother and Child*, 1913

Goss took this tender shot of a mother and child on
October 29, 1913. The two are sitting in the corner of a
small, dark, multi-purpose room, in The Ward or another
poor part of the City. No lights of any sort are visible, not
even an oil lamp; the home would have been a dark one,
indeed. No window is visible, so the pair may have lived in
one of the "dark rooms," rightly condemned by Hastings as
being particularly unhealthy. Still, life went on. Diapers
dangle from a clothesline; an ancient stove provides heat;
a calendar decorates the wall; and what appears to
be an alarm clock stands at the ready. The family
was poor, but the infant apparently well-cared for.
CITY OF TORONTO ARCHIVES: Series 372, Subseries 32,
Item 242

unpaved and filthy yards and lanes,
sanitary conveniences so-called which
because of their position or condition, or
for various other reasons, have become
a public nuisance, a menace to public
health, a danger to public morals, and, in
fact, an offence against public decency.[26]

Bounded by Yonge, University, Queen, and
College Streets, "The Ward" was a tough and crowded immigrant reception area
in the heart of a rapidly growing city. The Ward was not the only area in Toronto
with appalling housing conditions, but it was the largest, densest, and most
notorious.[27] Dr. Hastings' 1911 report, quoted above, looked at six areas.[28] Over
a third of the 4,696 houses surveyed were in The Ward, where the density was
82 people to the acre, far higher than any other district surveyed. Moreover, the
total number of families (1,275) and individuals (11,645) investigated was also
far greater than anywhere else.

Dr. Hastings, like most other social reformers, looked at such areas with
middle-class, British-Canadian eyes, failing to see underlying social strengths
(e.g., the various synagogues and other community institutions)[29] or to accept
differing concepts of "home" and "work" spaces (e.g., the "untidy" yards, where
junk dealers stored their wares), and generally blaming, at least in part, the
"foreigners" for the conditions of their environment. Such attitudes are amply
evident in the summary quotation at the beginning of this section, which cites
not only physical, but also "moral" defects as part of the problem facing the
City. On the other hand, Hastings did take exploitative landlords to task, did
understand at least some of the underlying economic factors, and did make

DEPT. OF HEALTH No 244 OCT 29 1913

2.7: *Three Children,* 1913
Goss photographed these three children in a sleeping corner of their crowded home. Just who these children were or whether there was an adult nearby is unknown. What we can know is that their home was crowded (two beds are pushed slap up against each other and other beds may have been out of camera range); the children are apparently downcast; and at least the little boy is quite dirty. Whether the little girl should have been at school is unrecorded, but even if that was the case, she may have been in charge of younger siblings. Distinct touches of "home" nevertheless, grace the impoverished surroundings: lace curtains at the window, and pictures, possibly torn from a magazine, on the wall.
CITY OF TORONTO ARCHIVES: Series 372, Subseries 32, Item 244

both straightforward recommendations (such as instituting more follow-up inspections to ensure that repairs were made) and more wide-ranging recommendations (such as building Garden Cities on the British model). Over the next six or seven years, some of the most egregious problems were fixed. For example, by 1919, nearly 16,000 backyard privies had been eliminated, although many distressing problems remained.[30]

Goss took hundreds of photographs of The Ward and other poor districts. Sometimes he took them specifically for Hastings' public-health department,

and sometimes he took them for the Board of Education. Often, he visited several places in the course of one day and rattled off a series of moving images, like the three shown here, which are only some of the ones he took for the Health Department on October 29, 1913. In each case, we learn a good deal about the people, as well as the spaces they inhabited. (See 2.6–2.8.)

All too many of the people photographed in The Ward, by Goss or other photographers, remain anonymous. They have no pasts and no futures, only a brief present immortalized by the camera. Such anonymity contributes to the

2.8: *Marriage Certificate*, 1913
Goss took this photograph immediately after recording the three children, but there is no way of knowing if the two pictures are related. The wallpaper is different, so the rooms are most certainly different ones. Despite the peeling and stained paper (indicating ongoing dampness), the inhabitants have personalized the space in many distinctive ways. Vases and knick-knacks cover the "mantle"; and diverse objects, including a wicker basket, a family photograph, and a religious picture, decorate the walls. A print labelled "The Nursery" suggests that small children may have lived here with their parents. Another print, of a young woman paddling a canoe (behind the skirt hanging from a hook on the far wall), provides a nice Canadian touch. And a framed "Marriage Certificate" is prominently displayed in the corner. The inhabitants may have been poor, but they were morally honest, in a way that Dr. Hastings would have applauded.
CITY OF TORONTO ARCHIVES: Series 372, Subseries 32, Item 245.

distance placed between modern viewers and the subjects of old photographs. Very occasionally, the subjects' identity becomes known long after the fact.

The Donn Family represents one such lucky instance. Sixty years after Goss photographed an anonymous group, both inside and outside an equally anonymous Ward dwelling, a descendent miraculously saw and recognized his ancestors.[31] As a result of this chance encounter, we know that the house was at 9 Alice Street, just northeast of Holy Trinity Church, on what is now the northern edge of the Eaton Centre, and that the people photographed were members of the Donn family. Mrs. Dinah (Silverman) Donn emigrated to Canada from England between 1905 and 1908 with her husband, two sons, and a daughter. We also know that by the time Goss took his three photographs of the Donns for the Board of Education on August 14, 1913, there was at least one more child, and no husband evident. Whether Mrs. Donn was a widow (as the City Directory indicates), or abandoned (as her descendants believe), she was a single mother, carving out a meagre existence for herself and her offspring.

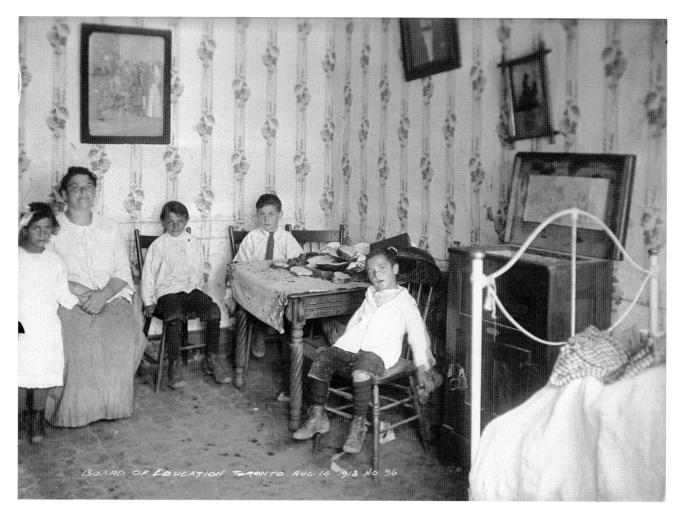

BOARD OF EDUCATION TORONTO AUG. 14 1913 No 96

We know from descendants that The Ward took its toll on the Donn family: the beribboned girl in the photograph died in childhood of one of the diseases that swept through the crowded and impoverished area. Of the other people shown, we know that one little boy, Harold, became a furrier on Yonge Street near Dundas (also now absorbed into the Eaton Centre); and that many of Dinah's descendants prospered, thus fulfilling the immigrant's dream.[32] (See 2.9.)

"Public" Housing

Some of the housing in The Ward was squalid. Much of it was extremely crowded. And none of it attained the ideal set either then or now for truly livable space. In response, the city's first government-sponsored housing was built at 74 to 86 Spruce Street in today's Cabbagetown. The newly formed Toronto Housing Company (THC) hired prominent architect, Eden Smith,[33] to

2.10: *Spruce Court "Living Room"*, ca. **1914**

"Sanitary conveniences, adequate bedroom accommodation and domestic privacy are the primary requirements for proper housing," proclaimed the Toronto Housing Company's 1915 publication, *Cottage Flats*, where this photograph by William James first appeared. At that time, "cottage flats" ranged in size from small, one-bedroom flats to four-bedroom, two-storey units, with monthly rents ranging from $14.50 to $29.00, depending on the size and location of the unit. This 1914 photograph shows the "Living Room" in one of the larger cottage flats at Spruce Court, obviously furnished as a model suite. Both the layout and the furnishing reflected the aspirations of the Company to house well the lower-income "wage earner." The aspirations of the architect and his sponsor were perhaps a tad unrealistic. Few potential tenants would have been able to afford the Tiffany lamp or even have wanted the exceptionally well-stocked bookcase.
CITY OF TORONTO ARCHIVES: Fonds 1018, Item 26

design two, non-profit, rental housing projects on sites relatively close to the downtown, rather than on cheaper, but more remote land in the suburbs. The first opened in 1913 at Spruce Court, on land leased from the General Hospital Trust;[34] and the second opened in 1914 at Riverdale Courts, across the Don Valley at 100 Bain Avenue. In both cases, Smith's basic unit of design was the "cottage flat ... a modern apartment with its own front door to the street," clustered around grassy "courts"[35] that were overseen by each flat.

Built for working people with low incomes, Spruce Court and Riverdale Courts could hardly have been more different from The Ward and its ilk: solid, well-built, brick buildings; open, grassy common spaces where children could play and be easily supervised; individual entrances; airy, well-ventilated, well-lit interiors; modern gas stoves and electrical fixtures; and careful detailing throughout. The only comparable quality, perhaps, was the human scale evident in both types of housing, a scale so often flouted in later public housing.

This early housing experiment was not a financial success. At a time when the "average wage [was] still considerably under $15.00 a week,"[36] the rents charged by the THC proved too onerous for the target clientele. Just twenty years later, in the middle of the Great Depression, the THC ceased operations. Fortunately, the physical fabric of the projects was neither razed nor renovated into oblivion. Both Spruce Court and Riverdale Courts were eventually transformed into successful, City-housing co-ops, catering to groups similar to those originally envisioned for them, with monthly rates in 2005 ranging from $696 to $1257, depending on the size and location of the unit. (See 2.10.)

Middle Class Struggle & Propriety

Just as Mrs. Dinah Donn's story was a classic immigrant's tale, Mrs. Catherine Agnew's was a classic, middle-class widow's tale. According to City records, Mrs. Agnew bought and moved to 244 Jarvis Street in 1875. It was a traditional Toronto bay-n-gable, semi-detached house of modest proportions, located on lower Jarvis Street, a site later covered by the massive Sears Building, south of Gould Street. In the 1880s, a "proper" middle-class widow's options were distinctly limited. Without an adequate inheritance or

2.12: *Tea Time at 39 Huron Street*, 1909

William James, the sternly staring patriarch at the centre of this large family grouping, emigrated from England in late 1906. By 1909, when this photograph was taken, he was an established professional photographer and living in the first of his four Toronto homes, 39 Huron Street, a tiny, half-worker's cottage located south of Grange Avenue (and still standing in 2005). The James family undoubtedly lived in crowded conditions. Here, we see eleven people and one cat, gathered around a fold-out table in the corner of the kitchen/dining/living room. All the proprieties are being observed: a proper English tea is set on a white tablecloth; solid furniture rings the room; numerous knick-knacks are neatly displayed along the mantlepiece; leather-bound books are piled atop the highboy; and the alarmingly loud, water-lily wallpaper is decorated with an abundance of prints, photographs, and calendars.

CITY OF TORONTO ARCHIVES: Fonds 1244, Item 3554

2.13: *Parlour Portrait, 1893*
Taken in 1893 at 697 Spadina Avenue (south of Bloor), this parlour portrait is devoid of people, but full of information about both the house and its occupant(s). Although bigger than the James' cottage and located in a more affluent neighbourhood (Dr. W. Warren Baldwin occupied #699), this mildly Romanesque-Revival residence is still modestly proportioned. The main staircase, visible through the string curtains, is a switchback, rather than a straight bank; the parlour and dining rooms appear to open off either side of a small entrance hall, rather than directly into one another as in many middle-class semis. The kitchen is tucked discreetly out of sight in the back. As for the parlour itself, it speaks volumes about the activities, taste, and even aspirations of its occupants; or possibly of its real estate agent, since the first occupant, Gutta-Percha cashier, Stacey Lake, only moved in around the time the photograph was taken. Everything is laid out and carefully displayed for the camera. Here, we see the ubiquitous parlour piano and, on the tiered table, the wildly popular stereoscopic viewer. Slightly less expected are the large, 5-string banjo (they must really have been music-makers), and the issues of *Scribner's Magazine* (they must have been intellectual, or had intellectual pretensions).[38]
CITY OF TORONTO ARCHIVES: Series 379, Item 1234

independent income, she could live in penury; she could become a teacher, a nurse, a governess, or a companion; and/or she could take in boarders. Whether Mrs. Agnew was a teacher before her husband died is unknown. But while residing at 244 Jarvis, she did teach at Winchester School in nearby Cabbagetown, and apparently took in boarders to augment her income. (See 2.13.)

Photographers did not enjoy wealth and status, not at the beginning of their careers, and often never. Based on the evidence from William James,

among others, the photographer was regarded more or less as a skilled craftsman who, by diligence, talent, and diplomacy might rise above this modest station.[37] But modest income did not imply modest pretensions. (See 2.12.)

The quintessential middle-class room was the parlour, where the family could gather, friends be received and entertained, and the family's precious items be put on display. In some cases, the family actually gathered in the kitchen, and the front room was used *only* for formal receptions. (See 2.13)

2.14: *Hallway, The Grange, ca. 1910*

This full-length portrait of the eminent poet, Henry Howard (Earl of Surrey), presided over the oak-panelled front hall of The Grange and all who entered there. Whether hung by the builder of The Grange, arch-Tory D'Arcy Boulton Jr., or by its last male occupant, arch-Liberal Goldwin Smith, Henry Howard was beheaded in 1547 by his fickle patron (and fashion model), Henry VIII.

Among those who flocked to the elegant Georgian home were several generations of prominent Canadians, ranging in political persuasion from Family Compact founder Bishop Strachan to Liberal spokesman George Brown. Whether linked to the Howards by blood, or only fantasy, the owners of the great portrait, and the English Renaissance chest below it, set an aristocratic tone for their home on The Grange, a tone captured by William James ca. 1910, the year Goldwin Smith died. A portrait of The Grange hangs just to the right of the Howard portrait.

CITY OF TORONTO ARCHIVES: Fonds 1244, Item 321A

Upper Class Comfort and Display

Housing provides much more than mere physical comfort. When moving up the social scale, the balance between need and desire shifts radically, although the occupants may often confuse the two. When money is no object, or far less of an object, the nature of the comforts and display varies more according to taste and values, tempered by technology and geographic location, than sheer need. Entirely new rooms and spaces appear on the domestic landscape — drawing-rooms, private studies, libraries, music rooms, billiard rooms, conservatories, large hallways, art galleries, and so on. These are illustrated here and elsewhere in the book. (*See also* Chapters 3, 7, and 8.)

Two of Toronto's most elegant, still extant mansions are The Grange near the Art Gallery of Ontario,[39] and Spadina House atop Davenport Hill just east of Casa Loma.[40] Each offers visitors a grand entrance. Built by Family Compact member D'Arcy Boulton Jr. in 1818, The Grange gives

THE ENTRANCE HALL AT "SPADINA."
This gives also a glimpse of the reception room. The large portrait is that of the late Mr. James Austin.

2.15: Spadina House Hall, 1915

By the time this photograph was taken for *Saturday Night* magazine in January 1915, the second generation of Austins had made many changes to Spadina House, including adding extensions to the north, south, and top of the house, and a port-cochèred main entrance to the west. Inside, the main staircase (featured here), had been reconfigured: a telephone room had been added, the drawing-room converted into a music room, and the doorways connecting the principal rooms enlarged so that dancers could swirl in a great, uninterrupted circle — through the hall, music room (to the right), reception room (behind), and back to the hall. Even the distinctive gold-and-white wallpaper had been replaced by dark green Art Nouveau paper.[41] Through it all, James Austin (painted by his talented and socially dominant daughter, Anne Arthurs) kept watch from half-way up the stairs, while his original gasolier continued to illuminate the Edwardian glitterati and post-millennial tourists still drawn to Toronto's most elegant house on Davenport Hill.

TORONTO PUBLIC LIBRARY

The entrance hall is after the Italian manner; paved in black and gold marble. An interesting treatment of the stairwell is the coffered ceiling decorated in blue, grey, and deep ivory.

2.16: Mrs. Christie's Hall, 1927

Residential architecture in the 1920s tended more toward revival — Gothic, Classical, and Georgian — than Moderne or even Art Deco. Long-time Toronto architect, John Lyle, who worked in many styles, created this residence for Mrs. R. J. Christie of Frybrooke Road in 1927. Instructed simply to "design a beige stucco house with grey-green shutters," Lyle designed the eclectic mansion whose striking entrance hall was "paved in black and gold marble laid in the Italian manner." Lyle selected Emile Wenger to create the hall's "imposing wrought iron stair rail finished to a burnished steel effect relieved by gold." Among Wenger's papers at the City of Toronto is Lyle's description of the house, published in an unidentified magazine with this photograph and a detail of the stair railing.

CITY OF TORONTO ARCHIVES: Series 512, File 3

2.17: *Blake's Study*, ca. 1880
While most of the rooms photographed ca. 1880 are decorated-for-display in typically ornate, overstuffed, occasionally bizarre Victoriana, this upstairs room is clearly lived-in. Here is Blake's study, giving the impression that the great man has just stepped out for a moment and will return shortly to work on the legal papers strewn across his desk. The sun-drenched windows face south; heavily laden bookcases line the east wall, and contain a copy of Adam Smith's *Wealth of Nations*; and an empty chair appears to await the arrival of a statesman or a favour-seeker to consult the Leader of the Liberal Party. A rare glimpse beyond the public rooms of a big house.

Torontonians a touch of red-brick, late-Georgian elegance. Over time, owners of The Grange amassed an art collection that formed the basis of the Art Gallery of Ontario (initially the Art Museum of Toronto), which was bequeathed the property by the last Boulton to live there, Harriette Boulton Smith, who died shortly before her second husband, the notable Liberal, Dr. Goldwin Smith, in 1909. The entrance hall at The Grange is suitably and conspicuously dominated by artwork. (See 2.14.)

James Austin built the current Spadina House in 1866, on the site of two previous Baldwin Spadina Houses. Spadina House boasts extensive gardens, a conservatory, an unusual gold-and-white drawing-room, and an entrance hall still lit by the gas that Consumers' Gas President Austin brought to the property in the 1860s. Hallways link principal rooms and provide corridors for servants to go about their business discreetly and inconspicuously; but in the great scheme of things, the grand entrance hall is superfluous, and therefore a mark of distinction. (See 2.15.)

Architectural styles may change, but luxurious design in luxurious space is a constant, as John Lyle knew when he, with the help of master metal

worker, Emile Wenger, created a sumptuous twenties' hall for an affluent client. (See 2.16. For more about Wenger, see Chapters 6 and 8.)

Only the wealthy could afford either the very public forms of display or the very private comforts of home offered by the rooms illustrated here. For example, the study. Not everyone would want, or could afford, such a room. But one of Toronto's most distinguished citizens did, and could: the Hon.

Edward Blake, who purchased Homewood in 1879. Blake was the first Liberal premier of Ontario (1870–71), the mentor of long-time Premier, Sir Oliver Mowat, a prominent lawyer, and the only Federal Liberal Leader never to become Prime Minister. After purchasing a pair of picturesque, Second Empire-cum Italianate semi-detached residences on the east side of elm-lined, ultra-fashionable Jarvis Street, he adaptively recycled the buildings according to the needs of his family.[42] One of those needs was obviously his own, well-used, private study. (See 2.17.)

Architect Frederic W. Cumberland built Pendarves between 1857 and 1860, while creating his nearby masterpiece, University College. Pendarves was

2.19: *Conservatory, Cumberland House,* ca. 1890

Inspired by Paxton's great Crystal Palace in 1851, Toronto's first quasi-crystal palace was Sanford Fleming's 1858 Palace of Industry.[44] Just when a domestic conservatory, or glass house, was built at Cumberland House is unknown, but Bruce's photograph provides an early glimpse into the genre. Here, an elegant glass dome shelters a wide variety of palms and other exotic plants, imported from remote corners of the Empire, purchased locally from a thriving nursery business such as Stone & Wellington on Church Street, or even exchanged among the active members of Toronto's thriving Horticultural Society.[45] However obtained, the plants and their glass homes were elegant status symbols.

the first building on St. George Street, although it initially fronted onto College Street. After designing University College, Cumberland gave up architecture, entered into even more lucrative businesses, and moved into Pendarves, where he lived until his death in 1881. Now generally known as Cumberland House, the mansion at 33 St. George Street was redesigned in 1883 by Cumberland's former partner, William Storm, and was sold a few years later to Robert Hay, the co-founder of the famous Jacques & Hay furniture company. Hay moved into the house after retiring from his furniture companies and was probably the occupant who hired Josiah Bruce to photograph the handsome, mid-Victorian mansion that is now owned and operated by the University of Toronto. (See 2.18.)

The Victorians were keen naturalists and mad collectors — of shells, butterflies, beetles, plants, and much else. It's not surprising, therefore, that the "glass house" or "conservatory" became a distinctly Victorian addition to the domestic landscape. Such rooms, or buildings, were made possible by two innovations: the introduction of that great new building material, cast iron, which also supported railway stations, crystal palaces, and such newfangled,

2.20: *Baronial Hall, Holwood, ca. 1910*
Photographed by William James around 1910, Sir Joseph Flavelle's vaulted baronial hall boasted a magnificent, carved oak mantel, a (copy) of Raphael's High Renaissance Vatican fresco, the *School of Athens*, and (genuine) Art Nouveau frescoes by Gustav Hahn that still give the room a "subaqueous effect."[47] The Raphael aptly points to Flavelle's long association with the University of Toronto, while the Hahn underlines his tasteful material success. Gustav Hahn, who lived in the Arts & Crafts enclave of Wychwood Park, also decorated the Legislative Chamber at Queen's Park, Chester Massey's Art Gallery on Jarvis Street, and Sir Edmund Walker's library at Long Garth on St. George Street. A work by Hahn was a mark of distinction for the late-Victorians and Edwardians, but apparently not for later generations, since little of his work has survived either the decorator[48] or the wrecker.[49]
CITY OF TORONTO ARCHIVES: Fonds 1244, Item 372

multi-storey buildings as department stores and skyscrapers; and the introduction of exotic plants from the far-flung reaches of the Empire.[43] Seen from these perspectives, the conservatory was a perfect focus for upper-middle-class conspicuous consumption. (See 2.19.)

Arguably the "grandest of the Edwardian Georgian houses in Toronto"[46] was Sir Joseph Flavelle's Holwood built in 1901–02 at 78 Queen's Park

Crescent. Entered through a monumental Corinthian portal, the interior has been substantially altered since Flavelle's time. Only his vaulted baronial hall, created a decade or so before he actually became a baron, has been preserved, in all its dark, Jacobean splendour. (See 2.20.)

Joseph Flavelle was one of those self-made Victorian men who rose from humble beginnings to fame and considerable fortune. (Timothy Eaton and

2.21: *Drawing-room, Flavelle House, ca. 1910*

Unlike Sir Henry Pellatt, his far more flamboyant contemporary, Sir Joseph Flavelle refused to allow photographers into the family's private spaces. But he did allow photographs of the mansion's public rooms. This photograph by William James shows one of the many formal rooms, created more to impress the visitor than to comfort the sitter. Only the elaborate plaster ceiling can now be detected in parts of the University of Toronto Law School, along with other Edwardian touches such as elaborately encased radiators. What struggling photographer James, of tiny 39 Huron Street, thought of Flavelle's overhoused splendour goes unrecorded.

CITY OF TORONTO ARCHIVES: Fonds 1244, Item 307

Daniel Massey were others.) In Flavelle's case, he was born in Peterborough where he began his business career as a clerk, migrated to Toronto in 1887, and became co-owner of the William Davies Company, which he expanded into the largest pork-packer in the British Empire, and the first nationwide retail grocery business in Canada. With this secure base, he went on to diversify his wealth in banking and insurance, and became one of Toronto's foremost philanthropists, including stints with the Toronto General Hospital, the University of Toronto, and the Toronto Housing Company, which built Spruce Court and Riverdale Courts. During the First World War he headed the Ottawa-based Imperial Munitions Board, earning a knighthood and a considerable amount of post-War criticism for the huge profits the Davies Company had made supplying meat to the armed forces.[50] Public ambivalence, about his success and his

2.22: *Tea Time at the Castle,* ca. 1914
Even before Sir Henry's horticultural delights[53] had been moved into their new Conservatory, the Pellatts entertained in grand, but waning, Edwardian style. (The picture may actually have been taken after the death of Edward VII in 1910, but before the "long" Edwardian Era was obliterated by the Great War.) Approached through three sets of Italianate bronze doors, the Conservatory was bathed in translucent light, good for growing plants and taking high-society pictures.[54]
CITY OF TORONTO ARCHIVES: Fonds 1244, Item 4073

2.23: *Library Corner, Casa Loma, 1922*

Never meant to be a quiet place of contemplation, Pellatt's grand Library perfectly describes his devotion to opulent display: glazed bookcases with room for 10,000 books — but relatively few on shelves; elaborately carved Jacobean furniture, beautiful to behold — but not to settle on; and many well-lit paintings — but a paucity of decent reading lights. William James photographed the Library in August 1922, exactly a year before the collapse of the Home Bank and Sir Henry's fortune. Within two years, all the books, paintings, and other furnishings shown here were sold at auction. In the late 1920s, when a hotel-apartment scheme was undertaken (with Pellatt as one of the backers), the Dining Room and Library were folded into one dining room for the residents. This, too, failed.

un-Methodist worldly display, was reflected in the popular epithet for Flavelle's magnificent mansion: "Porker's Palace."

The height of Edwardian excess, not only in Toronto, but in all of Canada, was undoubtedly Sir Henry Pellatt's 98-room castle on Davenport Hill: Casa Loma. Built between about 1909 and 1914, this well-known Toronto landmark was designed by Pellatt's future neighbour, E. J. Lennox, himself no stranger to grandiose display.[51] Lennox ably fed Sir Henry's Scottish baronial appetites by selecting choice bits from such Victorian splendours as the Queen's own Balmoral in Aberdeenshire, and from more ancient and equally romantic castles in Europe. When (relatively) completed, however, Casa Loma was no military fortress, but a megalomaniacal monument to romance and cupidity.[52] "Pellatt's Folly," as the work was aptly christened, did include a 50-metre-long shooting

gallery and space in the basement to drill the Queen's Own Rifles, but more importantly, it included every convenience known to Edwardian man: 5,000 electric lights (Pellatt earned much of his fortune in hydro-electricity), over 30 well-appointed bathrooms, a central vacuuming system, a temperature-controlled wine cellar, and an electric-powered elevator. It also included such Gilded Age necessities as a truly Great Hall, an Oak Drawing-room, a two-tiered billiard room, a marble-floored Conservatory, and a huge Elizabethan Library. (See 2.22–2.24.)

In style and substance, Pellatt was the archetypical "bloated plutocrat." Along with Senator George A. Cox, Pellatt was arguably the best-connected money-man in Edwardian Toronto.[55] Having once won the American championship for running the mile,[56] the svelte young man who had entered the Queen's Own Rifles for love and social advancement, evolved into the 300-pound baronet who dined (well) with royalty, resolved to build a castle "worthy of a Knight of the British Realm,"[57] and risked everything (of his own and of his family, friends, and servants) to make his dream come true. Given the flight of his fancy, and the ignominy of his fall, Casa Loma stands as a suitably grand architectural rebuke to the knight dubbed by Dennis Duffy as "the sinister clown prince of heroic Canadian capitalism."[58]

3

Rooms for Comment

Over time, domestic interiors evolved from the single, all-purpose room —

that sometimes included animals as well as humans — to collections

of specialized rooms or sections of rooms.

heir names, functions, and locations relative to one another, also varied, according to such factors as level of available domestic technology (the outhouse versus the indoor toilet), class (kitchen-as-centre-of-family-life versus kitchen-as-servants'-work-area), ethnic background (British "parlour" versus American "living room"), geographic location (city versus country, Upper versus Lower Canada), and so on.[1]

Architectural Plans & Sketches

Photographs are only one, very rich, resource for studying how people built, shaped, and used domestic spaces. Some questions — such as what a room was called, or where it was located in relation to other rooms — cannot be answered by photographs alone. Other types of records, such as architectural drawings, are invaluable, complementary sources of information. Unfortunately, few residential plans and drawings were ever drawn, and fewer still have survived to help us unravel vexing issues — such as when bathrooms entered the average Toronto house (toward the end of the nineteenth century[2]); or what Torontonians called the formal sitting area ("parlour" or "drawing-room," depending mostly on social status); or where servants lived (generally in either the basement or the attic); or whether Torontonians ever used the very Dutch New York term "stoop" (they did, very occasionally[3]).

Plans were more likely to have been created by architects (the designers of a relatively small

percentage of all residences), and for major residences (such as Casa Loma). Most buildings never generated plans at all, at least in the period under consideration here. But occasionally, researchers get lucky. They may stumble on a little sketch or a published plan or an unprepossessing drainage plan that helps dispel some of the uncertainty. Here we look at two outstanding issues: room names,

3.1: *Sketch for House on Selby Street, 1882*
The size, location, and functions of rooms varied across time and space, but the very *names* of rooms also varied, and now reveal a good deal about the original builders, inhabitants, and the society in which they lived. For example, the "parlour" was more-or-less ubiquitous in nineteenth-century British Toronto, but has virtually vanished from modern, multicultural Toronto where "living room" is the current favourite. The significance of room names is nicely illustrated by a small sketch found with the City of Toronto's building permits. In November 1882, Toronto surveyor, H. J. Browne, wanted to apply for a permit to build a modest brick house on Selby Street, near Sherbourne and Bloor Streets. In order to support his application, he sent the Commissioner a rough (and now very rare) drawing of his proposed structure. Although the house was a modest, middle-class structure (a seven-room house, with a 20-foot frontage on a 30-foot lot), Mr. Browne clearly had pretensions. He labelled his sitting area a Drawing-room, rather than just an ordinary Parlour; and a tiny 3 x 3-foot, storage nook, with the more-impressive-sounding Conservatory. Browne got his permit on November 30, 1882, and erected his house on a site now covered by a high-rise building.
CITY OF TORONTO ARCHIVES: Sketch by J. Browne. RG 13, Series C, Subseries 4, Box 1, Permit 188, Nov. 30, 1882

and arrangement of rooms, especially in modest, middle-class homes.

Turn-of-the-century Toronto's cultural location was between British and American traditions, so it's not surprising that even the naming of rooms can be emblematic and problematic.[4]

Informal sketches, like H. J. Browne's, and formal architectural drawings offer invaluable insight into the history of domestic space. For example, the room known as a den. A. J. Denison's blueprints for upscale Spadina Gardens, an early apartment house on lower Spadina Road, indicate that the term "den" had entered the local architectural lexicon by 1905.

E. J. Lennox's plans for Casa Loma suggest that the term "den" should not be used loosely or without confirmation. Contrary to the labelling of a lantern slide created by William James, of "Sir Henry Pellatt's Private Den," Sir Henry probably didn't have a den among his 98 rooms. He *did* have a fashionable "nook" in the corner of his massive Library, and across Peacock Alley from the Library, there was a large room labelled "Business Office."[5] Both of these had plenty of space for his massive desk.

Photographs provide useful, but limited information about the size, shape, and relationship of rooms to one another. Without a thorough documentation of interior space, which seldom occurs, the overall layout of the space, or even the total number of rooms, remains a mystery. Again, surviving plans provide essential information. E. J. Lennox's plans for Sir Henry Pellatt's mansion on Davenport Hill included plans not only for the main buildings, but also for such ancillary buildings as a pair of Workmen's Cottages, located north of the first structures completed on the site: Pellatt Lodge at the corner of Austin Terrace and Walmer Road, and the fabled Stables. These "cottages," in reality a pair of semi-detached brick houses, reveal a good deal about domestic technology (they included a 3-piece, indoor bathroom on the second floor), as well as disposition of space (the main floor was composed of parlour, dining room, and kitchen at the back, a very common form of middle-class housing in Victorian and Edwardian Toronto). (See 3.2–3.4.)

The Kitchen

No matter where it has been located, how it has been arranged, what it has contained, or what it has been called, the kitchen has always shaped domestic

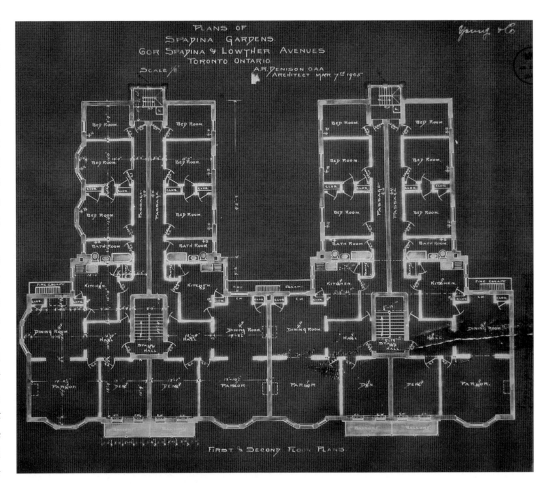

3.2: "The Den," Spadina Gardens, 1905. Private Collection
The den has had a somewhat checkered career in Toronto architectural history. It was clearly a later addition to the architectural vocabulary than the kitchen or parlour or drawing room, and an earlier entry than family room or rec room. Here is A. R. Denison's 1905 rendering of the concept, on the First and Second Floors of his elegantly appointed Spadina Gardens at 41 Spadina Road. Each unit has a "parlor" with a bay window, and a smaller den opening off the entry hall.
PRIVATE COLLECTION

3.3: *Sir Henry Pellatt's Desk, 1922*

William James photographed Sir Henry Pellatt's "private" desk at Casa Loma in August 1922, either in the Library "nook" or the "business office" indicated on Lennox's 1909 plan. Despite the paintings lining the wall, Pellatt was no art connoisseur. Unlike American robber-barons like Frick, Mellon, and Morgan, Pellatt neither collected great art nor left a public legacy to burnish socially tarnished reputations. According to Lady Eaton, Sir Henry bought and installed the finely carved, gold frames before choosing the art.[6] The narcissus flowers on Pellatt's desk seem suitable ones for the flamboyant builder of Toronto's fantasy castle.

CITY OF TORONTO ARCHIVES: Fonds 1244, Item 4140

GROUND FLOOR PLAN.

3.4: *"Workmen's Cottages,"*
Casa Loma, 1905

In July 1905, Sir Henry Pellatt's architect, E. J. Lennox, filed this plan for a pair of semi-detached houses labelled Workmen's Cottages. Located immediately north of Pellatt's vast, and luxuriously appointed, stables, these houses were unusually well-designed homes for "workers," such as the gardeners and grooms who lived here. Each cottage was smallish, with a frontage of 19-feet, but had a traditional ground-floor plan of parlour at the front, dining room in the middle, and kitchen at the back — a layout seen over and over in Toronto and in other urban housing. One of Metro Toronto's most powerful bureaucrats from the 1950s to the 1970s, Parks Commissioner Tommy Thompson, was born and raised here, because his father, George Thompson, was Pellatt's chief gardener.

CITY OF TORONTO ARCHIVES: Series 454, File 1, Ground Floor Plan

3.5: *A Home made Xmas Pudding in the Making, 1910*

Even pushed into a corner of a room, the "kitchen" was often a richly symbolic centre of family life. Clearly, making plum pudding was a vital part of the James' Christmas ritual. "The family see that nothing but the best produce is minced," a family member noted on the back of this 1910 photograph. The photographer has captured both the physical process ... and the transcendently joyful expectation of the end product, which was being created in a corner of their crowded home at 39 Huron Street. By moving furniture around (opening and closing tables, and so on), the family could transform this multi-purpose room into a parlour sitting area, a dining /tea room, and a kitchen.

The little fellow with the blond curls is Norm James, who grew up to be a well-known photographer for the *Toronto Star*.

CITY OF TORONTO ARCHIVES: Fonds 1244, Item 3518

life, practically and symbolically.[7] From the era of the open fire to the era of the microwave oven, the preparation of food has occupied a central position in "the home," sometimes quite literally, as in the crofter's peat-fired cottage, more often metaphorically, as in many of the photographs illustrating this book.

Between the 1880s and the 1920s, the Toronto kitchen underwent radical revisions, moving from human mechanical power to gas and electric power; from candles and oil lamps to gas and electric lighting; from wood and coal-fired stoves to gas and electric ranges; from buckets filled at a communal pump to indoor sinks with hot and cold running water; from no refrigeration or only (real) iceboxes, to gas and electric refrigerators. The changes were vast, and they constituted a move from the pre-Industrial to the almost-Modern kitchen.[8] As always, personal resources governed the level of technology and the nature of the space available to any particular household.

The poor had to make do with cramped quarters, no gas or electrical assistance, and only the most basic equipment — coal or wood stove, multi-purpose table, kerosene lamps, and maybe indoor water. City photographer, Arthur Goss, documented many kitchen areas in The Ward and other poor areas of Toronto; some were in chaos, others were immaculately clean. (See 3.6.)

The middle and upper levels of society had more space and more options. Middle-class households often had servants, but many housewives, like Mrs. Arthur Beales, also worked in the kitchen. These households had many amenities: more workspace and storage cabinets; more easily cleaned linoleum floors; running water (sometimes even hot as well as cold); gas or electric stoves; and lighting. The larger space available was a mixed blessing.

3.6: *Thirteen Centre Avenue, 1914*

Arthur Goss photographed this neat little kitchen as part of Dr. Hastings' documentation of "slum conditions" in pre-World War I Toronto. Why this place was chosen is unclear, since it appears to be immaculately, even lovingly, tended. A framed horse-print and an elegant Coca Cola ad enliven the wall, while a decorative curtain is drawn across an already closed door. No smoke smudges the walls or ceiling. No dirty pots or dishes clutter the work area. A sleeping couch is far too close to the wood or coal "Home Comfort" stove for either sleeping comfort or safety, but it is hardly an unsanitary arrangement.

CITY OF TORONTO ARCHIVES: Series 372, Subseries 32, Item 323

3.7: Mrs. Arthur Beales In Her Kitchen, ca. 1914

Arthur Beales, the long-time official photographer for the Toronto Harbour Commissioners, photographed his young wife in their kitchen, probably at 114 Summerhill Avenue, between 1910 and 1915. Mrs. Beales' large kitchen was located at the back of the house, where most Toronto kitchens were and still are. Unlike the multi-purpose kitchens photographed by James and Goss, this kitchen is distinctly separated from the rest of the house by a wall. This shields the front of the house from the sounds and odours of cooking, and isolates the housewife (and/or the servants) from the rest of the house. Mrs. Beales enjoyed certain new conveniences, such as a hot-water boiler beside, and probably attached to the stove, and a small sink with hot and cold running water (two exposed pipes run along the wall between the pantry door and the closet).[9] Yet the stove is still coal or wood-burning and there is no evidence of electric or gas lighting, although one or the other seems likely. The large size of this kitchen probably created more work for the cook than a smaller, more efficiently planned arrangement. The big bag of flour in the wooden drawer, the flour-sifter, bowl of eggs, and rolling pin on the work table, suggest that Mrs. Beales is baking. The walls were comparatively dark, the cabinets and furniture were all wooden, and the floor was covered with patterned linoleum.

LIBRARY AND ARCHIVES CANADA: PA800211

3.8: *Summering at the Island*, 1890s
Roughing it in the bush, on the lake, or at the Island has long been a Canadian tradition. At the cottage — or in the tent — summering Torontonians often tolerated cramped quarters and lower technologies than they might accept during the rest of the year. F. W. Micklethwaite and his family are having a meal in one part of their marquee tent, which was located between the Lakeside Home for Little Children and the Gibralter Point Lighthouse. Despite their camping status, the Micklethwaites' furnishings are impressive and include a substantial stove. Like other Islanders, they did not have running water or indoor plumbing, and had to share communal pumps and outdoor privies. But unlike many Islanders, the Micklethwaites' kitchen area does not seem to be relegated to a separate tent at the back.
CITY OF TORONTO ARCHIVES: Series 388, Item 36

economically important to society. As a result, Frederick Taylor's principles of scientific management, based on close analysis of how people and machines actually performed their work, swept through the industrial and business worlds during the late-nineteenth and early twentieth-centuries, but had virtually no impact on the domestic world until after

Sometimes the technical advances seemed modest, but were far-reaching in impact, such as fashioning old utensils out of new materials, like lightweight tin, and applying proper "time and motion" planning to domestic spaces like the kitchen. (See 3.9.)

the First World War. In June 1919, household efficiency expert, Katherine M. Caldwell, commented on this fact in an early Canadian women's magazine, *Everywoman's World*:

Planning-for-efficiency, not to mention comfort, came late to the kitchen. Most kitchens, if they were "designed" at all, were designed by men who never used such spaces, and domestic kitchens were simply not regarded as

The most personal, most-used and frequently, alas, the most inconvenient room in the average home, is the kitchen. This is especially true of the kitchen in the old-fashioned house ... fortunately,

3.9: *Tin Pans,* **1890s**

One of the often unsung advances in domestic technology that eased the burden of many servants and housewives was the creation of tin pans, as displayed in this photograph of George and Mabel Parker's 10th (Tin) Anniversary presents at 190 Cowan Avenue, around 1900. Early cooks had to work with extremely large and heavy iron pots, which were back-breaking, cumbersome and potentially dangerous.[10]

CITY OF TORONTO ARCHIVES: Fonds 1649, Item 14

the subject of kitchen planning has of late years assumed something of its proper importance in architectural eyes, and we not so often find the window so placed that it can light neither stove nor table, the place where the stove must stand far distant as possible from table and sink, the whole arrangement of the room predestined to be as awkward and step-making as possible.[11]

As for the legacy of old kitchens, which formed the bulk of kitchens in 1919 or any other year, Ms. Caldwell was optimistic: "Even an old-style kitchen ... may frequently be improved, if it is carefully studied and recognition given to the fact that its sanitary, cheery and convenient nature is of the very greatest importance, not only to the woman who works in it, but *to the whole family.*" Place the major appliances and work areas conveniently around the central workspace (a table) and relative to light sources like windows and a central electric light. Cover hard-to-clean old pine floors with up-to-date materials like linoleum. Ban dark colours — "Who could happily concoct a poem in gelatine, eggs and whipped cream, whilst dour-looking walls of an unhealthy brown hue, glowered upon her?" Put the sink "at a proper working level — absolutely the first improvement every woman should insist upon in her kitchen." Install plenty of (white or light-coloured) cabinets and storage spaces around the room. And place the "hub of the kitchen," a table, in the most logical and convenient place for it to be, "in the middle of the room."

With respect to *new* kitchens, where more choice was possible, too much space was the enemy, not the ally of happy kitchen life:

> In the first place, the great, spacious kitchen of our grandmother's day, is as out of date as hoop-skirts and side-curls. The miles of walking in a year, from sink to table, from table to stove, from stove to cupboard! The thousands of strokes with the scrubbing brush, to keep the wide expanse of pine floor snowy!

So ... "no more immense kitchens, for the moderate-sized house," she declared (with good reason). "Rather a small, compact apartment, where every foot of space counts, and provision is made for the ideal placing of each piece of equipment."

The Parlour[12]

Only the poorest of the poor did not have a designated "parlour," or so it seems from surviving photographs and plans.[13] As elsewhere, the poor had to make do with a single, not-so-large, multi-functional area for kitchen, sitting, and sleeping. (See 3.11.) Nevertheless, even the corner of an apartment could provide an appropriate setting for sitting and personal display, although human occupation was sometimes superfluous. (See 3.12.)

Cooking, eating, and sitting were the major activities accommodated by the ground floor of the typical, middle-class Toronto home, with the kitchen at the back, the dining room in the middle, and the parlour at the front of the house. Such an arrangement was, and still is, found with great regularity in narrow, detached houses, as well as semi-detached, row, and other multiple-housing forms. Dedicating an entire room to sitting, entertaining and formal display enhanced the scope for personal display ... and increased the terror for young visitors, like Helen Murphy when she visited her grandmother's ultra Victorian parlour. "My grandmother's parlor (sic) was an awesome room. Its very air whispered 'Helen, don't touch.'" The parlour in her own home on Collier Street was "much less forbidding with its pale green satin-striped wallpaper, its lovely cream-coloured lace curtains and its airy, if formal, feeling of welcome." And it was in such parlours that proper little girls like Helen Murphy learned the social proprieties of her class, such as passing the tea and cream for her mother's "At Home" event every third Thursday.[15] (See 3.13.)

The parlour piano was almost ubiquitous. Some were small and extremely plain — see the Micklethwaite piano in *Photographer's Parlour*, 2.1. Others were of modest dimensions, like the James' family piano illustrated in 3.14. And others were extremely elaborate, such as the upright photographed at Cumberland House and the drawing-room grand found at Spadina House. Numerous Canadian firms built and sold pianos, notably Toronto's Heintzman, Mason & Risch, and Nordheimer companies.[17] Many Victorian homes even had a "piano window," a small stained- or bevelled-glass window set five or six feet above the floor to provide space for an upright. Most entertainment

3.11: *9 Alice Street*, 1913
On August 14, 1913, Arthur Goss photographed both the exterior and interior of 9 Alice Street for the Toronto Board of Education. On this hot summer day in The Ward, Goss captured not only a very tired and dirty little fellow falling asleep on a chair, but also the occupants' clear delineation of their space into functional areas, and their efforts to personalize and decorate the space. An ornately coiffed oil lamp sits on a cloth-covered table in the sitting area; and the walls are papered and decorated — with a portrait, a drugstore calendar, and a print of an aproned cook. The patriarchal portrait and the female cook reflect the (so often unattained) family ideals of the time. Certainly, Mrs. Dinah (Silverman) Donn, who is sitting nearly off-camera to the right, was abandoned by her husband and left with the daunting task of raising at least four children.[14]
CITY OF TORONTO ARCHIVES: Series 372, Subseries 11, Item 95

3.12: *Parkers' Wedding Gift,* ca. 1899
George Parker, a clerk at dry-goods wholesaler, Cockshutt & Co., lived with his family at 22 Spadina Avenue, just south of Wellington, near Clarence Square. An anonymous photographer posed the Parkers' prized wedding gift, a rocking chair, in the corner of their apartment. Here it shares pride of place with family photographs, potted aralia, framed prints, mounted china saucer, and frilly daybed.
CITY OF TORONTO ARCHIVES: Fonds 1649, Item 6

3.13: *Grandmother's Parlour,* ca. 1900
Helen Murphy Ball aptly described the furnishings and the temptations associated with her grandmother's parlour in Parkdale, which is shown in this photograph, "The mantel, surmounted by a towering wall cabinet, was high enough for its own safety but what a glorious wreck a small child could have made of its bric-a-brac, photographs, artificial flowers, etc., had she succumbed to temptation, jumped up and yanked on the fringe of the silk scarf so carefully draped around Venus."[16] Although no piano is shown in this corner of her Grandmother's parlour, another popular instrument of the day is prominently displayed: a mandolin.
CITY OF TORONTO ARCHIVES: Fonds 1228, Item 7

3.14: *The Parlour Piano,* ca. 1909
William James photographed his daughter, Gillian, playing the family piano at 39 Huron Street. James was a struggling photographer, but provided a piano for the family. Here, under a photograph of her maternal grandparents and next to two brothers, Gillian plays "Sabbath Melodies," illustrating yet another use to which the popular instrument was put.
CITY OF TORONTO ARCHIVES: Fonds 1244, Item 3565

was home entertainment, and much of it involved the piano. You didn't have to be rich to own a piano, although, if you *were* rich, you could own a better instrument — a Steinway (like Lady Eaton's) or a pipe organ (like Sir Joseph Flavelle's) — set in its own "music room."

Although there were phonographs during most of this period (the phonograph was invented in 1877 and the record in 1887), the piano was still king; and sheet music sold in the millions. Although many of the songs were "foreign" — from Britain and Broadway — many were home-grown, like those revived by Canada's Primadonna on a Moose, Mary Lou Fallis: "Paddle Your Own Canoe" (1862), celebrated the independence of spirit associated with that most Canadian of vessels; "Since the Hydro Came" (1912) bemoaned the romantic implications of bright street lighting in formerly dark parks; "Have Courage My Boy, To Say 'No!'" (1910) was a temperance admonition; and "We Dye to Live!" (1890) was an early jingle for the R. Parker & Company Dye Works, designed to stimulate business and brand-loyalty. The songs, of course, reflected the attitudes, events, and concerns of their times. As such, they are well worth studying. They are also good fun, as Ms. Fallis has demonstrated.[18]

In the grandest homes of all, the various functions of the modest, middle-class parlour evolved into collections of distinct rooms, such as morning room, drawing-room, library, music room and art gallery. Take, for example, Lady Eaton's music room at *Ardwold* (3.16) and Chester Massey's private art gallery at 519 Jarvis Street. (3.17.)

Both the piano and the room reflect the wealth of the homeowner, John H. Mason of *Ermeleigh,* at the corner of Sherbourne and Wellesley. Here, the "parlour" has grown into the "drawing-room," and the parlour "upright" has grown into the drawing-room "grand." Although Mason's house was electrified, and various kinds of light fixtures are evident (both overhead electrolier and table lamps), it is not clear how the piano might have been lit. Perhaps romantic old candelabra were dragged out for appropriate occasions. More likely, one of the era's distinctive "piano lamps" stood off-camera.
CITY OF TORONTO ARCHIVES: Fonds 1212, Item 7

3.16: *Ardwold Music Room,* **ca. 1922**

After Timothy Eaton died in 1907, his son took control of the family retail empire. The newly appointed president and his wife decided that they needed a larger house befitting his new job and their new social position. The couple built a 50-room, neo-Georgian, red-brick mansion on the brow of Davenport Hill where both Eatons could indulge their musical talents. Sir John C. Eaton had his mechanical aeolian organ in the Great Hall where he pumped away with great enthusiasm of an evening, and Lady Eaton had her own, exquisitely carved Steinway in the nearby Music Room. Flora Eaton was a genuinely talented pianist, who had even performed at Massey Hall, and was a frequent host of concerts that featured everyone from Dr. Vogt, head of the Toronto Conservatory of Music, to Harry Lauder, the irreverent London wit who frequently visited Ardwold. How the ukele-playing Lauder saluted the dancing cherubs goes unrecorded.[19]
ONTARIO ARCHIVES/EATON ARCHIVES: AO 3740

3.17: *Chester Massey's Art Gallery, ca. 1910*

When the somewhat reclusive Chester Massey was forced by family obligation to take over the Massey manufacturing empire in 1884, he moved into the second Massey mansion on Jarvis Street[20]; started a family, which included future Governor-General Vincent Massey and future acting star Raymond Massey; helped run the family business; and collected art. In order to house his growing collection, Chester bought the house to his north in 1905, demolished it, and made major renovations to both the interior and exterior of the old E. J. Lennox building. William James photographed Chester Massey's Art Gallery around 1910. The distinctive skylight contained McCausland stained glass (of the sort that graced the new Parliament Buildings at Queen's Park, and presumably Joseph McCausland's own house down at 411 Jarvis Street). The Art Nouveau frieze below the ceiling was painted by noted Art Nouveau painter, Gustav Hahn. Dark brocade wallpaper set off the Old Masters, which are now at the National Gallery in Ottawa. It was in this formidable room that young Raymond Massey told his ailing father that he had decided to become a professional actor rather than join the family business, news that the old man took well.[21]

CITY OF TORONTO ARCHIVES: Fonds 1244, Item 322

3.18: *Crowded Kitchen, 1913*

Arthur Goss captured many eating arrangements in his photographs of poor housing conditions in Toronto. The eight people here, probably three generations of the same family, are crammed into a corner of the kitchen area ... where at least one member of the family could enjoy a blissful dinner. The non-babes-in-arms would have had to jockey for room, and possibly for adequate food. It is unclear what the older woman is doing, but it appears she may be involved with "piece-work" sewing for a local garment manufacturer. Obviously, there was no separate dining room for families like these.

Plan No. 3.

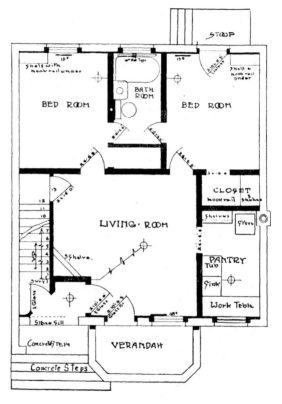

3.19: *Plan No. 3, Riverdale Courts,* ca. 1914
Eden Smith designed a range of "Cottage flats" for the Toronto Housing Company's Spruce Court and Riverdale Courts. This plan for a unit of middle size shows that this ground level "flat" had a verandah overlooking the central common, a well-appointed kitchen and pantry area, two bedrooms, a three-piece bathroom, living room (rather than "parlour") ... but no dining room or designated dining area. Where eating actually happened is unclear. The rent for such a unit was $19.00 or $20.00 per month, depending on where it was located.[23]

3.20: *James Family Christmas Dinner,* ca. 1913
According to the wallpaper, the James family had probably moved to new quarters by the time this photograph was taken by father William, ca. 1913. But whether the family had a separate dining room, or only the corner of a multi-purpose room, they are certainly enjoying a very traditional Christmas feast: the table is elaborately set, an adult male is carving the turkey, and everyone is on his or her best behaviour ... even baby Norman in his high chair. No doubt the Christmas pudding was as fine as usual.

3.21: *Dr. Rea and Daughters, ca. 1892*
Dr. James Rea was a physician and surgeon whose office was at the back of this 3-storey, brick house at 1265 (formerly 301) Dundas West. The house at the corner of Dundas and Dovercourt was modest in size, but big enough for a dining room, here seen from the doctor's parlour, and a live-in servant. In the 1890s, Toronto was undeniably racist at all levels of society. According to Dr. Rae's younger daughter, Lillian, "The [white] servant slept in the third floor & strongly objected to a 'nigger' living on the same floor so [Sam the "colored" coachman] had to sleep in the stable (now of course a garage)...." Neither Sam nor the racist servant ever ate at this highly polished table.[24]
CITY OF TORONTO ARCHIVES: Fonds 1467, Item 3

The Dining Room

Eating is basic to life. But just where and how eating occurs has always depended not only on economic resources, but also on agricultural, technological, and cultural factors of the sort made famous by classicist Margaret Visser.[22] The menu, for example, depended on what food might be available, how much money the family had to spend, what national traditions the family shared, and so on. Plans and photographs confirm that the dining room was something of a luxury: if space was in short supply, a separate dining room did not exist. (See 3.18.)

Plans for the well- and humanely-designed Spruce Court and Riverdale Courts housing for the working poor illustrate the disposable nature of the dining room. While including such relative luxuries as bathroom, gas stove, and electric overhead lighting, none of the units had a dining room, or even a designated dining area. (See 3.19.)

Even when shoved off into a corner, however, dining can be the most ceremonial of domestic routines, as evidenced by the traditional (in some homes) Sunday lunch, Thanksgiving Dinner, and many more religious meals. (See 3.20.)

When separate rooms did exist, they tended to be used only occasionally for food, but always for display, as is shown in this one and the following two, increasingly splendid, dining rooms. (See 3.21–3.23.)

3.22: *Table Setting*, ca. 1900
This gaslit table — with its lavish display of the "right" silver and crystal, the shaded candles and vases of flowers at each place — could have been set at any point during the period covered by this book. The unidentified dining room, photographed by Alexander W. Galbraith, displays solidly expensive Jacques & Hay-style sideboard and chairs, and opens from a corridor through which servants may have quietly entered and exited.
CITY OF TORONTO ARCHIVES: Fonds 1545, Item 53

3.23: *The Simpsons: Dining in Grand Style,* **ca. 1898**

Around 1897, Ernest Simpson and family moved into their new home at 12 Admiral Road. Simpson, a director of the Toronto Knitting Factory on lower Berkeley Street, had hired company architect, Charles J. Gibson, to ply his considerable talents in Toronto's newly fashionable Annex district. Here, an anonymous photographer focussed on a corner of the resplendently embellished dining room. Surrounded by painted stags, stained glass, exquisite woodwork, plaster garlands, and naughty naked caryatids (not a knitted garment in sight), the Simpsons dined in high Victorian style. A highchair was even provided for baby Simpsons over near the patriarchal decanters. In late 2005, retiring Governor-General Adrienne Clarkson and her husband, John Ralston Saul, moved from Rideau Hall into Simpson House.[25] Even with many of the exuberant Victorian details removed, the Vice-Regal couple will dine in grand, twenty-first century style. Perhaps Mr. Saul will also derive inspiration from the spirit of Lester B. Pearson, who once toiled away on the third floor as a young history professor in the mid-1920s.[26] This photograph was probably taken around 1898, perhaps to illustrate the skill of the architect, who went on to design another exuberant Simpson House on fashionable Wellesley Place and many houses in the up-and-coming district of Rosedale.

TORONTO REFERENCE LIBRARY: 992-2-10

3.24: Reflections on Blake, ca. 1880
Although passably well-lit during the day when the front curtain was pulled back for the photographer, Edward Blake's front parlour[29] on Jarvis Street must have been a symphony of light and shadow at night. Despite the clever addition of a reflector, the corner standing oil lamp might not have shed enough light, or shed it in the right direction, for Blake or any of his family to read under. Assuming that the floral fire screen was removed, the room would be lit by flickering flames, enhanced oil lamp, and a pair of overhead lamps, probably fuelled by gas. This kind of jumbled technologies was typical of the time.
CITY OF TORONTO ARCHIVES: Fonds 1146, Item 10

Let There Be Lights

From parlor to bedchamber, from front hall to kitchen, from cellar to attic, there was a gradual but clearly discernible transition from darkness and shadow to brightness and clarity. It is nearly impossible for us to appreciate this transition from a vantage point lighted with fluorescent tubes and halogen bulbs.[27]

The quantity, quality, and location of domestic lights shaped domestic life as much as any other technological change that occurred between the 1880s and 1920s. As Ierley suggests, it is even hard to *imagine* life without having bright, reliable lighting at the tip of a finger. Interior lighting moved from candles and lamps to gas, and, ultimately, electric lighting,[28] although there were long periods of overlap among the various kinds of light.

Generally speaking, internal household changes followed external public changes such as gas street lighting which came to Toronto in the 1840s and electric street lighting, which followed in the 1880s. Gas lighting, at least in newer and wealthier households, dominated domestic lighting from about the 1860s until around the First World War; and electric lighting, which began entering private homes in the late 1880s and early 1890s, came to dominate domestic lighting after the Great War.[30]

Gas and electric fixtures could not be used until gas pipes and electric lines were installed. Even when such services were available, however, the nature of domestic lighting also depended on the taste and resources of the residents.

3.25: *Lamp Lighting, 1914*
The two oil lamps shown here would have done little to brighten the lives of the poor, African-Canadian family who lived at Rear 512 Front Street on August 27, 1914 when Goss took this photograph for the Department of Health's survey of crowded housing conditions. A related photograph showing family members standing outside their home indicates that a dozen or more people lived in this inadequate space, with its windowless walls, damp-damaged ceiling, and extremely cramped quarters. Both natural and artificial lighting was in short supply.

3.26: *Agnew Dining Room,* **ca. 1886**

The two oil lamps on the mantel in this middle-class dining room were elegant, "student lamps," which were portable, fuelled by kerosene, and designed to cast no shadow over the student's work.[33]

Mrs. Agnew's bay-n-gable house at 244 Jarvis Street may have had gas lighting when this photograph was taken around 1886, although there is no evidence in the picture. What is evident is that plenty of natural light could pour into the dining room where this contented group was enjoying a summer treat of watermelon. The Widow Agnew had to take in boarders to supplement her income after her physician husband died, but her household appears to have been a congenial, and well-lit one.

CITY OF TORONTO ARCHIVES: Fonds 80, File 4, Image 1

3.27: *Spruce Court Lighting*, ca. 1914
Light was important to the designers of Spruce Court, who provided a window in every room and electricity to every flat. Probably taken by William James and published in a promotional report,[34] this photograph shows the "pantry-kitchen" portion of the "living room" in one of the smaller cottage flats at Spruce Court. The room may have been multi-purpose, like many living areas photographed by Arthur Goss in the poorer parts of Toronto, but it was much better laid out, had more storage space (shelves over the stove), and, above all, had overhead electric lighting. The outlets were limited to two overhead lights (one in the sitting area and one in the kitchen-pantry area, but none in the bedrooms or bathroom). Still, having any electricity at all was a rare amenity for poor, working people in pre-War Toronto.
CITY OF TORONTO ARCHIVES: Fonds 1018, Cottage Flats, p. 9

For example, the Austin family at Spadina House resisted introducing electric lighting until long after it was physically possible to switch from gas, because James Austin was president of Consumers' Gas and had brought gas to Davenport Hill in the 1860s. James' son, Albert, was also a president of Consumers' Gas and continued to live by gas alone. (See 3.29.) By contrast, their immediate neighbour, Sir Henry Pellatt, was one of the "private power barons"[31] who had made millions from bringing electricity to Torontonians, so he brought electricity to Davenport Hill around 1910, and flooded his castle with electric lighting and appliances.[32] At less-elevated levels of society, options were far more restricted, and economic resources played a key role in domestic opportunities.

While many working-class residents of Toronto had to make do with assorted lamps before the First World War (3.25), the lucky occupants of Spruce Court and its sister development, Riverdale Courts, benefited from electricity, another example of the Toronto Housing Company's desire to house lower-income, working people decently. (See 3.27.)

When land-developer Simeon H. Janes installed electric lighting in the art gallery of his fashionable home at 375 Jarvis Street, he became one of the first Torontonians to brighten his home electrically.[35] Although his experience does not appear to have been a happy one — he used gas to light his grand new home, *Benvenuto*, on Avenue Road in 1890 — electrical lighting was in Toronto to stay. Naturally, it first penetrated the homes of wealthier, and sometimes hipper, Torontonians. New fixtures, service, and so on were expensive, but demonstrably "modern." (See 3.28.)

As newer residential areas, like North Rosedale and Casa Loma, were opened up in the teens, they tended to be serviced with a gas pipe for cooking and heating, and electricity for lighting and, eventually, a multitude of labour-saving devices. Such a pattern of mixed power-sources has persisted, with various permutations, throughout the residential history of Toronto, and many other North American cities.

Just when John H. Mason brought electricity to his mansion at 477 Sherbourne Street is unknown, but it was clearly in use by the time this photograph was taken, around 1912. The aging founder of Canada Permanent[36] adapted the modern marvel to his entrenched Victorian tastes, best symbolized by the shaggy lampshade on the electrical standing lamp, shown in this view from his Drawing-room toward the Library with its central "electrolier." Other photographs of his home show a range of electrical fixtures ... and shaggy objects. The Earnescliffe apartment building at Wellesley and Sherbourne stands on the site of Mason's Second Empire mansion.
CITY OF TORONTO ARCHIVES: Fonds 1212, Item 8

3.29: *Donning the Gas Mantle*, 1915
Consumers' Gas President, James Austin, brought gas to Davenport Hill when he built the third Spadina House on the site in the 1860s. In the 1880s, gas lighting was immeasurably improved by the invention of the Welsbach gas mantle, which produced a bright white light and prolonged its life for domestic lighting.[37] This photograph, which appeared in a January 1915 issue of *Saturday Night*, shows the Austins' 42' x 98', formerly gold-and-white Drawing-room, with its Toronto-produced Jacques & Hay furniture, converted into a moss-green Music Room, with imported 1882 Steinway grand piano, busts of composers, oriental rugs, and flocked "tree-of-life" wallpaper. Through all the changes, crystal gasoliers shone over many an elegant event. For sentimental, and perhaps financial reasons, the Austins of Spadina House clung to gas lighting long after most Torontonians switched to electricity.[38] Their flamboyant next-estate neighbour, Sir Henry Pellatt, was a flashy, perhaps flashing, beacon of modernity, with some 5000 light bulbs illuminating his castle on the hill. (See, *Sir Henry Pellatt's Desk* and *Peacock Alley* in Chapter 2, for examples of domestic lighting at Casa Loma.)
TORONTO PUBLIC LIBRARY

The Servant Problem

We know a good deal about the lives of the rich and famous, but relatively little about the lives of those who served them. It is extraordinarily difficult to find out how marginalized people, like domestic servants, lived their lives. Few records were ever created; and fewer still have survived. Sometimes servants live on as characters in records left by their employers, for example, standing respectfully in the background of photographs featuring the household principles. (See "Farewell Dinner at Government House," in Chapter 5, which records not only the Lieutenant-Governor, but also his butler in attendance.) Occasionally, the camera peaks into the work areas of a household, such as the kitchen, where servants performed their duties. But intimate glimpses directly into the private spaces inhabited by domestics are rarer still and sadly missing from *Inside Toronto*.

In the absence of either written accounts (letters or diaries created by the workers, not their employers) or photographic accounts (snapshots focussing on the servants, not their employers, in their own rooms or other domestic surroundings), other records, like architectural drawings of houses that label "maid's room" or "housekeeper's room," must suffice. Generally, these indicate that domestic servants lived either in the basement or in the attic.[39] In a large household, the more important servants might live on the same floor as the family (the housekeeper and/or the governess), or even in a wing of their own, as was the case at Casa Loma. (See 3.30.)

The Bedroom

Only the moderately wealthy were allowed the luxury of privacy. Providing separate bedrooms for adults and children, let alone for each child, was expensive. The poor, therefore, had to cram themselves into inadequate spaces,

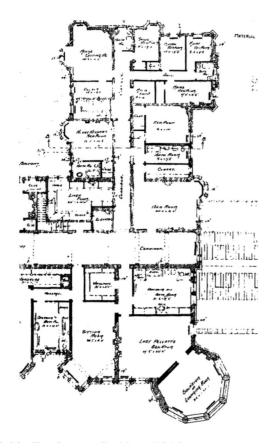

3.30: *The Servant Problem, 1910.*
E. J. Lennox's 1910 plan for the second floor of Casa Loma indicates that Sir Henry and Lady Pellatt's grand bedroom suites stretched along the southeastern facade; a couple of other large bedroom suites (each with its own bathroom) were distributed around the same floor; and servants quarters were located in the northeastern wing of the castle. We do not know how many people were assigned to each of the "maids rooms," but we can instantly see that they were much smaller (the smallest being 9.5 x 9.5 feet) and less amply lit (although each did have a window). The Housekeeper had a large bedroom with its own bathroom, but the other maids had to share two small bathrooms and a general sitting room. Each of the bathrooms had the full complement of tub, sink and water closet, something of a luxury even in 1910.
CITY OF TORONTO ARCHIVES: E.J. Lennox, PT00632-5

3.31: *No Privacy for the Poor*
Just how many people shared this space is unclear. Three beds are visible along the left side, two in the small area that could be curtained off, and one closer to the photographer. Whether any children shared the space with the adults is also unclear, but the clothes indicate that both men and women lived in very tight quarters. They had no running water (only a pitcher and washtub), no electric light (only two oil lamps), and precious little privacy. Kitchen functions stretch along the right side. City photographer Arthur Goss took this picture on October 30, 1913. The occupants remain anonymous.
CITY OF TORONTO ARCHIVES: Series 372, Subseries 32, Item 247

68

3.32: *Bedroom, 1880s*

Just why photographer J. Bruce was allowed to photograph this 1880s bedroom in Cumberland House is unclear, but photograph it he did, along with all the principal public rooms of this splendid residence at 33 St. George Street. The key to Bruce's being given access to private space may be that Cumberland House was occupied by Robert Hay, of Jacques & Hay furniture fame. Perhaps Mr. Hay wanted publicity photos of his very expensive furniture. Whatever the reason, Bruce documented this fine, Jacques & Hay-style bedroom.

CITY OF TORONTO ARCHIVES: Fonds 1155, Item 7

Sir Henry Pellatt was not shy. So it is not surprising that both the public and private parts of Casa Loma were documented for posterity. At a time when separate bedrooms for children were far more unusual than they are now, the Casa Loma child received characteristically overblown treatment: a great, Jacobean-style bed and Chippendale chairs. There was probably also a private bathroom attached to the suite.

creating the illusion of privacy by stretching cloth across the room, or giving up entirely on the notion of privacy. (See 3.31.)

Perhaps not surprisingly, relatively few pictures of either middle-class or upper-class bedrooms have survived. Most professional and amateur photographers focussed on the more public areas of the house, where family members gathered and special events were celebrated. And Sir Joseph Flavelle, like most prominent Torontonians, refused to have the family areas of Holwood photo-graphed. Very occasionally, however, photographers did gain access to the private realms of their wealthy clients. (See 3.32, 3.33.)

The Bathroom

What we know euphemistically as the "bathroom," encompassing at least the triumvirate of tub, toilet and sink, began life as a literal room for a bath, not necessarily with running water, and certainly not with a toilet or a sink nearby. The development of the modern bathroom was a relatively late phenomenon, which depended on technical advances (such as provision of water and sewerage services) and cultural changes (such as attitudes toward sanitation, body odours, and personal privacy). According to Merritt Ierley, historian of domestic technology, only about 15% of American (US) homes had complete bathrooms in 1900.[40] There is no reason to believe that Torontonians fared much better, or worse. The 1901 Eaton's Catalogue, which offered consumers a vast range

of domestic items, contained no bathtubs (only wooden laundry tubs), no toilets (except in the sense of hair brush "toilet sets"), and no sinks. Obviously, there wasn't enough of a market yet. Most residents continued to bathe in one room and use a toilet (or water closet[41]) in another, either inside or outside, depending on their economic resources and geographic location.

Modern tubs required indoor plumbing (both running water and drains) and a stationary location in a private room. These conveniences were late in coming to The Ward and other poor parts of Toronto, so Toronto's poor had to make do with the pitcher and wash basin, the traditional tub, public baths ... or no bathing, far longer than more affluent citizens.

The sink was the last of the three fundamental components of a "modern" bathroom to enter the room. Plans drawn up by Eden Smith for Spruce Court and Riverdale Courts illustrate the late and uneven arrival of the sink: the smaller and cheaper units had only two-piece bathrooms (bathtub and toilet), whereas the larger more expensive units had three-piece bathrooms. Of course, in 1914, it was pretty unusual for lower-income people to have any decent indoor bathroom at all.

"[T]he outdoor privy remained a near-universal feature of the Canadian home until the late nineteenth century," according to historian Peter Ward. "Indoors the chamber pot and the commode or *chaise percée* were in daily use, dumped regularly in the small house at the back of the lot ... The processes of meeting bodily needs were neither

3.34: A Bath ... But No Room
This little fellow is enjoying a bath in a small, but traditional tub ... somewhere inside the Hill's Centre Island cottage in August 1892. Baby Hill's bathing experience reminds us that a bathtub was, for many centuries, just that: a movable tub, filled by hand, and located near a fire or stove for warmth.
CITY OF TORONTO ARCHIVES: Series 379, Item 1163

3.35: *Ad for "Steel-Clad" Baths, 1894*
The history of modern conveniences can be traced through advertisements, such as this one for "Steel-Clad" Baths which appeared in the 1894 City Directory. By then, new houses always contained a "bathroom," so the Toronto Steel-Clad Bath & Metal Company had a market for their product.
CITY OF TORONTO ARCHIVES: 1894 *Toronto City Directory*, p. 33

carefully hidden nor artfully disguised, and the odour of human wastes blended into the rich bouquet of everyday life indoors and outdoors alike. The triumph of the toilet was to change all this."[42]

The triumph of the toilet was, however, uneven in arriving. Even when central Toronto was fairly well-served by public water-and-sewerage services,[43] many existing residences did not benefit. For example, The Ward area was theoretically served by the 1880s,[44] but few individual homes benefited. Toronto's first comprehensive house-to-house public health inspection revealed that in 1885, 60% of all dwellings were still served by outdoor privies, half of which were either full or foul. By 1911, when Dr. Hastings surveyed conditions in Toronto's poorest areas, almost half the homes still relied on outhouses, although indoor plumbing was more-or-less universal elsewhere in the city. And even when the outdoor privy *had* made its "dignified march from the back of the lot to a small room inside the home,"[45] its addition to the dwelling was not always a happy one. A case in point was 154 Terauley Street (now Bay Street) where cap-maker Isaac Soloman and thirteen other residents had to share a single toilet tucked away in the corner of the kitchen area in a half-basement. Their living conditions summarized just about everything that was so horribly, and inhumanely, wrong with The Ward. (See 3.37.)

Sir Henry Pellatt spared no expense where plumbing and personal luxury were concerned. His 98-room mansion contained *thirty* bathrooms,

3.36: *Pedestal Sink, 1905*
In 1905, architect E. J. Lennox published a book to promote his business. In addition to photographs and brief descriptions of his work, there were ads by various contractors and suppliers with whom he had worked ... or who were willing to support his book. The pedestal sink illustrated in this ad represented the height of bathroom style at the time.
CITY OF TORONTO ARCHIVES, Research Hall Library: *E. J. Lennox, Architect*, 1905, Advertisement for Ontario Lead and Wire Co.

3.37: *Foul Indoor Conditions, 1913*

Arthur Goss' legendary technique and unblinking eye documented the squalid conditions that *thirteen* residents at 154 Terauley were forced to share. The authors of a report published in 1914, which was illustrated by this photograph, describe both the conditions and the desperate need of Ward residents for *any* housing: In the rear of the kitchen, which served as a dining room with no ventilation except through the two sleeping rooms, was found a toilet. The height of the toilet room was five feet eight inches; the entrance door was narrow and only four feet high. In one of the corners of the toilet room were old clothes and kindling wood; in the other was a box containing vegetables and food stuffs. The health department had taken action and closed these premises once, but due to the great demand for living facilities and the lack of inspection facilities for a "follow-up," tenants had again entered the premises and were living in almost as unsanitary a condition as had their predecessors.[46]

CITY OF TORONTO ARCHIVES: Series 372, Subseries 32, Item 251

DEPT. OF HEALTH No 251 NOV. 25 1913

this at a time when most houses contained, at best, one indoor bathroom. Sir Henry did share the luxury to a certain extent. He provided bathrooms for the workers who lived in E. J. Lennox's "Workmen's Cottages" — one three-piece bathroom per semi-detached house. He also provided several three-piece bathrooms to be shared by live-in servants at the castle. For himself, his wife and his guests, Pellatt provided large, elegantly appointed, ensuite bathrooms. His own was the most elegantly appointed of all. And he was positively eager to have someone photograph this most intimate of living spaces. (See 3.38.)

73

3.38: *Gold-plated Fittings,*
ca. 1915
William James noted on the back of this photograph: "Pellatt's bath room with its gold plated fittings," which were of intense interest not only to James, but also to legions of other Torontonians. Sir Henry's bathroom was the height of fashion ca. 1915: marble walls, floor, tub and fixtures; double pedestal sink; gold-plated fittings; and a jazzy multiple-jet shower (at a time when *no one* had showers). Alas for poor Pellatt's memory, his ultra-bathroom is far less impressive to modern eyes than many other parts of his grand creation on Davenport Hill. Where size matters (as in Great Halls and Conservatories), Pellatt wins. Where technology matters, modern bathrooms can at least stay in the race.
CITY OF TORONTO ARCHIVES:
Fonds 1244, Item 4062

4

From Factory Floor to Corner Office

The work world changed dramatically between the 1880s and 1920s.

During this period of intense urbanization, industrialization, and corporate concentration,

Toronto's paid workforce grew by migration, immigration and annexation[1] from about 32,000 in 1881,

to about 170,000 in 1911, and nearly 280,000 in 1931.[2]

Not only did the scale of business change, but also the nature of work.

*F*actories expanded and multiplied. Office buildings became skyscrapers. Department stores dwarfed small retailers. Self-employed artisans disappeared. Assembly-line labour replaced skilled labour. Clerical and service jobs abounded. Professions proliferated. And women entered the non-domestic workplace in ever-increasing numbers.

The period leading up to the First World War is often considered one of great prosperity — the golden Edwardian afternoon that immediately preceded Armageddon. Fortunes *were* made. Consumption *was* conspicuous. And many *did* prosper. But not everyone, and not always. In fact, despite the much-ballyhooed prosperity, ordinary, blue-collar workers were no better off in 1921 than they had been in 1900.[5] Unemployment — a relatively new concept[6] — was a constant threat. Recessions and depressions hit, and hit hard, in 1907–8, 1913–15, and 1921, just as they had hit in the early 1890s. Economic progress was uneven, and unevenly distributed. For all too many Torontonians, work life was nasty, brutish, and short: wages were low, hours were long, conditions were dangerous, and life expectancy was shorter than for the managerial classes.

City Jobs

City jobs, both blue-collar and white-collar, were prized. They paid relatively well, though not lavishly, and, perhaps most importantly, they were relatively steady. Whereas the average blue-collar worker could expect to be off two months a year even in good times[7] (and much more in recessionary times), City workers could expect steadier employment.[8] Such reliable work meant the difference between destitution and mere poverty.

Turn-of-the-century Toronto experienced a major influx of non-English-speaking immigrants, many of whom laboured anonymously, under the most dangerous and unpleasant conditions, to build the city.[9] During a period of phenomenal urban growth, there were miles of streetcar tracks to be laid, streets and sidewalks to be paved, and tunnels to be dug. There were also dozens of public works to be built, from the new (now old) City Hall on Queen Street and the Filtration Plant on Toronto Island, to the great Prince Edward Viaduct across the Don Valley at Bloor Street. Although frequently working on City projects, many of these non-English-speaking immigrants were hired by contractors — the proverbial *padrone* — rather than by the City itself. The padrone hired the men, set their wages (about $1.75 per day in 1905),[10] supervised their work, and generally negotiated with the City. Some provided valuable services for a reasonable reward; others exploited the newcomers.[11] (See 4.3.)

Toronto has long been famous for her clean streets.[15] According to the Board of Trade in 1897–8, the Street Commissioner "revolutionised the street cleaning business" in Toronto, not only by eliminating the contractor and (apparently) running an efficient department, but also by designing, building, and repairing equipment in City shops:

....out of scanty annual appropriations [Commissioner Jones] has actually built and equipped shops where the entire construction and repair work of the department is executed. And not that alone; here sprinklers, rotary sweepers, automatic loading carts and snow scrapers of patterns devised by the Commissioner or under his direction, are produced specially adapted to the climate, pavements and conditions of Toronto, so that four teams and four men now do what nine teams and seventeen men were required formerly to accomplish.[16]

By 1911, the Street Cleaning Department had 1000 employees, who collected and disposed of garbage, as well as cleaning and ploughing the streets.[17] If the Street Cleaning Department was like the Works Department, most of its employees were English-speaking, male Protestants.[18] (See 4.4.)

Toronto's firefighters and policemen were definitely male, white, and English-speaking during the period under investigation. Most were also Protestant and many were of Irish background. Toronto's Fire Department was created by City Council in 1874. Prior to that, firefighters had all been

4.3: *Sewer Tunnelling*, June 5, **1912**

Some of the immigrant workers mythologized by Michael Ondaatje's *In the Skin of a Lion* paused and posed for Goss' camera. Arthur Goss, the newly appointed official photographer for the newly created City Works Department,[12] documented this tight little group under Barton Street in the West Annex, where they were building a storm overflow sewer to help drain the "open sewer" then flowing through nearby Willowvale Park.[13] Whether they were contract or City workers, the miners laboured away in damp, very constricted conditions, to drive a tunnel through almost impenetrable clay soil, using pick-axes and shovels. A white-collared supervisor in hip waders notes progress, as patchy timber-work provides indifferent safety supports. Excavators such as these made about 25-cents an hour or $10 to $12 per week during the construction season. Many also developed rheumatism and arthritis, "finding their bodies knotting up and useless at a time when honest pensions were rare and social security unknown."[14] The Works Department inspector made about $23 per week.

CITY OF TORONTO ARCHIVES: Series 372, Subseries 59, Item 47

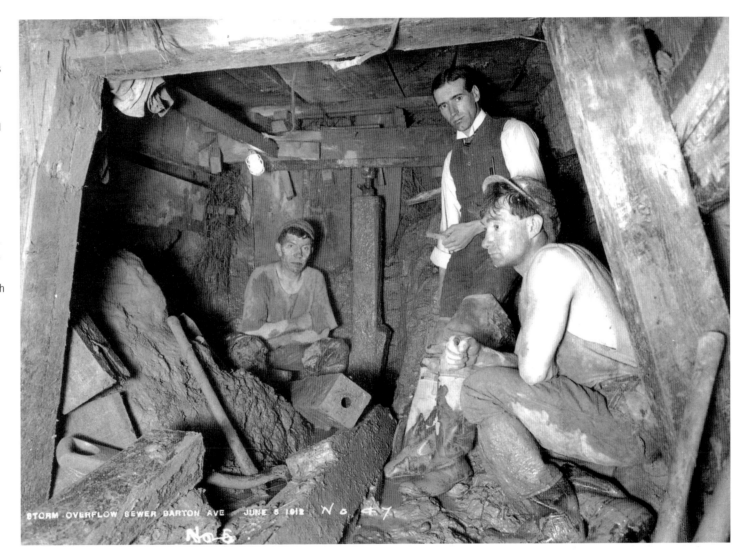

STORM OVERFLOW SEWER BARTON AVE   JUNE 5 1912   No 47.

No 5.

4.4: *Western City Yard, ca. 1896*
Cartwrights, wheelwrights, blacksmiths, and carpenters were among the skilled City workers who made and repaired equipment at the Western City Yard, 1118 King Street West, in the late 1890s. Although the men photographed by Josiah Bruce were City employees, their workshops had an independent, pre-industrial feel to them. By the time Josiah Bruce documented the Western Yard, more and more manufacturing, processes once carried out by small numbers of skilled craftsmen, were being analyzed, broken down, and split up among numerous, (relatively) unskilled factory workers. The days of the independent artisan were numbered.
CITY OF TORONTO ARCHIVES: Series 372, Subseries 100, Item 720

4.5: *Fire Chief Richard Ardagh*, ca. 1890
The Toronto Fire Department's second chief, Richard Ardagh, joined the volunteer force when he was only 15, perhaps as a torchbearer who lit the way along dark city streets. Here he poses in the safety of Dixon's photographic studio, with the accoutrements of his trade, a distinctive fire helmet and ceremonial speaking trumpet. Trumpets were used by the Chief to bellow commands in the era before electronic megaphones, microphones, or earphones. Ardagh died in the line of fire, from injuries sustained at the *Globe* blaze of January 6, 1895.
CITY OF TORONTO ARCHIVES: Fonds 1246, Item 57

4.6: *Fireman Descending*, ca. 1915
An anonymous photographer captured this quasi-action shot at the Yorkville Firehall around 1915. A firefighter sliding down the burnished brass fire pole is about to land behind his Captain. Meanwhile, the flash-startled Captain (with two bugles on his cap) answers the phone used to alert stations about fires; a harness hangs from the tin ceiling, ready to be dropped onto the backs of the three horses that would burst from the station with their ladder truck; and George W. Phillips, whose son preserved this photo, stands second from the right, behind the carriage lamp and fire helmet on the truck. Built in 1876, the parti-coloured Yorkville Firehall had an 80-foot hose-and-bell tower, bays for two rigs (this is the eastern bay), sleeping quarters above, and a seldom-used sleigh shed at the rear. By 1915, Yorkville had replaced one of its horse-drawn vehicles with a motorized one and the era of the horse was fast drawing to a close, with the final team being withdrawn in 1931.[20]

1915 proved to be a year of change for the TFD. City Council established a judicial inquiry to investigate charges of gambling, politicking, drinking, and consorting with loose women at various fire stations.[21] Irish-born Chief John Thompson resigned and was replaced by Toronto-born Chief William Smith. Smith increased the pace of motorization and allowed — at long last — the creation of a union.
COURTESTY OF DISTRICT FIRE CHIEF: R. PHILLIPS (retired)

expansion of the city to about 875 members, distributed over the twelve divisions that covered the entire former City of Toronto.[22] From a predominantly British, lopsidedly Irish Protestant force,[23] the police remained a British-dominated force whose senior officers were still largely Irish, but whose rank and file were much more Canadian in origin.[24] Significantly, the ethnic diversity of the city — and especially of the population hauled before the Police Magistrates — was almost completely absent from the force.[25] Then, as later, the police failed to mirror the population they were policing. (See 4.7, 4.8.)

From a completely male force, the Toronto police evolved into an *almost*-completely male force that hired its first female "matron" in 1888, added two bone fide policewomen in 1913, and had a total of eight women on the payroll in 1925 — three matrons and five policewomen. One of the matron's primary roles was to look after the female prisoners held in cells at Division One, where the matron also had slightly more lavish living quarters. The first two policewomen were attached to the Staff Department (aka, morality squad)

volunteers, organized into companies — often competitive companies, eager to be first to the fire. In 1874, the new fire department consisted of 36 full-time, paid firemen, manning five firehalls. Growth was rapid. Between 1890 and 1930, the fire force grew from under 100 men operating out of 10 firehalls, to over 650 staffing 33 fire halls, including the Yorkville No. 10 Firehall shown here.[19] (See 4.5, 4.6.)

Between 1880 and 1925, the Toronto Police force grew and changed in many significant ways ... and failed to grow and change in others. From a compact force of about 130 members distributed over four, essentially downtown divisions, the force grew with the population and territorial

4.8: *Holding Cells*, nd

Each police station had holding cells, usually in the basement and often in wretched condition, where predominantly lower-class prisoners were detained until their appearance before a Police Magistrate. Most of the occupants were charged with vagrancy or drunkenness, neither state contributing to the cleanliness of the cells. Division One on Court Street, near King and Church Streets, had cellblocks for both men — shown here — and women. Not surprisingly, less attention was paid to the condition of the cells than the condition of the rest of the station.

In the early 1880s, however, the condition of the cells became so bad that prisoners actually had to be removed to Division Two for several years until the ventilation was improved. Conditions must have been truly Dickensian to warrant prisoners being removed. Although probably taken after the 1920s, this grim photograph shows cells that are decades old, still overcrowded (why else would one man be sleeping outside the padlocked cells?), still occupied by members of Toronto's underclass, and still emitting an almost sensible stench. Whether the women's holding cells supervised by female matrons were as badly kept, remains unknown.

to work specifically with women, and especially women with "domestic complaints" relating to abuse or abandonment. In 1919, two more policewomen were hired for "outside patrol service," which included duties such as patrolling dance halls.

Public transportation was another absolutely vital City service that grew dramatically between the 1880s and the 1920s, from about 25 kilometres of track and 77,000 riders in 1880 to an absolute peak of 547 kilometres (or 16 miles) of track and over 197 million passengers in 1928.[28] Although streetcars were initially privately operated, the City got into the streetcar business when the private operator refused to service outlying areas, such as St. Clair, Lansdowne, and the Danforth. Then, in 1921, the private lines were taken over by the newly created, publicly owned Toronto Transportation Commission. The new TTC immediately did an inventory of its property, and launched a huge expansion of service. (See 4.9, 4.10.) Meanwhile, City engineers, like the engineering profession in general society, were gaining professional status and increasing influence over the operation of the City.[30] (See 4.11.)

4.9 (left): *Motorman's Controls, 1918*

Fondly known as "the dinkies," the small cars of the Toronto Civic Railway rattled and swayed along five routes that the Toronto Railway Company (TRC) refused to provide. The covered vestibule and the driver's chair shown here were both innovations only gained by intense union pressure. In the early days, the driver (of both horse and then electrified streetcars) had to stand outside, for 12 to 14 hours a shift, in all weather. The worse the weather, the slower the trip, and the longer the standing and exposure to the elements. Ironically, the TRC treated the horses better than the men. "About every two hours the horse or mule was taken from the car and a fresh one put on. The two-legged critter, the human mule, had no such release," an old streetcar driver recalled in 1939. "If the company overworked an animal and if it died it cost them about $75. In the overworking and killing of a man it cost them nothing. They could get a new man at less wages."[29] Here the controls of Civic Railway Car No. 203 (later TTC 2174) are protected by a vestibule and awaiting the arrival of the City driver. The photograph was probably taken by City photographer, Arthur Goss.

CITY OF TORONTO ARCHIVES: Fonds 1231, Item 217

4.10 (right): *Streetcar Building Shop, 1921*

Ever since 1882, streetcars had been built in this Car Building Shop at Front and Frederick, which was later transformed into a children's theatre. Even as the TTC was taking over, Toronto Railway Company cars continued rolling off, not the assembly line, but the second-storey elevator. (The wooden streetcars were still more handcrafted than Henry Ford's 1913 assembly-line motor cars.) Alfred Pearson's camera documents the moment when private TRC employees became public TTC employees. And his lovely, backlit photograph casts either an aura of nostalgia, or a halo of modernity around the car and and its proud creators.

CITY OF TORONTO ARCHIVES: Series 559, Item 682

4.11: *City Engineer's Department, ca. 1899*

In an era of unprecedented civic growth — both in physical and bureaucratic terms — the City Engineer's (later the Public Works) Department occupied a position of considerable importance. Here, City engineers at the Front Street City Hall plot the growth of the public services built by work crews such as the one illustrated earlier. Apprenticeship was still the dominant way into the profession, so even a child of poverty, like Arthur Goss, could start as an 11-year-old office boy in 1892 and work his way up, in his case to the position of Official Photographer. (Goss is the bow-tied young man with arms akimbo near the centre of this photograph.) Many of the maps, drawings, and other records created by the City Engineer's Department are now open to public perusal at the City of Toronto Archives.

CITY OF TORONTO ARCHIVES: Series 372, Subseries 51, Item 733

4.12: *Toronto Health Department,* **1915**
On January 27, 1915, City Health inspectors posed for Arthur Goss's camera during their daily roll call at the Health Department's general office. All the meat, milk, housing, and other inspectors, as well as the central planners, were male. Their female colleagues were probably out in the field making home visits. The already overcrowded office in the new (now old) City Hall, displayed most of the accoutrements of an early-twentieth-century office: shared telephone, card files, wire wastebaskets, big roll-top desks, and papers of all shapes and descriptions. Only the typewriters — both machine and human — were missing from the picture.
CITY OF TORONTO ARCHIVES: Series 372, Subseries 32, Item 381

4.13: *Public Health Nurse,* **March 28, 1912**
While the public-health bureaucracy was dominated by males, the public-health nursing staff was exclusively female. Not tied to desks or offices, as many of their male counterparts were, these nurses spent much of their time out in the field. Here, a nurse visits a home in The Ward or one of Toronto's other poor areas. Just what she is explaining to her solemn, young client is unclear, but the poverty of the surrounding is all too clear.
CITY OF TORONTO ARCHIVES: Series 372, Subseries 32, Item 96

Another centre of civic growth and activity during the late-nineteenth and early-twentieth centuries was the City's Department of Public Health, established by Dr. William Canniff in 1883, and driven forward during the Progressive Era by Dr. Charles Hastings, who had been one of Toronto's first, full-time obstetricians before entering the arena of public health. During his tenure, 1910 to 1929, Hastings campaigned for a wide variety of causes, including purification of water, pasteurization of milk, and improvement of slum housing. He also established an internationally renowned system of public-health nursing. The Department employed more women than most City Departments, but the gender roles were very precisely demarcated, as indicated by these two photographs.

4.14: *A North End Smithy*, 1898
Amateur photographer and future City Architect, John J. Woolnough, photographed workers at their places of work. Here we see an anonymous, but quintessentially independent, artisan: the leather-aproned village smithy at his forge ... somewhere in (still independent) North Toronto. A glass-chimneyed oil lamp hangs on the wall, a circular whetting stone and a sturdy anvil stand on the floor behind him, as the muscular artisan pumps the bellows and heats a piece of iron in the intensifying fire before him.
CITY OF TORONTO ARCHIVES: Series 974, Item 2

Artisans

The day of the independent artisan was drawing to a close. In the pre-industrial world, much work was organized along craft lines — masons, carpenters, printers, and so on — and most work was accomplished either by peripatetic artisans or in small workshops. Apprenticeship was the normal method of training, and craft association the normal method of establishing working conditions and looking after members of the trade. Industrialization and the factory changed all that. Nevertheless, though reduced in numbers and relative importance, the artisan still had, and has, a place in the industrial and even the post-industrial work-world of Toronto. (See 4.14–4.17.)

BAILEY & OBEN
56 RICHMOND ST WEST
TORONTO

4.15: *Baily & Oben, Plasterers, ca. 1901*

Fine plaster work was a hallmark of both Victorian and Edwardian Toronto. Here, the master plasterers of Bailey & Oben stand among the future ruins, dwarfed by over-life-sized creations, such as the Duke and Duchess of Cornwall and York (later King George V and Queen Alexandra) on the left and right sides of their Richmond Street workshop. The profusion of royals, and the large crown on the floor, suggest the craftsmen might have been preparing for the Duke and Duchess's 1901 Royal Visit, when Toronto plastered the town with festive bunting and, well, plaster crowns for triumphal arches and royal events. Mr. Oben is the bearded man on the right, in front of the pile of decorated capitals.

CITY OF TORONTO ARCHIVES: Fonds 1268, Item 24

4.16: *Wenger Studio*, after 1926

For nearly 50 years, Swiss-German master metalsmith, Emile Wenger, worked out of a studio in an old stable near Ossington Avenue and Bloor Street West. With the help of apprentices like these, Wenger created metal marvels in both traditional and modern styles. Wenger's records — now at the City of Toronto Archives — include photographs and drawings of the gates, grilles, windows, tables, lamps, chandeliers, sconces, railings, firedogs, handles, knobs and knockers that he created for some of Toronto's most prominent architects, including John Lyle and Baldwin and Greene. In an era that was moving ever more swiftly toward standardization and mechanization, Wenger was able to hold his own and leave a precious legacy of handcrafted metalwork that can still be admired in a dwindling number of locations, including the Seagram residence in Rosedale, the Claridge apartment building off Avenue Road, and the Concourse skyscraper on Adelaide Street West.

CITY OF TORONTO ARCHIVES: Series 512, File 1, p. 82

4.17: *James Little in his Workshop*, 1925

Traditionally, the master craftsman owned his own tools. Here 90-year-old carpenter, James Little, posed for *Globe* photographer John Boyd the younger,[31] in his workshop at the Salvation Army. Little had seen major transformations in both society and his work world. Born in Glasgow, he served in the Crimean War and during the Indian Mutiny before emigrating to Canada in 1887. The details of his Canadian work-life are sketchy. But, according to a *Globe* caption on May 13, 1925, Little was "still active in the workaday world, laboring eight hours each day at the carpenter's bench in the Industrial Department of the Salvation Army." Under his heavy apron, Little sported a leather vest and tweed tie, marks of his status, just as the tool box behind him was a mark of his trade.

CITY OF TORONTO ARCHIVES: Fonds 1266, Item 5192

The Building Trades

Toronto's construction and manufacturing industries employed about 60 per cent of the workforce between 1900 and 1920.[32] In contrast to the manufacturing industry, the construction industry was virtually entirely male, organized along traditional craft lines (carpenters, plasterers, lathers, stonecutters, brick-layers, and so on), and relatively highly unionized. As a result, construction workers tended to have (relatively) high hourly and weekly wage rates.[33] On the other hand, construction workers, even more than factory workers, were vulnerable to seasonal and cyclical unemployment. Winters were cruel. The Depressions of 1907–08, 1913–1915, and 1921 were crueller yet.

Construction workers fared better than factory workers, as a group, but neither group fared very well. According to Michael Piva, "the majority of building trades workers lived at or below the poverty line during the entire period [between 1900 and 1921]." Moreover, "their economic position deteriorated after 1902." Even when the economy boomed and the city grew at a phenomenal rate, the workers failed to share in the wealth. When the economy stalled, the workers crashed.

4.18: *Pantages Theatre Under Construction*, ca. 1920
The times were still buoyant when these grim-faced-but-employed construction workers gathered to have their picture taken by F. W. Micklethwaite under one of Toronto's early entertainment Domes. Designed by Thomas W. Lamb, the Pantages Theatre was plush, elegantly plastered (by W. J. Hynes Ltd.), and big. In fact, when it opened in 1920, it was the largest vaudeville house in the British Empire. After life as a luxury picture palace and a less luxurious multiplex cinema, the grand old Pantages was restored in the mid-1980s for live theatre, complete with Edwardian phantom and crashing chandelier. As for the workers, the phantom of hunger stalked their every waking moment. Lathers like these men made a relatively high $27.30 per week, but only worked an average of 37.2 weeks a year in 1921.[34]
CITY OF TORONTO ARCHIVES: Series 387, Item 17

One of Canada's greatest building projects during the teens provided Toronto with one of its grandest public spaces and Toronto workers with substantial employment: Union Station. Toronto's citizens, however, had to wait for over a decade before they could actually use the station. Because of bickering among the railways, and between the railways and the City, John Lyle et al's Beaux Arts station, still lacking tracks, was ceremonially opened in 1927 by the Prince of Wales and only put into use a few years later. (See 4.19, 4.20.)

4.19: *The Great Hall, Union Station, 1919*

By May 6, 1919, when this progress photograph was taken by Peake and Whittingham, the neo-classical exterior of Toronto's grand new Union Station was essentially finished and the interior was nearing completion. Arguably still the grandest and most monumental room in Canada,[35] the modestly named "ticket lobby" measures 260 feet long, 86 feet wide, and 88 feet high. Beyond sheer size, many of the features that endow this room with its special character are already evident: ample natural light flowing across a still-unfinished floor (pink and grey Tennessee marble would be added later); softly toned Missouri Zumbro stone walls; frieze of names celebrating railway cities across the continent; monumental Corinthian columns demarking the entrance to the concourse; and gently arching coffered ceiling.
CITY OF TORONTO ARCHIVES:
SC 172, Series 2, Item 19

4.20: *Union Station: Ceiling, 1919*

Balancing 80 feet above floor level, tile workers created this distinctive vaulted ceiling over the Great Hall. On April 4, 1919 photographers Peake & Whittingham ventured aloft to take a close-up of the vitrified Guastavino tile selected by the architects for its immense strength and light reflective qualities.[36] Today, during special events like Doors Open,[37] tourists can get a close look at the ceiling by climbing the stairs to a gallery, not the rungs of a scaffold.

4.21: *Time Office, Gooderham & Worts, 1918*
Just as Canadian surveyor and engineer Sir Sandford Fleming sought to standardize railway — and ultimately world — time in the 1880s, the American guru of "scientific management," time-and-study engineer Frederick Winslow Taylor, sought to analyze, standardize, and control every aspect of industrial production, including both human and machine parts. The time clock became ubiquitous and symbolic of the times. (Significantly, by 1907 many leading manufacturers of time clocks had been bought up by the International Time Recording company ... which became International Business Machines, or IBM.[40]) The Gooderham & Worts Time Office, pictured here just after World War I, was located near the front entrance to the plant. Supervisors, timekeepers, and telephone operators remained behind closed doors, while factory hands rang their time (as the sign cautioned) en route to work. The large clock near the door was probably set to synchronize all clocks and signals in the plant, another common feature of the day.
CITY OF TORONTO ARCHIVES: Fonds 1583, Item 144

The Factory

By 1914, Toronto was the leading industrial centre for Ontario[38] and boasted some of the largest companies not only in Canada, but in the world. The Massey-Harris Company, headquartered at King and Strachan, was the largest manufacturer of farm implements in the Empire, and the Gooderham & Worts plant on the lakeshore, east of Parliament Street, was one of the largest distillers in the Empire. (See 4.21.) Even major retailers, like Eaton's and Simpson's, had become significant manufacturers of goods, just as Hog Town's giant-pork packer, the William Davies Company, operated huge slaughter-houses, meat-packing plants, and a growing number of grocery outlets. (See 4.25.) In 1911, therefore, over half of Toronto's blue-collar workers were employed in manufacturing. By far the biggest industrial employer was the clothing industry, followed by iron and steel, food and allied products, printing and engraving, wood products (including paper), and leather and rubber goods.[39]

The transformation of industrial life was very rapid. "With us the factory system has not grown slowly," observed the Second Report of the Royal Labor Commission in 1889, "it sprang into existence almost at one bound...." bringing with it both "the material prosperity of the country" and "the evils which accompany the factory system," which were so amply illustrated by

4.22: *J. & J. Taylor Safe Works*, ca. 1904
The metal trades were the second largest, and among the most dangerous, of Toronto industries. Fatigue, combined with inadequate safety equipment, created conditions for disaster. In 1902, for example, an exhausted metal worker at Canada Fairbanks Morse Company "collapsed while carrying a full ladle of moulten iron," severely burning his leg and foot.[43] Since 1855, metal workers had been manufacturing J. & J. Taylor safes, at the corner of Front and Frederick Streets, that had "withstood the fierce attacks of the devouring elements and the desperate burglar when many others of different manufacture [had] succumbed."[44] A photograph of safes retrieved from the rubble of Toronto's Great Fire of 1904 confirmed the earlier advertising copy.[45] The contents of the safes may have been safe, but the metal workers most assuredly were not. Wearing only aprons and no goggles, gloves or other protective gear, these men banged red-hot ingots and poured molten metal to make Toronto safes for plutocracy.
CITY OF TORONTO ARCHIVES: Fonds 1268, Item 1804

4.23: *Gutta Percha Workers*, ca. 1906
Although originally intended to be an exclusive residential area, distant Parkdale caught the industrial fever that was sweeping across the province in the early 1880s. Parkdale Town Council, like boosterish politicians everywhere, relaxed anti-noxious industry bylaws and welcomed a variety of industries to the area. One of the major beneficiaries was the Gutta Percha & Rubber Manufacturing Co., which built a plant near the tracks on West Lodge Avenue in 1884. Among the rubber products created by workers, such as those posing here in 1906, were industrial belting, firehoses, and rubber boots. According to an 1885 letterhead, the company was "the only rubber factory in Ontario" and had factories in New York and San Francisco, as well as Toronto. The plant closed around 1960.[46]
CITY OF TORONTO ARCHIVES: Fonds 1264, Item 5

4.24: *British Forgings Melting House: Tipping Molten Steel, 1917–18*

At the height of its production in 1917–1918, the British Forgings plant at Ashbridge's Bay employed 1600 workers, including this furnace operator at one of the ten electric furnaces. The Ministry of Munitions of War and the Imperial Munitions Board of Canada produced a photo album to document the work of this plant. According to its commentary, "The melting of each heat was a matter of skill and judgment on the part of the furnace operators." When the molten mix was just right, part of the floor in front of the furnace was raised, the ladle was moved directly under the spout of the furnace, the furnace was tilted (as shown here), and the molten metal was poured into the ladle. The ladle, in turn, was suspended over cast-iron ingot moulds, and the operator filled each mould in turn. The operator appears to be wearing dark glasses, but precious little other protective clothing. All in all, it was hot, dirty, dangerous, and vital work.

CITY OF TORONTO ARCHIVES: Fonds 1634, Item 24

VIEW OF FURNACE BEING TILTED DURING POURING.

witnesses before the Commission.[41] Take the casual attitude toward industrial accidents. A Toronto box manufacturer testified that one of his workers lost part of his hand, and another his life out of sheer foolishness and carelessness, rather than any possible wrongdoing on the part of the manufacturer.[42] In an era before strong unions, strong legislation, and adequate enforcement, workers were routinely under-protected, over-worked, and labouring under flagrantly dangerous conditions — noxious fumes, dust-filled air, inadequate light, little ventilation, unshielded machinery, and so on. (See 4.22–4.23.)

The Great War only increased pressures and dangers for industrial workers. As wartime industries ramped up, the demand for steel and shells climbed ever higher. With nearly half of the steel used in the manufacture of shells being lost to scrap, the search for a way to recycle this material was intensified and finally successful in late 1916. The result was the creation of Toronto's largest "national factory," and the largest electric steel-plant in the world: the 127-acre British Forgings plant that came to dominate the waterfront wasteland south and east of Gooderham & Worts.[47] (See 4.24.)

After emigrating to Canada, non-English-speaking immigrants gravitated to different occupations. Jewish immigrants, for example, comprised a very high proportion of the garment workers. Italians were heavily represented in the construction industry, both as artisans and general labourers. And Macedonians moved into the dyeing, tanning, and meat-packing industries. In fact, Lillian Petroff commented wryly, Macedonians were not only "men of the factory," but also took a "perverse sort of pride in their ability to endure near [the] 'smelly' fur dressing and dyeing works," as well as the equally repellent slaughterhouses and meat processing plants that grew up in the lower Cabbagetown, Niagara Street, and Junction areas of Toronto.[48]

As noted earlier, the clothing industry was by far the most important industrial employer in Toronto.[51] In 1901 the garment industry employed about 12,800 people, far more than any other sector and a third of all manufacturing workers in the city. After 1901, the clothing industry became less important, but still employed a great many workers, including large numbers of women and children, as well as men. In fact, more women than men worked in the needle trades,[52] which helps to explain the often appalling conditions under which they laboured, whether working at home, in small shops, or in large factories. In October 1897, Toronto's normally Conservative *Daily Mail and Empire* ran an exposé of sweat-shop conditions in the city, citing at length the following desperate case:

A woman with a large family, some of whom were sick, was the next person visited. She was about to move to a new residence, and the clothes at which she had been working were lying with a heap of rubbish on the dirty floor. She could hardly speak with a consumptive cough, which is fast taking her life away. She had worked at the garment trade for many years, but had been unable to save enough to permit of her children getting a proper schooling. A little girl, sixteen years of age, who was thin and sickly in appearance, stood by her side and related how she had worked for eight years past for a large wholesale house, most of the time at $2 a week. She now intended to help her mother at the machine. She had a little sister, nine years of age,

4.26: *J. D. King Company, 1897*
Hunched over tightly packed sewing machines for ten to twelve hours daily, the women at J. D. King & Co.[54] stitched their way to continued poverty. Without a trace of embarrassment, Manager R. C. Winlow matter-of-factly told the 1889 Labour Commission that he paid his 75 female workers under $5.00 per week, while paying his 125 male workers between $7 and $15 per week to make shoes and boots. Even at this, Winlow was exaggerating the take-home pay of his piece-working women.[55] According to labour historian Linda Kealey, the women actually made between one and four dollars weekly in the depressive early 1890s.

These women may have been exploited, but they didn't always take abuse quietly. In January 1894, when the company tried to lower rates for the second time in two months, the women struck. J. D. King refused to meet with the strikers. Seven women and one man were arrested outside the Wellington factory, which generated a good deal of support from other unionized workers, but failed to win the day, or the strike.[56] The evidence of this photograph, and four others that appeared in a book published by the 1897-8 Board of Trade, suggests that conditions didn't improve. As for the unresponsive J. D. King, he lived in a Second-Empire mansion on ultra-fashionable Jarvis Street,[57] while many of his sweated workers probably lived in the impoverished Ward.[58]
CITY OF TORONTO ARCHIVES: Series 654, File 18 (upper)

4.27: *Making Ladies Waists*, 1910

Another more famous but equally unsuccessful strike by garment workers occurred in February 1912, when Eaton's workers refused to co-operate with management dictates to do more work for no more money. Ultimately, over a thousand men and women walked out and stayed out for four months, gaining a place in Toronto's labour history, but no more pay in their packets or respect from their employer, arch anti-unionist John Craig Eaton. Sir John, of course, lived in neo-Georgian splendour atop Davenport Hill (see *Ardwold* in Chapter 3), while many of his Jewish immigrant employees lived in squalor, perhaps in a slum dwelling owned by the T. Eaton Company itself. [59]

This view, created by an unknown photographer but marketed by Eaton's as part of its peppy stereoscopic tour of

the Big Store, illustrates the gap between management and labour world-views highlighted by the strike. Company copy on the back of this stereograph enthuses, "On this floor over 450 operators are engaged. Factory is light, clean, bright and airy, and we keep a superior class of help." "Help"? The women bent over their clattering sewing machines were industrial workers, not domestic "help." They might have liked the description "superior," but undoubtedly would have preferred superior wages, to superior advertising. As it turned out, their response to the bright, airy, labour-saving conditions was to walk out. Their employer's response was to let them starve, in some cases quite literally; hire scabs (even from abroad); and keep on advertising in the local newspapers that refrained from criticizing one of their main advertisers. [60]

CITY OF TORONTO ARCHIVES: Fonds 1125, Item 34

who also sewed at the machine. Another sister got $3 a week in a large shop for making button-holes in coats, the button-hole contractor had to clear a profit after sub-contracting the work. They had made up knickerbockers at five cents a pair, and were supplying the thread themselves. [53]

No matter where they turned — to a large wholesale house, to a small contractor, or to their own home — these females were exploited miserably and piteously by a system designed to maximize profits ... no matter what the human consequences. (The 16-year old had been working since the age of eight, and her nine-year-old sister already knew how to use a sewing machine.) At least women — and men — sweating in factories could find companionship, and sometimes solidarity. (See 4.26, 4.27.)

Female garment-workers continued working under exploitative conditions, which were obtained during the First World War when greater numbers of women were being lured into the workforce and manufacturers stood to make huge profits. In 1915, for example, sweating conditions were purportedly so bad that suffragist, labour supporter, and pacifist, Laura Hughes, worked, under cover, for several different companies, including the Joseph Simpson Knitting Mill, which was filling a militia contract at the time of her appearance. Working from 8 a.m. to 6 p.m., she netted 71 1/2-cents for her first day's work:

4.28: *Folding Machines, June 1898*

Founded in 1878, the Toronto Lithographing Company became one of Toronto's most successful printers, turning out well-known prints of Sir John A. Macdonald, the Gooderham & Worts distillery, and Massey-Harris farm implements.[63] After fire destroyed its Jordan Street factory in January 1895, the company built "the Largest & Best Equipped Establishment of the kind in Canada"[64] at the northwest corner of King and Bathurst Streets, where photographer A. A. Gray documented the building from basement bicycle storage to upper-floor printing, design and office work. More highly feminized than other industries, printing plants employed women in lower-echelon jobs, such as binding and folding. Here, we see properly dressed Victorians at the folding machines, working with a chromolithographic poster advertising the World's Cycling Championships in Montreal. Other photographs in this series depict men (and only men) at both the regular and the lithographic printing presses, as well as at artists' benches and in the photography room.

CITY OF TORONTO ARCHIVES:
Fonds 1137, Item 5

4.29: *Litho Artist at Work,* **1898**
The Toronto Lithographing Company employed some of the finest chromolithographic artists in Canada, notably Arthur H. Hider who created a magnificent poster advertising Massey-Harris' No. 7 Mower, featuring a pair of high-stepping horses and a nattily overdressed farmer. In this photograph by A. A. Gray, two male employees have retreated to a spacious, probably quiet, corner office, where one reads while the other one draws. Two of the three windows have been blocked by curtains, leaving only one window uncovered to shed (possibly northern) light into the artistic office. Diverse artwork on the walls ranges from a Rembrandt self-portrait to paintings of the Rockies and a buffalo hunt. Tools of the artist's trade, including drafting board and paint brushes, are spread across the large, executive desk.
CITY OF TORONTO ARCHIVES: Fonds 1137, Item 10

4.30: *Private Office of Charles E. Goad,* **1890**
This office portrait by F. W. Micklethwaite was taken around the time that surveyor and cartographer Charles E. Goad published his 1890 *Fire Insurance Atlas of Toronto.* Although "the founder of systematic mapping in Canada"[66] was extremely successful, and ultimately created fire-insurance maps for 1300 places in Canada, as well as cities throughout the Empire and around the world, his office in the Quebec Bank Chambers on Toronto Street was modest. No telephones, typewriters, or other business machines are evident here, or elsewhere in the office.[67] Only the large, probably lockable, desk was symbolic of both his occupation and his position. The desk's high back would have provided visual privacy if located in a more exposed position. Its numerous drawers and coverable pigeonholes, as well as its high back, are all reminiscent of the famous Wooten "a place for everything and everything in its place" desk of the period.[68] The clerical revolution, however, does not yet seem to have penetrated Goad's head office.
CITY OF TORONTO ARCHIVES: Fonds 1109, Item 2

4.31: *The 1890s Office*

Financial services, like other office functions, grew dramatically in the late-nineteenth century. Located in the heart of the business quarter, the office of R. G. Dun & Company illustrates the male domination not only of managerial positions, but all office work in the 1890s. Here, in Room 314 of the Board of Trade's new Romanesque Revival building at Yonge & Front Street, even the proto-typing-pool was all male. All characteristic of this period are the classic, black, upright typewriters, and new filing systems (card files and file folders were recent inventions that swept the record-keeping world); so are the glassed-in managers' offices that look out over the clerical corps massed in the centre. Only one woman, with puffy mutton-leg sleeves, can be detected, but her corporate function is unclear. The Dun office, and the very similar Bradstreet office, was photographed for the Board of Trade's 1897-'98 publication, *Toronto Canada.*

CITY OF TORONTO ARCHIVES: Series 654, File 18, Page 64 (upper right)

I was put to work inspecting garments, the pay being five cents a dozen. I worked as fast as I could all day, and even through the noon hour, and only inspected fourteen dozen. Once when the lacers were slow I laced a dozen for which I received one and one-half cents.[61]

Hughes' report ultimately encouraged Ottawa to set one dollar a day as the minimum wage, but not to do anything about other working conditions.

Workers in the printing trades were among the best paid, most consistently employed, and most highly unionized. They also included a relatively high number of women who, as usual, were relegated to the less prestigious and less remunerative positions — folding and binding, rather than engraving, compositing, and printing.[62] (See 4.28, 4.29.)

The Office

The white-collar revolution swept across the labour landscape,[65] not only dramatically increasing the numbers of workers employed in offices and other new services, but also changing the nature of the work — in many ways, "the factory" came into "the office" — and altering the gender balance of the workers. Many previously male occupations, such as telephone operator, typewriter, bookkeeper and office clerk, became female-dominated. Others remained distinctly male, notably middle and upper management, as well as most professions, each of which grew rapidly during this period. And others were shared: the accounting function was split into bookkeeping — female — and cost-control — male. Many of the changes were visible on the floor and behind (usually) closed doors. (See 4.30, 4.31, 4.32.)

Women's Work

Beginning in the 1880s, more and more women entered the paid, non-domestic workforce to become wage-earning factory, clerical, retail, and service workers of all sorts.[70] The change was rapid. In 1881, over half of Toronto's female workers were employed as domestic servants, but by 1911, only about a

4.32: *Department of Education,* ca. 1910

In 1898, Miss Scobie was the only female employee in the Ontario Legislative Building. In fact, her employment had been a bit of a mistake, and was not to be repeated, at least not any time soon.[69] Yet by 1910, around the time William James photographed the Ontario Education Department located in Egerton Ryerson's Normal School, where Ryerson University now stands, both the civil service and the number of women in the civil service had increased dramatically. This increase would only intensify after the First World War and the arrival of really Big Government. This trio of male manager and two female clerical workers illustrates many of the organizational and physical features then found in government and non-government offices around the world. Dressed for success in white "shirt waists" and (probably) dark skirts, the two women attend on the manager's wishes. One sits next to a slightly less upright, but industrial-looking black typewriter; while the other sits behind a wooden filing cabinet. Their well-fed secretarial superior sits at his large roll-top desk consulting notes, and perhaps preparing to dictate his thoughts to an alert stenographer. A large photograph of Trinity University (on the left) and a smaller photograph of the 1905 Royal Commission on the University of Toronto over the Shannon Filing Cabinet (at the back) indicate that this is the ante-office for the Minister of Education. The genre painting of an English cocker spaniel suggests more private interests of an occupant. (See also Chapter 7, *Inner Sancta,* for the Royal Commission photograph.)

quarter still worked "in service."[71] Upper-class observers and social reformers of all stripes remained puzzled as to why "nice" young women would leave domestic service to enter the morally ambiguous sphere of paid, city employment. The answers seem obvious: house-bound servants traded 24-hour supervision, 16 to 18-hour workdays, eternal subservience and frequent isolation, for on-the-job supervision, 8 to 10-hour workdays, relative freedom and social opportunity away from the home.[72] They may not have fared any better

economically — many traded the security of guaranteed room-and-board for insecure employment, and possible destitution.[73] But increasing numbers of women decided that the risks were worth taking. (See 4.33.)

Communications revolutions appear to be never-ending. From the telegraph of the 1830s to the internet of the 1990s, technology has almost constantly transformed both personal and business life. For the Victorians and Edwardians, the telephone was arguably the most significant new communications technology.

4.33: Domestic Workers in Training, Mercer Reformatory, 1903

The details of domestic service were seldom recorded, either in writing or on film.[74] Here we gain indirect insight into the life of service, both reformatory and domestic. Rejected by increasing numbers of working-class women, domestic service was still held up as a model by social arbiters, ranging from potential employers to social reformers and correctional services. Some correctional institutions, like the Mercer Reformatory, made taking a position as a domestic servant a condition of release. Here we see a somewhat sullen group of inmates in maids' uniforms learning the skills that will set them free. Published in Ontario's *Annual Report of the Inspector of Prisons and Public Charities for 1903*, the original caption for this photograph was *"'Fallen women' learn the virtues of domesticity."*

UNIVERSITY OF TORONTO LIBRARIES

Given final testing in Brantford, Ontario in 1876, Alexander Graham Bell's telephone radically altered both communications and business organization. Like the typewriter, which also first appeared in 1876, the telephone both eased women's way into the white-collar world and kept them in a subservient position. Nowhere was this more obvious than in the bosom of Ma Bell who then, as later, had difficulty paying women equitably.

Although the first telephone operators were male, women soon came to dominate the new service industry, supposedly because of their more pleasing voices and nimble fingers, but more likely because of their willingness to work for lower wages.[75] Their willingness to accept long hours, low wages, and minute supervision was, however, not unlimited. When Bell tried to reorganize their work schedules so that their hourly pay would decrease by 25%, four hundred of Toronto's "hello girls" struck.[76] "No job action better dramatized the plight, and the spunk, of Toronto's working girls than the strike of Bell Telephone operators in February 1907," writes historian Carolyn Strange in her ironically titled, *Toronto's Girl Problem*. Unfortunately, no strike better underlined the difficulties of organizing female workers or gaining concessions from an unwilling employer. Despite tremendous public sympathy, mass meeting at the Labour Temple, and the intervention of a Royal Commission, the women lost. Lured back to work when the Commission was appointed, they continued to work under the same, shocking (sometimes literally) conditions,[77] and received the same, patently inadequate pay until just before the First World War. Bell simply refused to implement the Commission's modest recommendations. (See 4.34.)

4.34: *Bell Operators, 1907*
All is not as calm as it first appears in this James photograph of Head Office Bell operators ca. 1907. By this time, factory-like conditions had entered the white-collar world. The workstations are tightly packed, the furniture is far from ergonomically acceptable, and supervisors hover over their charges. When Bell decided to cut already inadequate pay in early 1907, four hundred female operators struck. Their plight generated masses of publicity and weak intervention by the Federal Ministry of Labour under William Lyon Mackenzie King. Testimony before the Commission confirmed that the women were cruelly and deliberately underpaid. Bell Manager, K. J. Dunstan, asserted that the monthly pay of $20 was perfectly adequate for young "girls" who were only working for "pin money" or "to earn a fur coat or something like that and leave to get married after two or three years."[78] The facts were that almost half of the women were self-supporting and most of the others were making essential contributions to their family incomes. But because they were young, female, and single, they could be paid less than a living wage. The market, and society, would tolerate it.[79]
CITY OF TORONTO ARCHIVES: Fonds 1244, Item 138

Large retailers, like Queen Street rivals Simpson's and Eaton's, employed armies of low-paid female clerical workers. Again, early-twentieth-century Taylorism was immediately evident: rank upon rank of closely packed workers performed highly regulated, closely monitored, repetitive tasks. The paternalism was equally present, if less immediately obvious. For example, in 1917 Simpson's built a women's rest room in its downtown store to "help uplift the physical and moral welfare of [its] employees ... [providing a place] where they can spend their lunch hours instead of loitering through the store or being forced to walk the streets."[80] God forbid they should mingle with customers, meet young men, or go window-shopping in their own free time.

In the same year, Simpson's President, H. H. Fudger, built the city's largest boarding house for single working women. After purchasing the grand old Cox mansion on Sherbourne Street, Fudger built the 150-room Sherbourne House and converted the mansion into a clubhouse, complete with reading rooms, gymnasia, tennis courts and hockey rinks. Such an institution was designed at least as much to preserve the health and morality of company workers, as it was

4.35: *Mail Order Department,* ca. 1909
Tightly packed, closely supervised clerical workers processed mail orders for the Robert Simpson Company on Queen Street. Designed by Burke & Horwood in 1895, Simpson's department store was the first Toronto building to apply the metal-frame technology that was transforming Chicago and other North American cities. The open plan and rivetted steel skeleton characteristic of the new style provided the easily surveyed space so beloved of scientific managers everywhere.[82] In the shopping areas, the building skeleton was somewhat camouflaged. (See photograph of the Robert Simpson store in Chapter 6.) In the work areas, in a proto-brutalist architectural gesture, the structure was left uncovered, in all its naked glory.
CITY OF TORONTO ARCHIVES: Fonds 1244, Item 136A

to cater to their off-hour wishes. "Seventy-two per cent of the business girl's life is spent in 'home life' and on this depends her health and fitness for business," commented professionally trained Sherbourne House supervisor, Miss Bollert. Supervised boarding houses kept women "good," not in "a moral sense alone, but ... efficient so that they may go forth with health of body and spirit to do good useful work." Far better to spend time in properly supervised recreation than "walk the streets or go to a picture show."[81] No similar worries seemed to be expressed about male Simpson's workers, boys or men. (See 4.35.)

Retail Sales

In retail sales, as elsewhere, young men — never referred to as "sales boys" or "working boys" unless, of course, they *were* little office boys or messenger boys — fared better than the poor working girl. Inequities, as Timothy Eaton explained to the Labour Commission of 1889, were built right into the retail system. While an "average" salesman earned from $10 to $12 a week, a "first-class" saleswoman earned from $6 to $8 a week. A successful male clerk,

Restaurants, Bars & Hotels

"The Late Victorian and Edwardian periods were the great age of hotel-building," according to William Dendy and William Kilbourn.[85] Palatial hotels were built in London, New York, Montreal and, finally, Toronto. In late 1898, financier

capable of handling a department, might make $20 per week. Gender inequity even extended to the child labour employed. While a 12-year old message boy would get $2 a week, a little message or parcel girl would get only $1.50 per week.[83] Naturally, more fashionable stores employed more fashionable sales staff. (See 4.36.)

Family stores, however, operated according to completely different rules. Only a non-relative, hired assistant would be paid regular wages, while all members of the family were expected to pitch in, as required.[84] (See 4.37.)

Aemilius Jarvis got together with George Cox (of Canada Life and the Bank of Commerce) and George H. Gooderham (of Gooderham & Worts and diverse financial interests) to create the Toronto Hotel Company. Their aim was twofold: to make money, and to build a hotel where they could entertain and accommodate distinguished visitors without flinching. By the turn-of-the-century, both the grand old Queen's Hotel on Front Street (where the Royal York Hotel now stands) and the ancient and once honourable Rossin Hotel on York Street were fading fast. Perforce, the Duke and Duchess of York and Cornwall's retinue stayed at the Queen's during the 1901 Royal Visit. But the

4.37: *B. Sherman*, ca. 1920
Immigrant entrepreneurs set up shop wherever opportunity looked good, or even possible. Here, Jewish shopkeeper, B. Sherman, stands near his trusty National Cash Register machine, amid the casual clutter of his hardware and tinsmith's store at 549 Queen Street West, near Bathurst Street. Just outside, his wife and two children were also photographed next to the brooms, washtub and assorted other wares that might draw paying customers into the shop. Although photographed around 1920, this classic, small, family store looked more-or-less unchanged from the end of the previous century, and a world away from Harcourt's impeccably turned-out men's furnishings.

old Queen's no longer commanded the respect she once had. Perhaps the new King would.

The consortium hired E. J. Lennox to give reality to their idea. On a site at the head of ritzy-but-Ritzless Toronto Street, Lennox's quintessential Edwardian edifice rose. While the exterior had presence and dignity befitting its station, the interior was spectacular. The famously obsessive Lennox had ensured that craftsmanship was of the highest quality. Some of his sub-contractors later advertised in the architect's 1905 self-published, self-promoting book. For example, the plastering firm of Hoidge & Sons, included a photograph of the richly decorated restaurant that they had helped create. Lennox pulled out all the stops, in decorating and in fireproofing the hotel, a characteristic that was featured on much of its early publicity. (See 4.38, 4.39, 4.40.)

When the King Edward Hotel opened in 1903, it was an instant hit with the elite, business-class travellers, who often congregated in one of the hotel's banquet halls for annual meetings; and celebratory fêtes; and also with the homegrown, social elite, who now dined out and held many of their society functions here, rather than in a private home or a public hall. "Before 1900 Toronto society rarely dined out in the evening or entertained away from home," observed Dendy and Kilbourn. "The King Edward changed all that in the grandest manner."[86] The Rotunda became a major meeting place. The European Restaurant on the ground floor was decorated in an "opulent Edwardian version of the Louis XV style," and served expensive meals. A Ladies Parlour awaited weary shoppers emerging from King Street through the Victoria Street entrance. Tea and light refreshments were available at the Palm

4.38: *King Edward Hotel Rotunda,* 1905

On October 7, 1905, the *Toronto World* published this very rare view of workers creating the Baroque splendour that greeted guests when they entered Toronto's most fashionable new hotel, the King Edward on King Street East.

"The scaffold shown in the illustration was designed by Mr. Bailey for use in reaching all parts of the great rotunda of the big hotel. It is put together without nails or screws, and when taken down takes up very little room. It is 31 feet high."

CITY OF TORONTO ARCHIVES: Series 1144, Subseries 1, File 4

4.39: *Banquet at the King Edward,* 1913

Upstairs at the King Edward Hotel: F. W. Micklethwaite documented the perks of success. Surrounded by Toronto rococo, fifty formally dressed managers and salesmen from the Johns-Manville company wait for the banquet to begin. A solitary, equally formally dressed, hotel employee surveys the culinary battlefield before deploying his tray-bearing troops.

CITY OF TORONTO ARCHIVES: Series 387, Item 181

4.40: *Kitchen at the King Eddy, ca. 1916*

Downstairs at the King Edward Hotel, F. W. Micklethwaite trained his camera on the dreary kitchen where multi-course meals for the movers and shakers were prepared by the moved and shaken. Hired by the Consumers' Gas Company, Micklethwaite documented the new, gas-guzzling Garland stoves that had just replaced the phalanx of even grungier, coal-fired, industrial stoves that he had photographed in 1913. The placement of the pots, pans, and utensils is almost exactly the same in both photographs, evidence of an organized culinary mind behind the pans ... but not in the picture.

CITY OF TORONTO ARCHIVES: Fonds 1034, Item 792

4.41: *Vendôme Hotel Lobby, ca. 1913*
A cigar-smoking, commercial-traveller patron[87] pauses before the modest "Dining Room" door, in the small lobby of Vendôme Hotel at 281–283 Yonge Street. A large hotel register lies open on the front desk, where clerks registered guests, sold cigars, and handed out room keys from the board behind them. There is a spittoon near the stairs, a telephone on the desk, a Bank of Hamilton calendar (foul geographic calumny) on the wall, and a stuffed racoon surveying the scene from his glass cabinet overhead. A small sign informs the Vendôme's less financially reliable clientele that No Cheques or Drafts would be cashed. Around the time this photograph was taken, this dapper businessman was also photographed having a nip at the Vendôme's busy bar next door.
CITY OF TORONTO ARCHIVES: Fonds 1656, Item 2

Room on the mezzanine. Assorted banquet and reception rooms and another, less-expensive restaurant were spread across the second floor. Success was so obvious and instantaneous that additions began even before the building opened. King Edward had conquered Toronto.

A wide range of less-exclusive hotels — such as the Walker, the St. Charles, and the Vendôme — served the middle class of commercial and tourist travellers. (See 4.41, 4.43a.)

Despite the best efforts of the temperance zealots, Torontonians liked their drink. There were pubs, bars, and watering holes of all descriptions to serve the mostly male Torontonians of all descriptions; except for a brief period during and after the First World War. For this period of enforced abstinence, the wealthy could retreat to private venues, like the Albany Club, where spirits continued to flow. The middle class could find favour with physicians who were authorized to prescribe alcohol for medicinal purposes. And the desperate did what they

4.42: *They also serve who only stand and wait., ca. 1911*

Uniformed barmen at the old St. Charles Hotel at 70 Yonge Street paused and posed, before the next invasion of thirsty, non-teetotalling Torontonians. Twenty years earlier, the St. Charles was reportedly "the finest bar in the Dominion" and its bar-room described as being a "veritable work of art," with handsome mirrors, a "magnificent mahogany cabinet," cut-glass decanters, and a bar stocked with "the choicest and most popular brands of fine whiskies and light wines," and "cigars and cigarettes of all varieties." The best, the *Dominion Illustrated News* reported, could "always be obtained at the St. Charles." By the time William James snapped this picture, the St. Charles had dropped a notch, but was still serving a fairly exclusive clientele, who enjoyed a good drink, a good chew, and a good cigar. Brass spittoons were placed at strategic locations along the marble bar. Patrons' chewing tobacco created less unhealthy working conditions than their smoking, but second-hand smoke was all in a day's work for these turn-of-the-century workers.

CITY OF TORONTO ARCHIVES: Fonds 1244, Item 487

had to to feed their habit, even if it killed them, as it sometimes did. During periods of free-flowing booze, Torontonians headed off to their local or to a downtown spot like the St. Charles Hotel bar on Yonge Street. It wasn't the King Eddy, but it wasn't a dive, either. (See 4.42.)

"Men of every nationality ran restaurants or cafés," comment Richard Harney and Harold Troper about one of the entrepreneurial opportunities awaiting new immigrants.[88] Immigrant restaurants catered to both their own groups and the wider society, as opportunity allowed, although the ethnic association of the restaurant was not always evident, at least in the name. "Macedonians, perhaps reacting to a sense that they were perceived as alien, rarely used their family names on businesses intended for a general clientele," Petroff explains. "Thus restaurant names, such as the Queen's Tea Rooms Company, Florida Tea Room and the Harbord Lunch, were as much Macedonian enterprises as the Balkan Café or Hadji Peroff's."[89] (See 4.43b.)

4.43a: *Vendôme Hotel Bar*, ca. 1913
Lacking the spit, polish, and even the spittoons of the St. Charles, the Vendôme
Hotel Bar probably served a different crowd at its location farther up Yonge Street.
Both barmen and downtown workers seem to be enjoying this lunchtime or
after-work moment. (The clock in the Vendôme's lobby described earlier read
11:45, so this is probably a midday moment at the bar.)
CITY OF TORONTO ARCHIVES: Fonds 1656, Item 3.

4.43b: *Bulgarian Lodging House & Restaurant*, 1912
Located near the East End Macedonian and Bulgarian community, this restaurant
on King Street East catered to the single males who were "sojourning" in Toronto
(planning to work temporarily in Canada in order to save money before returning
home). Not only were such ethnic restaurants early entrepreneurial ventures that
enabled some immigrants to stay in Canada, but they also provided essential
culinary and social services to members of the community. Workers like those
pictured here may have only made a dollar a day, but a bricklayer back home in
Macedonia probably only made 20-cents for a ten-hour day.[90] They were
understandably attracted to what many called "Upper America." The pride of the
immigrant is well illustrated by the man at the back (second from the right) who
held several dollar bills aloft, indicating his success in the New World. Some of the
men photographed in the restaurant by Arthur Goss for the City's Health
Department also lived upstairs in the lodging-house part of the establishment.
(See Chapter 1 for that photograph.)
CITY OF TORONTO ARCHIVES: Series 372, Subseries 32, Item 57

4.44: *Doctor's Office, 1896*
Captioned "A Consulting Room (flashlight)," this photograph of an anonymous, but obviously successful, Toronto physician sitting in his quiet, home office, was taken by John J. Woolnough in 1896. The photographer may have been just as interested in the technical difficulties presented by taking pictures indoors, as he was in the details of his sitter, hence the notation that he took the photograph by "flashlight." But our attention gravitates more to the splendour of the physician's surroundings and the tools of the trade that are on display, such as an examining chair to his left, a metal-armed medical instrument behind, and diverse bottles arranged on a handsome desk before him.
CITY OF TORONTO ARCHIVES: Series 974, Item 28

Professionals

The drive to "professionalize"[91] picked up momentum in the late-nineteenth and early-twentieth centuries. It reinforced the traditional professions such as the law and medicine,[92] regularized related professions like social work[93] and nursing,[94] and created the entirely new categories of accountants,[95] civil servants, and stenographers.[96] The more prestigious, and usually more remunerative, professions remained almost exclusively white,[97] Anglo-Celtic, and male. A few females forced their way into medicine[98] and the law,[99] although the clergy and the academy remained closed to them. But nursing, school teaching, and the new social work were then, as now, dominated by women. For many members of the working class, entry into the proliferating, new professions enabled a rise into the growing middle class.[100] (See 4.44, 4.45, 4.46.)

The legal profession expanded, diversified, specialized, professionalized, and even admitted women to the bar during this period. Although successful lawyers, like successful doctors and businessmen, may have lived in luxury and enjoyed many perks in their private lives, they tended to work in quite Spartan offices. Rather than decorating to impress clients, as many twenty-first century Bay Street law firms do, late-Victorian lawyers clearly wanted to project an image of no-nonsense frugality and hard work. Linoleum often lined the floors. Furniture was sparse. Many firms had no waiting room. Juniors, clerks, and support staff shared a common area. Only partners and principals had private offices. And partners' wives were sometimes known to come in on Saturdays to do the cleaning.[103] (See 4.47.)

4.46: *Dentist's Office,* ca. **1900**

Architect Charles Gibson photographed the College Street dental office of Dr. Frederick T. Capon, presumably to illustrate the functional elegance of his own architectural work. Gibson's skylit baywindow area, combined with the doctor's strangely tasselled gooseneck lamp, cast good light on Dr. Capon's work area, although strong forearms were perhaps as important as good lighting to the practice of dentistry in these early days.

TORONTO PUBLIC LIBRARY: 992-2-8

4.47: *Anglin and Mallon, 1890s*

In the latter part of the nineteenth century, about 60% of all Toronto lawyers practised in small, one- or two-person firms, like this one. Here, successful lawyers, Frank A. Anglin and James W. Mallon, posed solemnly in their simply appointed offices in Rooms 32 and 33, at 34 Victoria Street. This downtown law firm boasted a linoleum-covered floor, a small and overstocked bookcase, no pictures on the walls, a workmanlike paper-strewn desk, and no telephone. Lawyers of the day tended to be conservative and late-adopters of technology: as late as 1908 and '09, most correspondence was still written by hand, not typewriter.[104] After Anglin became a judge, and eventually Chief Justice of Canada, Mallon went into government and their firm evolved into the long-lived Day, Wilson partnership.[105]

LAW SOCIETY OF UPPER CANADA ARCHIVES

4.48: *His Honour Judge F. M. Morson, 1899*

By the end of his long career, Judge Morson was "as much an institution in Toronto as the City Hall."[107] Moreover, he was popular in his profession, regarded as being "a friend to younger members of the bar in his chambers as well as in court."[108] Here, Morson poses at his docket-strewn desk, in the corner of his large, but sparsely furnished, judge's chambers on the south side of 57 Adelaide Street East. The major decorative element is a large photograph taken in the Court of Chancery at Osgoode Hall, discussed later. Although there are no books in sight, the well-stocked York County Law Association was down the hall and the splendiferous Osgoode Hall Library was only a few blocks away.

TORONTO PUBLIC LIBRARY: T-11828

4.49: *Great Library,* ca. 1908

Cumberland's Great Library is both a spectacle and a working space. As spectacle, none is better. As a working library, it has had its flaws, notably the sunny southern exposure, which is hard on books, and the (almost always) inadequate space for books. When William James photographed the Great Library in Osgoode Hall around 1908, its high, oak bookcases contained about 30,000 leather-bound volumes;[114] its environs were lit by new electric lights attached to the high bookcases; and Chief Justice Sir John Beverley Robinson peered down from the West Wall to encourage, or perhaps scare, ghostly readers labouring away at long tables supplied with ink pots and blotters. Legend has it that a *real* ghost occasionally still appears to workers at the eastern end of the Great Library near the War Memorial. The iron candelabra and clock visible here still grace the "flamboyant fireplace of colossal scale and doubtful historic parentage,"[115] but authentic historic plaques have been added for the benefit of students and tourists.

CITY OF TORONTO ARCHIVES: Fonds 1244, Item 2050

Even judges displayed austerity in their chambers. Take County Court Judge F. M. Morson, who was appointed to the bench in 1891, and became something of a fixture at the County Court House on Adelaide Street East. It was before Judge Morson that Canada's first female articling student (and lawyer), Clara Brett Martin, argued and won her first case, a dispute over rent.[106] (See 4.48.)

What judges and lawyers may have lacked in office surroundings, they more than made up for by plying their trade in some of the city's, and country's, most glorious workspaces, including the Great Library and Court of Chancery at Osgoode Hall. Inside and out, Osgoode Hall has long been one of Toronto's true architectural treasures, and the centre of the legal profession in Ontario.[109] Originally built by the Law Society of Upper Canada[110] in 1829–1832, Osgoode Hall has been significantly expanded and altered by many architects over the years, including Henry Bowyer Lane who designed the western wing in 1844–5; Frederic William Cumberland, who gave us the Palladian central block in 1856–1860; and William Storm, who created the less-well-known Romanesque Convocation Hall, opened in 1882 as an examination room and social centre. Despite the work of many hands, the final result is harmonious and suitably impressive.

Here is the majesty of the law incarnate, or perhaps, in carved oak. Located on the second floor, in the southwestern courtroom of Osgoode Hall,[117] the Court of Chancery could only be photographed out-of-session. In contrast to some crowded and crumbling lower courts, Mr. Justice Meredith's was elegant in the extreme. Approached through multi-vaulted splendour, everything in this courtroom was designed to impress — from the heavily corniced ceilings and tall arched windows (off-camera), to the brass gasolier and the splendidly carved bench. Respectful bows and hushed voices were *de rigour* in this august space. Both bread-and-butter and newsmaking cases were heard here. In fact, on October 1, 1892, one of the lawyers appearing before Meredith on a routine matter was Frank A. Anglin, shown earlier in his office. This Court of Chancery later became Courtroom 2, where important "Toronto" cases such as the 1997 Citizens' Legal Challenge to the enforced amalgamation of Toronto, have been heard.

Most impressive of all is Cumberland's palatial Great Library on the second floor, which is arguably the most beautiful interior space in Toronto, perhaps in Canada.[111] Stretching for 112 feet along the entire central block, and rising with Corinthian-columned splendour 40 feet toward "the most elaborate plaster ceiling created in nineteenth-century Canada,"[112] the Great Library, as Dr. Henry Scadding once suggested, "must, even independently of its contents, tend to create a love of legal study and research."[113] (See 4.49.)

Not all judges sat on elegant benches to dispense justice. (Frequent complaints were heard during this period from lower-court occupants.[116]) But some did. (See 4.50.)

The professionalization of teaching proceeded apace even, or perhaps especially after Egerton Ryerson[118] retired in the late 1870s. Ryerson's drive for compulsory mass education and centralized control of curriculum, training, and supervision continued to shape the Ontario, and Toronto, education system, as the population exploded, industry expanded, and women entered the workforce in ever-increasing numbers. Although revered by many as the father of public education in Ontario, Ryerson was very much a man of his times: a stern, patriarchal authoritarian, who promoted mass education of the working-class at least as much to provide adequately educated but docile workers, as to shape a "moral" populace.[119] His values both reflected the wider society and

4.51: *Crowded School Room, 1923*

These forty or so students, at the Frankland Public School on Logan Avenue in Riverdale, presented a daunting audience for any teacher, especially a young, female teacher like the woman who probably took this class. The Ryersonian rigidity of the discipline, not to mention the curriculum, is aptly reflected in the rigidity of attached desks.

TORONTO CITY ARCHIVES: Series 600, Subseries 3, File 10

imbued the new education system. (See 4.51.)

Throughout our period, men and women teachers continued to receive unequal pay for work of equal value, although the differential lessened between 1881 and 1920,[120] at least in part because of the establishment of female teachers' associations.[121] Both men and women studied at Toronto's Normal School to become school teachers. In fact, before the end of the nineteenth century, far more women than men graduated from that institution. Thereafter, their career paths diverged. The men (single or married) could become principals and inspectors, as well as teachers of the higher grades, but the women (only the unmarried or widowed) spent their entire careers standing before large classes of small students, condemned to a life of abject, if genteel, poverty.[122] More intellectually gifted, or independently wealthy, males could also become university professors, a career that was closed to all but the most exceptional women.[123] It was only in 1884 that women even gained entrance to the University of Toronto.[124] (See 4.52.)

Professors operated in a more rarified atmosphere than mere public-school teachers. While Trinity College allowed young women to become undergraduates in the mid-1880s, it did not have any women on its faculty until much later. Located in what is now known as Trinity-Bellwoods Park, the first Trinity College opened in the 1850s and was subsequently rebuilt at its present location on Hoskin Avenue to look much as it had on Queen Street West. Here, the Gothic Library exudes scholarly calm and male patronage, with photographs of notable males displayed on chairs and along the walls.
CITY OF TORONTO ARCHIVES, Research Hall Library: *Trinity College, Toronto.* 1914, Plate 21b

The Corner Office

Without doubt, Timothy Eaton was a retail genius. Through hard work and innovative selling practices, not to mention anti-unionism and worker exploitation,[125] he parlayed a small dry-goods store at 178 Yonge Street into a business empire, embracing not only large department stores in Montreal, Toronto, and Winnipeg, but also major manufacturing enterprises to supply "his" stores, and a booming catalogue business. He was also a man of his times. Like his contemporary and co-religionist, Hart Massey, the first Eaton focussed on his main business: he grew and diversified, but stayed within the same industrial sphere. Unlike the new breed of interconnecting plutocrats, like George Cox, Henry Pellatt, and Edmund B. Osler, Eaton was primarily a producer and seller of "goods," not a collector of directorships and manipulator of stocks.[126] (See 4.53.)

The growth and increasing dominance of Toronto's corporate power was amply reflected in the transformation of King Street, from "the city's specialty and retail street" in the mid- to late-nineteenth century, into "a canyon of Edwardian office towers," in the first decades of the twentieth century. According to historical geographers Gunther Gad and Deryck Holdsworth, the first structures over six storeys tall were built in the 1890s. By the late 1920s, over forty such buildings were located in the central business district.[127] These included the York & Sawyer's skyscraping, 34-storey Canadian Bank of Commerce Building that replaced the 1890 head office in 1929–31. It became the tallest building in the British Empire, and still graces the financial district along King Street, west of Yonge.[128]

Among the most magnificent of the Edwardian skyscrapers was Darling & Pearson's million-dollar, 12-storey Dominion Bank (now the Toronto Dominion Bank) at the southwest corner of Yonge and King Street West.[129]

4.53: *Timothy Eaton's Office, 1899*

Whether or not Timothy Eaton's private office was physically in a corner of 190 Yonge Street, it certainly was the locus of power for his retail empire. Here, the grey-bearded founding father discusses business with his second son and successor, John Craig Eaton. Lavish personal display was obviously anathema. These office surroundings were Spartan, aptly reflecting Eaton's stern Methodism and utilitarian approach to business. Eaton's Big Store probably provided the sturdy, oak, office furniture (a desk like the one shown here cost about $20.00, according to the 1901 catalogue). Photographs of family members and company stores offered the major decorative touches. No fine art or expensive knick-knacks competed for the occupants' attention, although the dangling electrical wire might have distracted a visitor with more refined sensibilities. Only a son would have dared drape an arm casually over the edge of the patriarch's well-used roll-top desk. John Craig took over Eaton's corner office after his father's death in early 1907. Given the younger Eaton's love of luxury, his corner office was probably more opulent than his austere father's.

ARCHIVES OF ONTARIO / EATON'S ARCHIVES: AO 1860

4.54: *General Manager's Office, 1914*
Located at the southeast corner of the Dominion Bank's ninth-floor head offices, the General Manager's private office was "richly decorated in walnut woodwork and florid tapestry of dull warm colors." The only dangling wire evident here is discreetly connected to controls on the desk. The lighting fixtures of dull bronze wall brackets and frosted chandelier were designed to be "expressive of the quiet and dignified treatment throughout." The mantel, with a mantel clock facing the occupant, was of black and white marble. All in all, an appropriate seat of power, conveniently located adjacent to the "most elaborately designed part of the bank,"[132] the holy of holies, the directors' Board Room. (See also Chapter 7, *Inner Sancta*.)
TORONTO PUBLIC LIBRARY: Construction, December 1914, p. 443

Combining bankerlike formality with Edwardian opulence, the Renaissance Revival Dominion Bank offered elegant banking services, and elegant offices for its own staff and its affluent tenants. Private offices were "fitted up with every convenience," including seamless imported Wilton rugs, filing cabinet, desk, and clothes-press. According to the December 1914 issue of *Construction*, the new Dominion Bank combined "a dignified and harmonious appearance, both upon the exterior and interior" with the ultimate in "practicability."[130] This practicability was illustrated in the General Manager's Office. Amid the Edwardian splendour, this top executive had access to possibly the first conference-call system in Toronto:

> An interior telephone system has been installed which connects all departments. The manager, by pressing down a series of levers built into his desk, can communicate with all the heads of departments at one time. This action is taken without the use of a receiver by means of two large openings above the row of levers; and should he desire not to have the conversation overheard by others in the room, he uses the receiver, which in turn disconnects the open annunciator.[131]

The occupant of this office was in control and well-connected in every sense of the word. (See 4.54.)

5

From City Hall to Government House

New Years Day

The new century was welcomed in by ringing the big new bells

for the first time in the City Hall — accompanied by other bells, firing of guns,

whistles blowing etc. — quite a time altogether at 12 P.M.

FANNY CHADWICK GRAYSON SMITH, DAILY JOURNAL FOR 1901[1]

*A*s Toronto grew, so did the public stages where politicians and public servants played their parts. In the 1830s, Toronto's population hovered around 10,000, fiery William Lyon Mackenzie was regularly thrown out of the Legislative Assembly, was briefly mayor of the new City of Toronto,[2] and ultimately led a Rebellion. Upper Canada's Parliament was on Front Street West,[3] Toronto's City Hall was on King Street East,[4] and no Government House had yet been built.[5] By 1901, when Toronto rang in the twentieth century,[6] the city's population hovered around 200,000, Ontario's Parliament had moved from Front Street to Queen's Park, Toronto's City Hall had moved from Front Street to Queen and Bay, and the Queen's Representative lived in a Second-Empire mansion at King and Simcoe. By 1915, Toronto boasted two ultra-modern, Romanesque Revival government complexes, and a brand new, but short-lived, French-chateau-style Government House in Rosedale. The times were optimistic, but the path to public magnificence was arduous, querulous, and expensive, for both the City and the Province.

City Halls

The old City Hall, on Front Street, built in 1845, served its purpose for more than fifty years. During that time it had been patched up, added to, and altered, till at length further alterations and additions could no longer be made with advantage, nor was the site any longer considered the best. A similar condition of things prevailed with regard to the Court House on Adelaide Street, built in 1853. The Accommodations were insufficient, the Court House unsanitary, and the City was threatened with an indictment in consequence. Under these circumstances new buildings were inevitable.

MAYOR JOHN SHAW[9]

A new City Hall may have seemed inevitable to Mayor Shaw when opening E. J. Lennox's magnificent new municipal buildings on September 18, 1899; but the idea of creating a *combined* Court House and City Hall had not occurred to City Councillors in January 1880 when they acknowledged the need for a new Court House, appointed a special Court House Committee to investigate, and indirectly set the new City Hall process in motion.[10] This process would last nearly twenty years, and consume the time, talent, and resources of untold Torontonians, from architect and politician right down to ordinary ratepayer and lowly bricklayer.[11]

In 1880, however, municipal politicians were still happily meeting in Henry Bowyer Lane's much revised City Hall-cum-Market on the south side of Front Street just west of Jarvis Street.[12] (Remnants of Lane's classically Georgian hall are incorporated into the 1901 Market that still operates on the site.) Over the years, as Shaw indicates, the civic bureaucracy had grown and taken over more of this civic building, including nearby St. Lawrence Hall,[13] and the centre of the city had gradually moved north-westward. (See 5.2–5.6.)

This Gagen & Fraser photograph appears to depict a City Council Committee in a Committee Room at the Front Street City Hall. Although the specifics of this photograph are unknown, it was before a Committee such as this, in a Committee Room such as this, that E. J. Lennox first laid out his plans, in February 1887, for a *combined* Court House and City Hall at Queen and Bay Street. At the time this photograph was taken, it was difficult to capture large groups of sitters in their original habitats — in this case, a gaslit public room. For both technical and social reasons (i.e., lack of light and the convenience of the sitters), the photographer took individual portraits, which were then mounted against a painted backdrop, probably created by the well-known artist, John A. Fraser. The mock-up was re-photographed for the final composite, which is the rare photograph shown here.

5.3: *City Treasurer,* **1898**

On May 18, 1898, Broom & Bryan composed this portrait of long-time City Treasurer, Richard T. Coady, at work in his busy Victorian gaslit City Hall office on Front Street. Naturally, Toronto's main money man was located near the centre of civic power, not exiled to a remote, off-site location. By the time this photograph was taken, Toronto's new City Hall was nearing completion and the civil service was about to move north-west to Queen Street.

CITY OF TORONTO ARCHIVES: Fonds 1268, Item 207

5.4: *Assessment Department,* **1898**

More money men (and they were *all* men) crowd into this Front Street City Hall office: the Assessment Department, where former mayor, R. J. Fleming, held sway as Assessment Commissioner from mid-1897 to 1903.[14] While their contemporaries may have detested them, their descendants have reason to be grateful: the Assessment Rolls prepared by these civil servants are now among the most frequently consulted and most valuable civic records maintained by the City of Toronto Archives.

CITY OF TORONTO ARCHIVES: Fonds 1268, Item 208

architectural competitions for the building.[18] Nothing proceeded quickly or smoothly.

In March 1885, the City circulated *Instructions to Architects*, prepared by prominent Toronto architect, William G. Storm. From 1852 to 1863, Storm and his partner, Frederic Cumberland, had created some of Toronto's finest buildings, including University College and Osgoode Hall.[19] This first competition netted 50 sets of plans, which were reviewed by three "experts": former carpenter and long-time developer, Mayor Alexander Manning,[20] and architects Matthew Sheard and Thomas Fuller.[21] On May 7, 1885 the expert trio reported that no design for the Court House should be adopted, but further plans should be requested from seven of the competitors, including the young, Toronto-born architect, E. J. Lennox.[22]

Although young — only 28 in 1885 — Lennox was well-connected, well-placed, and something of an architectural prodigy. He had grown up near the

It was only in 1884, Toronto's Semi-Centennial Year,[15] that Mayor John Boswell first uttered the fateful words "new City Hall" in his Inaugural Address,[16] words that were promptly ignored as Council continued onward with the Court House project alone. After having rejected two possible sites suggested by the legal people in 1883, Council, which would pay for 5/6 of the project, voted on June 27, 1884 to acquire 5.4 acres on Queen Street West at the head of Bay Street, and to spend $200,000 to expropriate the shops and other buildings on the site.[17] Council also decided to hold the first of several

Front Street City Hall (his father ran a hotel on Francis Street, just north of St. Lawrence Hall), and had won the Mechanics Institute's top prize in architecture at the tender age of 17.[23] More importantly, he had already produced major buildings for two of Toronto's most important businessmen: Hart Massey's new Massey-Harris head office at 701 King Street West and Alexander Manning's new Arcade at 22–28 King Street West, both designed in 1883. It's not surprising that *Mayor* Manning's trio of experts looked with favour on Lennox's first plans. And although Manning was no longer mayor when the revised plans came back in 1886 (that honour now fell to temperance terror, William P. Howland), he was still influential. On May 7th, Manning and the other experts selected Lennox's plan for the Court House, which was duly published in local newspapers and confirms that it looked much like the final building.[24] For the rest of the year, however, Council dithered over tendering for the new project.

In January 1887, the City changed course one last time. It asked Lennox to prepare yet another set of plans, this time for both a new Court House and a new City Hall. The architect was well-prepared for this request. On February 23rd, Lennox laid a sketch for the combined building on a table before the Court House Committee and explained its finer points. The Committee, then the Executive, and finally the Council were convinced ... and went to the people for approval for the (expected) $750,000 to complete the project. Meanwhile, Lennox visited American city halls, concluding, not surprisingly, that he had seen none "which is laid out superior or ventilated any better than the one

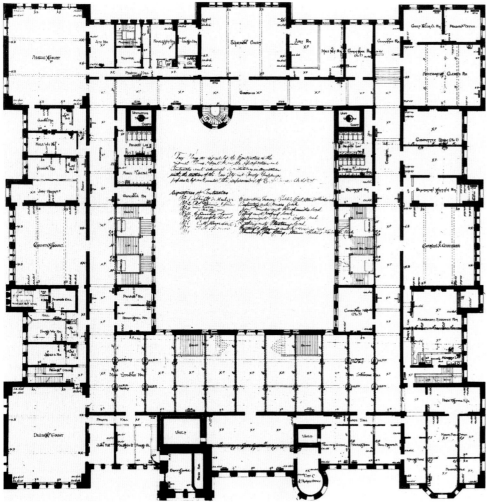

5.7: *Lennox's Official Plan, 1887/1889*
According to Lennox's final plans, Toronto's new "Municipal and County Buildings" were organized so that Court House functions were located on the first two floors of the West Wing; City Hall functions were located on the first two floors of the East Wing; police functions were distributed over several floors, with holding cells in the basement and the Police Magistrate's Court just above, at the northeast corner of the first floor; and the Public School department occupied the top floor. While the County and the Municipal Wings each had a separate entrance, the main, triple-arched entrance to the building overlooked Queen Street and directed foot traffic through an elegant "Main Staircase Hall." The Mayor's Office and City Council Chamber were on the second floor, which was reached either by the grand double staircase facing Queen Street, or the elegant Lennox-designed elevator opening directly across from the Council Chamber.
CITY OF TORONTO ARCHIVES: PT 365, "Second" floor

What had "the people" agreed to continue financing? According to the 1889 circular distributed to ratepayers prior to the vote, Lennox's pile on Queen Street was "a massive structure designed in modern romanesque style," composed of Credit Valley grey stone and New Brunswick brown stone trim, not only conforming "to the canons of quiet tastefulness," but also "expressive of vigor and go" appropriate to the booming city. Of particular note was the asymmetrically placed tower, rising 260 feet high at the head of Bay Street. The building was proclaimed to be not only elegant, but also practical, "arranged in the most perfect manner for the expeditious transaction of business with due regard for light, ventilation, appearance and durability."[26] A proud monument for a proud city.

Work could, and finally did, begin ... slowly. It took Elliott and Neelon nearly two years to clear the site, excavate the foundations, and move construction forward enough for City Council to formally lay the cornerstone on November 21, 1891. Given the decade of delays, Council was determined to make the most of the occasion, despite a downpour that recalled all-too-vividly the days of Muddy York. Mayor Clarke and his Council met at the Front Street City Hall and progressed in two large streetcars — each pulled by twelve grey horses — to Lennox's building site where they met the Governor-General and the Lieutenant-Governor.[27] By the time the party

which your Committee has seen fit to adopt,"[25] prepared final plans and specifications, and entered the prolonged tendering phase. It was only in August 1889, after Toronto ratepayers had voted another $600,000 for the project, that Mayor Ned Clarke and contractors Elliott and Neelon signed the contract, and Lennox's final, signed plans were deposited with the City Treasurer at old, old City Hall. (See 5.7.)

5.8: *Victorian Glass & Grotesques, ca. 1910*
City Hall officially opened on September 18, 1899 when Mayor John
Shaw orated from the Main Staircase, poised between E. J. Lennox's
wrought-iron, dragon-like grotesques, and under Robert McCausland's
glowing glass tribute to Toronto. Called "The Union of Commerce &
Industry," the 20-foot window depicted a benevolent goddess of
Commerce shaking hands with a realistic-looking worker (reputedly Robert
McCausland's father, Joseph, who had founded the stained-glass
company), standing before both the old City Hall on Front Street and the
scaffolded new City Hall under construction on Queen Street. Although
City Hall opened for business in 1899, thousands of Torontonians had
already enjoyed a sneak preview on July 1, 1898, when the buildings
were "hailed with joy by the long suffering citizens" eager to "view the
interior of the magnificent home they are erecting." While disappointed
that the building was not yet complete, the *Globe* reporter was impressed
by the marble mosaic floor "forming chaste designs calculated to
bewilder and charm the eye and lend elasticity to the step of the wearied
taxpayer" and by the fact that even on a national holiday (Dominion Day)
some twenty workers were down on their knees laying the floor... and
earning their pay packets.
CITY OF TORONTO ARCHIVES: Fonds 1244, Item 323 G

reached the platform, the politicians were mud-splattered and
nearly unrecognizable to the small crowd.

Undeterred, Court House Committee Chair, Alderman
Gibbs, waxed eloquent about early days in Little York, scenes
which were "daguerreotyped on [his] memory," and pointed out that "this
massive and imposing pile" was not only the largest building in Toronto, but
the second largest municipal building on the continent.[28] Mayor Clarke, for his
part, waxed equally grandiloquent about Toronto's history, and Lennox's rising
"stately pile" before burying a time capsule and formally laying (with the help
of a derrick) the six-ton New Brunswick cornerstone at the southwest corner of
the building. Just as the Mayor touched the cornerstone with a silver trowel, a
solitary ray of sunlight burst through the clouds, and spotlighted the mayor's
head. Then, according to the *Empire*, "the clouds closed in again, the Heavens

once more wept and so did most of the audience." For dry modern observers,
it is comforting to know that Toronto's 1889 City Hall was built on history,
both oratorical and written. One of the objects placed in the asbestos-lined,
hermetically sealed, copper "time capsule" was a copy of the first history of the
city, *Toronto of Old*, by Dr. Henry Scadding who attended the ceremony, read
the invocation, and is still watching over the building from one of George Reid's
murals in the Main Staircase Hall.[29]

The contractors did not improve their performance. Not only did they build
too slowly, they also did not build well. According to Lennox, much of the stone

they were laying was faulty. After prolonged disputation, Lennox, with police in tow, mounted a midnight raid on the lightly guarded construction site:

> It was midnight [September 8, 1892] on the Court House site. The mellow chimes of St. James' [cathedral] had died reluctantly away and the only sounds of life were the hurrying footsteps of belated home goers or the jingle of the car-horse bell. The huge derricks cast gaunt shadows across the moonlight....
>
> Just at this time his Worship the Mayor [R. J. Fleming] happened to come along. The city's Chief Magistrate is usually in bed long before midnight, so his appearance at the scene of action was in all reasonable probability more by design than accident.
>
> It was decided to take aggressive action and the Terauley [now Bay] street side of the block was once more sought. The practised hand of Mr. Lennox soon found a loose board in the fence, and it being ripped off he climbed to the top of the fence by the inside joists.
>
> And, oh, it was a goodly sight to see him standing on that Terauley street fence in the shimmering moonlight.
>
> "Follow me," he said, and jumped down, adding, "I call on the police to protect me in the execution of my duty."[30]

And so the youthful architect took over the site, physically and metaphorically when he was named chief contractor and supervisor of the construction. Thereafter, the building progressed, if not smoothly, at least to capstone and completion. Obviously given to daring, theatrical gestures, Lennox arranged, and City Fathers miraculously agreed to, a hair-raising Capstone Ceremony. On July 14, 1898, Mayor and Mrs. John Shaw clambered into a large, flag-draped bucket along with four courageous aldermen and one wryly triumphant architect, who commented as they were slowly hauled up to the top of the tower, "I guess I'll get all I ask of the board now I have them on this trip."[31] A game Mrs. Shaw laid the finishing stone in the southwest corner of the tower, the Mayor declared it "well and truly laid," and the party returned safely to earth.

Nearly one more year passed before the new municipal buildings were ready to receive Council and throw their doors open for business. All was apparently sweetness and light at the formal opening, although councillors had refused to allow the bold-but-prickly architect to attach a plaque with his name. Like architects before him, however, Lennox commemorated himself in the building itself: high above the ground, he had the letters of his name carved on stones dotted around the building; and right over the main entrance, legend holds, Lennox's benevolently mustachioed face beams out among the grotesques reputed to be caricatures of aldermen. So, on September 18, 1899, a beaming Mayor Shaw inserted a pearl-studded, golden key (made by Ryrie jewellers) in the lock of "Toronto's newest, most massive and most costly edifice," marched to a podium erected on the main staircase, and made a speech.[32] After reviewing the financial history of the building, taking pot shots at the Provincial Parliament Buildings in Queen's Park that had *also* cost far more than originally expected ("a very general experience in erecting large buildings"), Mayor Shaw commented on the meaning of great buildings:

> Why people will spend large sums of money on great buildings opens up a wider field of thought. It may, however, be roughly answered that great buildings symbolize a peoples' deeds and aspirations. It has been said that wherever a nation had a conscience and a mind, it recorded the evidence of its being in the highest products of this greatest of all arts.[33]

Certainly, Lennox would have applauded this sentiment, as would the modern Friends of Old City Hall, who mounted the historical preservation barricades in the late 1960s to prevent Eaton's from demolishing all but the tower of the much-loved landmark.

The creation of E. J. Lennox's civic *chef d'oeuvre* on Queen Street required two architectural competitions, four money referenda,[35] a midnight raid, several court cases (Lennox's own suit was only settled in 1912), and prolonged bickering. Despite all the delay and dismay, it is forever to the City's credit that, unlike the Province, it not only seriously considered, but actually hired a *Canadian* architect for its great project. (See 5.9–5.11.)

5.9: *Modern Times*, 1900

City Hall was not complete when Mayor Shaw declared it open for business in September 1899. There was a great hole near the top of the clock tower where the 20-foot diameter, 4-dialled, illuminated public clock was to be placed. Created by English clockmakers, Gillett & Johnston, the "works" for Toronto's Big Ben clock were only installed in late 1900, just in time to ring in 1901. According to Fanny Chadwick Grayson Smith, and confirmed by the clockmakers, "our 'Big Ben' [is] a bell which is the third largest in the world" after Moscow and London.[34] In fact, Toronto's clock tower boasted not one, but three great bells: the 12,000 pound "hour bell," and two smaller quarter-hour chiming bells. Although the dedication ceremony for the new clock, led by Mayor Howland, was well attended, Charlie Chaplin didn't drop by .... but Alexander Galbraith later photographed the works.

CITY OF TORONTO ARCHIVES: Fonds 1567, Item 168

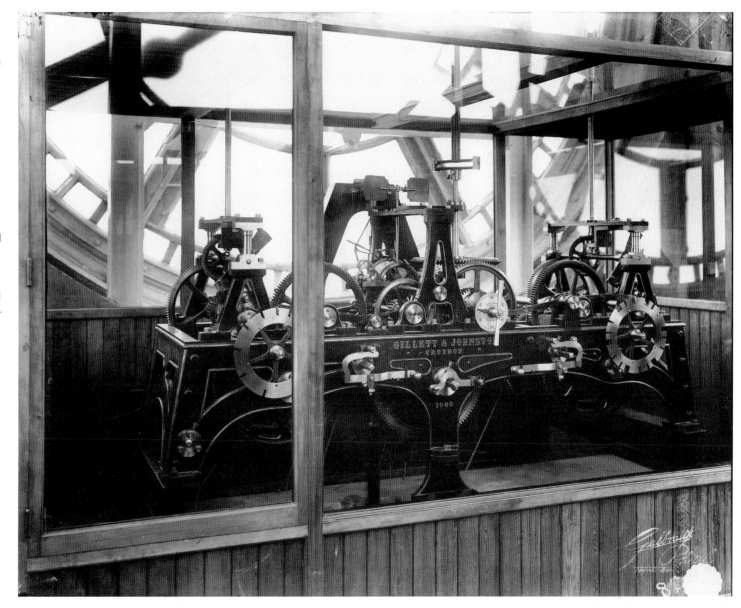

Inaugural Meeting City Council. Toronto Jan. 9. 1911.

Copyright Canada 1911. By F.W.Micklethwaite. 243 Yonge St. Toronto.

5.10: *City Council: January 9, 1911*

Contentedly ensconced in the Mayoral Chair is easily re-elected Mayor G. R. Geary, who looks out over an assortment of palms, plumes, and politicians, toward F. W. Micklethwaite's view-camera for the 1911 Council's official portrait. For a dozen years, City Councils had been meeting in Lennox's two-storey Council Chamber. On this particular occasion, with the galleries full and political wives sitting around the horseshoe, Mayor Geary expressed the optimism of the times, reviewed the previous year's accomplishments, and looked forward to solving some of the City's ongoing problems, especially regarding the recalcitrant railways (the companies continued to block the construction of a new Union Station), and the unresponsive street railways. Still showing "absolute disregard for the convenience and rights of the people of Toronto," the Toronto Railway Company was now managed by former Mayor R. J. Fleming, who, Geary noted pointedly, had once told Council, in frustration with the self-same company, "Every citizen is entitled to a seat when he pays his fare." More streetcars were needed, but none were forthcoming. A familiar scenario for the City then, and now.[36]

CITY OF TORONTO ARCHIVES: Series 387, Item 200

5.11: *Women at City Hall,* 1919
City Hall was a male preserve. Toronto
women got the local and provincial
votes in 1917, the federal vote in 1918,
and a duly elected woman on City
Council in 1920, when Constance
Hamilton broke through the gender
barrier.[37] Most civic departments, like
the Assessment Department illustrated
earlier, were male-dominated. The public
health department, however, was
somewhat unusual. Then, as now, public
health nurses, such as those shown in
this photograph, were predominantly
female. (The only male present on this
occasion was the Medical Officer of
Health, Dr. Charles Hastings.) Here,
Arthur Goss documented not only the
demonstration of how to properly bathe
a baby, but also Committee Room 3,
which was located near the northeast
corner of the second floor and had also
functioned as the Women's Court.
Although Committee Room 3 was the
smallest of the three committee rooms,
it was much more commodious than
the 1885 Committee Room depicted
by Gagen & Fraser, well able to
accommodate not only politicians,
but also citizens eager to observe
municipal politics in action. A young
Queen Victoria and Prince Albert
watch over the proceedings.

Provincial Parliaments

April 4th [1893]. This was an exciting day in Toronto being the opening of the New Parliament Buildings in Queen's Park ... About 3 o'clock Mr. Speaker Ballantyne read the prayer and soon after the Lieutenant Governor Kirkpatrick arrived preceded by a score of military officers and he immediately read the speech from the throne in clear tones ... [and] held a reception ... below the Speaker's throne on the floor of the House.... I suppose the elite of Toronto were there but it soon grew as weariness to look on such a moving mass although so charmingly attired, and we moved on to walk to some other part of the building. The corridors were spacious and lofty and some of the wood carving very fine. While we were in the west wing we were alarmed by hearing a fearful crash, a window had blown in and smashed, the wind being very boisterous, and we afterwards heard that that part was not quite completed.

MRS. CLOVER'S DIARY[38]

The 1893 opening of Toronto's fourth Parliament at Queen's Park was pompous, glamorous, and even a tad tempestuous — all distinctly appropriate for the decade's other most controversial public building. While hatchets may have been buried during the opening ceremony, the architectural controversy that surrounded the new Parliament buildings at the head of College (now University) Avenue lasted for generations, at least among Canadian architects.[39]

The 1829 Parliament, where Upper Canadian William Lyon Mackenzie had railed against the Family Compact and Ontario Parliaments had met since Confederation, had enjoyed a long and distinguished history, but it was time for a change. In 1884, for example, local historian, C. P. Mulvany, called James G. Chewett's red-brick Georgian complex, on Front Street between Simcoe and John, a "mouldering old pile" whose "decayed timbers make it the merest fire trap," inadequate for its parliamentary purposes, and for its preservation purposes.[40] (See 5.12–5.15.)

The push for new parliamentary digs had started as early as 1873 when

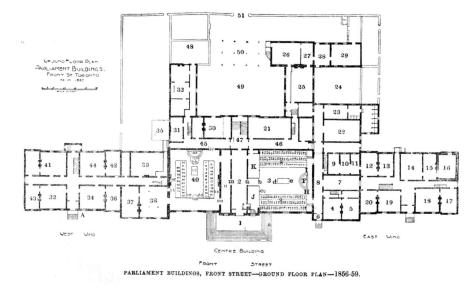

5.12: *Parliamentary Plan, 1857*
Published in 1898 by local historian John Ross Robertson, this 1857 ground floor plan shows William Hay's mid-century renovations to Chewett's old Parliament on Front Street. To accommodate the larger Parliament of the United Provinces of Canada, which met here between 1856 and 1859, Hay enlarged and repositioned the Legislative Chamber. Although renovations were also done after Confederation, to create the Ontario Parliament which obviated the need for a Legislative Council, the location of the legislative chamber (#3) remained the same. The old Legislative Council Chamber (#40) was transformed into additional library space.
LANDMARKS OF TORONTO, v. 3, p. 321

Provincial Public Works architect, Kivas Tully, argued that a new building was urgently needed.[41] By that time, the common assumption was that the new building would be located in pastoral and geographically prominent Queen's Park, about a mile north of the crowded and industrializing old site. Early in 1880, around the time that City Fathers were beginning to discuss their own domestic problems, Tully prepared a report on the "dilapidated and dangerous condition" of the old legislative building, for the provincial Minister of Public Works, the Honourable Christopher Findlay Fraser. He would provide the persistence and political muscle necessary to force the project through to completion ... 13 years later. Fraser asked Tully (the architect of old Trinity College) to draw up plans. In February, Tully outlined the basics of the building (its size, location, and general composition), and suggested a neo-Gothic style, but failed to find favour with his political masters.

Wisely, the government decided to hold an international competition for the building, which it advertised on April 26, 1880. But the competition was completely botched, or so Canadian architects like Eric Arthur have argued. The jury for the competition seemed fine. It included builder and former Liberal Prime Minister, Alexander Mackenzie (who had once bid on the construction of Ottawa's Parliament); prominent local architect, W. G. Storm (who later became involved in the City Hall design process); and outside architect, R. A. Waite (an English-trained architect living in Buffalo). But the rules established by the penny-pinching Fraser (a part of Mowat's very frugal Government), were "absurd," according to Roger Hall.[42] An equally absurd $500,000 cap was placed on costs, which Eric Arthur characterized as "niggardly in the extreme." And political interference, according to both commentators, ran amok.[43]

Sixteen competitors submitted plans: eleven Canadians and five Americans. The jury awarded first prize to Darling & Curry; and second prize to Gordon and Helliwell — all Canadian architects of some repute. In the end, however, neither firm received the commission, partly because neither scheme could be built for the specified $500,000, and partly because the Minister, inexplicably and inappropriately, asked jury member, Richard Waite, "to make a consultative examination" of the plans.[44] Perhaps not surprisingly, given the ultimate outcome, Waite found both sets of plans inadequate, more for their treatment of such mechanical issues as heating, lighting, and ventilation, than their architectural conception and design. What to do? Fraser decided to hold a run-off competition between the top two firms. Again, their proposals came in over the $500,000 limit. Again, Waite was asked to comment. Again, he found them wanting, even when the monetary limit was raised to $750,000. Again, what to do?

By now, five years had elapsed, political pressure was mounting, and newspapers were clamouring for an answer as to why the promised Parliament

5.13: *Sketch of Main Staircase*, 1892
In 1908, John Ross Robertson published a series of sketches by William Thomson, of the old Front Street Parliament that had been demolished in 1900 and replaced by Grand Trunk Railway freight sheds. (The CBC building now stands on the site, which is now much farther from the Lake than the Parliament had been.) This modest but graceful vestibule was located on the north side of the building. The stairway, with its nicely curved bannister, rose through a semi-elliptical Georgian archway toward the second floor galleries of each Chamber.
LANDMARKS OF TORONTO, v. 5, p. 568 (top)

had not yet been built. Perhaps in desperation, perhaps in relief, the Minister of Public Works asked *Waite* to draw up a new set of plans. Waite's plans found favour. On January 8, 1886 Waite was offered a contract, and shortly thereafter, in the old Legislative Chamber on Front Street, parliamentarians enthusiastically approved the plans for a new home, not to exceed $750,000. Ontario politicians may have been happy, but Canadian architects were so angry that they published a poster lambasting the hiring of an expensive, American architect over a competent, less expensive, Canadian architect.

5.14: *The Chamber on Front Street, 1892*

A rare photograph shows the Ontario Parliament in session at the Front Street legislative buildings where debates raged over the new parliament, among other lively topics. Sir Oliver Mowat, the decade's most important provincial politician, appears to be absent — he should be seated on the left-hand, Government side — although a number of ghostly figures drifted indistinctly across the open lens. Taken shortly before the move to Queen's Park, this view looks eastward toward the exquisitely carved Speaker's Chair, and the elaborate wrought-iron Press Gallery, where such ink-stained wretches as *Grip* cartoonist J. W. Bengough observed provincial politics from on high. (Our images of Sir John A. Macdonald and Premier Mowat come as much from Bengough's pen as any photographer's camera.) Ranks of bewhiskered Parliamentarians sit among young messengers, half-filled wastepaper baskets, heating vents, singular clock, scuffed desks, elaborately upholstered chairs set against the far wall, and the Provincial Mace placed on the Clerk's Table, facing toward the camera (indicating that the House was in session). Some of the desks occupied by the likes of Mackenzie, Baldwin, and Blake, the clerk's table, and the 1867 mace, are now at Queen's Park.

5.15: *Legislative Library, 1892*

Some time after Confederation, the old Legislative Council Chamber, where the likes of Sir Peregrine Maitland, Sir John Colborne, and Sir Francis Bond Head had once presided, was transformed into surplus library space. The only architectural evidence of the room's earlier use are the nearly blocked-off, elliptical arches that used to frame the Lieutenant-Governor's throne. Here, Parliamentary Librarian, the Reverend William Inglis, stands to the right, superintending his bibliographic domain; a pot-bellied coal stove stands to the left, emitting perhaps the only heat provided to the room; and diverse patrons consult books that probably disappeared in the 1909 fire at Queen's Park.

CITY OF TORONTO ARCHIVES: Series 406, Item 7

The competition for the Queen's Park Parliament may have been just as time-consuming as the competition for the Queen Street City Hall, and the cost-overrides may have been nearly as great, but the actual construction of Waite's Pink Palace moved along far more smoothly. The project was immense — inmates at Central Prison, for example, produced 10.5 million bricks for what is generally regarded as a stone building (mostly Credit Valley sandstone) — and was constructed in just six years.[45]

On April 4, 1893, Waite's "New Pile in Queen's Park"[46] opened to mixed reviews. A churlish *Saturday Night* reporter described the exterior as "a painful piece of architecture ... of no style or class," and the Legislature Chamber as "almost hideously decorated."[47] Obviously, the reporter was an admirer of neither the Richardsonian Romanesque style of Richard Waite's exterior nor the Canadian Art-Nouveau-style of Gustav Hahn's Legislative interior. A still-aggrieved *Canadian Architect* devoted most of its editorial to a diatribe that ended, "Draughtsman is writ large all over our greatest and most costly public building."[48] Not an accolade.

5.16: *Legislative Chamber*, April 1893

"The glory of the building" was, indeed, the Legislative Chamber, depicted in this faded-but-still-exuberant photograph, attributed to G. R. Lancefield and reproduced in the *Saturday Globe* of April 15, 1893.[49] Highlighting Waite's double-chandeliers, Lancefield's photograph shows the Ontario Parliament as it was originally intended, with Gustav Hahn's brilliantly coloured murals of maple leaves and allegorical figures adorning the walls and ceilings. Looking toward the Speaker's Gallery over the entrance and the Government benches and gallery to the east, this daylit image illustrates the profuse natural lighting that poured into Waite's building. (The Speaker's dais, press gallery, and triple-arched windows overlooking Queen's Park were off-camera to the right.) According to the reporter, the allegorical figures represented Moderation, Justice (on the left), Power, and Wisdom, while the arms of the cities were apparently tucked in among the arms of the province.[50] The massive chandeliers designed by Waite comprised a circle of gas, candle-like fixtures above a circle of electrified pendants exploding from the centre. Before long, however, major changes were required.

TORONTO PUBLIC LIBRARY: T 33356

5.17: *Legislative Chamber,* July 1929

Complaints about Waite's original sound and light effects, led to alterations. First, the cascading double-chandeliers were redesigned to cast enough light on Members' desks twenty feet below. Far more radically, when the acoustics in the Chamber proved inadequate, Hahn's polychromatic painting was masked by canvas-covered horse hair mufflers, and then more or less forgotten. For much of the twentieth century, the House was painted plain white, with deep red curtains, carpets, and upholstery, as seen in this view of a much more restrained Chamber. It was taken by TTC photographer, Alfred Pearson, perhaps to promote tourism by transit. It was only in the late-1990s that a preservation project led to the Chamber's being transformed by the Mike Harris Tories from Liberal red into "Parliamentary green" and to the Hahn murals being restored, bit by careful bit.

CITY OF TORONTO ARCHIVES: Series 71, Item 6939

But the daily press was ecstatic. "Legislators in Fairyland ... The Scene Within the Chamber Was Unrivalled for Splendor," trumpeted the Conservative *Empire*; and "No Province ever got more for its money than Ontario secured in the New Parliament building," suggested the equally Conservative *Telegram*.[51] The politicians were effusive. Premier Mowat, looking "brave but forlorn" after the recent death of his wife,[52] thanked his supporters for the gift of the Robert Harris portrait, which still hangs at Queen's Park. He recalled his earliest days in Little York, when there was no responsible government, no municipal government, no railway or even a paved street. He stood in some awe before the great building that his Public Works Minister, and long-time friend, C. F. Fraser, had seen to completion. "I am glad," commented the premier of 11 years, "to have retained my premiership long enough to see the erection and completion of the magnificent building in which we are assembled, and to take my place as premier of the province at the first session of the Legislature held here."[53]

"The people," for their part, were at the very least, curious — they came in their thousands to the opening — and were mostly enthusiastic about both the building and the opening ceremony. According to some estimates, 20,000

5.18: *Members' Reception Room, 1893*

The Members were well looked after. In addition to a richly carved, walnut cloakroom, well-appointed smoking room, and conveniently located private dining room, the Members enjoyed this large Reception Room. With its upright piano, brilliant chandelier, and plush furniture, the Members' Reception Room looked a bit like a gay-nineties bordello ... though just who was sleeping with whom was not always clear, as the infamous Gamey Affair underscored in the spring of 1903.[54]

TORONTO PUBLIC LIBRARY: T 10057

5.19: *Great Stairway, 1893*

One of the most dramatic elements in the new Parliament was the Great Stairway, an architectural beacon visible all the way from the main entrance. "Truly the change is a marked one from the old red-brick pile on Front street to the great brown-stone structure in Queen's Park," Frank Yeigh wrote, this time for the first issue of *The Canadian Magazine* where a photograph very like this also appeared. "It is a transition from gloomy corridors, dimly lighted offices, dust-begrimed desks, flickering yellow gas jets, and old-time grates, to spacious quarters, with high ceilings, handsome paneling, massive corridors, beautiful electric appliances, and perfect heating and ventilation."[55] Originally illuminated by two enormous windows over the landing, the stairs rose, in switchback fashion, from the Main Lobby directly up to the second floor, supplying a suitably grand entrance to the Chamber. Looking diagonally across brown-slate stairs (only later covered by luxurious red carpeting), Josiah Bruce's photograph illustrates Yeigh's "massive corridors," "handsome paneling" and delightful "electric appliances," as well as master smith Angus Macdonald's magnificent ornamental ironwork, and the blank surfaces where premiers' portraits would soon be climbing the walls.

ARCHIVES OF ONTARIO: F 1125-1-0-0-135

5.20: *Education Department*, ca. 1910
Not all bureaucrats worked at Queen's Park. Here, members of the Education Department — both male and a few female — hunker down, among piles of papers and approved schoolbooks, in their offices at Egerton Ryerson's old Normal School on Gerrard Street East. Given all the loose papers lying about, it's probably a good thing that the newfangled electric fan atop the cupboard was turned off. A tiny fragment of Frederic Cumberland's once-grand educational edifice now stands in a quadrangle at Ryerson University.
CITY OF TORONTO ARCHIVES: Fonds 1244, Item 3060

Torontonians flocked on foot, horseback, carriage, or streetcar to inspect their new building. From her crowded perch high up in the new "Ladies Gallery" (now the Western, Opposition Gallery), English tourist, Mrs. John Clover, found the great, brass chandeliers "very beautiful," the ceiling and walls "richly and almost gorgeously decorated," and Toronto's elite splendidly — if a bit gaudily — turned-out.

After the Opening of Parliament and the Lieutenant-Governor's Reception, dignitaries retreated to Government House for a State Dinner, and ordinary Torontonians continued investigating their new Parliament. Until late at night, they listened to military bands and quaffed non-alcoholic punch in the lobby; wandered the broad, richly panelled, multi-cuspidored corridors; marvelled at master woodcarver William McCormack's *chef d'oeuvre*, the mahogany Speaker's Dais; and generally inspected many a finely finished nook and cranny in the building, fully illuminated by both gas *and* electricity. They were probably *not* allowed into the Speaker's private apartments — now the Lieutenant-Governor's suite — to inspect the Speaker's bedroom, dining room, or exceptionally well-appointed bathroom, with its oversized tub, cherry toilet-seat, and silver-plated basin cock. (Lesser personages had to make do with walnut seats and nickle-plated basin cocks.)

When Sir Oliver Mowat first entered "his" new Parliament, he had chortled to the Speaker, "Now that we built it, Joe, how are we going to fill it?" With 200 rooms and a modest civil service, space did not seem a problem. But that was before the dramatic growth of the Province, and the dramatically activist approach of the Conservative Whitney government, caused the civil service to expand correspondingly. More space was urgently needed. (See 5.20.)

had been much closer to destruction than previously realized.[56]

Making a virtue of necessity, the Government hired E. J. Lennox not only to rebuild, but to enlarge and fireproof the West Wing. Respecting the original floor plan, Lennox, nevertheless, "took liberties" with the interior.[58] Rather than adopting Waite's, or even his own earlier City-Hall-style, Lennox now worked in a more "modern classic" style, reminiscent of his 1905 Bank of Toronto at 205 Yonge Street. Lennox's Wing, therefore, favoured marble, for its luxury and invulnerability, and more majestic proportions. The times had changed, and so had the dominant architectural style, as the history of Toronto's two Government Houses would also attest.

On September 9, 1909, disaster struck ... and helped solve the Parliamentary space problem. Tinsmiths repairing an eavestrough over the West Wing set fire to the building. Civil servants attempted, unsuccessfully, to douse the flames. By the time the fire brigade snuffed out the blaze, the western roof was largely gone, the second floor was a shambles, and the Legislative Library entirely destroyed. Fortunately, the Speaker's Apartment had been saved, and fire doors in the attic had prevented the blaze from sweeping through the entire building, although scorch marks found in the 1990s suggest that the Legislative Chamber

5.22: *The West Wing, Queen's Park, 1929*
R. A. Waite's original plan for Queen's Park — still evident in much of the building —
created marvellous pedestrian spaces along broad, beautifully carved and
colonnaded wooden halls. After a 1909 fire destroyed the 1892 Provincial Library
and much of the West Wing, E. J. Lennox was hired to create a new, fireproof West
Wing, with the results shown in this photograph by TTC photographer Alfred
Pearson. While scorned by some, like architectural historian Eric Arthur, Lennox's
classical, triple-tiered, marble interior has aged well, perhaps improving by
comparison to other downtown architectural developments.
CITY OF TORONTO ARCHIVES: Series 71, Item 6935

Government Houses

> Government House, for forty years a social centre in Toronto, will be
> vacated by Sir John and Lady Gibson early in May [1912]. It will then
> be pulled down to make way for CPR freight yards.
>
> MRS. FORSYTH GRANT[59]

Government House, whatever it was called and wherever it was located, lay at
the symbolic heart of Ontario public life, both political and social. Here, the
Crown's Representative (i.e., the Lieutenant-Governor) lived, entertained, and
performed a range of public and political duties, such as welcoming Royal
Visitors, bestowing recognition on local dignitaries, receiving Premiers bent on
"going to the people,"[60] and generally waving the Imperial flag.

Since Confederation, Ontario's Lieutenant-Governors had occupied
Gundry & Langley's Second-Empire showstopper, just north of the Front Street
Parliament Buildings, about where Roy Thomson Hall now stands. Located at
the southwest corner of the King and Simcoe intersection long-known as
Education — Damnation — Legislation — and Salvation,[61] Government House
was entered off Simcoe Street and was surrounded by large, *private* grounds,
suitable for skating parties in winter and garden parties in summer.[62] (See 5.23.)

By the time he completed his career, straight-backed, snowy-haired Thomas Lymer had served eleven Lieutenant-Governors and had become as well-known (at least to those in the know[64]) as any of the Government Houses over which he presided. Having emigrated from England in the mid-1870s, young Lymer presented himself to the household of Lieutenant-Governor Sir Donald Alexander Macdonald, which hired him on as butler. Two years later, Lymer became head of the household. Understandably, Lymer regarded Sir John Beverley Robinson's regime (1880 to 1887) as one of the happiest he'd known:

> So musical were Mrs. Beverley Robinson and her daughters, Mrs. Forsyth Grant and Mrs. Stewart Houston (then Miss Augusta), that during the winter a Gilbert and Sullivan opera was produced weekly in the ballroom in which a permanent stage had been built....
>
> Even the staff were not forgotten. Servants' balls were introduced and there was also an annual sleighing party to a Weston hotel for a jolly supper and ice-boat parties on the bay were other treats after a big function. While with one of his reminiscent smiles, Mr. Lymer adds: "There was always ale for supper every night for everyone."[65]

The "big function," however, was the point of Government House. Among the grandest occasions, ably overseen by Lymer, was the 1901 Royal Visit when the Duke and Duchess of Cornwall and York descended not only on Government House (where the principals and their nine servants stayed), but also on the nearby Queen's Hotel, where the rest of the party and their 28 servants, stayed.[66] It was during this visit that the future King, who disliked long meals, quietly shocked Toronto society:

> Even before the war had curtailed them, the state dinner given by [Lieutenant-Governor] Sir Oliver Mowat in honor of their majesties' visit as the Duke and Duchess of York began the revolution [of the shrinking menus]. For even then the present King did not like a dinner to be longer than an hour and three-quarters. But I remember, though we tried to shorten the 1901 menu, the Duke began to look restless and, to the consternation of the Toronto people of that period, he pulled out a cigarette while the sweet was being served and lit it. Local society almost held their breath, but afterward they gossiped and some people said they hadn't seen anything like it since a Russian prince had shocked a dinner party in Sir William Howland's time."[67]

Quel faux pas ... unless you happen to be a future King.

5.24: *Farewell to Government House, 29th April 1912*

Standing at attention immediately behind bespectacled Lieutenant-Governor Sir John Gibson, long-time steward, Thomas Lymer, surveys the last state dinner held at the old Government House on Simcoe Street. This "flashlit" portrait taken by F. W. Micklethwaite, and copyrighted by John Ross Robertson (the thirteenth figure on the right, just after Mrs. Forsyth Grant), was snapped right after the toast to the King. According to the gold-printed menu cards standing before each participant, all the known "descendants and other relatives of all the Lieutenant-Governors since Confederation" had been invited to the occasion, and nearly forty showed up.[68] Lymer's "table" was exquisite. The menu was not too long, featuring lobster a la newburg, spring lamb, and a selection of desserts. The conversation was bright, perhaps about the *Titanic* investigation that was just wrapping up, or the imminent return of well-known Toronto survivor, Major Arthur Peuchen, who had much to answer for for *not* having gone down with the ship. The portraits by George Théodore Berthon of Lieutenant-Governors overseeing this event, were transferred to Chorley Park and then to Queen's Park where they can still be viewed.

CITY OF TORONTO ARCHIVES: Series 387, Item 184

5.25: *Drawing-room, Cumberland House, ca. 1890*

It's unknown whether the Gibsons and their successors, the Hendries, had to live with the same kind of Victorian clutter as photographed here by Josiah Bruce long before they moved into Cumberland House. But architect Frederic Cumberland's lovely home had good bones, and was a worthy temporary gubernatorial residence from May 1912 to November 1915.

CITY OF TORONTO ARCHIVES: Fonds 1155, Item 6

The Torontonian Society Blue Book

IMPOSING MARBLE ENTRANCE HALL AT GOVERNMENT HOUSE

5.26: *Chorley Park Atrium, 1916*
A Canadian bear reclines, permanently, on the floor of Heakes' three-tiered, supposedly "Louis XVI," marble Atrium. Conceived on a scale far larger than even Rideau Hall in Ottawa, Chorley Park in Rosedale reflected the buoyancy of the times. With a frontage of 156 feet and a depth of 203 feet, this French Renaissance chateau was approached from Roxborough Drive on the south, and looked out over a still-natural Don Valley to the east. Despite the antiquity of the style, "no detail [was] wanting in the equipment to make the building up-to-date and self-contained in every way."[75] No radiators were visible. A central vacuum system was installed. Electricity had even been brought into North Rosedale for the first time. This photograph, looking north toward the Marble Staircase and Ballroom beyond, appeared in both *Construction* magazine and *The Torontonian Society Blue Book* throughout the 1920s — a testament to the building's favour among the building trades and the elite.

By 1912, as indicated by Mrs. Forsyth Grant, the area around Government House was no longer the aristocratic centre of the growing city. It was time to say goodbye ... and move to Rosedale.

Alas, Rosedale was not quite ready to receive their mini-Excellencies. For about three years, the Lieutenant-Governor and his family had to slum it ... at exquisite Cumberland House on St. George Street. (See 5.25 and Chapter 2.)

Toronto's second, grandiose Government House was planned and mostly executed in the palmy, pre-War days of Sir James Whitney. The first twentieth-century Conservative to win power in Ontario, Whitney brought Big Government to Queen's Park and Big Government House to Chorley Park.[69] After the usual toing-and-froing, which began in 1909, the Province decided to build the new official residence, not on Bloor Street near once-fashionable Jarvis and Sherbourne Streets, but in soon-to-be very fashionable North Rosedale. The choice of the remote Rosedale location was a risky, some even thought a laughable one. But frugality, and obstinance, won out over William J. Gage's

5.27: *Tea at Chorley Park,*
July 13, 1923
On the spacious verandah at
Chorley Park, Mrs. Cockshutt, wife
of the Lieutenant-Governor, pours
refreshments not long after George
Howard Ferguson's Conservatives
had defeated a labour/farmer
coalition. Tea, juice ... and smiles
(almost) all around. Tories and
prosperity (not necessarily causally
linked) were returning to Ontario
after a grim, post-War depression
and Drury's surprise occupation of
the Premier's office. John Boyd
captured the moment for the *Globe*
on a glass negative that has
deteriorated over time.
CITY OF TORONTO ARCHIVES:
Fonds 1266, Item 1113

generous offer for one near Wychwood Park and soon-to-rise Casa Loma.[70] As to the choice of architect, government frugality, and perhaps obstinance, won out there, too. Rather than engaging the winner of a design competition for the Bloor Street site, or holding a second competition for the new site, the Government chose Provincial Architect F. R. Heakes to design the residence.[71]

Heakes's million-dollar chateau in Rosedale took about four years to build. "Just before the New Year [1916]," reported an enthusiastic, but overly optimistic, *Construction* reporter, "it was occupied by Sir John Hendrie, and will no doubt continue for generations to come to be the official home of Ontario's Lieutenant-Governors."[72] Well, no. Sturdy and grand it may have been, but it was no "durable monument"[73] to Heakes or anyone else. As early as 1920, the United Farmers of Ontario made no secret of their distaste for such magnificence. By 1937, in mid-Depression, Liberal Premier Mitch Hepburn shut the chateau down.[74]

Life at Chorley Park may have been short, but it was definitely grand. It was here, for example, that the charming Prince of Wales stayed during his triumphant 1919 tour of Toronto and Canada. And it was here that the scale of entertaining grew vastly in size, if not "quality," at least according to the high standards of long-standing steward, Thomas Lymer:

"For the 1929 King's birthday garden party 6,900 individuals were asked and a record number at a public reception for ladies was 2,300," declared Mr. Lymer, who characterised Hon. W. D. Ross as a wonderful host. ...

"It's these societies they entertain now that makes the parties so big," exclaimed Mr. Lymer. "It used to be society that went to government house, but now it's all the members of all the societies."

... though more and more public guests come to Ontario's government house, its old major-domo shakes his head when he comments on the lack of breeding of many who go there now [1932]. Not only do rude guests throw cigarettes on even the ballroom floor, but many of its gold chairs [from Eaton's] have been burned.[76]

But grand or gauche, this Government House was gone within a generation. Chorley is once again a park, and Lieutenant-Governors entertain at what was once the Speaker's suite, at Queen's Park.

6

From Farmer's Market to Carriage Trade

Whatever else they are, cities are centres of commerce.

Toronto was founded as Upper Canada's political and military capital.

By 1803, it had evolved into a significant market town

in need of a regular, public marketplace.

By mid-century, King Street had become the city's most fashionable retail street. By century's end, Toronto was the province's dominant commercial power, and well on its way to becoming a national centre of trade and commerce. Throughout, Toronto's commercial life was also sustained by small, local players who provided the goods and services needed, and desired, by local residents and businesses.

Commerce, like other spheres of life, changed radically between the 1880s and 1920s. Once dominated by the small, independent business catering primarily to a local, or possibly a regional market, commercial firms not only grew in size and scope, but also changed many of their methods of operation. The small dry-goods store grew into a department store. The independent shopkeeper grew into, or was replaced by, the chain store, the franchise, or the supermarket.

New methods of merchandising were introduced, such as replacing bulk-goods by dispensing individually packaged, brand-name products, and new methods of marketing, like blanketing the country with mail-order catalogues and intensive advertising.

Moreover, new technologies, from the telephone to the cash register, transformed the way of doing business. Commercial life was economically stratified, both in terms of provider and consumer. There were crossovers: all classes mingled, to a certain extent, at the corner store or the farmers' market. But there were also stores catering explicitly to either "the shawl trade" or "the carriage trade."

The Market

Beneath [the St. Lawrence Hall] is a central arcade, the first half of which, opening on King street, is occupied by stalls teeming with children's toys, nick-nacks, cheap jewellery, and perfumery, the candies and sweet stuff which Disraeli, in one of his novels, calls "the opium of childhood," and second-hand books, which are the opiates of old age! After this comes the butchers' stalls, opening into the arcade, and each of them opening also into the east or west sides of the market square, where are ranged the farmers' carts laden with dairy produce, meat, and vegetables. The show of meat in the market, as also of cheese and butter, is well worth a visit; the writer has seen nothing equal to it in any other Canadian city.

C. PELHAM MULVANY, 1884[4]

In October 1803, Lieutenant-Governor Peter Hunter proclaimed Saturday to be little York's Public Open Market day, and the block bounded by Church, Wellington, King and Jarvis to be the Market Square where this weekly event would be held.[5] Ever since that time, the City of Toronto has owned and operated a *public* market near that site. In 1834 the "wooden shambles" that had functioned as stalls were replaced by a "collegiate-looking building of red brick" with arched entrances on King and Front Streets, and a wooden gallery running around its sides that sheltered the

6.2: *Window Shopping*, ca. 1922
Rileys was clearly an upscale, independent purveyor of groceries, provisions, fruits and vegetables. A sturdy NCR brass, cash register stands at-the-ready on the lefthand counter. Ethereal Consumers' Gas lights reveal an impeccably kept interior, and artfully arranged window displays. Fruit on offer include not only mundane, somewhat blotched, bananas, but also more exotic pineapples. The store is full of brand-name products — including American Quaker Oats, Heinz ketchup and Franco-American soups, and Canadian Christie's biscuits. An ad for plum pudding, and the oranges, pineapples, jams, and other fancy goods, suggests that Micklethwaite took this photograph around Christmas 1922. Shops like this one graced Toronto's streets for forty years or more, mostly, but not completely, unchanged.
CITY OF TORONTO ARCHIVES: Fonds 1034, Item 825

Meanwhile, south of Front Street another public complex had already risen: Henry Bowyer Lane's 1844 City Hall and Market, which continued both functions, in various combinations, until 1899. (See also *Chapter 5. From City Hall to Government House.*) During the 1890s, the commercial centre of Toronto had been moving north and west away from the King and Jarvis

merchants and customers below. After the terrible fire of 1849 wiped out this part of Toronto, including nearby St. James Church, William Thomas' elegant St. Lawrence Hall *and Market* was erected on the northern part of the site. Opened in April 1851, this complex was "one of the glories of Toronto, and one its greatest attractions for country visitors."[6] Comfortable, sheltered, even elegant, space was created to attract and hold shoppers, such as those described by local historian, C. Pelham Mulvany in the early 1880s.

area. When City Council also moved northwest, to E. J. Lennox's new Municipal and County Court (not Market) Building at Queen and Bay in 1899, the physical connection between City Hall and the St. Lawrence Market was severed. The future of the old market building became a subject of great debate. Should the City accept commercial realities and junk the site, or should it take the lead and reinvent the site as a larger, more modern, more commercially viable public market?[9] Ultimately, and largely through the persistent prodding

6.3: *Christmas at The Market,* ca. 1895

"But the best time by far to visit St. Lawrence Market is at Christmas or New Year season," wrote Mulvany in 1884. Then the huge beef-carcasses, rich with fat, hang side by side, some of the finest labelled with the name of some hotel proprietor or prominent citizen, who may have purchased that splendid provision for the Christmas feast; there, to use Chaucer's phrase, it seems "to have snowed of meat and drink; ... Brilliantly illuminated, brightly decorated, St. Lawrence Market is undeniably one of the things worthy of being seen in Toronto during the Christmas holidays." White-coated John Mallon would have agreed with Mulvany's assessments.

Here, the burly butcher stands among the beribboned Christmas carcasses at his north St. Lawrence Market butcher stalls around 1895,[7] before the radical changes of 1899–1902. Mallon had emigrated from Ireland with his parents in 1847. After apprenticing as a butcher, he opened his own stall in 1861. By 1865, his growing business occupied three stalls and was located near the entrance. (In 1899, annual rent for the three stalls was the substantial sum of $306.) By the time of this photograph, Mallon was Dean of the Market, and one of Toronto's most successful butchers and exporters of meat products. He was also a Separate School Trustee, Treasurer of the Village of Brockton, and Alderman in the City of Toronto.[8]

CITY OF TORONTO ARCHIVES: Fonds 1205, Item 9

of Alderman Daniel Lamb, City Council decided to refurbish the Market. On Saturday, November 15, 1902, "Siddall's Shed" was formally opened, to the evident delight of several thousand curious shoppers:

Amidst a melange of music, laughter, murmurings and speeches the new St. Lawrence Market was formally opened for business on Saturday. The music was furnished by the Grenadiers' Band, the

laughter by the crowd, and the speeches by the Mayor [Howland] and aldermen [Lamb and others]. The band was appreciated, the laughter was enjoyed, but as for the addresses nobody heard or knew what the speakers were talking about .... There was an air of prosperity about the new market on Saturday. The majority of the stalls are already tenanted, and the building is most complete and conveniently equipped. While the stalls were appropriately decorated with flags and

unto sardines in a box," according to the *Mail and Empire*. "The young man and his best girl were out in force, and the way in which the chrysanthemums of the dealers were 'snapped up' was a sight to behold. And throughout it all the band played on."

What did Torontonians get for their $250,000 investment? Architect John Wilson Siddall completely overhauled the old space, throwing a huge iron and glass roof across a 345-foot brick market shed that extended all the way from the Esplanade to the rear of St. Lawrence Hall, including a great Railway Age canopy constructed over Front Street between the South (retail) and North (wholesale) Markets. Siddall's architectural

bunting, still by far the most attractive part of the display was the tastefully arranged stalls with their rows of produce, meats, vegetables, flowers, etc.[10]

Especially delightful and popular was the evening's entertainment under the arc lights, when "[a]ll sizes and conditions of people were crowded together like

6.5: *North Market Day*, ca. 1917

Since Saturday, November 5, 1803, Saturday has been Market Day in Toronto. Here, bursting with fall produce, and gas arc-lighting, was the rebuilt North Market, which F. W. Micklethwaite documented for his client, the Consumers' Gas Company, ca. 1917. According to John Ross Robertson in 1905, the new, high-ceilinged, brick-floored, 340-foot North Market was far less convivial, but probably more efficient than its 1851 predecessor. Essentially a wholesale market, it was organized so that farmers could "drive directly under cover, and there leave their sleighs or waggons" open for business, so long as they took the team out and stabled it "away from the market."[15] Although open on weekdays, the Farmer's Market has always been most complete and crowded on Saturdays.[16] On February 1, 1969, a new, low-ceilinged version was rededicated and reopened for business.

CITY OF TORONTO ARCHIVES: Fonds 1034, Item 884

enterprise was dubbed "Siddall's Shed," either out of admiration or, perhaps, derision. Unfortunately, en route to creating the new South Market, he deconstructed almost all of the old one. Lane's late-Georgian-style clock tower, domed cupola, and pediment over the Front Street entrance were all knocked down. Thomas and Langley's restyled east and west wings were lopped off. At least the (now stumpy) central portion of the old City Hall was left embedded — and still eminently visible — in the fabric of the new Market.[11] To this day, a hundred and fifty years of political and commercial history remain writ large on the north wall of the South Market.

As for the organization of the South Market, the butchers, who had initially resisted moving, were in place for opening day, as were seven poultry, nine florist, and six provision stall-operators. Others would join them later.[12] To the right of the new, more broadly arched Front Street entrance, flower dealers displayed their splendiferous wares "in a way which could never have been even thought of in the old regime." To the left of the entrance, farmers' wives were doing a brisk business in the eggs, butter, "dead" fowl, and preserves presented in their "basket room." The butchers were located in the centre and along the sides of the big room, while "at the south end, the vegetable dealers ... lost no opportunity of catering to the epicurean mind and taste" of Toronto.[13] The Market, in sum, functioned much as it always had, and would. The location of the sellers and the mix of goods has varied over time, but Commissioner Coatsworth's concept of providing "an attractive, convenient and profitable emporium for the transaction of business" remains the same, even in the age of the Internet.[14]

After the turn-of-the-century, retail trade in urban Canada developed along relatively specialized lines. From the market and the general store evolved the single-line stores, specializing in such product groups as food, hardware, drugs, clothing, and so on. Earlier forms were not eliminated, but they became less important, and evolved, as new ways of doing business entered the marketplace.

Groceries

Not only did the store not advertise, but most of the goods we sold were never advertised. We bought our tea in bulk, our coffee in the bean, and most of the other staples came to us without any trade name to distinguish them from others, any more than if they had been potatoes. But a change was taking place before we left the store. Things were being packaged. Creamery butter had come in, and the first I remember was that of the Locust Hill Farm. It was a novelty.

J. V. McAREE, Cabbagetown Store[17]

Bread is the staff of life, and groceries the lifeblood of local commerce.[18] In 1897, for example, "groceries and liquors," at $10,000,000, represented the second largest "line of trade" in Toronto. Add related lines, such as "produce, provisions etc." at $7,500,000 and "live stock" at $4,500,000, and Toronto's food trades easily topped the first-ranked line, "dry goods, clothing etc." at $18,000,000.[19] Food was, and still is, big business ... even when the

business was carried out by hundreds of small operators, and a small number of large ones.

According to the Board of Trade, Toronto's 1897 retail grocery trade was "in the hands of perhaps 500 dealers," including about 25 major dealers, perhaps 150 modest dealers, and some 375 "small corner groceries," whose individual business may have been tiny, but whose cumulative trade was "considerable."[20] Whether a small, struggling store like The Cabbagetown Store at 283 Parliament Street contributed to the Board of Trade's statistics is unknown, but it certainly contributed to the life of the neighbourhood, as did pushcart vendors and corner store operators throughout the city.[21]

Cabbagetown-kid and future journalist, John V. McAree, witnessed the many changes that swept across Toronto's retail landscape in the 1880s and '90s from a front-row seat at his family's grocery store on Parliament Street. (Whether there were cracker-barrels at The Cabbagetown Store goes unreported, but there were certainly large, wooden tea chests to perch on.) Shopping tended to be daily. Purchasing was almost always on credit. Prices were seldom fixed. And most goods were packed in large, generic boxes, barrels, chests, and bags, rather than in small, individually measured, marked, and wrapped packages.

Take creamery butter. Before the arrival of standardized packaging, the shopkeeper would buy a tub of butter from the wholesaler, and dole out smaller portions on command. It was often a messy, imprecise, wasteful, and time-consuming process, as McAree remembered:

But here was creamery butter in a neat cube, wrapped in paper with a name on it. It was easy to handle. There was no waste. Nor was their [sic] any time lost in weighing, nor in calculating the price of one pound one and a half ounces of butter selling at 37 cents a pound that used to attend the cutting, weighing, wrapping and calculating of bulk butters to a customer's requirements.[22]

And so it was with other bulk goods, although something went missing in the transformation to standardized prepackaging:

Before the packaging of tea was invented to make the fortunes of Lipton [1888], Larkin and a host of others, the grocers bought tea in large chests, weighing perhaps fifty pounds or more. They were lined with lead foil, and the outside was formed of a thin layer of wood. It was one of the arts of the grocer to blend the tea he retailed from two or three different chests. ... Our Uncle John prided himself on the taste with which he blended his teas, and I think with justice, for we sold a good deal of tea in the store. When packaged tea began to appear on the market it had the advantage of taking up less room than the bulk tea in the chests, and this enabled the grocer to stock more goods in the same space. But our Uncle John had no enthusiasm for the innovation. He perceived that one of his arts was becoming outmoded.[23]

6.6: *We sell Lipton's Tea, 1890s*

These unidentified storekeepers on Queen Street West were obviously selling groceries after Thomas Lipton pioneered individual packaging of tea in 1888, and Christie's Biscuits in a box eliminated the proverbial cracker-barrel. In addition to displaying one of Lipton's metal advertising signs, this Victorian store is full of other brand-name products, signs, and chromolithographic ads for soaps, staples, and comestibles of all sorts: Old Dutch Cleanser, Gold Dust Baking Powder, Blue Ribbon Tea, and more. Very little bulk food remains, although the string needed to wrap up individual portions of cheese or other products hangs from the ceiling over the weighing scales on a ware-battered counter. Piles of neatly packaged butter appear to fill a large icebox behind the aproned shopkeeper in the centre. An expensive, glass-covered display case along the right suggests that the store is a successful one, as does the cash register on the counter, behind a pile of tins and in front of a second aproned keeper who looks very much like the central one. The ratio of four sales people to one customer seems a tad excessive ... and would not survive long.
CITY OF TORONTO ARCHIVES: Fonds 1268, Item 2018

Not only standardized packaging, but national branding and high-powered advertising changed the retail world. Everything from soap (Sunlight) to soup (Heinz) was packaged and sold by every available advertising medium: product packages, rooftop billboards, advertising cards, chromolithographic prints, daily newspapers, and monthly magazines. In 1886, an Atlanta pharmacist concocted a refreshing carbonated tonic from South American coca leaves and African cola nuts, thus creating what would become the world's most popular soft drink, Coca-Cola (now without the coca), as well as untold, perhaps overtold, legions of advertising campaigns, featuring richly coloured advertising cards in the 1880s and the first, of many, Coca-Cola Girls, around the turn-of-the-century.[24] Before long, Coca-Cola ads decorated not only

6.7: Michie & Company, 1897

Michie & Company was a carriage-trade grocer whose success was eminently apparent not only from its address on Toronto's finest retail street, but also from its elegant, new building. This photograph from the Board of Trade's 1897 publication illustrates local architect Gemmel & Smith's skylit store-interior with its highly polished, gently curving counters and stairway, tear-drop chandeliers, plentiful seating, and beautifully stocked, dark-wood shelves. Expensive cigars and fine clarets vied with fancy goods in brightly coloured tins for the attention of Michie's well-heeled customers. Brand names were present, but advertising was more subdued than elsewhere. Michie continued to operate until 1947, when the business was bought out by Simpson's department store, and the building was transformed into the Nag's Head pub. Sadly, the building that survived for a 100 years, and was described in 2000 by Toronto's Heritage Preservationists as a "fine example of commercial architecture" from the late-nineteenth century[27] didn't survive the dramatic renovation of its banking neighbour.

CITY OF TORONTO ARCHIVES: Series 654, File 18, p. 108 (lower left)

stores — both outside and in — but also home environments of the poor, as we saw in Chapter 3. Both manufacturers and store owners got into the act. A new industry — advertising — was born. For good or ill, mass retailing and the consumer society were launched.

Grocers opened stores in all parts of the city, to serve all segments of society. Michie & Company, for example, was one of the 1897 Board of Trade's featured "Dealers in High-Class Groceries, and Fine Liquors and Cigars."[25] Located next to the Dominion Bank's splendid Victorian Renaissance Revival office building at 1 King Street West (which, in turn, would be replaced by Darling & Pearson's even more splendid, Edwardian Renaissance Revival skyscraper), Michie & Company appealed to the financial powers of Bay Street, as well as to the society matrons of Rosedale and beyond.[26] In the 1890s, Michie & Company represented the height of fashion, both in architectural style and clientele.

First the chain, and then the supermarket transformed the retail grocery business in Toronto and across the continent. South of the border, the Great Atlantic and Pacific Tea Company evolved, from a single, pre-Civil War, cut-rate tea store in New York City, into a coast-to-coast grocery chain of about 80 stores by 1880, 400 by 1912, and 15,000 by 1929. Then, south of the Mason-Dixon Line, Clarence Saunders of Memphis took the next giant retailing step, founding the absurdly named Piggly Wiggly self-service grocery. "Through the turnstile to a land of Adventure!" became the company's advertising mantra. The idea was simple, and revolutionary: shoppers selected their own items, put them in their own baskets, carried them to a checkout counter, and paid a fixed price for the selected items. The self-serve supermarket was on its way.[28] Gone were the costly large staffs, personal service, idiosyncratic content, and general "charm" of the earlier era.

In Canada, the first supermarket chains were Steinberg's in Montreal (founded in 1917) and Dominion Stores in Toronto (founded in 1919). Earlier in the century, however, the phenomenally successful William Davies & Company of Toronto was already pointing the way to a supermarket future. Begun as a pork-packing company in 1854, the Company expanded its meat-packing and exporting business, opened retail outlets, diversified its product

6.8: *William Davies Company*, 1900s

Laid out more like a department store than a traditional grocery store, the large
William Davies Company store at Queen and Bay encouraged shoppers to browse
the aisles, inspect the products, consult the clearly marked prices, and make their
own selections. By the time Alexander Galbraith took this photograph, around the
turn-of-the-century, the Company was marketing its own brands, not only of meat
products (its core business), but also of baked goods (like the fruit-cake featured in
the foreground), teas, coffees, and ice creams. This proto-supermarket represented
a major break from the Company's meat stalls at the St. Lawrence Market (which it
gave up in 1919), and its chain of smaller, more traditional stores, such as the one
illustrated in Chapter 4.

CITY OF TORONTO ARCHIVES: Fonds 1177, Item 2

6.9: *Johnston's Drug Store*, 1892

Dark wood, shimmering chandelier, multicoloured bottles, and serene atmosphere
set the stage for Chemist and Druggist Thomas Johnston's successful practice of
pharmacy at 68 Wellesley Street. According to the *Dominion Illustrated* that
published this photograph, Johnston's "spacious and commodious" store (measuring
25 by 55 feet) was "handsomely fitted with all the requisite equipments for properly
conducting a first-class drug store." Among these were the "most desirable and
popular patent medicines, proprietary medicines of worth and merit, plush toilet
articles, brushes, soaps, perfumes, sponges, surgical apparatus," all handsomely
displayed in the modern plate glass windows, in the "attractive" glass-covered
showcase featured here, and on the dark-wood shelves lining the walls. Wielding the
traditional mortar and pestle of his trade, Johnston personally supervised the
compounding and dispensing of all "prescriptions and recipes" issuing from his
neighbourhood store. He also would have consulted the catalogues, almanacs, and
advertising cards issued by drug manufacturers (e.g., the Thomas Milburn Company,
makers of Burdock Blood Bitters) to explain their products and drum up business.

CITY OF TORONTO ARCHIVES, Research Hall Library: *The Dominion Illustrated
Devoted to Toronto (Special Number)*, 1892, p. 71 (bottom)

6.10: *Liggett's Drug Store*, 1920s

The 1920s neighbourhood drugstore, represented by this photograph of Liggett's in Riverdale, was bigger, brighter, and sleeker than its Victorian predecessor. The perhaps surprising appearance, let alone dominance, of the soda fountain is not really so surprising, considering that "soda water" was originally marketed as a cure for such ills as constipation, indigestion, and obesity, and the world's most popular soda pop, Coca-Cola, was invented by an Atlanta pharmacist to cure headaches. So, long before the advent of the post-World War II "teenager," the soda fountain was ready. Although the store's layout is very different from its predecessors, with a soda fountain along one wall, product displays along a facing wall, and dispensing from the rear, the product range is probably quite similar to Thomas Johnston's. And still evident was personal service. This Liggett's had not yet gone self-service.

CITY OF TORONTO ARCHIVES: Fonds 1525, Item 4

lines, and marketed its own, proprietorial products.[29] At least one store in the chain — the one located near City Hall at Queen and Bay Streets — could be described as a proto-supermarket, featuring large-scale operations, aisles (albeit still with sawdust on the floor), and quasi-self-service. (See 6.8.)

Other Neighbourhood Services

Grocery stores may have been most numerous, but other, essentially neighbourhood services proliferated, especially in the pre-automobile era. In the 1890s, for example, the intersection of Amelia and Sackville Streets, in the heart of today's Cabbagetown, boasted a pharmacy on the north-east corner (Lemaître's, later Cranfield's) and both a butcher (Gardiner's) and a baker (McMorran's) on the southeast corner. Meanwhile, sections of long streets (such as Parliament, Church, and Spadina, as well as Queen, College, and Bloor) functioned as mini-main streets, each serving a segment of the population located within easy walking distance. As well as the proverbial butcher and baker, the pharmacist, the barber, and the real estate agent were among those staking claims to neighbourhood commercial turf, throughout the ever-growing metropolis.

From his classic, High-Victorian pharmacy at 68 Wellesley Street,[30] Chemist and Druggist Thomas Johnston dispensed the pills, powders, elixirs, and wonder drugs of his era. Some helped, some harmed, and some hooked his trusting patrons. After all, dispensing laudanum for the ladies and morphine for the masses was common practice until outlawed in the late 1920s. (Even turn-of-the-century Eaton's dispensed morphine, but *never* alcohol, from its Drug Department; its Methodist principles forbade the latter, but not the former.) It was also common practice to lay in supplies of personal products — soaps, toiletries, enema bags — and non-medicinal products — candies, tobacco,[31] stationery, and even books.[32] Johnston, like most Toronto pharmacists before him and many after him, had learned his trade by serving

6.11: *Barber Shop*, 1920s

Although A. F. Bentley's barber shop, at 165 1/2 Yonge Street across from Simpson's, catered more to businessmen than neighbourhood residents, it contained the well-known accoutrements of both the big and the little barber shop of its day: the white porcelain, leather-upholstered, Koken barber chairs,[35] unframed, plate-glass mirrors, shoeshine stand at the back, and the easily mopped floor of hexagonal ceramic tiles. The uncluttered look, light-coloured walls and cabinetry, pop-top waste baskets, and generally sleeker design places this store in the post-World War I era, rather than the Victorian. The shaving mugs on the stands and the formal nameplates on the mirrors, however, place it considerably earlier than our own time.

CITY OF TORONTO ARCHIVES: Fonds 1525, Item 7

6.12: *McKibbin & Pentecost*, January 10, 1916

McKibbin & Pentecost was a Real Estate, Insurance & Loans firm operating from 835 College Street near Ossington Avenue. Mr. N. B. McKibbin is seated at the front desk, while his associate consults with a young businesswoman at the receptionist's desk in the rear. Behind McKibbin is a board with keys, presumably to local houses being shown for sale. On the walls are maps of the City (directly across from McKibbin) and the Dominion (published by Manufacturer's Life and posted on a back wall above the safe), various photographs, and a Bank of Hamilton calendar. Gone are the old, roll-top executive desks. In are the flat-top desks, card catalogues, wire in-and-out letter baskets, and, somewhat more unusual, a counter for writing cheques. Apart from the British Bull Dog print over the safe, there is little evidence that a war was raging across the world.

an apprenticeship — in his case, an arduous, five-year long, "old country" apprenticeship with an Edinburgh master whom he had pledged to serve "night and day" for a pittance. He apparently learned the art, and perhaps the science, of pharmacy well, since his store became such a success that within three years he had opened a second store in another neigbourhood, and inched toward becoming a chain-store operator. (See 6.9.)

Drugstores went the way of grocery stores: chains, franchises, and, ultimately, self-service came to dominate the market. In 1902, for example, Louis Liggett (founder of Liggett's drug chain) banded together with forty other druggists to establish the Rexall company, which franchised its name, logo, and products to local business people across the continent.[33] By the 1920s, the scale, the content, operation, and the look of local drugstores had changed dramatically. (See 6.10.)

The barber shop was another local institution. In some ethnic neighbourhoods, the barber shops "doubled as social clubs for a specific group of *paesani* or *landsmann*."[34] Ragamuffin boys and hirsute men patronized these bastions of maleness, from one end of the city to the other. (See 6.11.)

The major banks, insurance companies, and other financial services were headquartered downtown. But there was a place for smaller, multi-purpose financial and real-estate businesses out in the neighbourhoods, especially as the city grew ever larger. One of these, the McKibbin and Pentecost Company, served the west end of the city. An earlier McKibbin, George, was a "Financial and General Agent, Dealer in Houses and City Property," who had operated in the 1890s from an office at 17 Adelaide Street East.[36] By World War I, a later McKibbin had gone west ... and apparently prospered.

6.13: *Eaton's Main Floor, 1897*
Timothy Eaton's retail empire expanded rapidly once he moved to 190–196 Yonge Street, in 1883. This photograph, published by the Board of Trade in 1897, depicts a recently and grandly renovated department store, with central atrium and miles of aisles displaying thousands of products. The huge banners hanging from upper balconies suggest that the store owners were still in a celebratory mood. The comfort of patrons was uppermost in Eaton's design. Although Eaton's "sales girls" were not allowed to sit down during their 8 to 10 hour workday,[38] Toronto's Merchant Prince provided plenty of seating to encourage his predominantly female customers to linger over the goods, and make their purchases with ease. The lightness of being expressed by this photograph disappeared in the early years of the twentieth century, when additional commercial space was created by flooring over the atrium ... and shutting out much of the natural light.
CITY OF TORONTO ARCHIVES: Series 654, File 18, p. 113, (lower right)

The Department Store

We began with Dry goods and have branched out so as to include everything that sells well together, from Groceries to Tinware and from Bicycles to Patent Medicines. Advanced thought on retailing says that all kinds of goods must be united in one common system if each is to get the best. There are half a hundred different stocks here in charge of experienced men, who are capable enough to be in business for themselves, but who find here a larger sphere of usefulness. In reality, there are all kinds of stores under one roof....
T. EATON CO., 1896 Spring & Summer Catalogue

The department store, like the railway station and the skyscraper, became a symbol of urbanity and modernity in the closing years of the Victorian era.[37] Inspired by Paxton's great Crystal Palace, where a vast panoply of modern industrial goods was displayed under a single, gloriously modern roof, the somewhat more modest department store sought to stimulate shopping by offering "everything to everyone," under an almost equally splendid roof, and by making shopping an enjoyable "experience." Entertainment, special events, and plush appointments (even early forms of daycare), as well as lavish displays of merchandise along the aisles and behind the modern plate-glass windows, were all designed to attract, soothe, and generally stimulate shoppers to greater feats of conspicuous consumption.

When Timothy Eaton opened his little dry-goods store at 178 Yonge Street in 1869, he shocked his competitors by declaring that he would neither extend credit nor haggle over prices. Cash. One Price. Money Back Guarantee. These

6.14: Robert Simpson Company, 1897
Although never as big as his rival north of Queen Street, Robert Simpson's six-storey
department store was still one of the most modern and successful of Toronto's late
Victorian stores.[42] This picture was taken around the time that Robert Simpson died,
in December 1897, and the new, fireproof store was sold to a syndicate formed
by Joseph Flavelle, H. H. Fudger, and A. E. Ames. By that time, Simpson's had
35 departments and nearly 500 employees. The airy, metal-frame shopping
emporium designed by Burke & Horwood was far more comfortable and attractive
to shop in (as shown in this photograph of the Main Floor from the Mezzanine
Gallery) than it was to work in. See the photograph of the mail-order room in
Chapter 4.
CITY OF TORONTO ARCHIVES: Series 654, File 18, p. 111 (lower left)

were the precepts upon which the 35-year old Irish immigrant intended to
proceed.[39] While they may have shocked local Toronto merchants, the cash-
only and fixed-price tenets were well-established in the larger commercial
world. In 1852 they underpinned the commercial effort of Aristide Boucicault,
when he opened what is generally considered to be the first "department store,"
the Bon Marché in Paris. A decade later, Alexander T. Stewart used the same
approach for his "Cast-Iron Palace" off-Broadway in New York City. As Eaton
was making his way up in the local retail world — all the way up to 190 Yonge
Street in 1883[40] (see 6.13) — the department store was making its mark in cities
across the continent and across the seas. It clearly provided a goal and a pattern
for Eaton and his soon-to-be major rival, Robert Simpson. (See 6.14.) If Eaton's
Methodism was ever at war with his Commercialism, Commercialism won.
Dry good works, he might have concluded, were clearly a sign of salvation.[41]

Eaton's enjoyed phenomenal growth. "Canada's Greatest Store!" —
according to its own exuberant advertising copy — had grown from a store
with about 275 employees and almost 25,000 square feet of store area in 1883,
to one with about 1,500 employees and nearly 300,000 square feet in 1896.[43]
After the turn-of-the-century, the pace of growth quickened. In rapid succession, the company expanded floor space in the Yonge Street store; built
a separate Mail Order Building (1903), a 12-storey Factory (1910), and a
separate Furniture Building (1913); and made numerous other "improve-
ments." By 1910, the year when the company sold stereograph views of "The
Big Store" (50 cards for 10 cents), over 9,000 men and women worked at
Eaton's Toronto — in the store, the offices, the factories, and related services.
A hundred and fifty wagons, pulled by 298 horses, made three deliveries
daily to all parts of the city. The Big Store itself had a main aisle that stretched
330-feet from Yonge Street to James Street, operated fifteen elevators, and fed
three to five *thousand* customers each day at a "luxuriously furnished" (with
mission-style tables and chairs) Grill Room on the fifth floor.[44] (See 6.16.)

From his newly expanded department store at 190 to 196 Yonge Street,
Timothy Eaton issued his first mail-order catalogue in 1884, and initiated
a merchandising and advertising venture that helped link the country, and
ensured his company's success for three or four generations to come. Mail order

6.15: *Eaton's Ladies' Waists Department*, 1910
The stereoscopic photographer who created Eaton's mail-order Tour of The Big Store, worked after hours. Here, s/he captured a preternaturally quiet Ladies' Waists Department, which was usually the scene of intense shopping. Finished "waists" stand sentinel over an upper-floor department devoid of either customers or salespeople. By 1910, new commercial floor space had been created by decking over the central atrium. The result, at least in the stereographs, could be claustrophobic and grim ... but not nearly as grim as conditions in the new factory, where Eaton-brand waists were sweated into completion by hundreds of mostly immigrant women. (See Chapter 4.)
CITY OF TORONTO ARCHIVES: Fonds 1125, Item 17

was huge — both in the US where Montgomery Ward and Richard Sears staked their claims, and in Canada where Timothy Eaton and Robert Simpson staked theirs. Eaton used this novel form of marketing to both stimulate national sales and generally advertise his growing business. His first catalogue, published at the 1884 Industrial Exhibition in Toronto's ebullient Semi-Centennial year, featured a drawing of his 4-storey, elevator-serviced, new store with modern plate-glass windows, "an abundance of light" and "no dark corners," where 35 departments, thousands of articles, and "a live colossal business" were all to be found.

Eaton's, like many retailers, adopted a wordy (some would say verbose), informative (if hyperbolic) style of advertising.[45] Endlessly repeating the themes of reliability, low cost, high quality, great service, and bountiful choice, Eaton's catalogues transformed consumer habits across the country. "Merely the best service, the best goods in the largest variety, and the best values. That's the whole case," summarized one promotional publication.[46] Each "Farmer's

Bible," as mail-order catalogues were often called, was eagerly awaited by isolated farmers and small-town residents longing for a taste (sometimes literally, through the grocery department) of the big city. Eaton's was there for their buying pleasure, offering semi-annual catalogues, free delivery for orders over $25 (excluding potentially heavy items like sugar and flour), and numerous special deals. "You and we may be quite a distance apart, measured by miles," copy writers commented, "yet by reason of our Mail Order facilities, we're virtually next door to you."[47] And so Eaton's created a national retail system based on folksy neighbourliness, and retailing savvy.

The size of the mail-order business was astonishing. In 1910,[48] women spent their entire days just opening mail orders. A phalanx of order-fillers selected appropriate items, which were then deposited in each customer's basket. These orders were checked and then sent down to the packing department via a continuous conveyor belt — "one of the many labor, time, and money-saving devices" that accomplished mechanically what it would have taken 100 to

6.16: *Eaton's Packaging Department*, 1910
In this stereograph, an army of well-dressed packers wraps up mail-ordered goods under the careful scrutiny of even-better-dressed supervisors. According to the commentary on the back of this stereographic card, the basket in the foreground contained a customer's order that would be "wrapped, packed, baled or crated," as required. Each man was provided with "an abundance of all necessary materials such as wrapping paper, excelsior, straw and packing boxes," like those visible overhead. No bubble wrap for these boys. Throughout the mail-order process — from receipt of order to sending of goods — Eaton's assured its customers that "every precaution is taken to protect the interests of our thousands of out-of-town customers who purchase from us, the result being that we have an ever-increasing list of patrons who buy practically their every household need from Eaton's."
CITY OF TORONTO ARCHIVES: Fonds 1125, Item 50

200 humans to do, declared the caption on a company stereographic card. Not a word about the fate of the expendable workers. Viva industrialization of the workplace. (See 6.16.)

For the small, independent merchant, the arrival of the department store was, at the very least, frightening. No one was safe, or so it appeared. Grocers, clothiers, pharmacists, florists, furriers, jewellers, milliners, harness-makers, hardware dealers, and so on, all faced stiff competition from the retail behemoths rising at Yonge and Queen. Two strategies, however, provided some protection: niche marketing (especially of bulky and/or high-priced goods), and local marketing.

Pianos, for example, were big business — in size of product, price tag, and national sales. Pianos and sheet music were to turn-of-the-century parlours what CDs and surround-sound were to turn-of-the-millennium homes. Despite the piano's evident popularity, Eaton's wasn't particularly interested. In 1901, for example, Eaton's Catalogue offered piano stools, piano drapes, piano music, a few Eaton-brand organs, but not a single piano. Such large and potentially expensive items were left to specialists, like the Bell Organ & Piano Company, to make and sell. Founded in Guelph around 1864, the Bell Company became one of Canada's most successful — and, at least according to its own publicity, largest — piano makers. By 1884, it had produced 26,000 organs and pianos; by 1902, 100,000; and by 1928 when the now-failing company was taken over, 170,000. "After 1920 business gradually declined as consumers wound up gramophones, cranked up Model Ts, and found other forms of entertainment," summarized piano historian, Wayne Kelly.[48] (See 6.17.)

Small local merchants, like McAree's Cabbagetown Store, continued to offer credit, late-evening hours, and personalized service to counter the draw of

6.17: *Bell Organ & Piano Company Show Room,* ca. 1902

Based in Guelph, the Bell Organ & Piano Company sold pianos not only in Toronto, but around the world. (Queen Victoria reportedly had a Bell in her palace, as did the Sultan of Turkey in his.) Alexander Galbraith photographed the company's showroom at 146 Yonge Street in its palmy days, around 1902 when lush plants, wallpapers and carpets (Turkish, perhaps) set just the right tone. Bell, like its many competitors, didn't rely on price or quality alone to push its pianos into the parlours of the nation. It deluged the public with colourful advertising cards and song sheets bearing the company's name. The Bell Company even issued a proto-advertising jingle when it published *The Bell Two Step* so that customers or potential customers could sing the praises of its products.

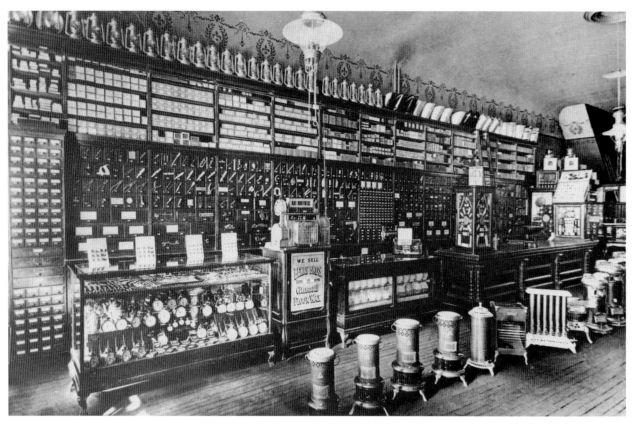

6.18: *May Brothers Hardware, 1905*

Department stores sorely tested, and often defeated, their smaller rivals. Eaton's hardware and stove department, for example, purchased the "total output of one of the largest and best equipped foundries in Canada,"[50] in order to offer its own brand of stove, the "Acme." The company's enormous buying power ensured that it could offer a wide range of relatively cheap wares that challenged local, independent merchants, like May Brothers at Dundas and Keele. Whether May Brothers succeeded, they had the virtue of proximity to and personal relationship with local residents, which are the abiding strengths of all good neighbourhood stores. May's was a classic, turn-of-the-century hardware store, stocking primarily "shelf hardware," like nails, knobs, knives, locks, screws, pliers, oil lamps, coal scuttles ... even space heaters and cheap alarm clocks. Cash register at the ready, May Brothers served West Toronto for many years.

CITY OF TORONTO ARCHIVES: Fonds 1268, Item 1920

the downtown department store. Occasionally, small retailers banded together in a vain effort to stop the big stores. On the other hand, the big stores conducted a relatively small proportion of total retail activity. There was still room for the little guy in the big city.[49] (See 6.18.)

By 1919, when the T. Eaton Company celebrated its 50th Anniversary, about 16,000 people worked for the Eaton Empire in Toronto. Beyond that, loyal publicists also trumpeted that "the Sun never sets on the Eaton Buying Organization."[51] The Company had buyers in such western locations as New York, London, Belfast, Manchester, Leicester, Paris and Zurich, and buyers in the more exotic locales of Kobe and Yokohama, Japan. The company had not yet branched out, except to Winnipeg, where it had built its second department store in 1905. But it had pumped up its advertising machine to such a fever pitch that "the average space per day occupied by Eaton Advertising in Toronto was 15,820 lines: two pages in each of the three evening papers and one page in each of the morning papers — besides an average of 596 lines per issues in a weekly journal," not to mention a steady flow of hand bills, catalogues, posters and such-like from its own Advertising Department (yet another novelty of the early twentieth century). No wonder local newspapers were reluctant to challenge Eaton's during the 1912 strike by its garment workers. According to the deep thinkers in advertising, readers of Toronto's evening papers wanted straight information, especially about moderately priced goods, such as those featured in the "Thursday Bargain" ads; and her morning paper-readers wanted softer, style chatter — "What's new, what's authentic, what's interesting in anything from frocks to refrigerators."[52] Eaton's was, and for a long time remained, a solid, reliable, moderately trendy, multi-faceted retailer.

Even at the height of the War, Eaton's Queen Street store was packed. Here, a multitude of shirtwaisted customers and employees pause and pose on one of Eaton's eight moving stairways. Eaton's was an early adopter of this people-moving technology, which had been created in the 1890s as a novelty ride for Coney Island, but was moved into the commercial mainstream around 1900. (Eaton had installed his first elevator in the mid-1880s, when that contraption was new and about to help revolutionize urban architecture by making skyscrapers possible.)

ARCHIVES OF ONTARIO/EATON'S ARCHIVES: F 229-308-0-1760

Refreshments

Victorians — not to mention Edwardians and Canadians of every generation — loved their candies and confections, soft drinks and hard. Naturally, entrepreneurs across the city did their best to titillate the taste buds and slake the thirsts of paying customers, from the most impoverished to the wealthiest.

One of the most successful early confectioners, caterers, and restauranteurs in Toronto was Harry Webb. The son of a local confectioner, Webb built a three-storey brick building at 447 Yonge Street, in 1880; employed a staff of 16 to produce his own "lines of confectionery, ice creams, water ices, sherbets, wine jellies, pastry, fancy ornamental dishes, French fruit glaces;" catered to "evening parties, receptions, banquets, etc." across the city; and generally

operated "one of the most handsomely fitted up establishments in the Dominion," according to the upbeat 1886 publication, *Industries of Canada: Historical and Commercial Sketches of Toronto*. Just looking at the accompanying engraving makes the mouth water.[53]

That quintessentially Victorian institution — the ice-cream parlour — had both temperance and even radical political overtones ... although mostly it was the sweetly nostalgic place that the term conjures up in the modern mind. The temperance connection is obvious: substitute refreshing, non-alcoholic beverages for the devil's brew.[54] The political connection is less obvious: in Toronto's Jewish communities, for example, neighbourhood ice cream parlours were social centres where unionism and other "radical" topics could be, and frequently were, discussed. The popularity of ice cream (a post-Civil War phenomenon

6.21: *Bingham's Palm Garden,* ca. 1902

Bingham's ice-cream parlour at 100 Yonge Street was a fashionable British version of the genre, attested by the flags and coat of arms decorating the far wall. Under slowly whirling fans — and nighttime bands of decorative electric lights — Edwardian soda-sippers and sundae-dippers perched on the wire chairs, around the small, round tables typically associated with this pastime. Bingham's Palm Garden boasted an especially fine onyx soda fountain, of the sort made by Toronto's successful manufacturer of such wares, the Fletcher Manufacturing Company.[57] Given the close association between pharmacies and soda fountains, it's not surprising that G. A. Bingham had operated a drug store at this location in 1889. But why Alexander Galbraith was hired to photograph it is unknown.

CITY OF TORONTO ARCHIVES: Series 394, Item 19

south of the border) and the ice cream soda (the 1874 invention of soda-fountain manufacturer, Robert M. Green[55]) contributed to the evolution of "the soda fountain" and "the ice cream parlour." Add the sundae and the ice cream cone — both apparently American creations[56] — and success was all but assured.

Some Torontonians liked their refreshments alcoholic. Calvinist Toronto was a major manufacturer of alcoholic drinks, with one of the world's largest distilleries growing apace on the eastern waterfront (Gooderham & Worts, creators of a classic, golden Canadian rye whiskey that is still sold around the world), and nine breweries "mak[ing] liberal provision for 'wetting ... the popular whistle,'" as the Board of Trade phrased it in 1897.[59] The market for Toronto's products extended "pretty generally throughout Canada" ... and across town. Despite the warnings of temperance fanatics like C. S. Clark, author of the ironically named *Of Toronto The Good,* 60 male Torontonians patronized an abundance of drinking places — ranging from the "blind pig" to the Albany Club, the local pub to the hotel saloon. For good or ill, the bar was here to stay. (See 6.24, 6.25.)

6.23: *Diana Sweets,* **1920s**
When this photograph was taken in the 1920s, the Diana Sweets food and confections chain operated three locations: at 153 Yonge Street, 187 Yonge Street (shown here), and 526 Bloor Street West. Its large scale and small touches (like fresh flowers on each of the little square tables), kept Diana going until late in the twentieth century. This local chain profited from economies of scale and standardized design. For example, decorative flourishes, like capitals on the piers and parti-coloured tiles underfoot, were the same at each location.[58] Ultimately, Diana failed to keep pace with modern taste and international competition.

CITY OF TORONTO ARCHIVES:
Fonds 1525, Item 9

6.24: *Oyster Bar at New Year's, ca. 1913*

Working under dim Consumers' Gas lighting, F. W. Micklethwaite, whose great rolofex camera is reflected in the right-hand mirror, captured atmosphere and details of this anonymous watering hole. Iced oysters and 25-cent beer attracted customers to this small oyster bar in downtown Toronto. For teetotalling travellers, Oyster Cocktail, Dairy Milk, and British Bovril were also offered. The decorations suggest the photograph was taken between Christmas and New Year, and the timetables posted on the wall to the left of the brass cash register suggest that it was located near Union Station, a traditional place for oyster bars to locate.[61]

CITY OF TORONTO ARCHIVES: Fonds 1034, Item 796

6.25: *Winchester (Lakeview) Hotel Bar,* **1898**

In the early 1890s, John Ayre's Lakeview Hotel, on "a commanding site" at the corner of Parliament and Winchester Streets, was regarded as "an excellent up-town hotel." From its high, cupolaed tower, and even from the plank sidewalk below, tourists could see the Lake at the foot of Parliament Street and Toronto Island across the Bay. With "telephone communication and convenient access to [street] cars for all parts of the city," the Lakeview was becoming a popular "resort for the travelling public,"[62] some of whom found their way, with Cabbagetown locals, to the ground-floor bar-room shown here. The liquor license over the cash register indicates that the photograph was taken in 1897 or 98. This old Cabbagetown saloon featured both the long, mahogany bar with brass foot-rail, and the elaborate pressed-tin ceiling so characteristic of the period.

The Lakeview's tin ceiling was so special, in fact, that this photograph was featured in a catalogue for *Metal Ceiling and Wall Finish,* issued by The Metallic Roofing Company of Canada (then located at King and Dufferin). According to the 1904 catalogue, customers could cobble (or nail) together their metal plates, borders, and cornices in a wide variety of more, or less, convoluted designs. The Lakeview ceiling, for example, was composed of elements in the "Empire" or "Colonial" style. The Metallic Roofing Company left its mark not only on Toronto and other cities of the Dominion, but in such far-distant locales as Cape Town, South Africa. Sadly, little remains of the original tin ceiling and virtually nothing of the Victorian bar.

COURTESTY OF BRIAN GREER

6.26: Main Banking Room, Dominion Bank, 1914

From boiler room to boardroom, the Dominion Bank's new headquarters at King and Yonge Street were not only state-of-the-art, but impressive beyond local measure.[67] The Main Banking Room shown here was the public pièce-de-résistance, just as the Board Room was its most eye-dazzling private space. (See Chapter 7, *Inner Sancta*.) Taken for *Construction* magazine in December 1914, this photograph surveys the opulent, 154 by 68-foot, marble hall with a Turkish-carpeted "officials' platform" at the south end. The classically coffered ceiling 33-feet overhead features richly coloured coats of arms of the nine provinces then comprising the "Dominion" of Canada, (Newfoundland joined Canada in 1949) but none of the bug-eyed modern lighting that later marred the effect. Designed both to impress and function efficiently, the banking hall was encircled by a monumental, 18-pier arcade, and was well-equipped with about two dozen tellers' windows, majestic marble tables, and a single telephone in the foreground. The vault in the basement was not only beautiful, but also the largest in the bank's Dominion, with among the heaviest doors ever made — 30 tons.[68]

The (Toronto) Dominion Bank's Main Banking Room is still one of Toronto's grandest commercial spaces,[69] but is no longer open to members of the public. Now, in the exquisitely renovated hall, members of the ultra-fashionable Dominion Club luxuriate under "new" grand chandeliers and network at the hundred-foot bar that replaces one bank of teller stations.

Banking

Banks and related financial services made the commercial world turn. "Until the 1880s Canadian banks were regionally based," write Gunther Gad et al, "but thereafter the banking system was increasingly dominated by large banks with nation-wide branch networks and significant operations overseas." The large banks — like the Canadian Bank of Commerce and the Dominion Bank in Toronto — developed by expanding their branch networks and merging with smaller, regional banks. Concentration of financial decision-making increased steadily. Between 1891 and 1931, the number of federally chartered banks dropped from 38 to ten, and the number of urban centres with head offices dropped from 18 to just two — Toronto and Montreal. Even the Bank of Nova Scotia moved its head office to Toronto in 1902.[63]

6.27: *Canadian Bank of Commerce Branch*, ca. 1893

No colourful chromolithographs, calendars, or other advertising come-ons decorate the stark walls of this 1890s bank. Like its competitors, the Canadian Bank of Commerce was branching out to provide better savings and loan services to local residents and businesses. By 1892, the Bank had moved into "new and commodious quarters at the corner of King and Jordan streets" downtown,[71] and was operating 47 branches across Canada, including nearly a dozen in Toronto. Here, confident Bank of Commerce staff members strike poses near the tellers' cages at their Yonge and College branch, while a caped patron checks her calculations at a side counter. The branch has the scuffed look of a well-used, but distinctly local, business.

CITY OF TORONTO ARCHIVES: Fonds 1268, Item 2097

In 1897, 14 chartered commercial banks were "furnish[ing] the sinews of trade for Toronto," of which seven were headquartered in the city.[64] These were the Bank of Toronto, Canadian Bank of Commerce, Dominion Bank, Ontario Bank, Standard Bank of Toronto, Imperial Bank of Canada, and Traders' Bank of Canada.[65] By 1914, seven of the eight banks making Toronto their headquarters had their head offices along King Street between about Yonge and Bay Streets.[66] For the moment, the grandest of these was the new Dominion Bank at the corner of King and Yonge. (See 6.26.)

In 1897, Toronto banks were operating a total of 26 branches in different parts of the city and suburbs "for the convenience of outlying business precincts and for savings deposits."[70] All but one of the branches were run by one of Toronto's "home banks." By far the largest were the Canadian Bank of Commerce with 11 branches in the city, and the Dominion and the Imperial Banks with six each. (See 6.27.)

Carriage Trade

Then, as York Street intersects [King Street], begins the most brilliant and long extended series of first-class stores of which Toronto can boast, her Palais Royal, her Regent Street. On the south side, the

6.28: *John H. Dunlop,* Florist, 1897

Ephemeral and extravagant, floral displays had definite carriage-trade potential. The flowers on a pedestal and Persian rugs on the floor set the tone for John H. Dunlop's fashionable flower shop at 5 King Street West. Dunlop was a flowering entrepreneur, who not only operated two shops (this one and a second one at 445 Yonge Street), but also grew his own materials, under 100,000 feet of glass at Landsdowne and Bloor Street West.

CITY OF TORONTO ARCHIVES: Series 654, File 18, p. 59 (upper left)

"dollar," or fashionable side, of King Street, continuously from York Street to the Market, are the spacious plate-glass windows, glittering with jewelry, with gold and silver plate, with elaborate china and bric-a-brac, with sheen of satin-shining tissues for Toronto's brides in esse and brides in posse, with more sober-hued, but still beautiful and elaborate materials for the adornment of Toronto's golden youth. Here are restaurants where men and ladies can dine in comfort, and as luxuriously as any in New York or London, photographers, art warerooms. Is there any luxurious taste you desire to gratify, any decorative art you would pursue? In that case, O reader, "put money in thy purse," (for that is an indispensable condition), and take a walk along the south side of King Street.

C. PELHAM MULVANY, 1884[72]

Since early in the nineteenth century, fashionable Torontonians had "promenaded" along fashionable King Street to see and be seen, as well as to peruse and to purchase the most fashionable goods and services the young city had to offer. For along King Street, as Mulvany described so exuberantly, the most fashionable photographers, furriers, and florists set up shop. In 1868, Notman & Fraser, for example, established their studio at 39 King Street East, which continued to house successive generations of fashionable photographers.[73] Both G. R. Renfrew and John H. Dunlop established their carriage-trade businesses at the late-Victorian, early-Edwardian power-corner of King and Yonge Street — Renfrew, a fur salon, and Dunlop, a flower shop. The pattern, as Mulvany suggested, flowed all the way to — or, more properly, from — the Market that had been the well-spring of commercial Toronto. (See 6.28.)

Jewellery was the ultimate carriage-trade item, and Toronto boasted a number of superior jewellers. In 1897, for example, Toronto had about seven "strictly first-class" jewellers, selected from a local pool of about 60 retailers who sold "jewelry of some sorts and in some degree."[74] Diamonds came from New York, but local workers provided most of the skills necessary to create fine jewellery. Among the foremost jewellers were Ryrie Brothers (born and bred in Toronto) and Henry Birks (branch planter from Montreal where the

6.29: *Jewellery Store,* early
1900s
The identity of this brilliantly
Edwardian jewellery store is
unknown, but its class and its
clientele are obvious. Even the
over-wrought-iron radiator serves as
a base for a marble platform
bearing bronze statuettes and a
gloriously excessive table lamp; and
the period ceiling was patterned
not only in tin, but also in electric
lights.[76] Satin swags, potted palms,
handsome mahogany cabinets,
and joyfully adjusted chandeliers
complete F. W. Micklethwaite's
period picture.
CITY OF TORONTO ARCHIVES:
Series 387, Item 28

head office still resides). In the late 1890s, Ryrie Brothers were still operating from 118 Yonge Street at the corner of Yonge and Adelaide, where they had fashioned the much-celebrated decorative "casket," presented by the City of Toronto to Queen Victoria on her Diamond Jubilee in 1897.[75] As Ryrie Brothers prospered, they moved up Yonge Street to settle in their own building, which is still known as the Ryrie Building, at 134 Yonge Street. Ultimately, Ryrie Brothers joined, and then was absorbed by Henry Birks & Sons, which continued to operate a store in the old Ryrie Building. (See 6.29.)

Fashionable early retailers may have congregated around the Market, but early hoteliers spread out from the wharves and the railways, where many of their patrons landed. In the early days, and on through the nineteenth century, no hotel was more fashionable than the Queen's Hotel at 100 Front Street West, which now holds the equally fashionable Royal York Hotel.[77] Virtually every commercial directory and local history sang the praises of Toronto's premier Victorian hotel, which was only eclipsed in 1903 when the King Edward Hotel opened on King Street East, ushering in a new monarch and a new age in carriage-trade hostelry. (See also Chapter 8.)

According to the 1886 illustrated compendium of Toronto industries, no hotel in Canada had "a more solid and wide-spread reputation than the really first-class establishment known as the 'Queen's.'" It had been "liberally patronized by royalty and nobility during their visits to Toronto,"

such as His Imperial Highness the Grand Duke Alexis of Russia, their Royal Highnesses Prince Leopold, Prince George, Princess Louise, the Marquis of Lorne, the Earl and Countess of Dufferin, and the Marquis and Marchioness of Landsdowne.[78] Not only did the Queen's offer spacious, well-laid-out grounds and a splendid view of Toronto Bay, but it was also supremely well-appointed. The public and many of the private rooms were furnished by premier Toronto furniture-makers, Jacques & Hay;[79] its cuisine was deemed unsurpassed for "excellence and luxury, every delicacy being furnished in season"; and bath-rooms were provided on every floor. True luxury indeed for the mid-1880s. The Queen's Hotel also inspired loyalty in its patrons and staff. When the Great Fire of April 1904 threatened to consume the Queen's Hotel, along with most of Toronto's central downtown area, guests and staff worked feverishly and well to save the grand old lady of Front Street. On the morning of April 20th, the Queen's distinctive Second-Empire tower still rose above the ruins.[80] At least one more generation would enjoy the cuisine and the character of the Queen's, before she was toppled in 1927 to make way for her replacement, the CPR's skyscraping chateau, the Royal York Hotel. (See 6.30, 6.31.)

Toronto, according to a promotional "guest book" issued by the King Edward Hotel in 1903, might not have had "the air and dash of London or New York," but it was surprisingly "metropolitan," and had a newly opened, three-million-dollar hotel that equalled "in elegance and excellence the

6.30: *Queen's Hotel Lobby,* 1904
It's unknown whether Alexander Galbraith photographed the lobby of the Queen's Hotel before or after she was saved from almost certain destruction by the Great Fire of 1904. But the reasons for the popularity of the forty-year-old hotel on Front Street are immediately evident. A pleasing, and eminently manageable fire lends warmth to one of the side reading rooms. Jacques & Hay furnishings, such as the mirror over the mantle and the great cabinet dominating the lobby, lend elegance and solidity to the environs. Coffered ceilings, dark-wood panelling, and curvaceous wall stencilling, lend character. Spacious, but not grandiose dimensions lend comfort, not pomposity, to the surroundings. By 1904, however, the Queen's Hotel perhaps had more of a lived-in look than Toronto's most striving and status-conscious Edwardians could tolerate. (Witness the permanently imprinted cushions on all the leather chairs.) For them and theirs, the King Eddy, not the Queen's, was the place to be.
CITY OF TORONTO ARCHIVES: Fonds 1587, Series 409, Item 8

6.31: *Queen's Hotel Bake-House,* ca. 1907
In the bake-house bowels of the gracious Queen's Hotel, time seems to stand still, as a white-suited cook removes loaves from his coal-fed oven. William James captured this moment around 1907, after the Great Fire had transformed the immediate surroundings of the Queen's, and the King Edward Hotel had transformed grand dining in Toronto. Cooks at the new hotel, however, did not fare much better than the cooks here. (See also Chapter 4.)
CITY OF TORONTO ARCHIVES: Fonds 1244, Item 617

most palatial hostelries of much more pretentious cities...." Not only that, it was also "absolutely fire proof," a quality of some psychological, as well as practical importance at a time when hotels, like office buildings and retail stores, scraped ever higher and higher. Whatever else he created, architect E. J. Lennox did not create a modest hotel on King Street East. His edifice was just about as pretentious — and High Edwardian — as buildings could be in turn-of-the-century Toronto. And it was just what his clients — the social and business elite of the city — wanted. (See 6.32.)

The automobile was originally a luxury item — an object of display more than a reliable form of transportation. Advertisers initially pitched their wares to the fur-wearing, golf- and tennis-playing crowd. Even when Henry Ford began to create mass production and a mass market for cars, the John Craig Eatons and Henry Pellatts were disporting themselves in Rolls Royces. The carriage-trade was rapidly, and inevitably, becoming the horseless-carriage trade — a group that took a different form of transportation, but still sought many of the same good things in life that it had always sought. (See 6.33.)

6.32: *King Edward Hotel Office, 1903*
Marble columns, mosaic floors, coffered ceilings, mural-covered walls, and monumental scale, combined to make E. J. Lennox's King Edward Hotel the toast of carriage-trade Toronto. This photograph appeared in a 1903 promotional booklet, with the great man, King Edward himself, on the cover. Intending to stir up high-end tourist trade, this richly produced brochure sang the praises of the hotel and the services it provided, including the special horse-drawn buses with coachmen in livery, that met trains and steamboats and whisked guests off to the hotel in the comfort to which they were accustomed.
CITY OF TORONTO ARCHIVES: Series 1144, Subseries 1, File 4

6.33: *Horseless-Carriage Trade, 1920s*
Cooke & Fogerty Jewellers welcomed the horseless-carriage crowd with the same polish that they had welcomed earlier generations of wealthy Torontonians. When patrons entered their store at 130 Yonge Street, they passed by a discreetly hidden porter/security guard, en route to the smoothly elegant show area beyond. Another Peake & Whittingham photograph of the store indicates that the style of the store might have changed — gone are the tin ceilings, the fussy chandeliers, and the overwrought clutter — but the cases contained, as always, the staples of the business — diamonds, diamonds, and more diamonds.
CITY OF TORONTO ARCHIVES: Series 958, File 110, Image 4

7

Inner Sancta

For the poor, especially poor women,

there was no privacy and there were no inner sancta.[1]

The camera of the powerful probed, often without permission,

the private spaces of the poor.

*I*t was unthinkable that anyone would have photographed the future Lady Eaton nursing her children in a kitchen, or any other part of the house. Yet photographing a poor, nursing mother in her own kitchen is exactly what City Photographer Arthur Goss did, on his search for "slum conditions" in The Ward.[2] For the rich and the near-rich, there were places of retreat, such as secret societies, clubs, backrooms, boardrooms, private offices and home libraries, which the camera, occasionally and definitely *with* permission, captured for posterity. As in so many other spheres of life, women fared less well than men. With little power and far fewer resources, women had fewer and less beautifully appointed clubs, virtually no offices or backrooms, and, ironically, little private space even in "the home," their own socially acknowledged sphere of influence.

Freemasons

For the uninitiated, it is hard to fathom the point of secret societies. With their funny clothes, bizarre symbols, obsessive hierarchies, and strange rituals, such fraternal associations often seem, at best, silly, and at worst, socially harmful.[3] But, however constituted, such organizations have often exercised considerable power. Take, for example, the oldest and the largest international fraternity, the monotheistic Freemasons, whose stated purposes are "mutual aid" and "brotherhood."[4] In Canada, at least six prime ministers, including Sir John A. Macdonald, have been Masons. In Ontario, some

16 premiers have been Masons. And in Toronto, many mayors and people of influence have also been Masons. The importance of the order to Toronto, and York before it, was symbolized by the fact that the first Masonic Hall, located in the 1820s on Colborne Street, was capped by the town's first cupola. "This ornamental appendage" was regarded by Dr. Henry Scadding in 1873 as "the first budding of the architectural ambition of a young town which leads at length to turrets, pinnacles, spires, and domes."[5] Because of their secrecy and their power, the Freemasons pique our historical curiosity, which, occasionally, the camera has satisfied. (See 7.2.)

The Freemasons expanded with the rest of the city. In 1897, the ten downtown lodges moved their headquarters to G. W. Gouinlock's striking, ten-storey IOF Temple Building[7] at Bay and Richmond, where they signed a twenty-year lease for a Blue Room, Royal Arch Room, and Dining Room. By the time the lease was up, other lodges had been created outside the downtown area. On January 1, 1917, they moved north into their own building, the Masonic Temple, at Yonge Street and Davenport Road. (See 7.3.)

Clubs

It cannot be denied that the Toronto people are what Dr. Johnson called "clubable." A considerable number of these pleasant social institutions exist in our city, of which the limits at our disposal permit us to give

7.1: *Revelry at the National Club, 1908*
Jackets off, vests unbuttoned and glasses raised, gentlemen of the National Club stand to toast ... photographer William James. The unclubbable James took this candid photograph in 1908 at one of Toronto's most elite men's clubs, which still occupies a neo-Georgian clubhouse at 303 Bay Street.
CITY OF TORONTO ARCHIVES: Fonds 1244, Item 3069

7.2: *City Masons*, ca. 1880
Under the all-seeing eye of the
Great Architect, these unidentified,
but probably aldermanic, Masons
posed for a group portrait by
Notman and Fraser around 1880.
Whether the setting painted by
John Fraser was real or imaginary
has not been determined. Around
the time this composite photograph
was created, Toronto's main
Masonic hall was located at
18–20 Toronto Street in a German-
Gothic-style building erected by
piano maker and Masonic brother,
Albert Nordheimer. According to
Mulvany, this hall was "the finest in
the Dominion," of lofty dimensions,
and even fitted-up with a Brussels
carpet of Masonic design that was
unique in Canada and seems to be
included in this picture. There were,
however, a number of other,
smaller Masonic halls, including
ones in Yorkville, Riverdale, and
Parkdale, so it is impossible to
locate this group with any degree
of certainty.[6]
CITY OF TORONTO ARCHIVES:
Fonds 1267, Item 398

7.3: *Masonic Reception, 1910*

Rank upon rank of aproned Masons gathered in their Masonic Hall at the Temple Building on October 18, 1910. Under the painted gaze of many long-past Most Worshipful Grand Masters, these Edwardian Masons gathered to pay tribute to their current M. W. Grand Master, Judge Daniel Fraser McWatt of Sarnia, and other, still-living past Grand Masters. Mulvany's unique, Masonic carpet is clearly visible on this floor.

CITY OF TORONTO ARCHIVES: Series 387, Item 183

7.4: *National Club Banquet, 1912*
In Toronto, the business, social, and military elites overlapped. Here, for example, the military elite, photographed by F. W. Micklethwaite, celebrates its own at the socially and economically elite National Club. On March 22, 1912, Brigadier-General W. H. Cotton and the Officers of the Toronto Garrison gave a dinner in honour of the corpulent, "vain, colourful, charming and splenetic" Conservative Minister of Militia and Defence, Sam Hughes, who was busy promoting citizen-soldiers over professionals.[10] Before long, both Hughes and many of the men in this room would be playing real war games on the fields of Flanders and around the world.
CITY OF TORONTO ARCHIVES: Series 387, Item 195

Albany and the Toronto Club, all of which still exist. A number of other exclusive clubs — like the York Club in 1909 and the Arts & Letters Club in 1908 — were formed after Mulvany's time and continue to flourish in one way or another.

In 1884, when Mulvany published *Toronto Past and Present*, the National Club occupied "a fine house" at 98 Bay Street, where it had a "handsome library, reception rooms, smoking and dining rooms," all the necessities for real club life. In those days, the "general tone" of the club was Liberal, and Lieutenant-Colonel (as well as Police Magistrate) George T. Denison was president. In 1907, the Club moved a few blocks up the street into its new, four-storey, neo-Georgian clubhouse at 303 Bay Street. Today, the club is dwarfed by skyscrapers, but still serves a business elite, which now includes women. (See 7.1, 7.4.)

little more than a bare catalogue. The clubs that most nearly represent the ideas attached to the name in English society are the National, the Toronto, and the Albany.

C. PELHAM MULVANY, 1884[8]

C. Pelham Mulvany was a snob[9] ... and therefore a good source for ranking early-Toronto's social clubs, which then included, as he notes, the National, the

7.5: *Albany Club Library*, ca. 1917
Closely modelled on the English gentlemen's political club, Toronto's Conservative Albany Club settled into its current home at 91–93 King Street East, in 1898. The Library, photographed by F. W. Micklethwaite for the Consumers' Gas Company, offered plush, overstuffed chairs, gas lighting and heating, and reading material appealing to the well-connected sportsman, the military man, the speech-maker, and the politico. On the magazine racks, for example, lie copies of *Forest & Stream*; on the bookshelves are *Naval List, Dictionary of Phrase and Fable, Ontario Statutes*, and *Who's Who 1917*; and over the gas fireplace hangs a painting of "The 1913 Derby."
CITY OF TORONTO ARCHIVES: Fonds 1034, Item 881

The Albany Club, established by friends of Sir John A. Macdonald in 1882, was, and still is, Conservative — not only in tone, but more especially in politics.[11] The Club's political bent was not left to the imagination. "No person shall become a Member of the Club unless a *Conservative*,"[12] stated the early Club bylaws. Nearly every Conservative Prime Minister since Sir John A.'s day; every Ontario Premier since Sir James P. Whitney; and most Federal and Ontario Provincial Leaders who never formed Governments, were all members of the Albany Club. For those wishing to rub shoulders with the Party elite, joining the Albany Club was a smart move.

The Club's first premises were at "Mrs. Dunlop's tenement" at 75 Bay Street, across the street from their Liberal political rivals at the National Club. The furnishings of the first clubhouse were not lavish, consisting mostly of household effects that went along with the house. In 1889, the Club moved to 34 Colborne Street, where it stayed until moving to its final resting place at 91–93 King Street East in 1898. Located in John George Howard's Victorian Row on fashionable King Street, the Albany Club has undergone many changes since 1898, making it impossible to identify the precise location of the Library illustrated here. (See 7.5.)

Established in 1837, the Toronto Club had "the repute of being a high-toned

BANQUET TO THE HON GEO A COX
PRESIDENT OF THE CANADA LIFE ASSURANCE CO
IN COMMEMORATION OF THE COMPLETION OF
— FIFTY YEARS OF SERVICE —
THE TORONTO CLUB. FEB. 1st. 1912.

F. W. MICKLETHWAITE
PORTS. 289 YONGE ST
TORONTO.

7.6: *Toronto Club*, 1912
Fashionable men repaired to fashionable clubs. Here, F. W. Micklethwaite photographed the popular, and supremely well-connected financier, Senator George Cox,[14] who was being feted at Toronto's oldest (and arguably North America's second-oldest) men's club, on the occasion of his 50th Anniversary at Canada Life. Despite the Club's externally eclectic, even eccentric, architecture,[15] eccentric male attire was not encouraged. In a velvet-curtained roomful of business and political leaders, including Lieutenant-Governor John Gibson, the only sartorial variation was between white tie or black. How the members greeted Oscar Wilde's colourful fashions when he dined at the Club in 1882, goes unrecorded. The *Star* of February 2nd ran this "flashlit" photograph on page one, a sign of Senator Cox's prominence in the city.
CITY OF TORONTO ARCHIVES: Series 387, Item 190

and somewhat exclusive society," a reputation that continued through the pre-War era documented by Micklethwaite's camera.[13] In 1888, the Club moved to the delightfully eclectic building it still occupies at York and Wellington.

Artists spend a great deal of time alone. Perhaps to counter the loneliness and encourage creative interaction, a group of artistic men met around 1908 in the old Palm Room at McConkey's Restaurant and decided to form what would soon become the Arts & Letters Club. Where should they meet? One suggested that they should stay true to their art ... and meet in a garret. After a

brief, nomadic life, the Club found a home in the old County Court House at 57 Adelaide Street East. Among the early members of the Club were such literary figures as poet Duncan Campbell Scott, journalist Augustus Bridle, and local historian Jesse Edgar Middleton; and such visual artists as Arthur Lismer, Lawren Harris, C. W. Jefferys, Fred Varley, and George Reid. Architect Eden Smith — George Reid's neighbour in Wychwood Park — designed the Club's Great Gothic Fireplace, which J. E. H. Macdonald depicted in a large painting that captured both the fireplace and the mood of the Club in those early years. Many other members contributed enthusiastically to the life of Club — putting on dramatic sketches, publishing a newsletter, and

7.7: *Arts & Letters Club Lunch*, ca. 1916
Toronto's men of the arts are lunching at their Arts & Letters Club in the old County Court House at 57 Adelaide Street East. Whatever the quality of the food, the splendour of the baronial hall — complete with huge fireplace and mock heraldic banners — was immense. Poets — like Duncan Campbell Scott — and painters — like Fred Varley and Arthur Lismer — were among those who enjoyed convivial, communal lunches at the Club.
CITY OF TORONTO ARCHIVES: Series 420, File 72

decorating the walls with paintings, banners, and other works of art. (See 7.7.)

In 1920, the Arts & Letters Club was forced to leave the Court building. With the timely intervention of architect Henry Sproatt — who was a member of both the St. George's Society and the Arts & Letters Club — the Club arranged to move to old St. George's Hall at 14 Elm Street, which Sproatt and his partner then renovated. Sproatt & Rolph (architects of Hart House) created another great, wood-panelled, baronial hall, featuring a recreation of Eden Smith's Great Fireplace, Gothic windows, and banners bearing fanciful heraldic crests. The Club — now with both men and women members — is still based at Elm Street.

Even if they couldn't join the high-powered, all-male Arts & Letters Club,

female artists *could* join the more modestly appointed Women's Art Association of Canada, which was founded in 1896 under the patronage of Lady Aberdeen and was devoted to both handicrafts and the visual arts.[16] (See 7.8.) Or there was the Toronto Heliconian Club, founded by professional artists in 1909 and initially devoted to music, art, and literature.[17] In both cases, they could enjoy pleasant, though not opulent surroundings, and the intelligent company of other women interested in many aspects of the arts.

While socially prominent men met at their exclusive clubs, socially prominent women had fewer choices. Members of such genealogically driven societies as the IODE (Imperial Order of the Daughters of the Empire), founded in 1900, tended to meet at the homes of members. The socially exclusive

7.8: *Women's Sketch Club*, 1894

In 1886, Mary E. Dingman invited a group of other female artists to meet at her studio in the Toronto Arcade on Yonge Street. Before long, they began meeting regularly to discuss art, hone their skills, and exhibit their work. Then, in 1896 under the patronage of Lady Aberdeen, Dingman and friends formed the Women's Art Association of Canada, which has been based at 23 Prince Arthur Avenue since 1916. Throughout the club's history, the handicrafts have been as important as the traditional high arts. Handicraft exhibitions were held at 594 Jarvis Street in the late 1890s, and a magnificent Historical Canadian Dining Service was created in 1897 and presented to the Aberdeens when they returned to Scotland in 1898. (This artistic testimony to Canadian nationalism still resides in Scotland.) In this photograph, mutton-sleeved artists, gathered around a fleecy spinning wheel, sketch one of their (well-clothed) members amid the organized clutter of a studio at the Canada Life Building, 40–46 King Street West. The spinning wheel — both symbol and tool of the handicrafts — may still be stored at the club's Yorkville headquarters.

WOMEN'S ART ASSOCIATION OF CANADA ARCHIVES

Toronto Ladies Club,[18] founded in 1904, operated from a third-floor room in the Toronto Arcade at 131–9 Yonge Street, until the mid-1930s when it moved to quarters in the (now demolished) Canadian Imperial Bank building at 2 Bloor Street West. A few, somewhat exclusive women's clubs did have their own clubhouses, such as the University Women's Club (1903) at 162 St. George Street. But most women — socially prominent or otherwise — enjoyed relatively few private spaces.

Backrooms

Many — most — important political decisions have always been made in such "backrooms" as the Mayor's Office, the Premier's Office, and the Prime Minister's Office. Because of its political status as the capital of Ontario, Toronto has hosted both mayoral and premiers' meetings in a variety of locations. Occasionally, a suitably subservient photographer was invited in to document an occasion, or just the surroundings. (See also Chapter 5.)

7.9: *YWCA Pool*, ca. 1909

The YWCA did not cater to the social, political, artistic or business elites of Toronto, but it did provide private recreational spaces for ordinary women, like these swimmers-in-training. This barren-looking pool area later became the luxurious, cedar-wrapped pool area for the relatively elite, late-twentieth-century women's club, 21 McGill Street and its successor, The McGill Club. Earlier in the century, when William James managed to gain access to the YWCA pool area, Miss Beaton seems to have spoken softly and wielded a big stick during her swimming lessons. Unlike the practice at the men's "Y," or even the later women's clubs, nudity was definitely verboten.

CITY OF TORONTO ARCHIVES: Fonds 1244, Item 2559

7.10: *YMCA Pool*, **1915**
The boys of the YMCA enjoyed not only more spacious quarters, but had considerably more sartorial freedom than their sisters at the YWCA. City photographer, Arthur Goss, photographed these frolicking skinny-dippers at the Broadview YMCA, in spring 1915.
CITY OF TORONTO ARCHIVES:
Series 372, Subseries 52, Item 529

7.11: *Mayor Fleming's Office, 1897*
Mayor Robert J. Fleming (silhouetted in centre)
meets with the 1897 Board of Control in the
Mayor's Office on Front Street. Here Fleming
is surrounded by the trappings of power
(photographs of predecessors piled high on his
walls) and Victorian taste (multi-patterned rugs,
multi-patterned wallpapers, potted palms,
tasselled light shade, and Japanese firescreen),
and also by the personnel of power. These
ranged from small office boy to snowy-bearded
aldermanic sage, Daniel Lamb, who preserved
this photograph by F. W. Micklethwaite with his
papers. Although the identity of the office boy is
unknown, many civil servants started their careers
this way. One such was the extremely successful
R.C. Harris who became the City's most powerful
commissioner in the first third of the twentieth
century; and another was Arthur Goss who
became the City's first, full-time official
photographer during that same period.
CITY OF TORONTO ARCHIVES: Fonds 1246,
Item 45

In the old, old (or second) City Hall on Front Street, the Mayor's Office was tucked away, conveniently close to the Council Chamber, and inconveniently away from the prying eyes of uninvited "guests," like reporters, irate citizens, or importuning lobbyists. Among the early mayors who called in the photographer was Robert J. Fleming. Fleming was a self-made man, who rose from relative poverty in Cabbagetown to the top of the civic hierarchy, both political (four-time mayor) and administrative (Commissioner of Assessment). During his first two mayoral campaigns in 1892 and '93, Fleming became known as the "People's Bob," an image he reinforced when he refused to wear the top hat, white gloves, and frock coat traditionally sported by a mayor. Also an ardent temperance advocate and moral reformer, Fleming hung a huge sign in his office which read: "Except the Lord keep the City/the Watchman waketh

392. TRANSPORTATION BOARD. AUG 12-1920.

7.12: *Mayor Church's Office,* **August 12, 1920**
One of the longest-serving and most popular mayors of Toronto was Tommy Church, who started his mayoralty during the first World War in 1915 and continued on until 1921 when he became a Tory MP.[21] Among the knottiest problems resolved during his long tenure was public transportation. Finally, after years of struggle and debate, the private streetcar system was replaced by the publicly owned Toronto Transportation Commission. (In the early part of the twentieth century, "Conservatives" were big boosters of such Big Government projects as public transportation and public hydro-electric power.) Under one of E. J. Lennox's exquisitely designed brass chandeliers, Mayor Church here signs into existence the first Commission, which gathers around for its first official portrait, along with such senior civil servants as Works Commissioner R. C. Harris (second from right). The Mayor's great, glass-topped "partners' desk" is impressively clear of papers, but holds two all-important telephones to keep the Mayor in touch with his staff and his constituents.
CITY OF TORONTO ARCHIVES: Series 372, Subseries 54, Item 392

but in vain."[19] During his second two-year stint as mayor, Fleming presided over the creation of the Board of Control to look after the day-to-day operation of the growing civic government, supposedly in a more businesslike manner.

In 1899, City Council moved to its grand new quarters on Queen Street. Here the Mayor's Office became a Mayor's Apartments, located in the southeast corner of the second floor, and just down the corridor from Lennox's new Council Chamber. The Mayor's Apartments consisted of a public waiting room, a public office, a private office, and an adjoining office for the Mayor's clerk.[20]

Provincial politicians, like their city brethren, were on the move in the 1890s. After great pomp and circumstance in April 1893, penny-pinching Premier Sir Oliver Mowat walked through R. A. Waite's amply proportioned and beautifully carved public corridors, into his own, quite stark, private space.

7.13: *Premier's Office, 1893*

Sir Oliver Mowat moved into the unadorned new Premier's Office at the southeast corner of the new Parliament building, around the time this photograph appeared in the Saturday *Globe*. Barely visible is the Premier's coal grate that created so much difficulty for a later occupant of the office: Premier E. C. Drury, head of the surprise post-War election victors, the United Farmers of Ontario. Drury was, personally, a frugal, teetotalling type. He also liked an open fire. Since his immediate predecessor, Conservative Sir William Hearst, had replaced the old coal grate with an electric one, Drury asked the housekeeper to put the old grate back in. Rising to the occasion, the housekeeper retrieved the grate and assorted brass accessories from the attic. The brass accessories, Drury commented, were polished until "they shone like gold." Unfortunately, a *Telegram* reporter thought they might *be* gold, and precipitated the great "Hundred Dollar Coal Scuttle" crisis that never really disappeared. The suggestion that Drury had redecorated his office at great public expense persisted and helped usher Conservative G. Howard Ferguson into the Premier's office in 1923 and for the rest of the decade.[22] Perhaps Mowat's more austere taste was also more politically astute.

TORONTO REFERENCE LIBRARY: T 10184

(See also Chapter 5, *From City Hall to Government House.*)

The only comment on the premier's office, made by a *Globe* reporter in a heavily illustrated, multi-page spread about the new legislative buildings, was that Mowat's walnut desk — "panelled and carved in the Byzantine style" suitable to the owner's occupation — qualified as "the finest writing table in the building."[23] Perhaps damnation by faint praise.

Boardrooms

Boardrooms, whether gloriously or only sparsely decorated, are hidden loci of power. Here are a few revealed in their ordinariness and in their glory.

The innermost sanctum of Ontario political life is the Cabinet Room, where the Premier's anointed meet and secrecy reigns. Not even agendas for

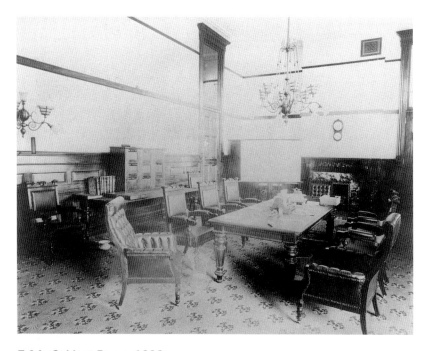

7.14: *Cabinet Room, 1893*

Located near the Premier's Office in the southeast corner of the second floor of the Legislature, the Cabinet Room did have impressive proportions, especially for a body that numbered only eight men when Mowat moved in. It was about 37 feet long, 22 feet wide, and 18 feet high. The architect's original specifications suggest that he intended this room to be very grand, with nine-foot high, butternut wainscotting around the walls; a cherry mantelpiece; fluted pilasters supporting an elaborate frieze, heavy mouldings, and beamed ceiling with painted panels.[24]

None of this German Renaissance plan was implemented, as this photograph makes abundantly clear. The wide mouldings were reduced to a thin picture rail. The cherry mantelpiece was reduced to brown-stained gumwood — a wood scornfully described by Eric Arthur as "outside the élite of Canadian woods such as walnut, pine, cherry, butternut, sycamore, and maple."[25] The ceiling was not coffered, and the walls were neither elaborately plastered nor pilastered. The room was definitely more Scottish Skinflint than German Renaissance. The only discernible touch of comfort was in the eight, high-backed, leather-upholstered oak chairs. Government secrets continue to be created in a much-changed version of this room at Queen's Park.

7.15: *Ontario Cabinet, 1893*

Photographer Josiah Bruce created a deceptive photomontage of Mowat's Cabinet meeting in the room as it was originally conceived. He photographed each of the eight members of the cabinet and affixed their individual photographs to a painted background of an imaginatively decorated room, with draperies, frescoes, pilasters, and book-laden shelves. The effect is both grander and warmer than the actual, photographed room.

7.16: *Royal Commission on the University of Toronto*, 1905

For about a year, the (apparently humourless) members of the Royal Commission on the University of Toronto met to map out the future course of the University. From left to right, this group of wealthy, cultural decision-makers, photographed by Alexander Galbraith, included: Rev. Bruce Macdonald, Rev. H. J. Cody, Sir William Meredith, Joseph Flavelle (Chair), A. H. V. Colquhoun, Goldwin Smith (who had once served on a Commission that reformed Oxford), and Edmund Walker. A copy of this photograph adorned the outer office of the Minister of Education.
CITY OF TORONTO ARCHIVES: Fonds 1568, Item 484

Cabinet meetings, let alone minutes or verbatim reports, are deemed open for public viewing until twenty years have elapsed. It is surprising, then, that this most important of private political spaces was far less richly finished than many of the public areas of Queen's Park. In fact, in Mowat's day, it was downright stark. The architect's intentions, however, were apparently grander than his political masters', as comparison of an actual photograph with a photomontage suggests. (See 7.14, 7.15.)

Around the turn-of-the-century, the University of Toronto moved into a new period of consolidation and growth. In 1905, Sir Joseph Flavelle, who lived in the heart of the University district, was appointed Chair of the Royal Commission on the University of Toronto. Also serving on this Commission was a wealthy, high-powered, occasionally intellectual group of men, including: Goldwin Smith (freelance intellectual and education reformer), Sir Edmund Walker (President of the Bank of Commerce, patron of both the Royal Ontario Museum and the Toronto Art Gallery, and a connoisseur in his own right), Sir William Meredith (Chief Justice and Chancellor of the University), Rev. Bruce

Macdonald (Principal of St. Andrew's boys' school), Rev. H. J. Cody (scholar and rising Anglican priest), and A. H. V. Colquhoun (Editor, *Toronto News*). As a result of this Commission, the Ontario Government passed legislation in 1906 that reorganized university governance (creating a Board of Governors and a more arm's-length relationship with provincial government), provided greater funding, and expanded technical education and research.[26] (See 7.16)

The ultimate "establishment" boardrooms in Victorian and Edwardian Toronto were created by the big (and getting bigger) banks. Designed to convey wealth, stability, and respectability, bank boardrooms tended to be subdued, wood-panelled, softly carpeted rooms of distinction, often containing portraits of The Founder or other Notable Male Personages to inspire, and perhaps intimidate, current directors.

7.18: *Dominion Bank Directors at Work*, 1922

Bank Chairman, Sir Edmund Osler (third from right), pauses briefly to pose with his General Manager (second from right) and Directors, including automobile magnate R. S. McLaughlin at the head of the table, and future president of the bank, A. W. Austin, at his side. With the departure of the photographer, Osler and the others undoubtedly pulled their chairs up to the Regency revival mahogany and leather table (crafted for the room by Francis Bacon of Boston), consulted the minute books, credit ledgers, and folders of documentation arrayed before them, and got down to business. Although it's not surprising to find a portrait of the bank's founder, James Austin, on display, it is surprising to see an American railway, not a Dominion Bank, calendar on the sideboard.

TD BANK ARCHIVES

By far the largest bank in 1914 Toronto was the Bank of Commerce, but by far the largest and most sumptuous bank boardroom was in the new Dominion Bank at 1 King Street West.[27] (See 7.17.)

On an ordinary Board day in 1922, a photographer was allowed — or summoned — in to document some of Toronto's most powerful men at work, reviewing every significant loan application and investment, discussing impending Bank Act revisions, and otherwise keeping a tight hand on the company they directed. In this view, the photographer zoomed in on a (still ample) corner of the boardroom. (See 7.18.)

The lavish boardroom remained in use until the Dominion Bank merged with the Toronto Bank in 1955. All the furnishings of the room, except the Donegal carpet, are still owned by the TD Bank.

When William James penetrated the innermost recesses of Casa Loma in 1917, Lady Pellatt's suite in the southeast tower looked neither lived-in nor especially idiosyncratic. It was perfectly decorated, immaculately kept, and large enough to accommodate a Canadian-made Heintzman grand piano in a side corner. Perhaps this was as telling as the facts that Sir Henry ordered books by the shelf-load, and ornate gold frames before he had the paintings. In any event, Lady Pellatt's suite at Casa Loma was probably large enough to accommodate the entire apartment down at Spadina Gardens, where she died in April 1924, shortly after Sir Henry lost most of his fortune, and all of Casa Loma.[31]

7.20: *Mary Hiester Reid,*
1911

For artists — whether male or
female — the studio is the ultimate
private space.[33] Mary Hiester Reid,
who had met her husband George
when they were both students of
Thomas Eakins in Philadelphia, was
an accomplished artist, a Heliconian
Club member, and one of the
earliest residents of Wychwood
Park. Here she sits, palette in hand
— but lace around her shoulders —
in the Arts & Crafts inglenook of
Upland Cottage. She is posing for
William James' 1911 series on
artists in their studios, surrounded
by the rough fireplace and exposed
beams characteristic of Morrisonian
architecture, and by artistic
touchstones such as a Japanese
print, copy of a Velasquez portrait,
and (perhaps) a study for
"Tranquility," her husband's painting
of nearby Wychwood Pond. Among
the many paintings left by Mary
Hiester Reid to the Art Gallery of
Toronto (now Art Gallery of Ontario)
was "Inglenook In My Studio," which
featured a bowl of daffodils rather
than a self-portrait in her inglenook.
CITY OF TORONTO ARCHIVES:
Fonds 1244, Item 703

7.21: O. A. Howland's Study, 1897
The Board of Trade published this photograph of once-and-future-politician Oliver Aitken Howland's study, when the occupant was between elected jobs.[39] Howland's study has a distinctly late-Victorian, almost Freudian, look to it. Tapestry-covered tables and couch, walls crammed with works of art, and a desk overflowing with papers, this was obviously the much-used study of a busy, late-Victorian gentleman.
CITY OF TORONTO ARCHIVES: Series 654, File 18, p. 169 (lower left)

A Room of One's Own

As Virginia Wolfe knew well, few women had access to a room — let alone a suite — of their own, where they could reflect, write, or do whatever else they wanted, away from the demands and probing eyes of other household members. "Studies," "libraries," "private offices," and so on were virtually always male spaces.[29] Lady Mary Pellatt was among the lucky ones. Although the library and office at Casa Loma were definitely allotted to her husband, Sir Henry Pellatt, Lady Pellatt did have a suite of rooms where she could entertain friends — especially when she was a near invalid — and pursue such good works as promoting the Girl Guides of Canada in their formative years before the first World War. On July 24, 1912, Lady Pellatt was tapped by Lady Baden-Powell to be the first Dominion regent of the newly created Canadian Baden-Powell Girl Guides. (Lord Baden-Powell was, of course, the founder of the scout movement, which his Lady wife was emulating and expanding.) According to one biographer, Lady Pellatt "held court in drawing-rooms across the country," drumming up support for the Guides.[30] Whether she also held similar confabulations in her private suite at Casa Loma is unknown, but likely. (See 7.19.)

Few were the women artists who had a studio room of their own, either inside or outside the home. One of the fortunate ones was Mary Hiester Reid, who was married to prominent artist and man-about-the-art-world, George Reid. In the 1880s, both Reids had studios in the Toronto Arcade on Yonge Street. By 1911, however, Ms Reid had set up shop in Upland Cottage, the Wychwood Park home designed by George in 1906. Fortunately for us, photojournalist William James gained access to the studios of 14 of Toronto's best-known artists while preparing a piece that appeared in the *Toronto World* of April 2, 1911. Mary Hiester Reid was one of only three women featured.[32] (See 7.20.)

Private work spaces — whether "study," "office," or "library" — provide insight into the tastes, lifestyles, and work habits of their (usually male) occupants. Edward Blake's study, for example, was practical, paper-strewn, and book-lined, with only one title evident: Adam Smith's *Wealth of Nations*, a singularly appropriate title for a Liberal free-trader like Blake.[34] (See also Chapter 2.) Sir Henry Pellatt's private office, which was built around a Napoleonic desk, and his grand library, overstuffed and understocked, were both pompous and showy, just like the romantic and overblown man who had created them. (See also Chapters 2 and 3.)

Oliver Aitken Howland was the last Victorian and the first Edwardian Mayor of Toronto. The

7.22: Goldwin Smith in His Library at the Grange, 1909

After Goldwin Smith moved into the Grange in 1875, William Henry Boulton's old grapery was replaced by a library, which became the centre of operations for one of Victorian Canada's most famous writers and intellectuals. From here, "this talented and acerbic political and literary critic would hurl his jeremiads at a world that irritatingly deviated" from the Liberal tenets of his youth and the passions of his old age.[45] Despite, or perhaps because of his intense intellectualism, The Grange became the centre not only of Toronto social life — the Boulton mansion had always functioned as that — but also of Canadian political and intellectual life. Through its very English portals passed many of the day's best-known figures, including Sir John A. Macdonald and Sir Wilfred Laurier (on separate occasions). William James took final photographs of the aged Sage of The Grange, not long after the death of Smith's beloved wife and about six months before he himself died on June 7, 1910. By this time, the mournful man of letters displayed little interest in such Arts and Crafts touches as the Morris wallpaper and the J. Moyr Smith fireplace tiles (Shakespeare series, of course). Frail and dwarfed by his material surroundings, Smith looked ready to lay down his pen and meet his maker.

son of a wealthy grain merchant — Sir William Pearce Howland — and the younger brother of another mayor — moral reformer William Holmes Howland[35] — O. A. Howland also delivered the twentieth century's first Inaugural Mayoral Address on January 14, 1901.[36] He took the opportunity to broach a subject that still intrigues Torontonians: provincial status for Toronto. On that ceremonial occasion about a hundred years ago, Mayor Howland proposed a new structure for the City:

> Commencing our duties ... at the beginning of a new century, curiously and significantly there is now apparently one of those tides in the affairs of men passing over this City which has caused the people to send us, charged with the duty of recognizing that we are indeed finishing with an old era and entering upon a new one....
>
> The late election was not so much, as far as the Mayoralty was concerned, a selection of persons because of their popularity or their merits as a determination by the public of Toronto upon an issue of policy upon a programme, which was deliberately submitted to them and which I believe was deliberately endorsed. That programme was to the effect that the time had come to recognize that the City of Toronto had grown to such proportions that its government ought to correspond with and be developed into something resembling the government of a province, handling as it does more money than are entrusted to the treasurer of any of the provinces.[37]

About a week later, Howland made the City's first Edwardian pronouncement: a message of condolence from the people of Toronto to King Edward on the death of Queen Victoria, who had "expired almost with the century she did so much to adorn."[38] Howland's messages were probably composed in either his large, new Mayoral Office at Lennox's City Hall, or his far more modest, personal office at home. (See 7.21.)

British-born "writer, journalist, and controversialist"[40] Goldwin Smith was arguably Toronto's most famous citizen at the turn-of-the-century. By the time he married Harriet Boulton[41] on September 3, 1875, Smith had been Regius professor of modern history at Oxford; guest professor at Cornell University, which later named a building after him; and was widely published on topics ranging from Irish history and Oxford University reform, to Greek tragedy and the American Civil War. After settling into The Grange, the lifelong Liberal continued his disputatious ways, which included founding several newspapers — notably the monthly *Bystander* — and contributing "a flood of articles"[42] to the international, English-speaking press, such as the *Nineteenth Century* in London and the *Atlantic Monthly* in Boston. Among his more controversial stances were anti-Imperialism (including opposition to Canada's sending troops to fight in South Africa) and pro-amalgamation with the United States. In fact, he was such an ardent proponent of the union of Canada with the United States that his opponents nicknamed him "Annexation" Smith. Less controversial, at least in his own day, were his stances against women's suffrage (as well as co-education and novels aimed at female readers), his anti-Semitism (although he had contributed to the building of a Toronto synagogue), his racism (especially against aboriginal peoples), and his anti-Catholicism (particularly with respect to the future of Quebec within Confederation). His ardent support for free trade and laissez-faire capitalism, however, would be perfectly acceptable in many twenty-first-century quarters.

Despite his strong views, or perhaps because of them, Smith was a notable host. He sat at the head of an impeccably laid-out table, courtesy of William Chinn who ran the Grange household for 52 years,[43] where he exchanged views with the likes of Matthew Arnold, Sir John A. Macdonald, Sir Wilfrid Laurier, and Canadian diva Madame Albani. At the time of his death in June 1910, Goldwin Smith was so famous that ordinary Torontonians flocked to The Grange to view his body, laid out in his personal *sanctum sanctorum*, the Library.[44] (See 7.22.)

8

From Late Victorian to Proto-Modern

I judge from the appearance of your principal business street [King]

that [Toronto] is a bright little town, and I have no doubt it is a commercial centre.

But I cannot help wondering why your citizens build their houses with

that horrid white brick when red brick is the same price. I think white brick

such a shallow colour — in fact it spoils the effect of the architecture.

OSCAR WILDE, 1882[1]

The Concourse Building is a modern of the moderns. It is frankly a skyscraper, not dressed up as a Doric temple, or as a Gothic hall: but a skyscraper exulting in its own inherent characteristics of strength and height.

CONSTRUCTION, 1929[2]

When publisher John Ross Robertson moved into his white brick Victorian mansion on Sherbourne Street in 1881, Toronto was a modest regional centre with about 80,000 residents, most of whom lived within walking distance of City Hall on Front Street.[3] St. James Cathedral was the tallest building. Public transportation was horse-powered. Victoria was still Queen, and would reign another 20 years. Sir John A. was still Prime Minister, and would serve another decade. Robertson himself had already founded several periodicals, including the *Toronto Telegram*, and was well on his way to becoming "The Tsar of Toronto."[4]

By 1929, when business tenants started moving into the city's jazziest new skyscraper — the 16-storey Art Deco Concourse Building at 100 Adelaide Street West — Toronto was a national centre and the second largest city in Canada. Municipal boundaries had been stretched to include suburbs such as blue-collar Earlscourt in the northwest, and middle-class North Toronto along Yonge Street. The TTC had been consolidating and expanding public transportation since 1921. The economy had been booming since mid-decade;[5] the population had topped 600,000;[6] the British

Empire's tallest building — the 34-storey Bank of Commerce Building — was under construction; the automobile was transforming urban transportation; and (many) citizens looked confidently to the future. Black Tuesday — October 29, 1929 — changed all that. Depression settled over the city. Stagnation and decline followed. The Concourse Building managed to fill up, but other commercial towers were left nearly empty. The only major building projects to proceed had been designed before the Crash. A distinct period in Toronto's architectural and social history came to an abrupt end.

This final chapter takes a chronological look at Toronto interiors, focussing primarily on the 1880s and the 1920s. The early period is viewed through the prism of one man's life: John Ross Robertson, whose wealth and interests enabled him to document his home and his business spheres. By drawing on related photographic resources, we can gain some idea of how other, less affluent, Torontonians lived. But we cannot follow the daily lives of most Torontonians as they passed through their usual rounds of activities. For some groups — such as servants or blue-collar suburbanites — we can find virtually no visual records at all. The lack of records speaks volumes about the marginality, poverty, and virtual invisibility of such groups.

The later period is discussed more thematically, emphasizing significant trends — such as the impact of the automobile, the apartment boom, and the dramatic change in scale — that were picked up and elaborated after World War II. Politically

and aesthetically, Toronto essentially remained a conservative city; in the 1920s and 1930s, architecture students at the University of Toronto were still being taught Greek Orders and Georgian ornamentation,[7] although practising architects, like John Lyle and Baldwin & Greene, were reflecting more progressive architectural ideas in their private and commercial commissions. Toronto was never at the forefront of the Modern, but it did take significant steps in that direction as it grappled with modern problems and modern ideas.[8]

John Ross Robertson

Eminent Victorian

John Ross Robertson was the complete Torontonian. According to one obituary in 1918:

> Few men, if any, ever lived in Toronto who became so much a part of the city as did the late John Ross Robertson. He was born in Toronto; he lived the greatest part of his life in Toronto, though he was a great traveller; his newspaper aims to be a local paper above all else; he wrote, or supervised the writing of a minute and detailed history of Toronto; and his finest monument, the Hospital for Sick Children, is built in Toronto. For him, the city apparently was the centre of all things....[9]

Born in 1841 of Scottish parents, John Ross Robertson grew up near the Georgian Parliament Buildings on Front Street West (see Chapter 5);

8.1: *Culloden House Exterior,* ca. 1888
Built in the mid-1870s and documented by an unknown photographer in the late-1880s, Culloden House was the home of John Ross Robertson from 1881 until his death in 1918. Robertson's residence slipped easily into its streetscape, used traditional materials, and employed traditional building methods. Although a substantial townhouse in late-Victorian Toronto, Robertson's 3-storey home was modest compared to such later Edwardian extravagances as Sir Joseph Flavelle's Holwood and Sir Henry Pellatt's Casa Loma (both illustrated elsewhere). Propping a heavy view-camera at the southwest corner of the property, the photographer captured the building, with its striped awnings and delicate verandah, and something of its inhabitants — Robertson's children, dogs and statuary at the front. The family's laundry, washed by anonymous servants, can be seen drying on a line near the coach house at the back. After taking three exterior shots, the photographer moved inside.
TORONTO PUBLIC LIBRARY: T10121

8.2: *Concourse Building Exterior,* ca. 1929
Celebrated by *Construction* magazine as "a modern of the moderns," Baldwin and Greene's Concourse Building, at 100 Adelaide Street West, brought a touch of Art Deco to Toronto's booming downtown. This photograph by Moore and Nixon-James, which appeared in *Construction* magazine of May 1929, shows the Concourse Building when it dominated its corner. Group of Seven member J. E. H. MacDonald's brightly coloured mosaics decorated the entrance arch with natural and industrial motifs, and reinforced the building's verticality with powerful native patterns at the top. Structurally, the building was of steel-reinforced concrete, enclosed in brick, and trimmed with stone. It displayed a style midway between masking new materials and structural techniques under layers of classical motifs, and exposing them to open celebration. The skyscraper presented a problem to both architects and architectural photographers. Here, the photographer sacrificed verticality to comprehensiveness by shooting from a nearby rooftop, rather than from street level.
CITY OF TORONTO ARCHVIES, Fonds 1654, Image 2

haunted newsrooms even before leaving school; won his reportorial spurs by tracking down Louis Riel during the Red River Rebellion in 1870; and launched his most successful enterprise, the *Toronto Telegram*, with backing from Goldwin Smith (see Chapter 7), in 1876. From day one, the paper turned a profit ... and five years later Robertson was able to move out of the Queen's Hotel (see Chapter 6) and into the mansion at 257 (later 291) Sherbourne Street, where he lived until his death in May 1918.

Robertson's Scottish roots were deep: he proudly traced his ancestry back to Duncan R, Chief of the Clan Robertson of Strowan in 1347.[10] Not only did he keep a sprig of "heather from Culloden Battle Field, Sept 1872" pressed into a scrapbook, now at the Archives of Ontario,[11] but he named his home after the famous battle where Bonnie Prince Charlie was defeated in 1746.

Home Life

In the late 1880s, Robertson decided to document — even memorialize — his home and his workplace. The reasons are unclear. Perhaps he wanted to celebrate his second marriage, in April 1888, to neighbour Jessie Elizabeth Holland, who lived at Culloden House until the 1940s. Perhaps, being a man of property, Robertson simply wanted to celebrate his domestic and commercial success. Whatever the reason, Robertson had 19 exquisite albumen photographs bound in a leather album with marbled endpapers and gold lettering. Each photograph is identified. None of the interior photographs shows people, either family members or servants. Many are taken with "flashlight" — a new invention that made such interior portraits possible. (See Chapter 1.) Each reveals a good deal about the man and the times he lived in.

The contents of the album are interesting, both for what they include and what they exclude. In addition to three exterior shots and the entrance hall, the album displays the following sequence of rooms, including both very public and very private spaces: the hall (8.3); the drawing-room (8.5); the dining room (both a north, 8.4, and a south view); the upstairs hall (8.6); the library (a north, 8.7, and a south view); the north bedroom (8.8); the south bedroom; the bathroom (8.9); and three photographs of the stable and the carriage house (8.10). Significantly, the album does not include photographs of the kitchen or any of the servants' quarters. Equally significant, the album includes two views of Robertson's workplace, providing an unusual glimpse of a Victorian gentleman at home and at work.

Unfortunately, no original architectural plans or drawings of Culloden House have surfaced. Fortunately, these 1880s photographs, a few modern interior photographs, and a much-renovated house remain, each adding pieces to the puzzle of how the house was originally laid-out and how it evolved over time. For example, where was Robertson's library? Which was the dining room and which the drawing-room? Although the heavily patterned wallpaper has been stripped from the dining and other rooms, the furniture removed, and the rooms painted light colours, much of the original plastering and anaglypta has survived renovations, by the Ontario Provincial Police in mid-twentieth-century, and City Community Services in the 1980s and 1990s. Together, these complementary sources help tell the story of the house.

Some time after this photograph was taken — perhaps in 1903–1904 when Robertson added a third storey and a new verandah[14] — the drawing-room was doubled in size. A second bay window was added to the front of the house; Corinthian columns were inserted between the old and new sections of the room; and the marble mantel shown here was moved northward to the new outer wall.[15] (See 8.5.)

John Ross Robertson was a journalist and writer of several books, an antiquarian, and an omnivorous collector of paintings, drawings, maps, and documents relating to the history of both Toronto and Canada. His 6-volume history of Toronto, *Landmarks of Toronto*, published between 1894 and 1914, is an exhaustive — if not always accurate — exploration of the people, places and events that created his Toronto.[16] His 2000-page discussion of Canadian Masonry is a testament to his research skills and his devotion to the secret society he once headed. (He was also a prominent Orangeman, although he limited his discussion of this order to articles in *Landmarks*.) Most of his Canadiana collection was donated to the Toronto Public Library, where it still forms a solid foundation for research into local history. The Culloden House photographs — which are part of material donated to the Library — document his collection at a relatively early stage in its history.

8.3: *Entrance Hall, Culloden House,* ca. 1888

With this photograph, John Ross Robertson's album welcomes visitors into his Victorian home on Sherbourne Street. The anonymous photographer is looking eastward, with Sherbourne Street at his back, and a window overlooking the stable yard before him. The first of ten house interiors photographed, this typically dark hallway is modest in dimension, but elegantly appointed, with crystal gasolier, elaborately plastered arch, and richly patterned ceiling. That quintessentially Victorian invention, the hallstand, dominates the south wall, with Robertson's top hat signalling that its owner is at home.[12] With door slightly ajar, the dining room awaits its guests.

TORONTO PUBLIC LIBRARY: T 10124

8.4: *Dining Room, Culloden House,* ca. 1888

Robertson's dining room ran along the south side of the ground floor, with the kitchen (not photographed) probably at the back of the house, on the north side. The arrangement wasn't convenient for servants, who had to cross the hall and enter by the door at the back of this picture. But such considerations were immaterial to the family and guests who dined here. Such occasions could be lavish indeed, especially Christmas when "dinner was a gala affair with a Scottish piper bringing in the turkey ..." and the turkey weighing up to 40 pounds.[13] Here, however, the dining room is set for its picture, not for guests. (A single periodical lies on the empty table.) Taken with the aid of "flashlight," which bounces off the dark furniture and light statues, this image shows the northern part of the room, with the southern half reflected in the mirror. The bay window on the south side is curtained, keeping the room in characteristic Victorian dimness.

TORONTO PUBLIC LIBRARY: T 10126

8.5: *Drawing-room, Culloden House, ca. 1888*

As is evident from the gold caption, Robertson's main public room was a "drawing-room," not a "parlour," let alone a "living room" or a "sitting-room" — each term adopted in various places and times by various classes, for this type of room. (See Chapter 3.) Based on surviving plaster work, it is clear that this room opened off the north, rather than the south, side of the hall, and that this photograph was taken from the Sherbourne end of the room — where a bay window still stands. As elsewhere in the house, there is a single, central light fixture, no smaller lights, and a single fireplace (in this case, with an elegant marble mantle similar to Edward Blake's on nearby Jarvis Street). The drawing-room shows Robertson-the-Collector at work, with tier upon tier of framed objects being offered for admiration, from floor to ceiling. The ubiquitous Victorian piano is tucked in a corner. The wicker and antimacassared furniture is typical, but not expensive.

TORONTO PUBLIC LIBRARY: T 34948

On May 31, 1918, John Ross Robertson died at home of pneumonia. During his final two weeks, he continued working on two of his major interests — the Hospital For Sick Children and the Masonic Order. In fact, the last cheque he wrote was for $111,000 to clear the debt for the hospital that he had patronized for a quarter-century. His funeral was a "private" one — nevertheless attended by many prominent Torontonians of the day — and held in the great library that had meant so much to him.[18]

After photographing the semi-private library, Robertson's chosen photographer moved into increasingly private areas. Just why Robertson allowed — even wanted — his intimate private life to be documented is unclear; but modern researchers can be exceedingly glad that he did.

8.7: *Library, Culloden House, ca. 1888*

The library — with its distinctive coffered ceiling — was John Ross Robertson's inner sanctum. Here — from early in his career, when this photograph was taken, until the end of his life in 1918 when he was laid out for his funeral in this room — he worked on his growing collections and on such philanthropic projects as the Hospital For Sick Children and the Masonic Order. This photograph shows the north side of the library. As elsewhere, the photograph was made possible by the invention of flashlight, which bounced off Robertson's leather chair, crystal chandelier, and numerous *objets d'art*. A later addition was a bookcase made from the counter in the City Treasurer's Office at Front Street City Hall, when it was vacated in 1899.[17] The painting reflected in the mirror may be of the Battle of the Boyne, with "King Billy" on a white charger. Robertson, like most men of power in Victorian Toronto, was a dedicated Orangeman who rarely missed marching in the annual July 12th parade.

TORONTO PUBLIC LIBRARY: T11462

Culloden House — or Robertson House as it is now called — is haunted, or so say various witnesses. Some claim that visiting children have reported playing with an "old man" upstairs ... when no such occupant was registered. Others have complained that "he" turns the water on ... and has even used the towels. If John Ross Robertson has returned, it makes sense that he would want to play with children (after all, he spent nearly every Sunday afternoon visiting young patients at the Hospital for Sick Children); and that he would be attracted to the upstairs bathroom luxuries, like running water (which he had) and showers (which he did not have).

8.9: *Bathroom, Culloden House*, ca. 1888

While John Ross Robertson was able to luxuriate in a long, marble bathtub, the warmth of gas heating, and the convenience of a second-storey indoor toilet (and toilet paper on a roll), most Torontonians were still using outhouses (and newspapers), and would continue to do so for many years to come.[19] In most photographs, Robertson looks like the successful, dour Scot that he undoubtedly often was. This photograph, however, reveals another side of the man: a sense of humour. On the mantelpiece stands a small statue of a photographer, pointing his view camera toward the bath.[20]

TORONTO PUBLIC LIBRARY: T 34953

8.10: *Carriage House, Culloden House*, ca. 1888
The carriage house was a two-storey building topped by a dovecote and a wrought-iron weathervane in the shape of a horse. (The weathervane has survived.) On the ground floor, shown here, were several vehicles, ranging from an open carriage with collapsable roof to a fully enclosed coach. Assessment records reveal that Robertson kept three horses. Stable boys probably lived in the dorm-style room overhead; and domestic staff likely washed the laundry (seen in an exterior photograph) in the washroom at the other end of this building.
TORONTO PUBLIC LIBRARY: T 34950

These photographs were taken during the Age of the Horse, as the final three domestic interiors reveal. By the late 1880s when Culloden House was photographed, Robertson had acquired not one, but an assortment of coaches and carriages. (See 8.10.)

By the end of his life, Robertson, like his wealthy contemporaries, had replaced horses with horsepower. On May 17, 1918, when he was falling prey to his final bout with pneumonia, Robertson asked his private secretary to phone for "one of his motors," which rushed him home from the office for the last time.[21]

Work Life
John Ross Robertson was a newspaperman who became a businessman, not a businessman who became a newspaperman:

> Probably, if the intimate history of the first few years of Mr. Robertson's life were available, it would be found that his early baby talk was of a "scoop." Certainly it is true that from the beginning the lad's mind and activities turned towards journalism.[22]

While still a student at Upper Canada College, Robertson learned the printing trade — becoming a pretty good compositor, a competent job printer, and an innovative journalist. He created in succession Canada's first student newspaper (the *College Times* for Upper Canada College), first sports paper (*Sporting Life*), first railway guide (*Robertson's Canadian Railway Guide*), and the first evening daily that was not linked to a morning paper (the *Daily Telegraph*). His most enduring and successful newspaper was the *Evening Telegram* — a paper "for the masses not the classes,"[23] which initially was backed by Liberal intellectual, Goldwin Smith, and always profitable.[24] (See 8.11.)

Robertson's keys to journalistic success were focussing on local, rather than national and international news; producing pithy paragraphs, rather than long-winded editorializing; and creating news, as well as covering it, such as providing band music in parks, projecting the election returns on the *Telegram's*

building, and importing an ambulance from Britain in 1888.[25] Robertson's key to financial success also depended on keeping labour costs low. Although he was an early member of the Toronto Typographical Union,[26] he became a patriarchal, tight-fisted, anti-union boss: the printers of the *Telegram* were the last in the city to be unionized.[27] By the time his photo album of domestic and worklife was produced around 1888, Robertson was "probably a millionaire,"[28] and well on his way to making a fortune that amounted to about $1,750,000 when he died in 1918.[29]

Robertson's album contained one exterior, and two interior photographs of his workplace, the 4-storey Second-Empire *Telegram* Building that he had constructed on the southwest corner of King and Bay streets in 1879.

The late-1880s album also contains a photograph of John Ross Robertson's private office. Studying a series of images of Robertson's office suggests how offices — and Robertson's in particular — changed over the years, and how different sources may provide different perspectives and different information. Both themes are illustrated throughout this book.

By 1879, the *Evening Telegram* was so successful that Robertson moved out of rented quarters on Yonge Street, into a purpose-built Second-Empire building at the southwest corner of King and Bay streets, where the Toronto-Dominion Centre now stands. Not long after moving into his new space, Robertson commissioned J. L. Telford to document his "model" newspaper building, from press room to proprietor's private office.[30] (See 8.12.)

According to *Canadian Architect and Builder*, Robertson's redecorated, 1888 private office overlooking Bay Street was small, but "in elegance of appointments and elaborate decoration ... perhaps not equalled in Canada."[31] In an article, illustrated by a drawing clearly based on the photograph in the album and reproduced here, the new architectural magazine provides details about location, colour and decoration that cannot be determined from the images alone. For example:

> The ceiling and walls are hung with Lincrusta Walton. The general tone of the ceiling is buff, while the raised designs are of delicate lilac and pale copper bronze. The cornice, enriched with artistically wrought

8.11: *Counting Room, The Evening Telegram*, ca. 1888
The Counting Room — an archaic term for the place where money flowed into the business — was one of only two workplace interior photographs contained in Robertson's leather album. Journalism may have been a calling for Robertson, but it was also a business ... and a successful one at that, as this elegant room attests. From the early 1880s, the *Telegram* had the highest circulation in the city. Not surprisingly, perhaps, its founder regarded this as a personal achievement ... and had his initials — rather than the paper's name — inscribed on the glass shown in this photograph. Less commercial instincts are represented by the small Venus de Milo statue just visible in the proprietor's private office in the background.
TORONTO PUBLIC LIBRARY: T 34951

8.12: *Manager's Room, The Evening Telegram*, 1880

In 1880, before the advent of flash photography, J. L. Telford produced a series of sketches of Robertson's new *Evening Telegram Building*, including this view of "Mr. Robertson's Private Office ... since altered." The room appears to be the same as the 1888 office. For example, the windows and radiators are in the same locations on the left, and mirrored walls/ doors flank the right side in both. Robertson's furnishing is different, most especially the desk and its placement. In the sketch, the desk is much larger and perhaps more imposing than the later one. Its placement along the mirrored wall emphasizes that wall. (The desk chair appears to be the same, but seems bigger and squatter in the drawing than in the photograph.) Only two small pictures decorate the space. The major differences are in size and lightness. Whether deliberately or not, Telford distorts the perspective and exaggerates the floor pattern, so that the room looks much larger than it was. The sketch technique makes the room appear much lighter and less cluttered than the 1888 photo. A number of other interesting details also emerge: the desk is draped with a work in progress, and a spittoon awaits use on the floor.

8.13: *Private Office, The Evening Telegram,* ca. 1888

The final albumen in the photo album shows a south view of Robertson's private office, which opened off the Counting Room. Taken by natural light and time exposure — which overexposes the area around the new, walnut "Wooton" desk against the far wall — this photograph makes the room appear smaller, darker, and more cluttered than the 1880 drawing. The spittoon has disappeared — or been hidden — but several interesting new items have appeared. "Speaking tubes" communicating with every room in the building protrude from the left wall. There are more pictures and statues — reflecting Robertson's collecting career — and also a special volume held aloft by a chubby Victorian putto. Close inspection of the original photographic print indicates that this is a "Memorial Volume" from the 50th anniversary of the "City of Toronto" in 1884, and a testament to Robertson's enduring love for his native city.

friezes, is olive shaded while the dull bronze of the lions' heads that adorn the upper frieze is relieved by electric blue which gives the room a bright and pleasant appearance.[32]

The stained glass and interior decoration was done by J. McCausland & Son, a stained-glass firm that is still active in Toronto and around the world. (See 8.13.)

The *Evening Telegram* continued to grow and prosper, causing it to move, once again, into a new, specially designed newspaper building, this time at Bay and Melinda Streets. The presses were started on February 26, 1900, and on April 19, 1904 the building "stood like a fire curtain" against the Great Fire. On April 20th, a sign in Robertson's building read simply, "Business as usual."[33] Photographs of Robertson's new, private and public offices reveal a more spacious, open approach to interior design. (See 8.14, 8.15.)

Not only Robertson's offices, but much of the new building at 81 Bay Street (1900–1963) was photographed in 1904 and 1905. For the first time, people appear in the spaces, at their desks, and beside their machines, providing a wider glimpse into the social and technological world of one of Toronto's major industries: publishing. (See 8.16, 8.17.)

Printing is an ancient craft, dating from Gutenberg's invention of the moveable-type press in 1455. As such, it became highly structured and, ultimately, highly unionized. In Toronto, the first printers' union was established in 1832 and, by the time these photographs were taken in the early 20th century, Local 91 of the International Typographical Union (ITU) was a presence in every city newspaper, and a power in local labour circles. Traditionally, printers had both set the type and operated the press. As mechanization entered the printing industry, it caused a split into "pressmen" who operated the new steam presses, and "compositors" who set the type, both before and after the introduction of the mechanized linotype machine. The composing room was "the preserve

8.14: *Private Office, The Evening Telegram, ca. 1904*
Robertson's second-floor private office in the new (1900-1963) *Evening Telegram Building*, shown in this photograph taken by an unknown photographer in 1904 or 1905, is larger, lighter, and more elegantly appointed than his earlier offices. Curtains have disappeared. The spittoon has reappeared. A square telephone sits on the new roll-top desk. Just outside the opaque glass wall is the stenographer's room where staff await the sound of their master's voice.
TORONTO PUBLIC LIBRARY: T 34942

8.15: *Business Office, The Evening Telegram, ca. 1905*
Located on the ground floor of the new building, Robertson's "business office" is much more open — both for viewing and being viewed. Looking more like a modern newspaper office, with editors behind glass partitions, Robertson's downstairs office has a small conference table (with a naked nymph poised to dive into the middle of the discussion) and a large executive desk ... with a billy club lying across some papers. The functional, glassed area to the left of the office seems to be the modern equivalent of the Counting Room illustrated earlier. (The word "Bookkeeper" arches over the opening.)
TORONTO PUBLIC LIBRARY: T 12375

8.16: *The Reporters' Room, The Evening Telegram, 1904*
This precursor of "the newsroom" captures a group of *Tely* reporters — such as "Jerry" Snider (C.J.H. Snider) who became a well-known columnist and local marine historian — and their support staff — an unidentified copy or office boy, and the only woman photographed in this series, "Miss Dawson," who appears to be scrutinizing copy or other print material at her desk.[34] In marked contrast to later reporters, no one is smoking (obeying the "NO SMOKING" sign); no one is pounding away at a typewriter; and no one is on the phone. Pen and inkstands perch on the desks.[35] The limitations of turn-of-the-century interior photography are also evident: despite the use of flashlight, subjects had to hold very still or end up blurred, like the mustachioed James Muir.
TORONTO PUBLIC LIBRARY: T 34943

machine was introduced in the late 1880s. After an initial struggle with the *Toronto News* in 1892, the Toronto printers' union won a settlement that established its right to control both the operation of the machine and the style of wages set.[38] Robertson's *Telegram* mechanized composing in 1894, and, a decade later, an anonymous photographer documented the scene. (See 8.17.)

of the printer" and lay at the heart of the process and of union power.[36] Despite his printer's skills — being a moderately fast compositor and able to operate small Hoe presses, in the 1860s[37] — Robertson was definitely on the side of management when these photographs were taken. Like radical William Lyon Mackenzie and Liberal George Brown, Conservative John Ross Robertson became anti-union. In his era, however, the union finally prevailed. The linotype

Photographs like those reproduced here, and elsewhere in the book, enable modern researchers to investigate the operation of old and the introduction of new technologies, in ways impossible to determine simply from verbal accounts.

8.17: *Composing Room, Evening Telegram Building, 1904*

During the first 18 years, every letter of the *Evening Telegram* was set by hand. Then, around Christmas 1894, the first machine-set issue of the paper rolled off the presses. In 1900, the first linotype machines with movable arms — like the Mergenthaler machines in this photograph — were introduced and regarded as "a marvel of ingenuity."[39] The man in charge of the composing room was foreman Michael J. Gloster, the vested and mustachioed older man in the middle distance on the left. Gloster had entered the Tely composing room in 1884, when type was still being set by hand, and remained with the paper for over forty years. In a union shop like this, the foreman was a force to be reckoned with — by both workers and management.

TORONTO PUBLIC LIBRARY: T 12367

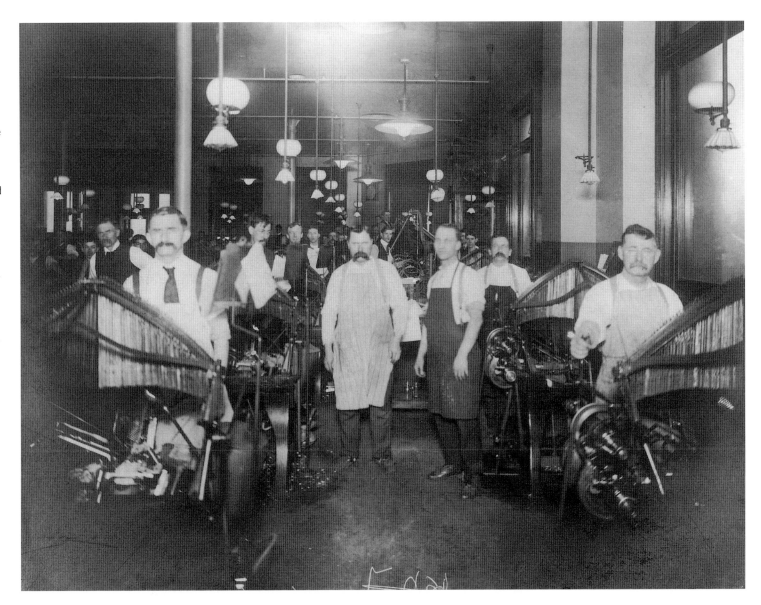

Social Life & Philanthropy

John Ross Robertson moved in the highest circles. He was a visitor to Government House, as illustrated by his attendance at the Farewell to Government House Ball, on April 29, 1912. He belonged to the Toronto Club, the National Club, the Arts & Letters Club, but not the Conservative Albany Club, with which he feuded over a property on lower Bay Street in the mid-1880s. (All these locations are illustrated in earlier chapters.) He was briefly an Independent Conservative member of Parliament, but preferred life in Toronto and behind the scenes to life in Ottawa and on the Parliamentary benches.[40] His obsession with political and journalistic independence was so strong that he proudly turned down both a knighthood and a senatorship, on the same day, December 31, 1916. He was a devout Presbyterian, lifelong Orangeman, and Grand Master of the Masons (Masonic symbols can be detected in photographs of the *Evening Telegram Building*).[41] His causes were many, his interests broad, and his life active.

Robertson's major philanthropic cause grew directly from the pain of losing his 2-year-old daughter, Goldie, to scarlet fever in 1882. By the time he made his last donation from his own deathbed in 1918, he had given about half a million dollars to the Hospital for Sick Children. Robertson's donations were used to establish the Lakeside Home for Little Children on Toronto Island in 1883 (and to replace it after a fire in 1891); to consolidate the mainland hospital into new Romanesque Revival quarters at College and Elizabeth Streets in 1891; and to operate such innovative programs as the 1909 installation of Toronto's first milk pasteurisation plant in the College Street hospital. Robertson's dedication to the hospital was both financial and personal: every Sunday he was in town, he visited the Hospital where he was instantly recognized and greeted by cries of "Mr. Wobson! Mr. Wobson!" according to his obituary in the rival *Toronto Daily Star*.[44] (See 8.20.)

John Ross Robertson started collecting historical pictures around 1853 when he was 12 years old, and went on to amass the largest Canadiana collection of his era.[45] Not only did he collect, but he also did research on his collection and his chosen

8.19: *A Quiet Moment with an Old Friend*, ca. 1910

This small (2 1/4 x 3 1/4-inch) photograph captures a rare, informal moment in the life of a public man. John Ross Robertson is visiting Susanna Hamilton Douglas (Mrs. George Byng Douglas), who had grown up at Terauley Cottage, 9 Trinity Square (near today's Eaton Centre) and had probably known John Ross all her life. On a hot summer day, the two converse on the vine-draped verandah of the Douglas home at Kew Beach, perhaps watching tennis being played on the lawn in front of the house, and certainly enjoying any breezes wafting off nearby Lake Ontario. Mrs. Douglas casts an adoring look at her quietly smiling companion.
CITY OF TORONTO ARCHVIES: Fonds 1203, Series 383, Item 10

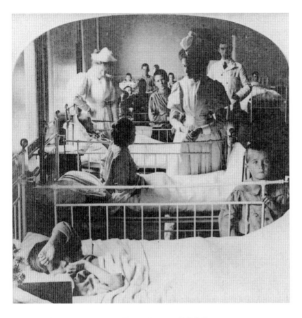

8.20: *Convalescent Ward*, ca. 1902

From 1875 until 1891, the Hospital for Sick Children was operated out of little houses in downtown Toronto. Robertson's new building on College Street was the largest, and arguably the best children's hospital of its day. This stereograph by American photographer, B. W. Kilburn, was taken around 1902, and shows some of the nurses, parents, and convalescent children who were supported and frequently visited by the tall, white-bearded gentleman known as "Mr. Wobson."
TORONTO PUBLIC LIBRARY: T 10242

topics, notably Toronto and its history. Just after Robertson's death, Ontario Archivist, Dr. Alexander Fraser, told a reporter that he had known the collector for about 32 years, long before the Ontario Archives was even established in 1903. "I came in contact with Mr. Robertson's historical research

first at that time [when Robertson was preparing an article on Upper Canada College]. Mr. Robertson impressed one at once with the thoroughness of his research. No stone was left unturned to find and identify the data of which he was in search."[46] (See 8.21.)

8.21: *John Ross Robertson with his Collection, 1912*
William James photographed John Ross Robertson with his collection when it was formally opened by the Toronto Public Library in January 1912. Here, he stands before a small selection of objects in the great hall of Toronto's 1909 Carnegie-supported library on College Street (later the University of Toronto Book Store). The paintings and drawings shown here were augmented by maps, documents, and photographs that can now be viewed at the Baldwin Room in the Toronto Reference Library at Yonge and Asquith streets. Although the City lent palms from Allan Gardens to enhance the occasion, none are visible here.[48]
CITY OF TORONTO ARCHVIES: Fonds 1244, Item 2309

By 1910, when his material exceeded his ability to house it, Robertson informed the Toronto Public Library Board that he wanted to donate his great "collection of prints and photos contained in portfolios in his private library, numbering about 15,000 pieces" to the Library in trust for the people of Toronto.[47] He also stipulated that "the pictures should be placed in a suitable room, with skilled attendants, covered by insurance, catalogued, and ... not be lent or removed from the library building on College Street." Thus was born the Robertson Collection — formally opened in 1912 — and the Baldwin Room, which is now at the Toronto Reference Library on Yonge Street.

John Ross Robertson died in May 1918, near the end of the First World War, and on the cusp of a new era in Toronto history. Because he was able to document significant spaces, and ensure that this documentation survived for future public inspection, Robertson's world has been preserved — at least in part — by an interrelated group of images. Few Victorian-Toronto lives are so well-documented. The final section of this book takes a different, more thematic approach.

Toronto in the Twenties

Approaching the Modern

This final section focusses on three icons of modernity that find their roots in the early-twentieth century: automobiles, apartments, and skyscrapers. For good or ill, by 1930 each had made a small but significant impact on Toronto. Their continued growth, however, would be delayed by the Great Depression and the Second World War. While the emphasis here is on change and portents of the future, it is important to remember that change was embedded in the fabric of the past. Most Torontonians continued to live much as they always had. Automobiles consumed more and more space, but most Torontonians continued to rely on feet and streetcars, with horses clopping onward through the thirties. Apartments had a growing impact, but most Torontonians continued to live in houses, whether owned or rented, large or small, single unit or broken into rooms.[49] Commercial buildings began to scrape the sky, but most Torontonians continued to work, shop, and pursue their daily rounds in buildings that hugged the ground.

Automobiles

It is only necessary to witness the vast number of industrial buildings used for its production, as well as ... its housing and distribution, which have come since the advent of the automobile twenty-five years ago, to realize the substantial contribution the motor car has made to building progress.

CONSTRUCTION, September 1928[50]

Although many would dispute the idea that the automobile should be regarded as a sign of

8.22: *Taking Tea in Her "T", 1910s*
From the age of the Model T to the age of the SUV, this
illustrates what advertisers have promised: freedom and
a peaceful ride in the country. Keeping that promise,
however, was easier in the early days. Far from the
madding crowds and congested streets of downtown
Toronto, photographer John Boyd, Sr. parked his Model T
in a field (perhaps near Islington), and photographed
his companion enjoying a cup of tea from the thermos
balanced on the running board. Personal mobility offered
some obvious perks ... so long as not too many other
drivers found the same spot.
CITY OF TORONTO ARCHVIES: Series 393, Item 17792A

unambiguous "progress," no one would
dispute the fact that the automobile (or "motor
car") has transformed the urban landscape.

Automobiles have allowed — even
pushed — people to live farther and farther
away from the city centre and radically
altered the balance of uses on city streets. But
they have also created entirely new kinds of
buildings — such as garages, gas stations, and showrooms — and promoted an
entirely new sense of style in line with modern materials and streamlined
design. The ultimate icon was New York's glorious Art Deco Chrysler Building,
completed in 1930, styled after a car, and named after a car company. Nothing
in Toronto reached the size or style of the Chrysler Building, but the automobile
had a profound impact here, as elsewhere.

By the late 1920s, the automobile was moving swiftly from being a luxury
item (of the sort snapped up by young John Craig Eaton who erected the
first purpose-built automobile garage in the Annex, and aging John Ross
Robertson who transformed his old coach house into a multi-car garage) to
being a mass-produced, mass-marketed product. Ironically — or perhaps
inevitably — products like cars, that are supposed to represent the ultra-
modern, often date quickly and look out-of-step, even amusing, to later
generations. Modern readers should try to imagine a time when the vehicles
in these photographs represented the height of both technology and fashion,
and when they were in harmony with the photographed surroundings that
now often seem more modern than they do. (See 8.23.)

Parking became a huge problem, especially in parts of the city designed and
densely built-up in the pre-automobile era. As early as the 1920s, calls were
being issued to radically reorganize downtown streets.[51] Had these calls been

8.23: *Automobile Showroom, 1926*

By the time the Automobile and Sales and Service Building shown here opened in 1926, Bay Street between College and Bloor was already known as "Automobile Row, " where showrooms, like this one at 1011–1027 Bay Street, and "some of the more prestigious filling stations in the city" were concentrating. The 1920s automotive impact still lingers on, along a much more densely developed Bay Street. Moore & Hughes' 1926 showroom for Dodge and Reo cars displays a typical combination of the modern (extensive plate-glass windows and splay-headed concrete columns) and the traditional (area rugs, checkered flooring, potted flowers, tasselled standing lamp, carved wooden furniture, and ornamental plastering). This photograph appeared in *Construction* magazine, which was devoting increasing space to the "motor car," or modern automobile.

TORONTO PUBLIC LIBRARY: Construction, November 1926, p. 363

8.24: *Bay-Adelaide Garage, 1928*

The Bay-Adelaide Garage shown here was the largest in Canada. With 14 levels of parking and 520 individual car "stalls" the new structure was a long way from Victorian livery stables and coach houses, like those of John Ross Robertson. In an effort to attract patronage, this garage offered luxury services, like valet parking, car washing, and light repairs. A brass sliding pole, such as those found in fire stations, connected each parking floor with the ground, enabling the valet drivers to "return rapidly to their post by the front entrance."[52]

TORONTO PUBLIC LIBRARY: Construction, April 1928, p. 141

heeded, even more of the historic fabric of the city would have been sacrificed to the almighty auto than has already happened. Among the "solutions" that emerged — and still emerges — was the multi-level parking garage. The 6-storey Bay-Adelaide Garage illustrated here was dressed up on the outside with neo-Gothic detailing, but remained as dark and ugly inside as most of its modern counterparts. This legacy of the automobile is not one of its happy ones. (See 8.24.)

Apartments

When *Construction* magazine declared this "is the age of the Apartment House" in November 1907, its pronouncement was still more symbolic than factual.[53] The apartment house came late to Toronto, as did other signs of the Modern. The first permit for building an apartment house was issued in 1899, thirty years after Stuyvesant Flats rose in New York City. The resulting 5-storey building — luxurious St. George Mansions — opened in 1903 on the southwest corner of St. George and Harbord streets (later occupied by the modernist Ramsey Wright Zoological Building), where it was surrounded by substantial Victorian villas.[54] And in 1907, the year when *Construction* magazine made its debut and its declaration, only five more permits were issued for apartment houses.[55]

Nevertheless, as geographer Richard Dennis has pointed out, the apartment house was a potent symbol of modernism, and a portent of changes that would transform the post-Second-World-War urban landscape. The city was growing rapidly — requiring places for new residents to live — and domestic conditions and technologies were also changing. Toronto's Victorian mansions, like John Ross Robertson's, and even the modest, middle-class households, needed domestic servants to keep them running smoothly.[56] But as jobs in manufacturing and retail opened up to women, they left domestic service in droves; upper and middle-class homeowners had to look for alternatives. Modern technologies — such as gas and electric appliances — began entering the home, making smaller households possible and a focus on "efficiency" more prevalent. Such trends gave rise to both the luxury and the efficiency apartments that came to dominate that housing sector.

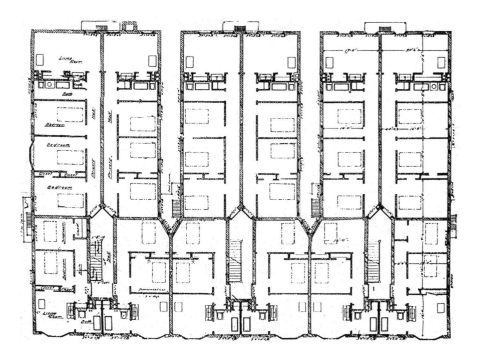

8.25: *Plan, Wineberg Apartments, 1907*
In a section entitled "Relieving the Overcrowding in the 'Ward,' Toronto," *Construction* magazine viewed the plan for Wineberg Apartments as "well adapted to provide convenient, cosy and sanitary places of abode for the poorer classes."[61] But Richard Dennis quite rightly suggests that "close inspection of the plans for Wineberg Apartments reveals just how narrow was the dividing line between apartments and tenements. Most bedrooms overlooked narrow light courts, little better than New York 'dumbbells,' and some rooms had to make do with 'borrowed light.'"[62] Contrast Wineberg's narrow light courts with the plan for Spadina Gardens, which opened in 1907 (see Chapter 3), and the plentiful windows indicated on the plan for a Claridge apartment (discussed later). Wineberg Apartments may have had indoor plumbing — unlike many of the houses in The Ward — but it provided far from healthy living conditions and was no harbinger of better housing to come for the poor.
CITY OF TORONTO ARCHIVES, Research Hall Library: *Construction*. November 1907, p. 51 (microfilm)

8.26: *Living Room, Stewart Manor, 1927*
Shoe-store manager, 55-year old Harry C. Knowlton, lived with three other people in Apartment 6, photographed for the gas company by F. W. Micklethwaite shortly after the building became occupied. Micklethwaite's task was to document gas services to the new building, which may have included the fireplace, lighting fixtures, and radiator in this room. But rather than simply focussing on individual appliances and fixtures, he provided an overall view of this late-twenties "living room."[64] Unlike the "tenements" so many Torontonians feared when they heard the word "apartment,"[65] this suite was light, airy, and quite spacious. Every room had natural light. And some, like this one, were flooded with it. Knowlton's light and uncluttered "living room" was in marked contrast to Robertson's grand but dark, multi-patterned "drawing-room" and the modest Victorian "parlours" illustrated elsewhere in this book.
CITY OF TORONTO ARCHVIES: Fonds 1034, Item 88

In the first third of the twentieth century, Toronto experienced two apartment-housing booms: one in the immediate pre-War period, which peaked in 1912 when 68 permits were issued for new apartment buildings; and another in the mid-to-late 1920s, which peaked in 1928 when 96 new permits were issued.[57] Some Torontonians — including municipal reformers like Dr. Charles Hastings — were virulently anti-apartment, in part because they equated them with the horrors of "tenements" like those found in New York's Lower East Side. Although Toronto saw relatively few real tenements built, one of the new buildings lauded by *Construction* magazine in 1907 came awfully close: Wineberg Apartments, located at the northeast corner of Agnes (later Dundas West) and Elizabeth Streets.

Promoted as a way of "relieving the overcrowding"[58] in Toronto's impoverished Ward area, Harry Wineberg's 3-storey brick building comprised eleven stores on the ground floor, such as a tailor, barber shop, and billiard hall,[59] and crammed 28 apartments into the upper two floors. At first, most of the residents were Jewish garment workers, and many of the tiny, dark apartments housed seven or eight people. By 1918, many of the tenants were Chinese — an indication of the movement of "Chinatown" from York and Wellington to the Elizabeth Street area — and units housed up to ten people.[60] During the twenties, as the Dundas West area became more commercialized, fewer people occupied the apartment building, but the mix of Jewish and Chinese tenants continued. (See 8.25.)

Most of the apartments built in the teens and the twenties were aimed at a broadly defined middle-class, but few photographs of these spaces were ever taken. When the Consumers' Gas Company sent F. W. Micklethwaite to document its services, at a new, suburban walk-up apartment building at 2269 Queen Street East, he came away with a rare glimpse into "efficiency apartment" life at lower-middle-class Stewart Manor. Built and opened in 1927, the 3-storey, red brick building was small (16 suites), located at the corner of a commercial and a residential street (Queen Street East and Scarboro Beach Boulevard[63]), and well served by public transportation (Queen Street streetcar) — all common characteristics of apartment buildings from this period. (See 8.26–8.29.)

8.27: Bedroom, Stewart Manor, 1927
This bedroom was probably in the same apartment
as the parlour, and was certainly photographed on
the same occasion by Micklethwaite.[66] Two people
may have shared this modest room — one using the
iron bedstead on the right and the other a daybed
on the left — making it quite cramped. But here, as
in most other apartment shots, the ceiling is light in
colour and the wallpaper (when present) a soft
pattern, making the overall effect far less
claustrophobic than it might otherwise have been.
CITY OF TORONTO ARCHVIES: Fonds 1034, Item 90

Owned by Kathleen Vaughan in Suite
16,[67] this first stage of Stewart Manor
was rapidly occupied by people of modest
means, ranging from a baker and a
mechanic to an auditor and a photographer.[68] Households were small —
usually two or three people[69] — and
children were few, if evident at all. While
modest, the building had — and still has
— pleasing bay windows at the front
and back, but no reception area, and no
accommodation for automobiles. A year
or so later, two similar apartment houses
(also called Stewart Manor) were built
just to the west, at 2265 and 2263 Queen Street East — a local reflection of the
general apartment boom across Toronto.[70] All still stand in Toronto's Beach
area and demonstrate the continuing value of this form of housing.

Most early apartment houses were built for the luxury end of the housing
market, providing all the modern conveniences of the era, as well as servants
quarters, elegant lobbies, spacious layouts, and even common dining rooms for
bachelor businessmen, who were presumed unable to cook for themselves.[71]
One of the earliest, and chicest, apartment buildings was the 7-storey Alexandra
Palace that opened in 1904 on University Avenue, where Mount Sinai Hospital
now stands.[72] Named after Edward VII's queen, the Alexandra Palace promoted

8.28: *Bathroom, Stewart Manor, 1927*
Using the number of toothbrushes as a guide, this small but efficient bathroom was shared by four people. Not surprisingly, this middle-class (even lower-middle-class) room lacks the marble and dark-wood grandeur of John Ross Robertson's upper-class luxury. The little radiator tucked in the corner has no elaborate cover. And there's certainly no room for a fireplace, decorative or otherwise. The fixtures, however, are up-to-date and available to a much broader public than similar fixtures were in Robertson's day. By the later 1920s, the bathroom looked, and worked, pretty much as it does today (although the tub stands on little claw feet and no shower is evident). The toilet tank, for example, had been lowered from near the ceiling (where it had been located in John Ross Robertson's time), to near the toilet seat (where it continues to be in our time).
CITY OF TORONTO ARCHVIES: Fonds 1034, Item 89

8.29: *Kitchen, Stewart Manor, 1927*
Apartment living was promoted as being more "efficient" — a trait that was increasingly valued as domestic servants became harder to find. "Efficiency" was certainly primary in the design of this small, galley-style kitchen, which may or may not have been in the Knowlton apartment. Unfortunately, the damaged photograph shows only part of the kitchen. A slight, 4-burner gas stove has replaced the heavy, black, coal-fired range. A white, gas refrigerator — boasting Consumers' Gas "flames that freeze" — has replaced the dark-wood "ice-box." Free-standing, white "hoosier" cabinets maximize storage space in this era before built-in cabinets. And, with a flick of a switch, a central, overhead light banishes shadows from counters and corners.
CITY OF TORONTO ARCHVIES: Fonds 1034, Item 85

8.30: *Alexandra Palace*, 1934
Bordered in gold and printed in blue, this ad in Toronto's 1934 social register was designed to appeal to the city's bluebloods. Clearly, the Edwardian Alexandra Palace on University Avenue stinted on neither size nor luxurious decoration in its appeal to another generation of Toronto's chic elite.
CITY OF TORONTO ARCHVIES, Series 654, File 46, [p. 4] of front matter

The Torontonian Society Blue Book

Lounge Room
at the Alexandra Palace

An attractive Suite
in the Alexandra Palace

itself as "Distinctive as to Location, Service and Patronage," successfully attracted elite tenants like Ontario's Chief Justice, and even advertised in the *Torontonian Society Blue Book*.[73] (See 8.30.)

Apartment building continued and accelerated. By the 1920s, the importance of luxury apartments may have lessened compared to the efficiency apartment, but the genre continued to impress and even point the way to the future. In January 1928, for example, *Construction* magazine commented:

> The present tendency of metropolitan living, away from the town house, and towards the higher type of group dwelling ... has even led to the prediction that the next twenty-five years will see an almost complete abandonment of the individual city house, due to the uneconomical aspect of the cost of maintenance, repairs, taxes and other items ... as well as to the increasing difficulty of securing and keeping the satisfactory servants necessary for proper service in the individual city house.[74]

8.31: *Reception Room, The Claridge, 1929*
"The Claridge possesses an entrance hall that must be the most beautiful in the city," William Dendy and William Kilbourn enthused in 1986. The judgment still stands. This photograph of the east end of the room, taken by Moore & Nixon-James in 1929, was republished in architectural journals[77] and provides ample evidence for this judgment: elegant proportions, triple-arched Moorish casement windows, baronial fireplace, Art Deco chandeliers and sconces, exquisitely wrought-iron detailing created by master metalworker Emile Wenger, and boldly patterned ceiling decoration designed by J. E. H. Macdonald and painted by Carl Schaefer. Taken for architects Baldwin & Greene, this photograph also amply illustrates W. F. Moore's artful approach to architectural photography which, he wrote in 1932, required careful lighting, careful preparation of the room and its furnishings, and a desire not only to represent a room or a building, but "interpret [the architect's] underlying idea or *motif*." Photographs intended for exhibition, Moore suggested, should be printed on "cream paper"[78] of the sort that can be seen in the original print of this image.
CITY OF TORONTO ARCHVIES: Fonds 1654, Image 6

The height of 1920s apartment luxury was reached on the site of Simeon H. Janes' mansion, Benvenuto, at Avenue Road south of St. Clair West. Here, three distinctive apartment buildings rose in 1927 and 1928: The Balmoral, The Clarendon, which inspired the above quotation, and The Claridge, which has been described as "the queen of Toronto apartment buildings."[75] Designed by Martin Baldwin of Baldwin & Greene architects, the 6-storey Claridge married convenience and efficiency (underground garage and the first automatic elevators in the city) with beauty and delight (decorative detailing in brick, stone, and wrought iron), to create a building deemed "comparable in luxurious finish and eccentric vitality to the firm's Victory and Concourse Buildings in the Bay Street Canyon."[76] The Claridge is eclectic in the extreme — and a far cry from the Stewart Manor ... which didn't even have a lobby, let alone an exquisite one.

Construction magazine concluded its description of The Claridge lobby by saying, "It has a suggestion both of novelty and old-established style, and expresses something of the modern tendency in a free use of, and benefit of color"[79] — an apt summary of Toronto's cautious approach to adopting the modern. (See 8.31.)

Scale

Size matters. The most obvious point of comparison between Toronto in the 1880s and Toronto in the 1920s is size: its population (both resident and working), physical extent, density of development, business activity, and so on. These changes have been documented throughout the book, including the previous section on apartments. Here, the point is reinforced by juxtaposing illustrations drawn from three aspects of Toronto life that reflect the distinct impact of size and scale: retail, communications, and tourism. The examples are meant to be indicative, not comprehensive.

The retail sector changed dramatically between the 1880s and 1920s. (See Chapter 6.) Small, general stores grew, became specialized, and ultimately multiplied into chain stores or were brought together under a single roof as department stores. Both developments are illustrated here.

In 1884, newlyweds Annie and Thomas Smith became the first residents on

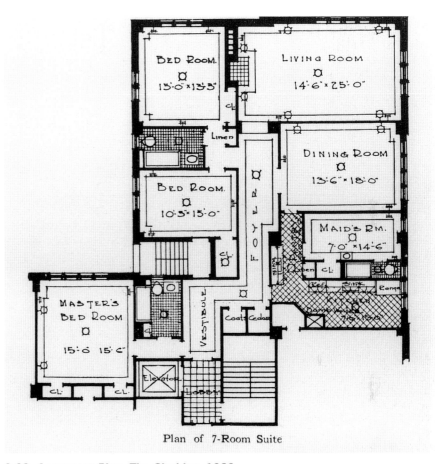

Plan of 7-Room Suite

8.32: *Apartment Plan, The Claridge, 1929*
Apartments at The Claridge originally ranged in size from six to ten rooms. This plan for a seven-room suite illustrates several distinctive features of luxurious apartment living in 1920s Toronto: large principal rooms; a small maid's room next to a modest but well-equipped kitchen; three bathrooms (two for the "family" and a small one for the maid); built-in closets (to replace Victorian wardrobes); and separation of "public" rooms (living room and dining room) from "private" rooms (bedrooms), by a hall (or "foyer").[80] The plan does not indicate the interior decorating details lovingly described in *Construction*, such as ceilings and walls painted in "delicate tones of light ivory and gray giving a soft lustrous finish," heavily stippled painting in halls and living room giving "the added beauty of a delicate textured surface," and "oak block floors in parquetry pattern" laid over the concrete base.[81] Although some of the large apartments have been subdivided into smaller ones, The Claridge retains many of its exquisite details, both inside and out.
TORONTO PUBLIC LIBRARY: Construction, March 1929, p. 95

8.33: *Mrs. Smith's Store*, ca. 1908
By 1908 when this photograph was taken, Annie Smith, who is standing at the counter, was helped by her daughter Hilda Victoria, who is seated between her mother and a dark wooden cabinet. This pre-modern appliance was an "icebox," which was chilled by blocks of ice harvested from Lake Ontario in winter, and preserved the ice cream that the Smiths sold in summer. Other items obviously sold here were Quaker Oats — from a top shelf — and Tona Cola — one of the many early competitors to Coca-Cola, which even adopted Coca-Cola typography on its signs. A stack of dimly lit cans seems to be labelled "Canada First." The contents of these nationalistic tins are unidentifiable.
PRIVATE COLLECTION

8.34: *Loblaw Head Office & Warehouse*, 1928
In 1928, the Loblaw Groceteria Company opened its Art Deco "monument to the success of the groceteria idea,"[85] at 500 Lake Shore Boulevard West. While lavishing attention on exterior detailing — designed to deal with the (perceived) problem of giving the appearance of height to a huge, low-lying building — *Construction* published, but said very little about this photograph of the interior. (No photographs of the warehouse part of the building were included at all.) These administrative offices on the second floor, near the unphotographed executive offices, have a distinctly solid-but-modern feel. The windows are uncurtained industrial; the huge room unpartitioned (for good or ill); and the reinforced concrete structure clearly stated in the splay-headed columns (similar to those found in nearby Terminal Warehouse, now Queen's Quay Terminal). Given the lack of desk clutter, the photograph was probably taken before the building was occupied and served as promotional material for both architects and client.
TORONTO PUBLIC LIBRARY: Construction, June 1928, p. 210

Fisherman's Island, which lay off the foot of Cherry Street, east of today's Toronto Island. Thomas fished, operated a boat livery, and saved over thirty people from drowning. Meanwhile, Annie raised a family and operated a small grocery store/ice-cream parlour that served the tiny residential community and summer tourists for over 30 years. While retailing changed dramatically on the "mainland," Mrs. Smith's neighbourhood store continued on relatively unchanged. (See 8.33.)

In 1916, the Smiths were forced to leave their "cosy home" on Fisherman's

Island, because the Toronto Harbour Commission was filling in Ashbridge's Bay to create a huge port-industrial area at the eastern end of Toronto Bay. They retired to the mainland and withdrew from the grocery business.[82] By then, the entire retail sector had already changed dramatically, with the growth of grocery chains, like Loblaw's, and department stores, like Simpson's and Eaton's. After the Great War, the pace of change accelerated.

"One of the most romantic of post war developments in Canadian commerce has been the spectacular growth of the Loblaw Groceterias," enthused *Construction* magazine in June 1928. "The growth of this chain store business has been phenomenal" — so great that the wizard of self-service, T. P. "We Sell For Less" Loblaw, built a grand new warehouse-cum-head-office on other land created by the Toronto Harbour Commission.[83] In 1928, Loblaw Groceterias opened one of the most sophisticated warehouses in North America at the northeast corner of Bathurst and Lakeshore.[84] Later disrupted by the dread Gardiner Expressway, the 4-storey Loblaw's Groceteria Building, together with the Crosse and Blackwell Building (1928), Tip Top Tailors (1929), and Terminal Warehouse (1927), formed part of an important Art Deco enclave on Toronto's ever-evolving waterfront. (See 8.34.)

8.35: *Advertisement for Canada Cement Company, 1927*
According to *Construction* of January 1928, the use of steel-reinforced concrete in the United States had skyrocketed from next-to-nothing around the turn-of-the-century to use in over 10,000 projects per year. On Toronto's waterfront, the Queen of Concrete was another occupant of the Harbour Commissioners' new land: the Toronto Terminal Warehouse. Built by the railways, Terminal Warehouse had a gross floor area of 1,000,000 square feet, was the largest warehouse in Canada, and was so solidly built that when redevelopers later wanted to knock the building down (despite loud cries from conservationists), the building refused to budge. It was more expensive to flatten the building than to renovate it — into the splendid residential-and-commercial complex now known as Queen's Quay Terminal. Not surprisingly, the concrete industry was proud of its association with the Terminal Warehouse. This ad, showing the Terminal Warehouse under construction, appeared in the October 1927 issue of the *University of Toronto Monthly*.
CITY OF TORONTO ARCHVIES, Series 600, Subseries 4, File 54

Interior view of new Toronto Terminal Warehouse
showing massive concrete construction

Our Service Department Will Be Glad to Hear from You

Our Service Department is maintained for the special purpose of co-operating with you in any line of work for which concrete is adapted. Our library is comprehensive and is at your disposal at all times, without charge.   Write us.

Canada Cement Company Limited

Canada Cement Company Building
Phillips Square   Montreal

Sales Offices at:

MONTREAL   TORONTO   WINNIPEG   CALGARY

The department store was a Victorian innovation that dramatically transformed retail activity by drawing together many different services under one roof. (See 8.36 and Chapter 6.)

In the late 1920s, the department store took another great leap forward, both in scale and style: Simpson's erected a 9-storey Art Deco addition at the corner of Bay and Richmond; and Eaton's started — but never finished — its own 40-storey Art Deco complex at Yonge and College.[86] Art Deco — a highly decorative, colourful, eclectic, and abstract style — drew on influences ranging from ancient Egypt to abstract cubism, from stylized natural forms to streamlined machine-age creations. Notoriously hard to define, Art Deco offered a stylistic buffer between "nineteenth-century fussiness" and the "comparative starkness of extreme modern architecture" in the 1960s.[87] Toronto's duelling retail giants raised their competition to a fine Art Deco, as revealed in the photographs and illustrations from that period. Unfortunately, only one interior has survived the intervening years relatively unscathed. (See 8.39, 8.40.)

Rather than moving "uptown" with Eaton's, Simpson's expanded its downtown store. *Construction* critic, "Sinaiticus," was delighted by the ongoing conversion of lower Bay Street, from a "late Victorian, shabby-genteel shopping street" to "the dignity of a genuinely 20th Century main thoroughfare" worthy of being known as "the Fifth Avenue of Toronto."[88] Of prime importance to this transformation was Alfred Chapman's Art Deco addition to the Robert Simpson store. The critic was somewhat ambivalent about the exterior of the "Greater Simpson Store," but he was unstinting in his praise for its interior. "Coming to the interior of the building," he wrote, "we find that the creative genius of the architect has been given full play."[89]

Sadly, only a hint of Simpson's Art Deco interior remains: a touch
of Botticino among the drywall; fragments of original metalwork; the
occasional patch of original floor; and the hexagonal entrance from Yonge
Street. Virtually the entire Bay Street Arcade is buried under or (more frequently) replaced entirely by later generations of retail design. All the Moderne
display cases are gone. Franz (Frank) Johnston's mural has disappeared. The
patterned terrazzo floor, classical columns, "Egyptian" doorway, richly
decorated elevator doors, and slender lights have all vanished.

The critic reached an ecstasy of enthusiasm when he came to The Arcadian
Court restaurant on the eighth and ninth floors. "The show feature of the entire
store is undoubtedly the new dining room," he declared. "While the accompanying illustrations of the dining room give a certain impression of its design
it is impossible to describe either by pen or picture the successful scheme of
decoration used in this room." But the critic did his best, "Its proportions
are monumental, the detail of silver skilfully touched with pink is delightful
both in colour and in the modernity of its design, while the entire scheme of
three huge bays finds its completion in the three round ceiling lights of exquisite
and lace-like tracery."[90] Of particular note was the spectacular metalwork on
elevators and balcony, and the elegantly arched ceiling, windows, and bays.
Virtually all traces of the room's Art Deco origins are gone, along with the
ladies-who-lunched and their sophisticated companions. (See 8.37, 8.38.)

Sinaiticus was equally enthusiastic about Eaton's plans (1928–1930) for
the southwest corner of Yonge and College streets, where the department-store
giant planned to expand its empire by building a huge new store: a stepped,
30-plus-storey tower set atop a 7-storey base that would combine "the spirit of
modernity with classical motifs."[91] The Depression nixed the tower, but the

8.38: *Simpson's Arcadian Court,* 1929

The ultra-chic Arcadian Court, depicted in this 1929 photograph for *Construction* magazine, is where Margaret Atwood's scheming society matron, Winifred Griffen Prior, took her awkward future sister-in-law, Iris Chase, for lunch and display in *The Blind Assassin*. "This was where the ladies lunched ... done in lilac and silver, with streamlined contours for the lighting fixtures and the chairs," Iris recalled. "A balcony ran around it halfway up, with wrought-iron railings; that was for men only, for businessmen. They could sit up there and look down on the ladies, feathered and twittering, as if in an aviary." The balcony is no longer reserved for men, and women seldom wear hats or twitter.

TORONTO PUBLIC LIBRARY: Construction, 1929, p. 86

8.39: *The Round Room,* 1930

The epitome of Toronto Art Deco was reached in Eaton's new "restaurant in modern style," illustrated in this drawing from a special issue of *The Eaton News* devoted to the new, uptown, upscale College Street Store, and the Auditorium across the hall. The drawing neatly captures both the simplicity of design — a domed circle within a square — and the hoped-for clientele — all perfectly shaped, coiffed and attired. Only an architectural photograph with no real people could attain a similar perfection.

CITY OF TORONTO ARCHVIES: Series 682, Subseries 1, File 34, p. 23

EATON AUDITORIUM, EATON'S·COLLEGE STREET, TORONTO

Art Deco base was built and formally opened in October 1930, providing a clear contrast to the company's (now-demolished) Victorian/Edwardian "Big Store"complex at Yonge and Queen.

From Sinaiticus onward, architectural critics have lavished praise on Eaton's Art Deco gems, the Round Room (8.39) restaurant and the Eaton Auditorium (8.40), both designed by eminent Parisian architect, Jacques Carlu, in the height of French Art-Deco fashion.[92] According to the contemporary critic, the design of the restaurant was "a very successful, ultra-modern essay in banana yellow, black, silver and beige" with concealed lighting, Lalique glass fountain, Natacha Carlu mural paintings, and radio suspended from the central dome — all constituting a "revelation of the spirit of the Twentieth Century"[93] and a marked contrast to such Edwardian baroque dining rooms as McConkeys or the King Edward Hotel.

Across a long streamlined foyer opened Carlu's equally streamlined French Art-Deco Auditorium, with its boldly tiled floor, translucent lighting, and modish gallery. The Carlus' work for Eaton's is widely regarded as the epitome of Art Deco interior design in Toronto.[94]

Increase in scale was evident in other sectors, including communications (e.g., newspapers) and tourism (e.g., hotels), discussed here. When John Ross Robertson slipped the first sheet of paper into his hand-fed Hoe press on April 18, 1876, his *Evening Telegram* staff numbered 23 and his press could churn out 1,750 four-page papers an hour. By April 1926, when the Tely's 50th anniversary paper appeared, the staff numbered 463, operations were split between two locations, and the paper's battery of roll-fed presses could churn out 140,000 thirty-two-page papers per hour. Between these two dates, Robertson's paper had grown steadily, equalling the combined circulation of all his rivals by 1884; Robertson had built two downtown newspaper buildings, each regarded as a model of its era (1879 and 1900); an annex had been built on Dupont Street (the first branch plant in Canadian newspaper history); and the paper's circulation had more than kept up with the city's growth in population. This growth is clearly captured by two images: a drawing from the 1880s and a photograph from the 1920s. (See 8.41, 8.42.)

8.41: *Power of the Press*, 1880

This is actually the second *Evening Telegram* press room, which was located in Robertson's first purpose-built newspaper building at King and Bay streets, where the Toronto-Dominion Centre now stands. Robertson's first, hand-fed press was even smaller than this 4 by 13-foot, roll-fed Potter-Scott model near the stairs. The new press could churn out a then-astonishing 10,500 eight-page papers an hour, and was nicknamed the "E. W. Gardiner" after the Tely's advertising agent. In 1888, Robertson purchased a second, similar press, which was nicknamed the "Goldwin Smith" in honour of his financial backer. J. L. Telford's sketch was probably created to document the grandeur of Robertson's new, preternaturally clean, press room in 1880; and was certainly used in 1926, when it was republished in the 50th anniversary edition of the paper, to illustrate the "remarkable contrast with the monster presses" of the twenties.

TORONTO PUBLIC LIBRARY: T 12357

8.42: *Power of the Press*, 1926

By 1926, the *Evening Telegram* was printed in two locations, here in the paper's crowded main press-room at Bay and Melinda streets, where presses were packed "as closely as the works in a watch," and at the paper's more spacious 1921 branch office at Dupont Street, where both pressmen and "gigantic six-roll press" enjoyed much more favourable "conditions as to air, light and room." In contrast to the 1880 press, which made "little more noise than a sewing machine," the monster presses shown here operated with "an even hum" that rose to "a continuous roar" as full speed was reached.

CITY OF TORONTO ARCHIVES: Series 655, File 27, *The Evening Telegram*, Monday, April 19, 1926, p. 25

Hotels provide a final case study of the impact of scale on the Toronto landscape. The Queen's Hotel on Front Street was the grandest of the Victorian hotels. (See also Chapters 4 and 6.) This cupola-capped dowager grew up near Toronto's bustling wharves, and maintained her dominant position when the railway inserted itself between water and city. Although the 4-storey, 17-parlour, 200-room Queen's remained the largest and most gracious of her era, many other Victorian hotels popped up across the city. In the central area, the Queen's was joined by such prominent rivals as the Rossin House and the Walker House. To the east there was the Lakeview Hotel on Parliament Street (discussed in Chapter 6). And to the west was the Gladstone Hotel at 1204–1208 Queen Street West. The Gladstone, which has entered a period of renewal, has played a significant role in west-end Toronto life for over a 100 years[95] and is now the oldest, continuously operated hotel in the city.

Although a small hotel had stood at the corner of Gladstone and Queen for at least a decade, it was Susanna Robinson who, in 1890, built the 4-storey, red-brick hotel that still graces that corner. By 1893, her family business included not only the new hotel, but also the adjoining stores, which had an impressive combined value of over $45,000, a value that remained constant through the hotel's early period of comfortable success.[96] This success was due in no small measure to its location across the street from the Parkdale Railway Station. By 1910, the hotel had been (temporarily and grandly) rechristened the "Hotel Gladstone" and become the property of Victor E. Gianelli — the son of an Italian aristocrat, who had been a long-time travelling salesman and then local manager for Reinhardt's beer company. It was Gianelli who had the newly refurbished hotel photographed for publicity and posterity. (See 8.43.)

Unlike the Gladstone, the era of the magnificent but declining Queen's Hotel came to a metaphorical end in 1903 with the appearance of the King Edward Hotel, and a physical end in 1927 when it was demolished to make way for the Canadian Pacific Railway's newest and grandest chateau-skyscraper.[98]

8.43: *Smoking Room, Gladstone Hotel, ca. 1910*
Located across from the Parkdale Railway Station, the Gladstone Hotel was a convenient resting place for tourists and, especially, travelling salesmen who would have enjoyed this recently refurbished Smoking Room. Four interior photographs accompanied owner Victor E. Gianelli's entry in the 1911 publication, *Toronto and the Men Who Made It*. Although markedly smaller and less grandly appointed than either the Victorian Queen's Hotel or the interwar Royal York Hotel, the Gladstone Hotel provided "first-class cuisine"[97] and manly furnishings (including brass spittoon) for its commercial travellers. An adjoining Reception Room was of a similar modest scale, but slightly more feminine in feel, with artfully draped curtains and a grand piano.
CITY OF TORONTO ARCHVIES, Research Hall Library: *Greater Toronto and the Men Who Made It*, 1911, p. 126 (upper right)

8.44: *Ball Room, Royal York Hotel, 1929*
This postcard shows the third-floor Ball Room of the Royal York Hotel in the year it opened, 1929.[103] *Construction* magazine's pseudonymous architectural critic, Sinaiticus, nearly exploded with purple prose when describing this "most perfect of hotels" as a "veritable poem in stone" with the "promise of the outside [being] splendidly performed within" and nowhere more perfectly so than in the Ball Room shown here. Noting the double-arched windows (that create one of the dominant features on the exterior, Front Street facade), the groined and painted-panelled ceiling, and the "majestic" crystal chandeliers, Sinaiticus pronounced this one of the "greatest halls of its kind upon this continent."[104]
CITY OF TORONTO ARCHVIES: Series 330, File 407, Image 1

In June 1929, Canadian Pacific ran an ad proclaiming its new hotel, the Royal York, to be a "symbol of Toronto's growth and power."[99] And so it was. Rising on the site of the old Queen's Hotel, the hulking, grey, 26-storey Royal York Hotel was briefly the tallest building in the British Empire,[100] and remained a dominant feature of Toronto's landscape until the Toronto-Dominion Centre — Mies van der Rohe's sleek and gloriously Modern black towers at King and Bay — initiated the next city-transforming skyscraper boom in the mid-1960s.[101]

Designed by the same architects who created the new Union Station across the street, the 1,000-room Royal York Hotel exploded the scale of hotel building; represented a new form of corporate — rather than family or personal — financing;[102] and included every then-imaginable luxury and convenience — not only ten passenger elevators with polished-walnut cabs, bathrooms with every room, and the city's first hotel convention facilities, but also the world's largest public-address system, Canada's largest organ, motion-picture projectors with provision for those newfangled "talking pictures," and even "television" when "that time arrives." That time didn't arrive until after the Second World War ... but the Royal York was ready and waiting. In the meantime, luxurious hotel-living continued, at both the individual suite level and the grand, communal level. (See 8.44.)

Construction magazine devoted 25 pages to the Royal York Hotel, published over 20 photographs of the interior, but captured only three people: the maître-d', a waiter and a waitress, all standing — as immobile and impersonal as the furniture — at the entrance to the main dining room. Neither patrons nor behind-the-scenes workers were allowed to sully the pristine beauty of the architectural photographs. Utilitarian and commercial Consumers' Gas Company, however, had different interests. Fortunately, it went behind the scenes to capture the gas works and, sometimes, the workers. (See 8.45.)

8.45: *Kitchen, Royal York Hotel,* **1929**

Consumers' Gas commissioned this photograph of one of the kitchens at the newly opened Royal York Hotel. There is no way to tell if it was taken in a corner of the "banquet kitchen" across from the ballroom on the third floor (reportedly "one of the largest in the world" in 1929[105]), or in one of the other ultra-modern kitchens in the new hotel. But the men pose at their stations — including one of Consumers' newest industrial ranges — in a quiet moment between servings. By this time, the hotel kitchen has acquired a stainless-steel glint of modernity, both a material and a feel distinctly lacking in the grungy old King Edward Hotel kitchens shown in an earlier chapter.

CITY OF TORONTO ARCHVIES: Fonds 1034, Item 1015

> Moreover this mountain has been an integral part of the metropolitanization of the city, a process both exhilarating and destructive, loved and hated.
>
> DETLEF MERTINS, Toronto Modern[106]

The most obvious evidence of increased scale and a modern sensibility was the skyscraper. Evolving from an older form — the "office building" that emerged as a distinct building-type in the late 1880s — the skyscraper was a building of great height (a relative, but important term), constructed on a metal frame.[107] The new form — made possible by such technological innovations as the elevator and steel skeleton-construction — originated in the United States, especially Chicago and New York City, and evolved over the next half-century from vertically extended traditional structures (such as New York's 60-storey neo-Gothic Woolworth Building), to stepped-profile buildings[108] (New York's 102-storey Empire State Building), to post-war glass-and-steel prisms (Mies van der Rohe's Seagram Building in New York and TD Centre in Toronto).

Skyscrapers

Seen from a distance, the city at night gives pause.... Toronto appears like a crystalline mountain of lights rising up gradually to a height of some 72 storeys and punctuated at its side by a single shaft thrusting 1,815 feet into the heavens. This image of Toronto is now so pervasive that we take it for granted. And yet this is a distinctly Modern aspect of a city whose morphology begins during the building boom of the 1920s and does not peak again until the next boom, during the 1960s.

8.47: *Capping Canada Life*, ca. 1930
Once again, William James risked his life to take this heart-stopping shot. From a position *above* the action, James photographed workers capping the Canada Life Building at 15 stories. The new Canada Life Building was the first, and ultimately the only, building to rise on University Avenue, according to plans laid down in 1929 by local Beaux Arts visionaries. It was also among those cut down to a smaller size by the Depression. Like Eaton's, Canada Life had bigger things in mind. As originally designed, the now-truncated tower was to have climbed higher, in a series of dramatic setbacks atop the (existing, massive) Classical Revival base. Even without the final tower, the insurance company has become a University Avenue landmark and a beacon of weather-forecasting for the city.
CITY OF TORONTO ARCHVIES: Fonds 1244, Item 116

Toronto approached the skyscraper cautiously and never reached the heights or the extremes of a New York (with its Empire State and Chrysler Buildings both rising to unimaginable heights in the late-1920s). While not intentional — the Depression squashed many thoughts of grandeur before they made it off the drawing board — the result was perhaps salutary and even ironic. By the time the second skyscraper boom got going in the mid-1960s (with the TD Centre soon to be followed by Commerce Court and Royal Bank Plaza), the counter-high-rise-revolution had also got rolling. It slapped a 45-foot-height limit on all downtown buildings, began re-thinking Toronto's approach to Modernism, and began demanding a modern city-building that was more respectful of the past and responsive to actual users. Ironically, the struggle continues, with the older skyscrapers themselves being under threat of demolition and replacement by the new new thing, whatever that might be.[109]

The earliest stage of the construction of skyscrapers in Toronto skyscraping occurred in the late-nineteenth and early-twentieth centuries, with buildings like the 1895 Romanesque Revival Temple Building, that

popped up all over town. Like local Babbitts — businessmen-boosters who liked to look out their office windows onto the glittering towers of Zenith — the compilers of *Might's City Directory* for 1928 presented "A Few of Toronto's Skyscrapers," most of which fell in the 12 to 15-storey range. And in the last

once rose to "a headline-grabbing ten storeys"[110] at Queen and Bay, and the 1914 12-storey Renaissance Revival Dominion Bank at King and Yonge,[111] applying familiar architectural styles to the new built form. But Toronto's first real skyscraper boom occurred — like the apartment and other commercial booms — in the mid- to late-1920s, when a slew of new commercial buildings

two years of the decade, both buildings and plans for buildings continued to pour forth, only once piercing the 30-storey plateau that held fast until the 1960s.

Two new buildings lauded in the May 1929 *Construction* magazine — just six months before the Crash — capture the style and enthusiasm of Toronto's

8.49: *Concourse Building Lobby, ca. 1929*
This fine exhibition print by architectural photographers Moore and Nixon-James documents both still existing and sadly lost details: the delicate Canadian deer on the ceiling, encircling triangular motifs, words of Canadian poets (such as Bliss Carman), quintessentially Art Deco lamps, and stylized iron flowers and jazzy grille work by Emile Wenger.

late-twenties skyscraper boom: the 23-storey *Toronto Star* Building at 80 King Street West, and the 16-storey Concourse Building at 100 Adelaide Street West. The first is long gone; and the other is nearly gone.

The power of the press was made evident not only by the stories on the page, but also by the storeys on the ground. The skyscraper was, of course, the ultimate status symbol for high-flying businesses in the 1920s, as in the 1960s, and perhaps still today.[112] By 1928 when the *Toronto Star* moved to its new home at 80 King Street West, "skyscraper" certainly equalled "success." (The *Chicago Tribune* had recently set a high standard with its 34-storey Tower in the Windy City.) By 1928, the *Star* produced the biggest daily in Toronto.[113] It was also moving ever closer to becoming as much a "business" as a "news" organization, so it is not surprising that the new *Star* Building included 18 stories of revenue-producing office space atop the 5-storey base devoted to the paper.

Once the Queen, now the Grande Dame, and soon to be the Ghost of Toronto Art Deco office architecture, the Concourse Building illustrates both the on-going dilemma of historic preservation in Canada's largest city,[114] and the power of photographs to document and preserve the memory of that past. In the case of the Concourse, the rare photographic record could have helped developers, bent on replacing the "small" 16-storey structure with a massive 41-storey tower, recover or recreate some of the most distinctive interior features of the original. Alas, the desire was not present, and another glorious and authentic Toronto interior will disappear.[115] (See 8.49.)

Now dwarfed by its downtown neighbours, Baldwin & Greene's 16-storey Concourse Building at 100 Adelaide Street West once dominated its piece of sky. In contrast to its direct contemporary, the *Star* building on King Street, the Concourse was light, colourful, and very Canadian. J. E. H. Macdonald, Group of Seven member and creator of the Concourse decorative scheme, compared the exterior of the building — in its verticality and its colourful detailing — to "a brightly illuminated letter in a fine manuscript, beginning, perhaps, some greater chapter of our future development" in the city.[116] That was not to be: the Concourse barely escaped crushing by the Depression that left other such structures as Baldwin & Greene's slightly younger Victory Building empty for most of the thirties.[117] But even during the dreary Depression, the Concourse stood as a colourful exclamation point on the landscape. And the colour was carried right into the lobby, which was also lovingly described by Macdonald:

The color idea is carried into the floors, walls and ceilings of the foyer,
the floors being of bold angular designs in green and buff terrazzo

inlaid with bronze stars. The walls are mostly of a warm, ivory travertine and the ceiling designs show Canadian motifs in definite coloring in gold on a warm, reddish-grey ground. There are running deer, Canadian trees and flowers, various types of sporting fish in gold, with flying birds, wild ducks and cloud forms.... There seems to be no reason why business and building should not be entertaining as well as efficient.[118]

In the mid-twentieth century, the colourful Art Deco lobby of the Concourse Building was unsympathetically renovated. The ceiling motifs, the quotations from eight Canadian poets,[119] the patterned terrazzo floors, and Emile Wenger's decorative metalwork were covered over or taken away. Still, the basic dimensions, marble walls, and some detailing survived that onslaught. Now the building faces another assault. Fortunately, a single display photograph by architectural specialists, Moore and Nixon-James, has survived to recall, celebrate and — developers willing — help recreate some of the vanished glories of the original.

The twin themes of this book are easy to express, although more difficult to elaborate: that both interior spaces and contemporary photographs are important. Until now, most attention has been devoted in Toronto — as around the world — to the city's exterior face; and photographs, like prints and drawings, have tended to be regarded as pleasant illustrations, rather than primary sources of information about those spaces. I hope *Inside Toronto* has shifted both perceptions, and added to our collective knowledge about the city and her people. Perhaps more efforts will be taken to celebrate and preserve not only exterior, but also interior spaces. Such efforts cannot come a moment too soon.

Acknowledgements

Every book has a history. *Inside Toronto* began in the fall of 1996 in the basement Archives for the old City of Toronto. A seasoned researcher but newly-minted archivist, I had been hired on contract to describe about 20 of its photographic collections, some well-known but in need of updating, others virtually unknown to me or potential researchers. I plunged into the task with characteristic enthusiasm, was privileged to work with wonderful materials, and regretted the day when my contract ended. Fortunately, my life with these historic materials was just beginning.

Not long after completing the archival contract, I realized that the images that remained most vividly with me were interior shots — of storm-sewer tunnels, jewellery stores, hotel kitchens, barber shops, city halls, downtown flop houses, Victorian parlours, Edwardian boardrooms. An idea was born. Before long, and long before I became a full-time archivist for the City, I had started combing archival holdings for rare — but fascinating — interior views of Toronto, and was well on my way to creating this book. Whenever I got bogged down in the writing or promoting of the manuscript, I simply returned to the original images and was reinvigorated.

Many people have helped along the way — friends, colleagues, specialists, even total strangers whom I now count among my friends. I can only pay formal tribute to a small number among the many whom I consulted. I am forever grateful to each of you.

First on my list are my colleagues at the City of Toronto Archives, especially long-time photo archivist, Steve Mackinnon; architectural-records expert, Patrick Cummins; master of the stimulating proto-idea, Lawrence Lee; and government-records maven, Elizabeth Cuthbertson. My archival companions have not only made numerous helpful suggestions, but have also weathered with grace and wit the mini-tirades emanating from my corner.

My explorations began in the City of Toronto Archives, but expanded well beyond it. I am grateful to archivists and special librarians at the Archives of Ontario (especially Carolyn Heald, Mary Ledwell, Stewart Boden, Christine Bourolias, and Judith Emery), the Toronto Public Library (notably Alan Walker), and the Library and Archives of Canada. I made targeted forays into such specialized archives as the Law Society of Upper Canada (fulsome thanks to research director, Susan Lewthwaite, and curator, Élise Brunet), TD Bank Archives (cyber-thanks to Roy Schaeffer), the Toronto Police Museum, the Women's Art Association of Canada, the Fisher Rare Book Library, the United Church and Victoria College Archives, the Hospital for Children, the Albany Club, and the McCord Museum in Montreal.

I am especially grateful to individuals who willingly shared personal photographs, notably: Dr. Lillian Petroff (Macedonian Ice Cream Parlour); retired District Fire Chief Russell Phillips (Yorkville Firehall); and master tinsmith, Brian Greer (Winchester Hotel Bar). I am equally indebted to Professors Dennis

ACKNOWLEDGEMENTS

Duffy and Susan Houston, who shared unpublished manuscripts on Henry Pellatt and Louisa Sims Rogers.

Among the many heritage cognoscenti consulted, my thanks go to: Cathy Nasmith (heritage preservation in all its diverse aspects); Steve Otto (works by Charles J. Gibson); Carl Benn (Toronto material culture); Doug Fyfe (Spadina House); heritage activist, Janice Etter; and restoration architect, Martha Werenfels. Also playing a key role during a difficult period was Heritage Toronto (huge thanks to both the Board and the Staff).

Creating a book presents many challenges. Eternal thanks to the Ontario Arts Council and to the Toronto Arts Council for grants that bought me time off work to make serious headway on the manuscript.

Inside Toronto might never have found its way from my computer into tangible, book form without the help of two amazing Toronto women: acute, urban observer, Martha Shuttleworth, and her Neptis Foundation; and heritage developer nonpareil, Margaret Zeidler of Urban Space. I am forever indebted to you both, not only for practical financial support, but also moral support during some very trying times.

Finally, I want to acknowledge my publisher, Marc Côté, the driving force behind Cormorant Books, who assembled the creative team that transformed a raw manuscript and hundreds of photographs into such an elegant book.

On the personal side, I am deeply grateful to my tough, witty, insightful, and empathic therapist of long-standing, Maridene Johnston. Meanwhile, the newest member of the family, Lindsay, has brought ineffable delight and renewed sense of wonder to her Granny Sal. Because I admire and love them beyond measure, I dedicate *Inside Toronto* to my daughters, Katie and Meg.

Notes

CHAPTER I
A Little Bit of Light Magic

1. "Photography," *The Quarterly Review*, vol. 101 (April 1857), p. 465. Emphasis added. Lady Eastlake, née Rigby, was a successful writer and critic who was married to Sir Charles Eastlake, English painter, National Gallery director, and first president of the Photographic Society. Lady Eastlake traced the evolution of photographic processes, and lauded new forms of photography as being among the "recent wonders of the age," (p. 453), but denigrated their artistic potential. She was neither the first nor the last to get tangled up in this unproductive, but inevitable, discussion. But her phrase "new form of communication" hit on a truth about the new medium that has engaged modern minds, especially from the time of McLuhan onward.

2. For discussions of the historical understanding and social construction of photographs see Alan Trachtenberg, *Reading American Photographs: Images as History, Mathew Brady to Walker Evans* (New York: Hill and Wang, Division of Farrar, Straus and Giroux, 1989); Abigail Solomon-Godeau, *Photography at the Dock: Essays on Photographic History, Institutions, and Practices* (Minneapolis: University of Minnesota Press, 1991); Susan Sontag, On Photography (New York: Doubleday Anchor Books paperback edition, 1990); John Tagg, *The Burden of Representation: Essays on Photographies and Histories* (Minneapolis: University of Minnesota Press, paperback edition 1993); and Joan M. Schwartz, "'Records of Simple Truth and Precision': Photography, Archives, and the Illusion of Control," *Archivaria* 50 (Fall 2000), pp. 1–40.

3. The address and date are inscribed on the back of this photograph. The name of the sitter is indicated on the back of a related photograph taken on the front porch of the same house. The name of the grandfather — but not the grandmother — is evident from the Assessment Roll and the City Directories. The directories also indicate that the Browns rented and resided at 1050 Bloor West for only one year — 1902. Other family relationships are evident from various photographs in Fonds 1185, including the apparently close relationship of Merle Foster's mother and her aunt Emily. The amateur nature of the hand-tinting is evident from close inspection of the photograph, which reveals a number of places where colours have flowed beyond their boundaries, for example on the green potted palm. Merle Foster's career as a sculptor is evident from other items in Fonds 1185, including photographs of her work and newspaper clippings about her.

4. "There is no more evocative image of fin-de-siècle interiors than a black-and-white photograph of a richly paneled room with chintz-covered furniture and, almost inevitably, the elegant fanlike leaves of a kentia palm ... the kentia [had] established itself as a sure sign of graceful living." Around the time this snapshot was taken with a modest Kentia palm, Queen Alexandra was posing for an official coronation portrait, in front of several huge Kentia palms. George Plumptre, "Strange Tale of the Kentia Palm: Exotic Origins of the Ubiquitous Houseplant," *Architectural Digest*, pp. 90–96.

5. During the Iraqi War, Susan Sontag presented a particularly potent argument about the power of context to shape the meaning of photographs. Even the "simple" and common practice of cropping

photographs can radically change what the image means and how it is interpreted. In an essay about photographs of prisoner abuse perpetrated by American soldiers on Muslim prisoners at Abu Ghraib prison, Sontag underlined the radically different impression given by images closely cropped to show only the prisoners being abused (as a horrible but perhaps infrequent act by a single, "aberrant" soldier), compared with uncropped versions of the same images, showing other soldiers looking on, or just passing by (a more repellant abuse as a common practice, engaged in by many "ordinary" soldiers). Susan Sontag, "The Photographs are Us: Regarding the Torture of Others," *The New York Times Magazine* (May 23, 2004), pp. 24–29, 42.

6. Ralph Greenhill and Andrew Birrell, *Canadian Photography 1839–1920* (Toronto: The Coach House Press, 1979), p. 1. The Quebec article said little about Daguerre's new process because it was still secret, but devoted most of its report to Fox Talbot, who had described his "photogenic drawing" to the Royal Society in London on February 21st. In part because Talbot patented his process in England, it became less widely disseminated than Daguerre's, which the French government opened to the world, while rewarding Daguerre with a life-pension. It was only in the mid-1850s that Talbot lost his patent and his "positive-negative" process became popular around the photographic world. From a single "negative," many "positive" "calotype" prints could be made. As with most new inventions, the early history of photography involved a great many new processes and new terms, before common terminology and standards were accepted.

7. Lilly Koltun, "Pre-Confederation Photography in Toronto," *History of Photography: An International Quarterly*, vol. 2, no. 3 (July 1978), p. 249. *The Patriot* reprinted a letter written on March 9th by Samuel Morse from Paris that described Daguerre's results, although not the process itself, which Daguerre only revealed on August 19th of the same year. Daguerre's process produced an exquisitely detailed, but unique image on a silver-coated copper plate. For the first 15 years or so of photography, the daguerreotype dominated the photographic field.

8. Graham W. Garrett, "Photography in Canada 1839–1841: A historical and biographical outline," *Photographic Canadiana*, vol. 22, no. 1 (May/June 1996), pp. 5–6. Finch was mentioned in the *British Colonist* of July 7, 1841; and Pauling was mentioned, not by correct name, in *The Patriot* of July 27, 1841. Mr. Garrett tracked down Pauling's real identity. Until this article appeared, L. W. Dessauer and C. Barns, who first advertised in July 1843, were commonly thought to be Toronto's earliest known photographers. Like Finch, they opened a business in the Wellington Building on King Street. See Koltun, *op. cit.*, p. 250; and Greenhill and Burrill, *op. cit.*, p. 26.

9. Quoted by Koltun, *op. cit.*, p. 251. Interestingly, the first amateur photographs as well as the first published photographic images by a Canadian were daguerreotypes taken by Quebec seigneur Pierre-Gaspard-Gustave Joly de Lotbinière, who happened to be in Paris when Daguerre made his dramatic announcement on August 19, 1839. Joly de Lotbinière, like so many others, was "seized by the miraculous process," acquired the necessary equipment, and learned the new craft well enough, before setting off on extensive travels, that he was able to supply a Parisian book publisher with views of his travels to Greece and Egypt. In 1842, N. P. Lerebours published *Excursions daguerriennes*

with engravings based on photographs. See Andrew Burrill, "The Early Years/1839–1885," in Lilly Koltun (ed.), Private Realms of Light: Amateur photography in Canada/1839–1940 (Toronto: Fitzhenry & Whiteside), pp. 2–5.

10. Koltun, "Pre-Confederation Photography in Toronto," *op. cit.*, p.254–255. The business section of the City Directory for 1859–60 lists seven photographic firms, all located on fashionable King Street — six to the east and one just to the west of Yonge Street.

11. The 25 Armstrong, Beere and Hime photographs of Toronto are so important to the history of the city that the British Government presented Toronto with a fine set of copy prints in 1984 as a Sesquicentennial gift. These are now at the City of Toronto Archives, Fonds 1498. The originals are still in the Foreign and Commonwealth Office library in London. Also of interest is the fact that William Armstrong was the noted watercolourist who painted the well-known 1856 view of Toronto from Toronto Island, which was "drawn from photographs taken on the spot," and became the first item in the City's fine-art collection. "View of Toronto," *The News of the Week*, February 6, 1857, p. 6.

12. The firm had been hired by the University to document the construction of its magnificent new building, now known as University College. In November 1858, for example, they billed the University for 291 photographs (at 15 cents apiece) and for mounting 251 photographs in books. In January 1859, the firm put in a bill for another 100 photographs. From the state of construction revealed in these photographs, the museum photograph could not have been taken before 1859 or 1860. For details of the design and building of University College see Douglas Richardson,

A Not Unsightly Building: University College and Its History (Toronto: Mosaic Press for University College, 1990). More specifically about the museum, see pp. 82, 93–95, 128–129. The exterior photographs were large, wet-processed prints. Whether the Museum stereograph was part of the set invoiced or simply a commercial venture on the part of the firm, it is not surprising that the interior was a stereograph rather than a print, since stereographs required less light to produce.

13. Boston writer and physician, Oliver Wendell Holmes, wrote an exuberant and insightful essay about the wonders of stereography in 1859, and actually coined the name "stereograph." He also invented one of the simplest and most popular of stereoscopic viewers. "The Stereoscope and the Stereograph," *The Atlantic Monthly*, vol. 3 (June 1859), pp. 738–748 (online version at: http://www.cis.yale.edu/amstud/inforev/stereo.htm, April 2001). Seen without the aid of a stereoscope, stereographs lose much of their panache and all of their three-dimensional appeal. With the it, however, it is easy to understand the enthusiasm of nineteenth-century viewers. Even in 21st-century Canada, appeals are still made to the magic of 3-D photography. See *Toronto Star*, April 21, 2001, which came with special glasses to view the apparently off-register photographs in the paper. According to Koltun, the craze for stereographs peaked between 1858 and 1861, being superseded by the craze for cartes-de-visite after 1861. Koltun, *Pre-Confederation*, *op. cit.*, p. 257. Stereographs, however, remained extremely popular through the Victorian era and on into the early twentieth-century, as is made evident in later chapters.

14. Because of the smaller size of the negative plates and the shorter focal length of the lenses, stereoscopic cameras needed less light to fix an image than did other cameras of the day. The absolute rarity of this stereograph in Toronto's photographic history is made all the more evident from the fact that Octavius Thompson's 1868 photographic masterwork, *Toronto in the Camera*, which contained no interior views of Toronto buildings. Octavius Thompson, *Toronto in the Camera*. (Toronto: O. Thompson, Photographic Publisher, 1868).

15. Richardson, *op. cit.*, p. 93. At the time of Hincks's 1853 appointment, his brother, Sir Francis Hincks, was premier of Canada, a "qualification," Huxley remarked, "better than all the testimonials in the world." Quoted by Richardson, *op. cit.*, p. 93.

16. Stephen Jay Gould, "Cabinet Museums; Alive, Alive, O!" in *Dinosaur in a Haystack: Reflections in Natural History*, p. 241. Gould's article discusses the exactly contemporary Dublin Museum of Natural History, whose foundation stone was laid in March 1856.

17. Koltun, Pre-Confederation, *op. cit.*, pp. 257–259.

18. Alan Thomas, "Fashionable Display," in *The Expanding Eye: Photography and the Nineteenth-Century Mind* (London: Croom Helm, 1978).

19. Alan Thomas, "Fashionable Display," *op. cit.* Thomas's discussion of Victorian portrait photography shows how conventions of dress, posing, and stage-setting were created and passed down the social scale ... but not quite to the level shown in this Children's Aid Society photograph.

20. Kodak came to Canada before the Brownie did. Although Kodak "demonstrators" had regularly visited the country through most of the 1890s, it was only in 1899 that the Rochester-based company established a Canadian company. In November 1899, Canadian Kodak Company set up in rented premises at 10 Colborne Street, near King and Church Streets, with 10 employees. The company grew rapidly, along with the explosion of amateur photography. In 1902, Canadian Kodak moved into a 4-storey building of its own on King Street West near Portland Street. About 10 years and two locations later, in 1913, Canadian Kodak moved its 400 employees to a new plant among the rolling farmlands of Mount Dennis. During the First World War "Kodak Heights" became "Camp Kodak," housing the 127th Overseas Battalion of the Canadian Expeditionary Force, York Rangers. "Kodak Canada: Celebrates its 100th Birthday 1899–1999," in *Photographic Canadiana*, vol. 25, no. 2 (Sept./Oct., 1999), pp. 16–18.

21. For discussions of the arrival and impact of dry-plate photography, see Ralph Greenhill, *op. cit.*, especially pp. 112–117; and Lilly Koltun (ed.), *Private Realms of Light*, *op. cit.*, especially Birrell, op. cit., p. 15, and Peter Robertson, "The New Amateur/1885–1900," in *Ibid.*, pp. 16–18.

22. This thesis is explored by Koltun (ed.), *Private Realms*, *op. cit.* In the Preface, for example, Koltun explains that the National Archives' project on amateur photography, which was confirmed and resulted in her book, was based "on the belief that had long circulated among photo-researchers, that amateurs were the true innovators of their time...." Amateurs certainly were active in Toronto as early as the 1850s when members of the Royal Canadian Institute attended demonstrations and published articles about new photographic alchemies.

23. Andrew Oliver, *The Toronto Camera Club: The First Hundred Years* (Toronto: Toronto Camera Club, 1988), p. 23.

24. Alfred Stieglitz was the charismatic guru of "pictorialism" and pure, "art" photography, who established Photo-Secession in 1902 New York City. He promoted his vision by creating exhibitions (he sent a batch of photos to a Toronto

Camera Club Salon in 1903), publishing *Camera Work*, and writing for other periodicals. See, for example, Alfred Stieglitz, "Pictorial Photography," *Scribner's Magazine*, vol. 26 (1899), pp. 528–537. *Scribner's* published a number of interesting photographic articles, including James B. Carrington, "Night Photography," *Scribner's Magazine*, vol. 22 (1897), pp. 626–628; and Jesse Lynch Williams, "The Walk Up-Town in New York," which was illustrated by Stieglitz photographs, *Scribner's Magazine*, vol. 27 (1900), pp. 44 ff.

25. Several of Woolnough's published images were interiors. See "some Recent Pictures in Amateur Photography," *Massey Magazine*, May 1897.

26. Lilly Koltun, "Art Ascendant/1900–1914," in Koltun (ed.), *op. cit.*, p. 38.

27. No doubt the commercial photographer had little interest in photographing something so familiar, unless someone paid him to do so. Meanwhile, the early amateur photographer, especially a pictorialist like Goss, would have regarded the subject as unartistic and unworthy. Here, TTC photographer Alfred Pearson may have been documenting a new darkroom as part of his job of documenting TTC operations between 1920 and 1944.

28. Physicist, astronomer, and photographic innovator, Sir John Herschel, is generally credited with coining, or at least successfully promoting, the term "photography," which is a combination of two Greek words: "photos," meaning light; and "graphos," meaning writing. Herschel also coined the words "positive," "negative," and "snap shot."

29. Michael Hiley, *Seeing Through Photographs* (London: Gordon Fraser, 1983, p. 75.

30. Riis quoted in Alexander Alland, Sr., *Jacob A. Riis: Photographer & Citizen* (Millerton New York: Aperture, Inc., 1974), p. 26. Elsewhere, Riis commented on the great power of photography,

saying his writing alone "did not make much of an impression — these things rarely do, put in mere words — until my negatives, still dripping from the dark-room, came to reinforce them. From them there was no appeal." Or so he thought. According to Alland, the man who resurrected Riis's photography and reputation after the Second World War, the first published account of the use of flash-powder photography was written, anonymously, by Riis, and published in the *New York Sun* on February 12, 1888 under the title "Flashes from the Slums, Pictures taken in dark places by the Lighting Process...." See *Ibid.*, pp. 26–27. The first publication of Riis's photographs — or, more properly, engravings based directly on his flashlit photographs — was an article entitled "How the Other Half Lives," in the December 1889 issue of *Scribner's Magazine*. Riis expanded this article into the book by the same name, which advanced his cause and made him famous. Jacob A. Riis, *How the Other Half Lives: Studies Among the Tenements of New York* (New York: Dover Publications, Inc., 1971), with 100 photographs from the Jacob A. Riis collection, Museum of the City of New York.

31. By the early 1900s, flashlight photography was a bit more regularized and slightly less hazardous than Riis's pioneering frying-pan process. Flash powders then came in three forms: in bottles for use in a flash lamp; in cartridges having fuses and requiring no extra equipment; and in "flash sheets," which were pinned against a cardboard (preferably white for maximum effect) and ignited by a match. Obviously, the process was still an awkward and potentially dangerous one. One 1903 handbook provided suggestions for placing the flashlight and the sitters, to avoid both mishaps and the "staring effect" that so often characterized early flashlit

portraits, and prevent other potential problems, such as a "foggy" effect: "When more than one flashlight [was] to be taken," the manual also advised, "the windows should be opened and time allowed between each flash to free the room thoroughly from smoke...." The chapter ended with a series of warnings, such as "WARNING! WHERE USING A FLASHLIGHT LAMP ALWAYS TURN THE BURNER AWAY FROM THE FLASH PAN WHEN THE LATTER IS BEING FILLED," and "NEVER FILL THE PAN WHEN THE BURNER IS LIGHTED AND TOWARD THE PAN." T. Stith Baldwin, *Picture Making for Pleasure and Profit: A Complete Illustrated Hand-Book on the Modern Practices of Photography in All its Various Branches* (Chicago: Frederick J. Drake & Co., 1903), pp. 105, 108.

32. Oliver, *op. cit.*, p. 9.

33. Oliver, *op. cit.*, p. 21.

34. One of Woolnough's published photographs was "A Reverie," which showed an old lady sitting in a rocking chair, silhouetted by the light of a fire, and recalling the love of her youth — depicted by a young man and a woman in a bubble floating over the mantle. Victorian sentimentality coupled with Victorian ingenuity combined to create this early "special effect." *Massey Magazine*, May 1897. The unpublished version, now at the City of Toronto Archives, was called "A Memory of the Past."

35. Roger Hall et al aptly describe the Toronto of 1868 as "a British bulwark in an American midwest setting." Roger Hall, Gordon Dodds, and Stanley Triggs, *The World of William Notman; The Nineteenth Century Through a Master Lens* (Toronto: McClelland & Stewart, 1993), p. 26.

36. Jesse Edgar Middleton. *The Municipality of Toronto: A History.* (Toronto: The Dominion Publishing Company, 1923), p. 361.

37. J. M. S. Careless. *Toronto to 1918: An Illustrated*

History. (Toronto: James Lorimer & Company, 1984), pp. 200–201. These figures are for ethnic background, not land of birth. In terms of birth, British-born also dominated the immigrant category. In 1881, 35% were British-born (60% were Canadian-born, and 5% were other Foreign-born); and in 1921, 29% were still British-born (62% were Canadian-born, and 9% were other Foreign-born). Such general comparisons obviously mask extremely important trends and differences.

38. It was only in 1952 that Vincent Massey became the first Canadian-born Governor General. By contrast, between the 1880s and 1920s all occupants of Toronto's Government Houses, the state residence of Ontario's Lieutenant-Governors, were *Canadian* — mostly Canadian-born — political and/or financial success stories.

39. Because women photographers were far less likely to open a commercial studio downtown, than to work for someone else or out of their homes, their lives as professional photographers are especially difficult to document. Neither business directories nor assessment records would pick them up. According to Peter Palmquist, "100 Years of California Photography by Women: 1850–1950," women represented about 10% of all photographers working in California during the nineteenth century; and by 1910, the figure had risen to about 20%.

On the other hand, Gary Saretzky reported to the PhotoHistory listserv on April 11, 2001 that only 1 to 2% of his database on 19th century New Jersey photographers were women.

40. For a pioneering view of Canadian women photographers, see Laura Jones, *Rediscovery: Canadian Women Photographers 1841–1941* (London, Ontario: London Regional Art Gallery, 1983). For a study of an almost-lost American photographer, who photographed Canada from Atlantic to Pacific between the 1890s and the 1930s, see Frances Rooney, *Working Light: The Wandering Life of Photographer Edith S. Watson* (Ottawa: Carleton University Press, 1996).

CHAPTER 2
From Homelessness to Opulence

1. Four books provide valuable context for this chapter on domestic life: two deal with the evolution of Canadian homes; one traces the evolution of domestic technology in the United States; and one investigates Victorian domestic life in British semi-detached and terrace housing. For Canadian domestic life, see: Peter Ward, *A History of Domestic Space: Privacy and the Canadian Home* (Vancouver: UBC Press, 1999); and Peter Ennals and Deryck W. Holdsworth, *Homeplace; The Making of the Canadian Dwelling over Three Centuries* (Toronto: University of Toronto Press, 1998). For domestic technology, see Merritt Ierley, *The Comforts of Home: The American House and the Evolution of Modern Convenience* (New York: Clarkson Potter/Publishers, 1999. For the British experience, see Judith Flanders, *The Victorian House: Domestic Life from Childbirth to Deathbed* (London: Harper Perennial, 2003).

2. The examples of shaping domestic, or other places, to reflect personal values, tastes, and experiences are endless. For a general discussion of "sense of place" and of the themes "sense of identity" and "house as reflection of self," see Sarah Duane Satterthwaite Gibson, *Sense of Place — Defense of Place: A Case Study of the Toronto Island* (Toronto: University of Toronto, Department of Geography, unpublished dissertation, 1981).

3. For dating photographs via fashions, see: Alison Gernsheim, *Victorian and Edwardian Fashion: A Photographic Survey* (New York: Dover Publications, Inc., 1963, 1981), *passim*; and Joan Severa, *Dressed for the Photographer: Ordinary Americans and Fashion, 1840–1900* (Kent, Ohio: The Kent State University Press, 1995), especially the chapters on the 1880s and 1890s. Gernsheim investigates British fashion; and Severa looks at U.S. forms of dress.

4. Photographers like William James and F. W. Micklethwaite left good documentation of family life in Toronto during the period covered by this book. Consumers' Gas sold not only gas and service, but also gas appliances, such as stoves and irons and lights, and it documented many of its appliances *in situ* in middle-class houses.

5. Late-twentieth-century Toronto experienced numerous trickle-down effects from the Thatcherite Reaganomics that dominated many Western agendas, notably the Mike Harris government in Ontario. These effects included homelessness not seen on a similar scale since at least the Great Depression of the 1930s.

6. A June 1911 statement by architect Eden Smith indicates that a house erected in Wychwood Park for E. T. Owen cost $6,378.09. City of Toronto Archives, Keith Miller fonds.

7. Police Duty Books for Division One, Series 92. See also Annual Reports of the Chief Constable, for annual and city-wide statistics; and *Aims and Objects of the Toronto Humane Society* (Toronto: Wm. Briggs, 1888) for examples of real-life cases told with characteristic Victorian sentimentality and rectitude.

8. See, for example, the *Scrapbooks* created by the House of Industry, City of Toronto Archives, Series 806.

9. See, for example, William James's photograph of a family sleeping on the streets of Toronto ca. 1910. City of Toronto Archives, Fonds 1244, Item 1033.

10. See, for example, the photograph of a Children's Aid Society child, in Chapter 1. Statistics compiled annually by the Chief Constable indicate that, contrary to our modern usage, the word "waif" included adult men and women. The housing of homeless people at police stations was common in North America. Jacob Riis, for example, provided harrowing views inside wretched police shelters 1890s New York City. But no similar photographs of Toronto shelters seem to exist.

11. A reporter for *The Globe* visited the House of Industry in January 1891 and went to great pains to assure his readers that current beneficiaries were worthy of charity:

> The winter has borne with exceptional severity upon a large section of the citizens of Toronto. It seems incredible, but it is nevertheless true, that there are hundreds of homes around us passively surrendered to destitution, where men, women and children are ignorant whence the next mouthful of bread is to come. They all tell the same story — no work to be had and nothing in the house to fill the mouths of the famishing little ones. This is the unvarying experience of those who visit the dwellings on behalf of the House of Industry [to ensure that the potential recipients of charity were worthy]. It is not alone among the thriftless and improvident that this state of things exists. The prudent, careful man found employment

uncertain and precarious during the summer months. The fall saw his little savings dwindle away, and the winter brought him [and his dependent family] to the verge of starvation. But for the timely assistance that has been rendered [of fuel and food from the "soup kitchen"] it is terrible to contemplate what their fate would have been.

"In Darkest Toronto'. Glimpses of Poverty in the Queen City," in *The Globe*, January 24, 1891.

12. See, for example, "The Tramp's Hotel," *Toronto Mail*, February 16, 1889, "Casual Callers. How They Are Cared For at the House of Industry. Interview With "Guest," *Toronto Mail*, April 20, 1889; "In Darkest Toronto': Glimpses of Poverty in the Queen City," *The Globe*, January 24, 1891; "Professor Goldwin Smith Interview In Regard to the Unemployed," *Daily Mail*, October 16, 1896; "Work of Relief Growing Steadily," *Mail*, April 16, 1913; "House of Industry Had a Big Year," *The Globe*, April 16, 1913. From *House of Industry Scrapbooks*, City of Toronto Archives, Series 806, *passim*.

13. Jacob A. Riis, "How the Other Half Lives; Studies Among the Tenements," *Scribner's Magazine*, vol. 6 (December 1889), pp. 643–662. Interestingly, Riis's article for *Scribner's* was illustrated by drawings based on his photographs, not the photographs themselves. This article led to the publication of his book by the same name.

14. The number of poor seeking assistance from the House of Industry nearly quadrupled between about 1885 and 1890, when nearly 10,000 people were helped. See Susan E. Houston and Susan L. Laskin, "Plate 56: Responses to Poverty, to 1891," especially the graphs dealing with the House of Industry. R. Louis Gentilcore (editor). *Historical*

Atlas of Canada: Land Transformed 1800–1891, vol. 2. (Toronto: University of Toronto Press, 1993).

15. "In Darkest Toronto'," *op. cit.*

16. Dr. Charles Hastings, *Report of the Medical Health Officer Dealing with the Recent Investigation of Slum Conditions in Toronto, Embodying Recommendations for the Amelioration of the Same* (Toronto: Department of Health, July 1911). Obviously, Hastings lacked Riis's (or his publishers') title-making ability. Apart from the traditional bureaucratic title, this was a most unusual report: it was published in pamphlet form, on glossy paper, with photographs. Although photographs had been used before to illustrate city reports (notably reports from the City Engineer), Hastings' prose and photographs were much more emotive.

17. Dennis Duffy, "Furnishing the Pictures: Arthus S. Goss, Michael Ondaatje and the Imag(in)ing of Toronto," in *Journal of Canadian Studies/Revue d'études canadiennes*, vol. 36, no. 2 (summer 2001), pp. 106–129.

18. For a contemporary view of Dr. Hastings, see "Little Sketches of Busy Men," in *Weekly Globe and Canada Farmer*, May 28, 1913. For a rare negative view of the Medical Officer of Health, peruse the crusading Toronto tabloid, *Jack Canuck* (City of Toronto Archives, Fonds 1255). *Jack Canuck's* founder was James Richard Rogers, a London compositor who emigrated with his wife Louisa Sims and their son Frank, to Canada via South Africa. After the devastating death of their only child at the Toronto Isolation Hospital, Rogers campaigned against the treatment his son had received and the public officials responsible for the hospital. After what they considered to be a whitewashing inquiry into the hospital, the Rogers published the first issue of *Jack Canuck*, on July 19, 1911. The death of their son helps explain

their tough assessment of Hastings. I want to thank Professor Susan E. Houston for sharing her biographical article on Louisa Sims (Rogers), who took over publishing the paper when her husband died, when the *Lusitania* was torpedoed in 1915, and continued until 1924 when it went bankrupt and she disappeared. See also "No Word of Rogers," *Toronto Telegram*, May 8, 1915, in A. R. Hassard's Scrapbook, City of Toronto Archives, Fonds 1087, p. 67.

19. In the pre-War period, immigration rebounded after a brief slowdown during the nineties. During the War, when no housing was being built, there was additional pressure as people, seeking to aid the war effort and capture the high wages, migrated to the city to work in munitions plants and other war industries.

20. For counterbalance, see Lillian Petroff, *Sojourners and Settlers: The Macedonian Community in Toronto to 1940* (Toronto: Multicultural History Society of Ontario, 1995), *passim*; and Robert F. Harney, ed., *Gathering Place: Peoples and Neighbourhoods of Toronto, 1834–1945* (Multi-cultural History Society of Ontario, 1985), *passim*.

21. Hastings, 1911, *op. cit.*, p. 8

22. BMR 1913, *op. cit.*, p. 14.

23. Lillian Petroff, *The Macedonian Community in Toronto to 1940* (Toronto: University of Toronto, Department of Educational Theory, unpublished Ph.D. thesis, 1983), *passim*. During her discussion of Macedonian "sojourning" and "settling" in Toronto, Dr. Petroff cites a 1910 church census by SS Cyril and Methody, which provides a more accurate count of the community than either the City Directories or Assessment Rolls, which woefully underestimate immigrant communities.

24. New York Bureau of Municipal Research, "Report on Physical Survey," *Report on Survey of the Treasury, Assessment, Works, Fire and Property Departments*, vol. 2, (1914), p. 10.

25. Hastings defined "tenement houses" as "a house where three or more families live independently," of which he found 92 in the districts investigated. Hastings, 1911, *op. cit.*, p.8.

26. Hastings, 1911, *op. cit.*, p.4.

27. The Ward's notoriety is indicated by the title of the Bureau of Municipal Research's 1918 study of slum housing which it called, *What is "The Ward" Going to Do With Toronto?*

28. The six areas investigated by Hastings were: the Eastern Avenue District (828 houses); the Central or City Hall District, aka The Ward (1,653 houses); the Niagara Street District (731 houses); the Parliament Street area, aka lower Cabbagetown (834 houses); the Bathurst Street area (499 houses); and the Spadina Avenue area (151 houses). The total number of houses inspected was 4,696. A few other, more scattered houses were also included in the survey. Five of the six areas named were located south of Queen Street. The Ward was the only one that poked north, as far as College Street. Hastings, 1911, *op. cit.*, pp.3–4.

29. Among these local strengths was Rivka (Rebecca) Landsberg Fox, wife of tailor Abraham Fox, mother of nine children and grandmother of feminist journalist, Michele Landsberg. Rivka emigrated with her husband and children from Russia, via England, to The Ward in the 1890s. She became one of the founders in 1899 of the Toronto Hebrew Ladies' Aid Society, which was the first formal charitable organization among Toronto's East European Jews. She served as the principal inspector for its investigating committee, which was formed after 1903 to seek out destitute families. Unlike the House of Industry and other Christian charities that gave only to the so-called "deserving poor," the Toronto Hebrew Ladies' Aid Society sought to help any who had fallen on hard times. Rivka's task was to ensure that the poor asked for what they really needed and to arrange for food and fuel to be delivered anonymously. In 1909, she became one of the founders of the Jewish Day Nursery, as well as the Jewish Children's Home, an orphanage on Simcoe Street. By the time of her death in 1917, she was so beloved and respected that her passing was front-page news in the *Daily Hebrew Journal*; and her casket was escorted through the Jewish neighbourhood to McCaul Street Synagogue where it was carried into the sanctuary, an honour reserved in Orthodox practice for great scholars and exceptionally righteous individuals. Stephen A. Speisman, "Fox, Rivka (Rebecca) (Landsberg)," in *Dictionary of Canadian Biography, Vol. XIV 1911–1920* (Toronto: University of Toronto Press, 1998), p. 375.

30. Department of Health, *Monthly Report for December 1919*, p. 9.

31. Karen Palmer, "Putting a face on the past," *The Toronto Star*, March 15, 2000.

32. *Ibid.*

33. Eden Smith knew the local area well, since he had occupied a bay-n-gable house at 34 Salisbury Place in 1890, when he was 29 years old. He is better known for his Arts and Crafts domestic architecture, however, than multiple-unit social housing. See for example, W. Douglas Brown, *Eden Smith: Toronto's Arts and Crafts Architect* (Toronto: W. Douglas Brown, 2003) and Annmarie Adams, "Eden Smith and the Canadian Domestic Revival" in *Urban History Review/Revue d'histoire urbaine*, vol. 21, no. 2 (March 1993), pp. 104–115.

34. The Toronto General Hospital was located on Gerrard Street, east of Parliament Street, for many

35. years before moving to its current location at College and University around 1913.

35. Toronto Housing Company, *First Annual Report, 1913.*

36. *Ibid.*

37. It is perhaps notable that one of James's sons became a butcher, while several of them became professional photographers like their father.

38. *Scribner's* was an immensely successful American general magazine that catered to progressive thinkers interested in both literary entertainment and self-improvement. Jacob Riis and Alfred Steiglitz both published here. Not long before this photograph was taken, the magazine published a long article by Russell Sturgis about "The City House," which looked at (mostly) semi-detached housing in New York City. Although American in origin, *Scribner's* published quite a few Canadian poets and fiction writers, such as Bliss Carman.

39. For a history of this house, see John Lownsbrough, *The Privileged Few: The Grange & Its People in Nineteenth Century Toronto* (Toronto: Art Gallery of Ontario, 1980).

40. For a history of this house, see Austin Thompson Seton, *Spadina: A Story of Old Toronto* (Toronto: Pagurian Press, 1975).

41. When Spadina House became a City of Toronto museum, the gold-and-white wallpaper was returned to the room. Restoration experts had discovered a fragment of the original paper behind the Jacques and Hay mirror over the fireplace.

42. Located at what is now 467–469 Jarvis Street, the Blake residence still stands, much changed, next to another, much changed building: the Red Lion pub.

43. Georg Kohlmaier and Barna von Sartory (trans. John C. Harvey), "The Idea of the Winter Garden" in *Houses of Glass: A Nineteenth-Century Build-*

ing Type (Cambridge, MA: The MIT Press, 19B), pp. 25–42. By 1886, Stone & Wellington of 24–26 Church Street (and Fonthill near Welland, Ontario) was the largest nursery business in Canada. According to their entry in *Industries of Canada* (Toronto M. G. Bixby & Co., 1886), Stone & Wellington was founded in 1868, operated a nursery farm of 450 acres at Fonthill with "extensive glass houses and conservatories," and could supply "all the rich and rare hothouse plants, including choice varieties of tropical plants, exotics and American flowers."

44. According to architectural historian, William Dendy, Fleming's 1858 "crystal palace" had a "frumpishly conservative appearance that nullified the lightness of the glass-and-iron walls." It had much structural iron, relatively little glass, and none of the lovely domes that graced later glass houses in Toronto, notably Allan Gardens, which opened in 1911. Still, its very construction was a landmark in local design and building, foreshadowing both the cast-iron construction of the 1860s and '70s, and high-rise design in the twentieth century. William Dendy, *Lost Toronto* (Toronto: Oxford University Press, 1978), p. 42–43.

45. See Pleasance Crawford, "The Roots of the Toronto Horticultural Society," *Ontario History*, vol. LXXXIX, No. 2 (June 1997), pp. 125–139. The THS was founded in 1834, drew members from across the social spectrum, created Horticultural Gardens, and built two horticultural pavilions on the site that later became Allan Gardens.

46. William Dendy & William Kilbourn, *Toronto Observed: Its Architecture, Patrons, and History* (Toronto: Oxford University Press, 1986), p. 173.

47. *Ibid.*

48. By the 1920s, Hahn's elaborate interior decoration of the Legislative Chamber had been painted over

and was more-or-less forgotten until recently.

49. In 1969, Walker's *Long Garth* was demolished in order to provide a parking lot for the Robarts Library, which angered architectural historian, William Dendy, who commented, "This demolition — sponsored, as it was, by the university — was more than an act of vandalism. It must be considered a classic example of the philistinism that Walker had hoped to eradicate by supporting and encouraging that same university and its sister institutions." Dendy, *Lost Toronto, op. cit.*, p. 171. Fortunately, the University of Toronto Law School later adopted a more enlightened position and preserved Hahn's work in the great hall at Flavelle's *Holwood*. Meanwhile, another Hahn work, at Chester Massey's house, was fighting for its life at the turn-of-the-millenium when the Ontario Government put the house up for sale.

50. See *The Canadian Who's Who, op. cit.*, p. 80; and Dendy and Kilbourn, *op. cit.*, pp. 172–174; and the muckraking, municipal reform paper, *Jack Canuck*, during the War years.

51. Lennox was the architect of many grand Toronto projects, including City Hall, St. Paul's Anglican Church, the King Edward Hotel, and the west wing of the Provincial Parliament. Lennox designed his own mansion, *Lenwil*, just west of Casa Loma at 5 Austin Terrace. Unlike Pellatt, who lost his fortune and had to move, Lennox lived out his life in his new home.

52. Pellatt never did complete his dream house. He started the project by buying up twenty-five lots on the Davenport escarpment, east of Walmer Road, between 1903 and 1905. After a "summer residence" was established at Pellatt Lodge (which still stands just northwest of the castle), monumental stables were built at a cost of about $250,000, and after both formal and market gardens had

been laid out, work on the main residence proceeded apace. Lennox's plans are dated 1909 and 1910, and work on the mansion started even before the final plans were completed. In 1913, the Pellatts moved in, while construction was still underway. At the time Pellatt lost his money (1923) and his house (1924), the Great Hall and billiard room had not received their panelling, and neither guest nor staff rooms were finished as Lennox had intended. Pellatt is said to have spent $3.5 building the estate and another $1.5 million on furnishings. The 1924 auction of interior furnishings raised only $131,600, suggesting that many Torontonians nabbed bargains that week in June. See Dendy and Kilbourn, Litvak, and Duffy, *op. cit.*

53. The Casa Loma conservatory in full bloom was a fitting tribute to Sir Henry's apparently genuine love of horticulture. He hired a professional gardener, Thomas McVittie, to oversee his estate gardens, and was the honorary president of the Toronto Horticultural Society in 1912. Created in 1834, the Society brought together professional horticulturalists (including gardeners and nurserymen), and enthusiastic amateurs: these included owners of substantial estates, like Pellatt and his neighbours in the Annex, as well as occupants of more modest, semi-detached houses on narrow lots. Pleasance Crawford, "The Roots of the Toronto Horticultural Society," in *Ontario History*, vol. LXXXIX, no. 2 (June 1997), pp. 125–139.

54. This image, like most from the period, was captured on a glass-plate negative, not celluloid film.

55. See "Toronto Plutocrats'," in Gunter Gad and Deryck W. Holdsworth, "The Emergence of Corporate Toronto," in Donald Kerr and Deryck W. Holdsworth (eds.). *Historical Atlas of Canada: Addressing the Twentieth Century* (Toronto: University of Toronto Press, 1990), Plate 15. See also Dennis Duffy's discussion of Pellatt's ignominious rise and fall in "Money to Burn: Chapter Four of Reservoir Ravine," unpublished manuscript.

56. In New York City, Pellatt won the 1879 American championship for the mile in 4 minutes 42.8 seconds. See Duffy, *op. cit.*, p. 4.

57. Marilyn M. Litvak, *Edward James Lennox: "Builder of Toronto"* (Toronto: Dundurn Press, 1995), p. 58.

58. Duffy, *op. cit.*, p. 3. In his article, Duffy quickly and acidly summarizes Pellatt's shady financial career. Particularly odious was Pellatt's having persuaded some of his servants to invest, and lose, their life savings in one of his stock schemes.

59. Dendy and Kilbourn, *op. cit.*, p. 182.

CHAPTER 3
Rooms for Comment

1. As with Chapter Two, four books provide valuable context for domestic life. Two dealing with the evolution of Canadian homes, one with the evolution of domestic technology in the United States, and one with Victorian domestic life in British semi-detached and terrace housing. For Canadian domestic life, see: Peter Ward, *A History of Domestic Space: Privacy and the Canadian Home* (Vancouver: UBC Press, 1999); and Peter Ennals and Deryck W. Holdsworth, *Homeplace; The Making of the Canadian Dwelling over Three Centuries* (Toronto: University of Toronto Press, 1998). For domestic technology, see Merritt Ierley, *The Comforts of Home: The American House and the Evolution of Modern Convenience* (New York: Clarkson Potter/Publishers, 1999). For the British experience, see Judith Flanders, *The Victorian House: Domestic Life from Childbirth to Deathbed* (London: Harper Perennial, 2003).

2. According to an unidentified newspaper article, the first house in Toronto for which the architect's plans included a "built-in convenience," was contractor Richard West's 1876 white-brick residence on Adelaide Street. According to the anonymous reporter (ca. 1930), "Half a century ago, 299 Adelaide west was one of the finest residences in Toronto and on account of its [indoor] bathroom it was acknowledged to be the most modern.... It is a matter of record that nearly every day, for months after the house was completed, architects, builders and prospective home-owners, visited it — 'singly and in groups' — to see its built-in bathroom and to plan to have one like it." City of Toronto Archives, Fonds 70, Larry Becker fonds.

3. See the plans for Riverdale Courts, City of Toronto Archives, Fonds 1018, Toronto Housing Company fonds.

4. Great care must be taken when examining period photographs. Sometimes, titles of photographs have been assigned, not by the original photographers or contemporary sources, but only after the fact by archivists, historians, or descendants of the originators, who may have applied modern terms to older and should confirm that the title was given by a contemporary source. Otherwise, non-photographic, corroborating evidence (such as a floor plan or a diary reference) is required.

5. See E. J. Lennox's 1909 First Floor Plan for Sir Henry Pellatt's "Mansion on Wells' Hill." City of

Toronto Archives, PT 13-00632 M-12; and William James's lantern slide, Fonds 1244, Item 22.6.

6. "When our tour was almost over and we were pausing in the corridor before a handsome carved oval frame that was still waiting for a painting, he said, 'I wish I had another million dollars. What do you think I would do with it?' There was hardly time for me to answer before he went on, 'I'd finish this house — and then I'd die happy.'" Lady Eaton, *Memory's Wall* (Toronto: Clarke Irwin & Company Limited, 1956), p. 109.

7. This chapter focuses on traditional domestic spaces, not institutional arrangements or more utopian, feminist, or communal arrangements.

8. See Ierley, *op. cit.*, for a comprehensive discussion of the evolution of domestic technology in the kitchen, and elsewhere in the house; also Peter Ward , *op. cit.* for a discussion of the arrangement and social implications of the kitchen. Sources like the Eaton's catalogue and contemporary publications with ads provide a wealth of information about the history of domestic technology in Toronto and Canada. The 1901 Eaton's catalogue, for example, offers only coal and wood fired cooking stoves, no toilets, and a good variety of oil, gas, and electric lamps. *The 1901 Editions of the T. Eaton Co. Limited Catalogues for Spring & Summer, Fall & Winter* (Toronto: Stoddart, 1970). The Eaton's catalogue, of course, was sent across the country, so its contents reflect nationwide tastes and technologies, not only those of urban Toronto.

9. The sink was a relative latecomer to kitchens. Despite the fact that running water was available relatively early in many areas (from wells and city water systems), bringing it into the kitchen to clean foods and wash up dirty dishes was delayed. For many years, people continued to use buckets to transport fresh water into the kitchen and tubs to wash dishes in. See Ierley, *op. cit.*, pp. 165–167.

10. Beginning in the 1850s, tin cookware began to replace copper and cast-iron pots. Tin was lighter and easier to use, but also more expensive and less durable. Ierley, *op. cit.*, p. 165.

11. Katherine M. Caldwell, B. A. "What Constitutes the Model Kitchen," in *Everywoman's World (June 1919)*, p. 13.

12. The naming of this room is more problematic than most other rooms. The following are all terms that have been applied to an area generally reserved for sitting and a variety of other, ancillary uses (like entertaining and personal display): sitting room, living room, salon, lounge, parlour, drawing-room. Drawing-rooms tend to be reserved for the rich, or the pretentious. Otherwise, the terms vary across time, class, and location. With respect to national differences, Ierley, *op. cit.*, indicates that turn-of-the-century Americans used the term "parlour" in much the way that Canadians have. Americans have long since abandoned the term in favour of living room or other designations, whereas some Canadians still use the term. See Ward, *op. cit.*, pp. 60–71. For an intriguing discussion of urban — rural differences in the American context, see Sally McMurry, "City Parlor, Country Sitting Room: Rural Vernacular Design and the American Parlor 1840–1900," in *Winterthur Portfolio*, vol. 20, no. 4 (Winter 1985), pp. 261–280.

13. For example, E. J. Lennox's 1905 "Workmen's Cottages" for builders of Casa Loma had a "parlour" in the front of each of the semi-detached houses.

14. Karen Palmer, "Putting a face on the past: Toronto man learns about his humble beginnings through a photo," *Toronto Star*, March 15, 2000, p. B2.

15. Helen Ball, "Tea in the Parlor on Mother's day at home," in *The Villager*, January 1978. City of Toronto Archives: *Helen Ball Scrapbooks* (on microfilm), Fonds 1228. Modern students of "material culture," such as Sally McMurry, have reinforced the idea that "Children especially were unwelcome in the parlor." Sally McMurry, *op. cit.*, p. 267.

16. Helen Ball, *op.cit.*

17. Wayne Kelly, *Downright Upright: A History of the Canadian Piano Industry* (Toronto: Natural Heritage/Natural History Inc., 1991). The 1885 City Directory for Toronto lists five piano manufacturers and fifteen dealers. Heintzman at 86 York Street was the largest.

18. Mary Lou Fallis, *Primadonna on a Moose*. CD. (Burlington, Ont.: Opening Day Recordings, 1997).

19. Flora McCrea Eaton, *Memory's Wall* (Toronto: Clarke, Irwin & Company Limited, 1956), p.105.

20. The first Massey mansion on Jarvis street was located immediately to the south at what later became The Keg restaurant. Chester's father, Hart Massey, bought the old McMaster residence, rechristened Euclid Hall, when he moved the great Massey-Harris Works from Newcastle to Toronto in 1879. Hart also purchased the adjoining property to build a suitable house for his oldest son and business heir, Charles. Massey architect, E. J. Lennox, who had just designed the company's Head Office on King Street West, both renovated Euclid Hall, and built the house at 519 for Charles. When Charles died unexpectedly in 1884, the Chester Massey moved in.

21. "The old man seemed quite proud," Raymond wrote in his memoirs. His older — and perhaps more snobbish — brother Vincent immediately asked, "What name are you going to use?" Raymond Massey, *When I was Young* (Toronto: McClelland and Stewart, 1976), pp. 268–269.

22. Margaret Visser, *Much Depends on Dinner* (Toronto: McClelland & Stewart, 1986).

23. Toronto Housing Company, *Cottage Flats At Riverdale Courts*, spring 1915, *passim*.

24. Lillian I. Morrow, *Memories* (City of Toronto Archives: SC 467). Ms Morrow was born in 1889 and left written memories that include evocative accounts of growing up in the west end of Toronto, where she sledded on biscuit-tin covers at Trinity-Bellwoods Park, attended the school where Alexander "The Maple Leaf Forever" Muir was principal, and ventured abroad on open streetcars. Her father was notable both for delivering well-known journalist Greg Clarke into this world and for inspiring the creation of Toronto Western Hospital, although he died just before it was founded. Late in her life, Ms Morrow recalled, but clearly did not endorse, the servant's ancient attitudes and use of the racist epithet.

25. Douglas Bell, "Crib Notes," *Toronto Life*, November 2005, p. 27

26. Patricia McHugh, *Toronto Architecture: A City Guide*, 2nd ed. (Toronto: McClelland & Stewart, 1985), p. 237.

27. Ierley, *op. cit.*, p. 132. For a history of Canadian domestic lighting, see Loris S. Russell, *A Heritage of Light: Lamps and Lighting in the Early Canadian Home* (Toronto: University of Toronto Press, 1968, reprinted with a new foreword, 2003).

28. For a discussion of electricity in Toronto, see Robert M. Stamp, *Bright Lights, Big City: The History of Electricity in Toronto* (Toronto: catalogue published in conjunction with "Bright Lights, Big City: The History of Electricity in Toronto," an exhibition at The Market Gallery of the City of Toronto Archives, 1991). For a discussion of the evolution of various services and public utilities in Toronto, including gas and electricity, see Bill McCourt (Works Department), *Outline of History of Roads in Toronto* (City of Toronto Archives: Papers &

29. Or front drawing room, although two drawing rooms was less common than two parlours in affluent Toronto homes.

30. Shortly before the war, gas and electric companies were battling for the middle-class consumer dollar. James Austin's Consumers' Gas Company began publishing *Gas News* in 1908 and Henry Pellatt's Toronto Electric Light Company started publishing *Electric Service Magazine* in 1910. Both were thinly disguised promotions for their respective technologies. And both contain information of great interest to modern material culturalists.

31. Stamp, *op. cit.*, p. 17. According to Stamp, Pellatt was the "real driving force" behind the Toronto Electric Light Company formed in 1883, and later lighting ventures that expanded his, and his partners' electrical empire in what was popularly known as "The Syndicate."'

32. According to Stamp, Pellatt "captured the headlines [in 1910] by outfitting his new mansion, 'Casa Loma,' with an estimated 4,000 to 5,000 electric lights." *Ibid.*, p. 39 and footnote 81.

33. According to Ierley, the popular student lamp was first devised in 1863. By placing the oil reserve to the side, the lamp avoided casting a shadow over the work area, which had been a common failing of other lamps. Ierley, *op. cit.*, p. 137.

34. Toronto Housing Company, *Cottage Flats At Riverdale Courts* (Toronto: The Toronto Housing Company, spring 1915).

35. Stamp, *op. cit.*, p. 38. This appears to have occurred in the mid- to late-1880s.

36. According to his entry in *The Canadian Who's Who* (Toronto: The Musson Book Company, 1910), pp. 150–151, Mason was born in England in 1827, had emigrated to Canada in 1842, and founded and managed for 50 years Canada Permanent Loan

Theses Collection, Box 10, File 4, ca. 1975).

and Savings Co., which became Canada Permanent Mortgage Company. He retreated to Chief's Island, Lake Joseph, Muskoka in the summer and at *Armeleigh* (sic) in winter.

37. Loris Russell, *op cit.*, pp. 296–298.

38. The transition occurred in the 1930s, although the family maintained gas lighting in many parts of the house, including the Drawing-Room, which can still be seen since it is now a city-owned and operated historical site.

39. Lillian I. (Rea) Marrow wrote in her memoirs, "We had a servant (maid nowadays) & a coachman, sometimes he was white & other times mostly colored. He always lived in the upstairs of the red brick stable at the end of the lot. The servant slept in the third floor & strongly objected to a 'nigger' living on the same floor so he had to sleep in the stable...." City of Toronto Archives, Fonds 1467. At a more exalted level of society, Raymond Massey recalled with great affection and occasional admiration the coachmen, cooks, and other servants who looked after the two Massey households at 515 and 519 Jarvis Street in the late-nineteenth and early-twentieth centuries. Although he includes a formal photograph of a maid and an exterior photograph of the coachman with coach, he includes no images of the servants' domestic lives. Raymond Massey, *When I Was Young* (Toronto: McClelland and Stewart, 1976).

40. Ierley, *op. cit.*, p. 220.

41. According to Ierley, the term "water closet" was used not only Britain, where it is still common, but also in the US, where it was used for many years before being replaced by the term toilet. Being between Britain and the US, Canada probably used the term water closet longer, and can still be bilingual where this modern convenience is concerned. Ierley, *op. cit., passim*.

42. Ward, *op. cit.*, pp. 51–52.
43. Catherine Brace, "Public Works in the Canadian City: the Provision of Sewers in Toronto 1870–1913." *Urban History Review/Revue d'histoire urbaine*, vol. 23, no. 2 (March 1995), 33–43; and Bill McCourt, *op. cit.*, *passim*.

44. Catherine Brace, Figure 5, "Extent of Sewers of all types and all sizes in Toronto 1880–1889," *op. cit.*, p. 39.
45. Ward, *op. cit.*, p. 53.
46. New York Bureau of Municipal Research, "Property Department," *Report on Survey of the Treasury, Assessment, Works, Fire and Property Departments*, part 2 of 2, 1913, p. 18 (CITY OF TORONTO ARCHIVES). See also Assessment Rolls for the property.

CHAPTER 4
From Factory Floor to Corner Office

1. "Migration" refers to movement of people within Canada, especially, during this period, from the agricultural hinterland into the city. "Immigration" is the movement of people from outside the country into Canada, which increasingly included non-English-speaking immigrants. "Annexation" means the political annexation by the City of Toronto of surrounding suburbs such as Yorkville (1883), Riverdale (1884), The Annex (1887), Parkdale (1889), Rosedale (1905), West Toronto (1909), and North Toronto (1912). When looking at population or other statistics, it's important to bear in mind the geographical changes in the boundaries of "Toronto."

2. More precisely, the Toronto workforce was 31,764 in 1881, 169,663 in 1911, 223,399 in 1921, and 280,383 in 1931. For 1881, see Carolyn Strange, *Toronto's Girl Problem: The Perils and Pleasures of the City, 1880–1930* (Toronto: University of Toronto Press, 1995), p. 218. For 1911, see Michael J. Piva, *The Condition of the Working Class in Toronto — 1900–1921* (Ottawa: University of Ottawa Press, 1979), p. 15. For 1921 and 1931, see James Lemon, *Toronto Since 1918: An Illustrated History* (Toronto: James Lorimer & Company, 1985), p.197. Perhaps surprisingly, more single women than single men lived in Toronto

through this period, with 1901, not post-War 1921, showing the greatest differential: nearly 121 single women for every 100 single men in 1901; nearly 113 in 1921. Strange, *op. cit.*, p. 217.

3. Conservative premier, James P. Whitney, brought in the first Workmen's Compensation legislation in 1914. See Piva, *op. cit.*, p. 107.

4. Percentages varied across occupations and over time. In 1921, Toronto women in manufacturing and services made 55.2% of what their male co-workers made. At that time, the average female wage in these sectors was $14.23, while the average male wage was $26.60. On average, women worked slightly more weeks per year than men: 46.9 compared with 45.4. "Table A.7, Female and Male Earnings in Toronto, 1921" in Strange, *op. cit.*, p. 221. Statistics also vary for base wages. In 1914, many female factory workers, salesgirls, and telephone operators, made around $6.00 per week, according to the *Report of Social Survey Commission of Toronto*, September 29, 1915, p. 35. (City of Toronto Archives, Reports Collection, Box 4, Folder 2.)

5. Piva devotes his book to analyzing how well, or badly, male blue-collar workers did during this period, concluding, "In all of the industries discussed earnings were well below the poverty line. Even though [Piva's] estimates of actual earnings are probably somewhat high, in no industry were

wages enough to cover the cost of the Department of Labour's [family] budget. Indeed, wages were well below this level of family expenditure." (Piva, *op. cit.*, pp. 54–55.) Among other things, this helps explain why women had to work, not for pin money, but for the survival of their families. When they did enter the workforce, which they were doing in ever-greater numbers, female workers were cruelly exploited, faring considerably worse than their working-class brothers. According to Piva, female blue-collar workers, averaged only $12.30 per week and $577.95 per annum in 1921, compared with the $1,053.32 earned by male blue-collar workers. Piva, *op. cit.*, pp. 31, 40.

The failure of the poor and the near-poor to share in boom-time prosperity is eerily familiar to the modern reader. Report after report in the 1990s and early 2000s documented the fact that already low-income people were actually losing ground during the Good Times, even — or especially — in Ontario. In November 2000, for example, 1.3 more Canadian children were living in poverty than in 1989 when the Canadian Parliament resolved to eliminate child poverty. Even more disturbing, according to one social activist, was "the rise in the number of children who [were] living in families who [were] working full-time for the full year and [were] still poor." As for the whole family, a United Way report in 1999 concluded that "despite the improving economy, low-income households had lost ground in the 1990s." Jim Coyle, "Sell this, Mel: The fight to end child poverty," *Toronto Star*, November 21, 2000.

6. "Unemployment" is a relatively modern concept, being recognized as a condition, or a problem, only when urban industrialism and the waged economy superseded the pre-industrial, agrarian economy. See Piva, *op. cit.*, and Peter Baskerville and Eric W. Sager, *Unwilling Idlers: The Urban Unemploye and Their Families in Late Victorian Canada* (Toronto: University of Toronto Press, 1998), pp. 3–40.

7. In 1921, male blue-collar workers averaged 43.8 weeks of work, annually. Construction workers, who were particularly vulnerable to seasonal and cyclical slowdowns, averaged 40.9 weeks, whereas transportation workers (such as those employed by the steam and the street railways) averaged 46.8 weeks. By contrast, male white-collar workers averaged $32.11 per week, worked an average of 50.0 weeks per year, and averaged $1,605.33. Piva, "Table 8. — Average Earnings of Toronto's Blue-collar Workers by Industry, 1921," *op. cit.*, p. 30.

8. According to Piva, "Not only did [male] labourers employed by the federal, provincial and municipal governments enjoy high weekly earnings [$24.84 in 1921], they also enjoyed comparatively secure employment [45.5 weeks per year in 1921]. The combination of these two factors meant that labourers working in the public sector had very high annual incomes [$1,130.12]." This "very high annual income" is only relative to non-government labourers, not to what was necessary for a family to live on. Piva, *op. cit.*, p. 33.

9. For an excellent discussion of the urban-immigrant experience in Toronto, see Robert F. Harney and Harold Troper, *Immigrants: A Portrait of the Urban Experience, 1890–1930* (Toronto: Van Nostrand Reinhold Ltd., 1975), *passim*.

10. *Ibid.*

11. Some acted as labour agents to help their comrades, not to earn money. According to historian Lillian Petroff, many Macedonians obtained jobs at the Kemp Manufacturing Company at Gerrard and River Streets through the efforts of two company employees, Lazo Evanoff and Staso Filkoff. "Among the earliest of Macedonian employees, Evanoff and Filkoff carefully learned the manpower needs of the various factory departments and then directed countrymen to the various employment opportunities. It is not clear whether these men profited in more than reputation and status for playing this role." Lillian Petroff, *The Macedonian Community in Toronto to 1940* (Toronto: unpublished dissertation, 1983), p. 137.

12. After an inquiry by Judge Winchester, the old City Engineer's Department was restructured, with the result that R. C. Harris became Commissioner.

13. City Works Department, Sewer Section, *Annual Report for 1912* (City of Toronto Archives: Reports Collection, Box 141), p. 9

14. Harney and Troper, *op. cit.*, p. 53.

15. Rev. Albert Shaw, "an expert in municipal matters," pronounced Toronto and New York "the two cleanest cities in America." Some might consider this a case of being damned by faint praise, but the Board of Trade was duly impressed. George W. Engelhardt. *Toronto Canada: The Book of Its Board of Trade. For General Circulation Through the Business Community. 1897–98* (City of Toronto Archives: Rare Books Collection), p. 44. The City's well-earned reputation for cleanliness took a severe beating, however, in the early years following enforced amalgamation in 1998.

16. *Ibid.*

17. Elizabeth Cuthbertson, *Toronto Above and Below: Public Works in Toronto 1910–1953* (Toronto: The Market Gallery of the City of Toronto Archives, 1997), [page 2].

18. Among the few City personnel records to survive are those of the City Works Department, from about 1912 on. These reveal that most permanent, and even temporary, employees were male, protestant, and of English background.

19. The history of the Toronto Fire Department may be found in: John Ross Robertson, *Landmarks of Toronto* (Toronto: John Ross Robertson, 1896), vol. 2, pp. 563–611; *History of the Toronto Fire Department* (Toronto, 1923); *History of the Toronto Fire Department* (Toronto, 1984); *History of the Toronto Fire Services, 1874–2002* (Toronto: Toronto Fire Services, 2002), pp. 113–158..

20. The Toronto Fire Department bought its first motor vehicle in 1911. In 1915 there were still 108 horses. *History of the Toronto Fire Department*, 1923, *op.cit.*, p. 81, and *History of the Toronto Fire Services, op. cit.*, p. 142.

21. "Report of His Honor Judge Denton re Fire Department Investigation," in *City of Toronto Council Minutes and Reports, Appendix C*, pp. 50–71.

22. According to Census figures, Toronto's population grew about 6.7-fold, from 86,415 in 1881 to 521,893 in 1921; and according to less-accurate, but more frequent Assessment figures, Toronto's population grew about 7-fold, from 77,034 in 1880 to 549,429 in 1925. Geographically, Toronto grew 3.7-fold by annexations, from 5,565.9 acres in 1881 to 20,678.4 acres in 1925. Meanwhile, resources consumed by the police force grew 21-*fold*, from about $91,000 in 1880, to about $1.9 million in 1925.

23. According to a list of the Force in the Chief Constable's Annual Report for 1881, the force of 134

contained 75 Irishmen; 35 Canadians; 14 Englishmen; and 10 Scots. Other listings indicate that force members were almost completely Protestant ... and all early Irish members were Protestant, several having served with the (in)famous Royal Irish Constabulary.

24. By 1913, for example, although the leadership remained dominantly Irish-born (11 of the 17 top officers — Inspector or above — were Irish, including one Roman Catholic), 236 or 38% of the 626 total were Canadian-born, 62 or 10% were Catholic (an overlapping group), and a handful were actually non-British (e.g., a couple of Italians, Germans, and Americans). By 1925 just over 40% of the 873 members were listed as Canadian, many of whom had served in World War I; 22% were English; 21% were Irish; and, again, only a handful were non-British. See the listings in the *Chief Constable's Annual Reports* for 1913 and 1925. There is no way to determine from these figures how many of the Canadian-born members were of Irish descent.

25. During this period, the Criminal Registers for the Police Court (listings of the people who appeared before the Police Magistrates) included an impressive range of nationalities — not only large numbers of Canadians, Irish Catholics, and other British folk, but also Italians, Greeks, Russians, Austrians, Chinese, Jews, "coloured," and so on. In 1925, the force, by contrast, was still 100% English-speaking, 99% British-Canadian, and 90% Protestant.

26. *Chief Constable's Annual Report for 1880*, p. 44.

27. City of Toronto Police Force, Duty Book, Division 1, Wednesday, October 16, 1889. City of Toronto Archives, Series 92, File 24.

28. Pursley, *op. cit.*, p. 144.

29. Magnus Sinclair, "It Was a Long and Bitter Fight..." reprinted in *100th Anniversary: ATU Local 113,*

1899–1999 (Toronto: ATU Local 113), pp. 18–19.

30. Thomas Schlereth discusses the growing influence exercised by engineers, like Frederick Winslow Taylor, over not only the design of industrial processes, but also the rapidly expanding, white-collar world of "management." Thomas J. Schlereth, *Victorian America: Transformation in Everyday Life* (New York: Harper Collins, 1991), pp. 62–65.

31. This John Boyd was the first staff photographer hired by the *Globe* in 1922. His father, also John Boyd, was a railway man and freelance photographer who sold many of his photographs to newspapers and magazines in Canada and the United States.

32. See Piva, *op. cit.*, pp. 46–50 for a detailed analysis of how construction workers fared between 1900 and 1921.

33. Piva emphasizes that not all skilled labourers were paid similar wages, and that not all construction workers were skilled. Stonecutters and bricklayers, for example, were paid significantly more than painters and electrical workers, and both skilled groups were paid significantly more than casual construction labourers. See especially "Table 16. — Real Annual Earnings Index for Seven Groups of Building Trades Workers, 1901–1920," p. 48.

34. Piva, *op. cit.*, pp. 33 and 38. Their annual earnings, therefore, were about $1095.04, at a time when a family of five needed to make $31.83 per week or $1,655.29 per year just to "rise above the poverty line."

35. Architectural historian, Patricia McHugh, described the Great Hall as "the finest room in Canada." Patricia McHugh, *Toronto Architecture: A City Guide* (Toronto: McClelland & Stewart, 1985), pp. 103–104. Meanwhile, William Dendy & William Kilbourn, state flatly, "In grandeur and space it is without peer in Canada." Dendy and

Kilbourn *op.cit.*, p. 213. And, at the time of its creation, the building's Toronto-based architect, John Lyle, challenged anyone "to name me a finer station room than the ticket lobby in the new Union Station, with the possible exception of the Great Room in the Pennsylvania Station, New York." Quoted by Douglas Richardson, "'A Blessed Sense of Civic Excess' The Architecture of Union Station," in Richard Bébout (ed.), *The Open Gate: Toronto Union Station* (Toronto: Peter Martin Associates Limited, 1972), p. 94. Since New York City's great room was demolished in the 1960s, Lyle's comment suggests that his "ticket lobby" is now the greatest railway room still standing in North America.

36. Richardson, *op. cit.*, p. 85.

37. In 1999, Toronto became the first city in North America to throw the doors of public and private buildings open to public inspection. By 2005, the phenomenally successful event included about 140 buildings of all types, attracted over 160,000 visitors, and generally raised public awareness of Toronto's built heritage from the early-nineteeth century through the late-twentieth century.

38. For a cartographic summary, see Gunter Gad and Deryck W. Holdsworth, "The Emergence of Corporate Toronto," in Donald Kerr and Deryck W. Holdsworth (ed.), *Historical Atlas of Canada: Addressing the Twentieth Century* (Toronto: University of Toronto Press, 1990), Plate 15.

39. Piva, *op. cit.*, pp. 17–18. According to Piva, 50.6% of all blue-collar workers in 1911 were employed in manufacturing industries, while the six largest industries employed 63.2% of all workers employed in manufacturing. Of the biggest industries, the clothing industry employed 11,828 workers, more than twice as many as the second largest industry, iron and steel.

40. Schlereth, *Victorian America, op. cit.*, p. 65.

41. Quoted in Greg Kealey (ed.), *Canada Investigates Industrialism* (Toronto: University of Toronto Press, 1973), p. 41. "Female and child labor, long hours, horrible working conditions, and low wages were," according to Kealey on p. xxi, "additional companions of Canadian industrialization," all of which were amply illustrated by the 1800 witness who testified before the Commission, including many proud capitalists like J. D. King and Timothy Eaton of Toronto.

42. Greg Kealey, *ibid.*, pp. 94–95.

43. Factory inspector James R. Brown, quoted in Piva, *op. cit.*, p. 89–90.

44. Advertisement in *Industries of Canada: Historical and Commercial Sketches of Toronto and environs* (Toronto: M. G. Bixby & Co., 1886), p. 94.

45. See "Safes Found in Ruins of 1904 fire" photographed outside the J & J. Taylor Safe Works on Front Street. City of Toronto Archives: Fonds 1268, Item 1808.

46. Margaret Laycock and Barbara Myrvold, *Parkdale in Pictures: Its Development to 1889.* (Toronto: Toronto Public Library Board, 1991), p. 53.

47. The creation of this dual purpose, steelmaking and shell-forging plant was an astonishing feat. Less than six months after breaking ground on January 31, 1917, the first "heat" of molten steel was "tipped" into shell mouldings on June 18th. Before the end of the war, the ten massive furnaces turned out 48,000 tons of steel, which created over 3,000,000 six- and nine-inch shell forgings.

48. Petroff, *op. cit.*, pp. 43–44.

49. *Ibid.*, p. 30–31. According to Petroff, such positions were a pragmatic solution to the presence of young boys in the immigrant community, and were "designed to minimise injury, escape possible suspicion and charges of the abuse of child labour laws, familiarise and set the stage for the young men to move into regular positions when the opportunities arose." For example, a future master butcher, foreman and union steward, Anastas Petroff, entered the world of the slaughterhouse as a Harris "battoir water boy." Harris Abattoir was located at 35 Jarvis Street.

50. Entry for Wm. Davies & Co. in *Industries of Canada, op. cit.*, p. 86.

51. "By far the most important industry in terms of employment in Toronto was the clothing industry. With 13,828 workers in 1911, it employed nearly twice as many workers as its nearest rival, iron and steel. Nevertheless, clothing declined in importance during the first decades of the century. According to the 1901 census of manufacturers, 35.4 per cent of all workers employed in manufacturing were listed as clothing workers. This compares to only 24.3 per cent in the census of occupations for 1911. By 1921, the proportion of workers in the clothing industry had declined to 18.3 per cent of the workforce in manufacturing." Piva, *op. cit.*, p. 18.

52. In 1911, for example, over 8,000, or 58.6 % of the 14,000 garment workers were women. Piva, *op. cit.*, p. 18.

53. Quoted by Piva, *op. cit.*, p. 95. The reporter was probably future Prime Minister and one-time labour sympathizer, William Lyon Mackenzie King. Not surprisingly, Joseph Atkinson's crusading new Liberal paper took up the cause of sweated labour right from the beginning. See "A Terrible Tale of Toil," *The Evening Star*, January 2, 1894, p. 1.

54. According to a promotional entry in a "special number" of *The Dominion Illustrated*, J. D. King & Co. was an innovative manufacturer of "Fine Boots and Shoes" at 122–124 Wellington Street West. Known for "style, quality of material and workmanship," (but not necessarily humane treatment of their high-quality workers), J. D. King was, apparently, among the first shoe manufacturers to recognize that "there is a great variety of feet; that one width will not fit all," and to create a range of shoe sizes. *The Dominion Illustrated*, 1892, p. 85.

55. Quoted in Greg Kealey, *op. cit.*, pp. 109–110. Since the average wage of all workers was five dollars, according to Winlow, and there were more men, who made more money than the women, the average female wage was undoubtedly lower than $5.00. Just how much lower is impossible to tell, especially since Mr. Winlow might have exaggerated the average. He was, however, careful to emphasize that very few workers made $15.00. He did not cite a wage for the dozen boys who also worked at the factory, but he did note that there was "no chance" for these lads to learn to become shoemakers. They might learn individual steps, but not the whole shoe. The process of de-skilling was well underway here, as elsewhere across the labour landscape.

56. Linda Kealey, *Enlisting Women for the Cause: Women, Labour, And the Left in Canada, 1890–1920* (Toronto: University of Toronto Press, 1998), pp. 52–53.

57. A picture of J. D. King's mansion at 428 Jarvis Street was also published in *Board of Trade 1897, op. cit.*, p. 31.

58. Despite prohibitions against home industry, many individuals and small contractors did piecework in The Ward, under dreadful physical and work conditions. "Two of our inspectors were born in St. John's Ward and have known it from their youth up to the present," Dr. Charles Hastings reported in his 1911 report on slum conditions. "One house there has been under observation for *forty* years. Forty years ago the basement used to

be flooded occasionally from the street sewer when it backed up. Damp and unsanitary forty years ago, it is damp and unsanitary still .... One of the worst features about the house is that one room has two sewing machines in it and tailoring is done there ...." A few pages later, he commented disapprovingly, "In several places two or three sewing machines were being used in the manufacture of men's clothing. Some of these were in unsanitary places. In one house, as many as eight of these sewing machines were concealed." *Report of the Medical Health Officer dealing with the Recent Investigation of Slum Conditions in Toronto* (Toronto: Department of Health, July 5, 1911), pp. 8–9, 11.

59. Around the same time, William James photographed 61–65 Terauley Street by moonlight, with the Eaton factory in the background. The workers' cottages were so dilapidated that they had been condemned and ordered destroyed by the City, and photographed — in daylight — during the strike by City Photographer Arthur Goss. City Assessment Rolls indicate that the slum landlord was none other than the T. Eaton Company, which ignored the City's order and continued renting the shameful dwellings to needy tenants like the Cohen and the Liebowitz families. Eaton's owned other rental properties in The Ward, as well.

60. The feisty new reform tabloid, *Jack Canuck*, was the only local newspaper that dared to support the strikers and directly confront one of the city's most powerful men. With no Eaton's advertising to lose, and a reputation to build, the paper's publisher, R. Rogers, threw himself into the journalistic fray with wit and vengeance. "We regret having to pillory so well known and in many circles, so popular a man as Mr. J. C. Eaton," Rogers apologized in his first post-strike editorial on February 24th. But

pillory he did and continued to do, and in the process bumping his own readership up to 100,000 per issue. Thanks to *Jack Canuck*, information about the store and the strike emerged for both workers and posterity. On April 6th, the paper published excerpts from a pamphlet then circulating in the city:

> The stories of injustice and suffering told by the locked-out workers from the so-called 'model' factory of the 'King of Canada' come as a great shock to the public after the pious pretensions of the T. Eaton firm. Frail children of fourteen years have worked from 8 a.m. to 9 p.m.; young girls on starvation wages have been subjected to gross insults and temptations from foremen and examiners; home work was common, and workers were forced to do it at night after long hours in the factory; graft was rife, where employees had to pay for a chance to earn a living wage; the much-bragged-of Saturday half-holiday was only a dream, during busy seasons, for tired little girls; the boasted sanitary conditions leave much to be desired in the way of suitable washrooms, lockers for wraps, etc, etc....

Ultimately, however, wealth and power won the day. The strike was crushed and the workers returned to the same working conditions they had left four months earlier. According to urban legend, one good thing did come out of the long strike. The largely-Jewish garment district that rose on Spadina Avenue owed much to the workers who were either fired or voluntarily left Eaton's to set up on The Avenue.

See Amanda Gregory, "The Strike of Toronto

Cloakmakers: Where the King Can Do No Wrong," *The Ladies' Garment Worker*, Vol. III, No. 4 (April 1912); Ruth Frager, "Class, Ethnicity, and Gender in the Eaton Strikes of 1912 and 1934," in Franca Iacovetta and Mariana Valverde, *Gender Conflicts: New Essays in Women's History* (Toronto: University of Toronto Press, 1992); Eileen Sufrin, *The Eaton Drive: The Campaign to Organize Canada's Largest Department Store 1948 to 1952* (Toronto: Fitzhenry & Whiteside, 1982), pp. 17–32; Linda Kealey, *Enlisting Women for the Cause: Women, Labour, and the Left in Canada, 1890–1920,* (Toronto: University of Toronto Press, 1998); and contemporary press accounts, including *Jack Canuck*, *The Globe*, and the *Toronto Star*.

61. Quoted by Linda Kealey, *op. cit.*, p. 151.

62. According to Carolyn Strange, female printing and bookbinding employees earned an average of $185 annually in 1901, while men earned more than twice as much, or $448. Strange, *op. cit.*, p. 24.

63. The City of Toronto Archives has one of the 1896 Gooderham & Worts prints and the only known surviving example of the 1904 Massey-Harris advertising poster. Both were designed by A. H. Hider.

64. Advertisement in *Massey-Harris Advertiser*, September 1896.

65. For example, between 1911 and 1921, the number of white-collar workers increased by nearly a third, or 33.1%. As white-collar employment became more important, opportunities for blue-collar workers to move up the social scale also increased. Piva, *op. cit.*, pp. 15–16. See also Graham S. Lowe, "'The Enormous File': The Evolution of the Modern Office in Early Twentieth-Century Canada," in *Archivaria* 19 (Winter 1984–85), pp. 137–151.

66. Lucy Booth Martyn, *The Mapping of Victorian*

Toronto(Sutton West & Santa Barbara: The Paget Press, 1984), [Introduction, p. 1].

67. The City of Toronto Archives has a series of photographs documenting Goad's office. Fonds 1109.

68. Thomas Schlereth, "The World and Workers of the Paper Empire," in *Cultural History & Material Culture: Everyday Life, Landscapes, Museums* (Charlottesville: University Press of Virginia, 1992), pp. 145–178. For a Canadian perspective on changes in administration and record-keeping, but not material culture, see Lowe, "Enormous File," *op. cit.*

69. Roger Hall, *A Century to Celebrate: 1893–1993* (Toronto: Dundurn Press, 1993), p. 58.

70. More single women than single men lived in Toronto throughout the period, with 1901, not post-War 1921, showing the greatest differential. Even in 1881, more women worked in manufacturing than in domestic service (3,218 compared with 2,888). By 1891, women comprised nearly a third of the manufacturing workforce, and the numbers continued to grow as Toronto moved into the twentieth century. Meanwhile, women left domestic service to take up other opportunities in such growth areas as retail sales and offices.

71. Strange, *op. cit.*, p. 37.

72. Muckraking reform paper, *Jack Canuck*, ran an exposé of domestic service in 1912 that castigated one, anonymous, society matron for paying her 15-year-old servant $8.00 *monthly*. "They work from morning to night," the outraged paper reported, "with the privilege granted them of a few hours off twice a week." Even at $18 a month, which was probably a more likely level of pay, young women were turning their backs on domestic service. See Carolyn Strange's fascinating analysis of the conditions of life experienced by young, independent, wage-earning females, and why so many (patriar-chal and morally uptight) Torontonians thought they had a "girl problem." Strange, *op. cit., passim.*

73. For all its limitations, the 1915 *Report of the Social Survey Commission*, established to investigate prostitution in Toronto, did investigate the widespread conditions of poverty that led some women to become prostitutes in order to survive. The Commission summarized the dismal economic situation faced by "working girls" in pre-First World War Toronto:

> ... obviously the first step was to find what are the prevailing wages and living conditions of working girls. To this end the Commission had an experienced woman investigator spend some time in interviewing many girls, whose occupations included department and other stores, telephone exchanges, laundries and factories of various kinds. The investigation was made before the outbreak of the war and the consequent depression, and may, therefore, be taken as representing normal conditions. The results indicate that the wages most commonly paid run from six to nine dollars per week. It is difficult to estimate the average from the data obtained. A limited number earn ten, twelve or fifteen dollars, the last named sum being the maximum. Only two of the factories covered by the investigation and only one of the laundries pay more than five dollars per week to beginners. A very considerable proportion of factory workers seem to be earning less than six dollars. A low wage prevails in a number of shops, those in the large departmental stores being apparently better off in this respect than on most others. The seasonal character of the work in the industries in which a great number of the woman workers are employed makes their living conditions much more difficult.

Report of Social Survey Commission of Toronto, September 29, 1915, p. 35. (City of Toronto Archives, Reports Collection, Box 4, Folder 2.) For a critique of the Commission's investigation into "the social evil," see Strange, *op. cit.*, pp. 106–115.

74. The lack of primary sources is a major problem for investigating domestic service. For an early, Canada-wide, rather than Toronto-specific, analysis, see Genvieve Leslie, "Domestic Service in Canada, 1880–1920," in Linda Kealey et al, *Women at Work 1850–1930* (Toronto: Canadian Women's Educational Press, 1974), pp. 72–125. For a British perspective on the drudgery of domestic service, see Judith Flanders, "The Scullery," in *The Victorian House: Domestic Life from Childbirth to Deathbed* (London: Harper Perennial, 2003), pp. 93–120.

75. Schlereth provides a brief technical and social analysis of the telephone in everyday American life. When the telephone was new, no one knew how to answer it. Thomas Edison, for example, suggested that the caller be greeted not with the simple "hello" that later became standard, but with a brisk, "Ahoy! Ahoy!" Before long, the Bell Company provided its thousands of operators with detailed instructions on how to do everything, from how to dress (neatly ... although no one outside the Exchange would ever know) to how to answer the phone ("Number, please?" with an upward inflection). Schlereth, *Victorian America, op. cit.*, pp. 187–191.

76. See Linda Kealey, *op. cit.*, pp. 75–77; Carolyn Strange, *op. cit.*, pp. 39–46; and Alice Klein and Wayne Roberts, "Besieged Innocence: The 'Problem'

and the Problems of Working Women — Toronto 1896–1914" in Linda Kealey et al, *op. cit.*, pp. 244–249.

77. Not only direct, electrical shocks, but other aspects of the operators' working conditions increased the mental and physical strain on telephone operators. "Certainly the [Bell Commission] report makes the case for the legitimacy of 'nerves'-based grievances," Klein and Roberts summarize. "It referred to the overloading of the lines, the flashing of lights, and the noisy clattering in the operator's ear if an impatient subscriber clicked the phone. All of this intensified the strain imposed by the pace of the work. It also noted that operating assaulted all of the senses, which distinguished it from other occupations that were equally fast and from physical work that was not as exhausting mentally." Roberts, *op. cit.*, p. 249.

78. Quoted by Strange, *op. cit.*, p. 41.

79. The Commission refused to even get into the question of pay, stating simply that "the question of wages [is] left to the market." Quoted by Strange, *op. cit.*, p. 40.

80. Quoted by Strange, *op. cit.*, p. 202.

81. Quoted *Ibid.*, p. 178.

82. For a discussion of Simpson's 1894 and 1895 stores, see Angela Carr, *Toronto Architect Edmund Burke* (Montreal and Kingston: McGill-Queen's University Press, 1995), pp. 114–121.

83. Timothy Eaton, quoted in Greg Kealey, *Labour Commission, op. cit.*, pp. 88–89.

84. See J. V. McAree, *Cabbagetown Store* (Toronto: The Ryerson Press, 1953), *passim*, for an evocative description of running a family store during the 1880s.

85. *Ibid.*

86. *Ibid.*

87. The identity of the man-in-the-hat is unknown, but

his dress and his demeanour suggest that he was a commercial traveller. If not that, he likely filled some other, modest business position.

88. Harney and Troper, *op. cit.*, p. 56.

89. Petroff, *op. cit.*, p. 19.

90. Petroff, *op. cit.*, p. 28 ; and Hastings, 1911, *op. cit.*, p. 8.

91. Professionalization was propelled by the establishment of professional associations, professional schools, and professional journals, as well as the passage of regulatory legislation. Considerable debate has swirled around just what constitutes a "profession," especially as the concept has been applied to more and more occupations. Usually, a profession is associated with specialized knowledge, education, and training; a legislative framework, often involving self-regulation; a written code of ethics; a professional association; and social prestige. Medicine and the law are the oldest self-regulating professions and still among the most prestigious and remunerative.

92. Professionalization of medicine was reflected in the establishment of the College of Physicians and Surgeons of Ontario in 1869, and the Ontario Medical Association in1880. Legal professionalization also proceeded apace through much of the nineteenth and early twentieth centuries. See G. Blaine Baker, "Legal Education in Upper Canada 1785–1889," in David H. Flaherty, *Essays in the History of Canadian Law* (Toronto: The Osgoode Society, 1981), vol. II, pp. 49–142.; and Christopher Moore, *The Law Society of Upper Canada and Ontario's Lawyers, 1797–1997* (Toronto: University of Toronto Press, 1997), pp. 135–185.

93. Social work grew out of charitable and volunteer assistance to the poor and needy. Canada's first training program for social workers was established at the University of Toronto in 1914, and

the new profession's first national organization, the Canadian Association of Social Workers, was founded in 1926. Glenn Drover, "Social Work," *The Canadian Encyclopedia Plus* (Toronto: McClelland & Stewart, 1996), CD-ROM.

94. Nursing as an avocation has a long history. But it was only in 1881 that the Toronto General Hospital established a nursing school; in 1907 the Canadian National Association of Nurses was formed; in 1910 the first provincial Nurses Act was passed in Nova Scotia; and in 1919 the first university degree programme for nurses was begun at the University of British Columbia. Throughout this period, and much later, nurses were underpaid and controlled by (mostly male) physicians. Phyllis Marie Jensen, "Nursing," *The Canadian Encyclopedia Plus* (Toronto: McClelland & Stewart, 1996), CD-ROM.

95. As companies grew in size and complexity, the profession of accounting became increasingly prominent in the white-collar world of management. In 1902, the first of three major associations for accountants was formed in Canada: the Dominion Association of Chartered Accountants, which is now called the Canadian Institute of Chartered Accountants. In 1913, the General Accounting Association was incorporated; and the Canadian Society of Cost Accountants, now the Society of Management Accountants, was formed in 1920. O. Croteau, "Accounting," *The Canadian Encyclopedia Plus* (Toronto: McClelland & Stewart, 1996), CD-ROM.

96. According to the 1911 Census, 13% of female workers were defined as "professionals," a new category that included artists, teachers, law clerks, stenographers, trained nurses, typists, and general "office employees." Only a tiny fraction of the more prestigious and established legal and medical

professions were female. Strange, *op. cit.*, pp. 51 and 234.

97. The son of a successful black businessman, Dr. Anderson Ruffin Abbott studied at Oberlin College in Ohio before matriculating from the Toronto School of Medicine in 1857, and becoming the first Canadian-born black doctor in 1861. During the American Civil War, Abbott applied for a commission in the Union Army, but was rejected. He then applied to become a "medical cadet" in a coloured regiment, and was ultimately taken on as a civilian surgeon under contract. He served at hospitals in Washington D. C., where he received commendations, participated in the vigil over the dying Lincoln, and later was presented with a shawl that Lincoln wore to his first inauguration. Although never formally graduating from any medical school, Abbott had a successful medical career, both in Canada and again in the U.S. He was also a journalist and an active member of Toronto's black community. Owen Thomas, "Abbott, Anderson Ruffin," *Dictionary of Canadian Biography* (Toronto: University of Toronto Press, 1998), vol. XIV, 1911–1920, pp. 4–5.

98. Dr. Emily Howard Stowe became the first woman to practice medicine openly in Canada. Having failed to gain entrance to any Canadian medical school, Stowe trained at the New York Medical College for Women, a homeopathic institution in New York City, and received her degree in 1867, before setting up practice in Toronto that year. She was only granted a licence by the Ontario College of Physicians and Surgeons in 1880. Because women had such difficulty gaining training and hospital appointments, she helped establish the Woman's Medical College in Toronto in 1883, which later became Women's College Hospital. Her daughter, Augusta Stowe-Gullen, who studied

at the Toronto School of Medicine, became the first woman to receive a medical degree in Canada, which was granted by Victoria College, Cobourg.

99. In 1891, Clara Brett Martin applied to the Law Society of Upper Canada for admission as a law student, but was refused. She gained entrance in 1893 only after receiving the support of such influential figures as Dr. Emily Stowe and Sir Oliver Mowat (a well-known layer and Premier of Ontario) and the passage of special legislation. Despite tremendous hostility from lecturers and fellow students, Ms Martin placed first in the Law Society's examinations. Once again, the Law Society tried to prevent her progress to the bar. But with the support of more influential figures, including Lady Aberdeen, and the passage of more legislation, she finally was admitted as a barrister. On February 2, 1897, she became the first woman lawyer in the British Empire. It wasn't until the middle of the twentieth century that significant numbers of women entered the legal profession in Canada. John D. Blackwell, "Martin, Clara Brett," *The Canadian Encyclopedia Plus* (Toronto: McClelland & Stewart, Inc., 1996), CD-ROM version.

100. According to material culture historian, Thomas Schlereth, these new professionals formed "a class with a 'vertical vision,' one that championed the rise of the expert in American life, whether in school administration, city planning, interior decoration, mortician services, certified public accounting, library science, physical education, child psychology, or mechanical engineering." Schlereth, *Victorian America, op. cit.*, p. 303.

101. The Women's Dispensary was started in 1896 by Anna McFee, a medical student at the Ontario Medical College for Women at 289 Sumach Street. Initially located in a house on St. David Street, the

Dispensary was a place where women physicians could treat their own patients. This clinic proved to be popular and soon moved to the Medical College itself. When the College merged with the medical faculty of the University of Toronto in 1903, the Women's Dispensary continued to operate on its own at Parliament and Queen, before moving to 18 Seaton Street in 1910, and then 125 Rusholme Road. George H. Rust-D'Eye, *Cabbagetown Remembered* (Erin, Ontario: Boston Mills Press, 1984), pp. 81–82.

102. See, for example, Goss's slightly later photograph, Series 372, Subseries 32, Item 339, dated March 8, 1919.

103. Elise Brunet, "The law office at the turn of the century," *Ontario Lawyers Gazette*, May–June 1999, p. 32. See also Christopher Moore, *The Law Society of Upper Canada and Ontario's Lawyers, 1797–1997* (Toronto: University of Toronto Press, 1997), pp. 196–197.

104. Brunet discusses recommendations, on how to organize a legal business, made by Halifax lawyer Reginald V. Harris in 1908 and '09. Harris "deplored that correspondence was still written by hand. He declared that the pen was obsolete and that it was unthinkable that an office should be without a typewriter." Brunet, *op. cit.*, p. 33.

105. Christopher Moore, *op. cit.*, p. 149.

106. "Toronto's Woman Lawyer," *The Law Society of Upper Canada and Ontario's Lawyers, 1797–1997*. (Toronto: University *The Empire*, September 22, 1894. The author of this article on the woman's page was an anonymous, female reporter, who had been drawn to cover the case partly out of curiosity about "just how unwomanly [Martin's] position would be." Martin's attire and quiet demeanour won the support of the reporter, as did her success as a lawyer. The message was: women can remain

feminine and be successful professionals if "oh you men, you men!" will only give them a chance. Not a hardline feminist position, but an expression of support nonetheless. For a nice discussion of this event, and the significance of fashion, see also Constance Backhouse, *Petticoats and Prejudice: Women and Law in Nineteenth-Century Canada* (Toronto: The Osgoode Society, 1991), pp. 311–312.

107. Quoted by Nancy Kastner, "The Notebooks of His Honour Judge F. M. Morson," in *The Law Society Gazette* (December 1981), vol. 15, no. 4, p. 417.

108. *Ibid.*, p. 415.

109. Although the courts have expanded and the law school has moved elsewhere, Osgoode Hall remains the symbolic centre of the profession, as well as the home of both the Law Society which governs the profession, and Ontario's highest courts.

110. The Law Society of Upper Canada was founded in 1797, making it the second oldest legal profesesional organization in North America, after the Boston Bar Association. It was incorporated in 1822, with a legislated mandate to oversee the education and admission to practice of lawyers in Ontario; to develop standards of professional conduct; and to discipline members of the legal profession.

111. "There is no grander room in Canada," according to William Dendy & William Kilbourn, *op. cit.*, p. 77. For original architectural drawings of the Osgoode Hall library, see Archives of Ontario, C 11.

112. Dendy & Kilbourn, *op. cit.*, p. 77.

113. Scadding, *op. cit.*, p. 227.

114. James Cleland Hamilton, *Osgoode Hall: Reminiscences of the Bench and Bar* (Toronto: The Carswell Company, Ltd., 1904), p. 4. Today, the Osgoode Hall Library still houses one of the largest collections of legal material in Canada, although not all in the Main Reading Room itself.

115. E. R. Arthur, "The History and Architecture of the Fabric," in C. H. A. Armstrong, *The Honourable Society of Osgoode Hall* (Toronto: Clarke, Irwin & Company Limited, 1952), p. 56.

116. Toronto's new (now old) City Hall on Queen Street was originally intended to be a County Court building to replace the then-crumbling County Court on Adelaide Street. It was only as the architectural program progressed that the City fathers decided they needed a new City Hall and hired E. J. Lennox to design a combination County Court and Municipal Building.

117. Goad's 1880 fire-insurance map indicates the location within Osgoode Hall of the Chancery Court, as well as the Common Pleas, Queen's Bench, Library and Lecture Rooms.

118. Neil Semple, "Ryerson, Adolphus Egerton," *The Canadian Encyclopedia Plus* (Toronto: McClelland & Stewart, Inc., 1996), CD-ROM version.

119. Elizabeth Graham suggests, "The growth of the cities was linked inextricably to both the growth of population and the rise of industrialization.... By mid-nineteenth century both of these developments had taken root and had implications for the field of education. Industry demanded employees who were amenable to training, competent at learning skills and used to authoritarian, hierarchical systems of control. Its needs focused on the institution of a system of compulsory education for the masses which could provide a pool of such malleable workers. At the same time women were beginning to explore new work roles outside the home; teaching became one of the new fields open to them." Elizabeth Graham, "Schoolmarms and Early Teaching in Ontario," in Linda Kealey et al, *Women at Work 1850–1930* (Toronto: Canadian Women's Educational Press, 1974), p. 166.

120. In 1881, Toronto's female teachers received $200–$400 per annum, while male teachers received $750–$1100, meaning that the top salary for a woman was lower than the bottom salary for a man. In 1920, women received $1000–$2400 per annum, while men received $1625–$2500, meaning that the top females *did* make more than lowest-paid males, but still 25% less than the top males. The lowest-paid females, where many female teachers spent their careers, made only 62.5% as much as their male colleagues. "Salaries of Teachers in Toronto," Graham, *op. cit.*, p. 194.

121. Graham traces the evolution of these associations, *op. cit.*

122. In 1900, the beginning salary for a female teacher in Toronto was $324, compared with $321 for a charwoman at the post office, $421 for a male street sweeper, and $546 for male labourers at the stock yards. Graham, *op. cit.*, p. 192.

123. Natural scientist, Carrie Matilda Derick, studied at McGill, Harvard, the Marine Biological Laboratory at Woods Hole, the Royal College of Science in London and the University of Bonn. She became the first woman on the McGill academic staff when she was appointed demonstrator in botany at McGill in 1891, and, the first woman in Canada to become a full professor when she achieved that status at McGill in 1912. Margaret Gillett, "Derick, Carrie Matilda," *The Canadian Encyclopedia Plus* (Toronto: McClelland & Stewart, Inc., 1996), CD-ROM version.

124. Graham, *op. cit.*, p. 179. By 1902, 277 women had graduated from the University of Toronto.

125. Eaton's exploitation of workers was arguably less extreme than other employers of the era. He did initiate shorter hours (reducing closing times progressively from 10 pm in the 1870s to 6 pm in the 1900s), and shorter weeks (instituting the half-day Saturdays in July and August during

the 1890s, which ultimately increased to full-day Saturdays on a year-round basis under his son in 1919). Whether everyone actually benefited from these policies is a different question, as indicated in the discussion about the 1912 strike at Eaton's. See also *Golden Jubilee 1869–1919* (Toronto: T. Eaton Co., 1919) for a hagiographic account of the founder and his business.

126. Gad and Holdsworth summarize "The Emergence of Corporate Toronto," *op. cit.*, Plate 15.
127. Gad and Holdsworth, *op. cit.*, Plate 15.
128. Kilbourn and Dendy, *op. cit.*, pp. 220–223.
129. Kilbourn and Dendy describe the Dominion Bank Building at 1–5 King Street West as "easily one of the most beautiful buildings in the city." Kilbourn and Dendy, *op. cit.*, p. 171.

130. "Dominion Bank Building, Toronto," *Construction* (December 191), vol. 7, no. 12, p. 427. The magazine devoted an entire article to the bank's mechanical equipment, as well as its general architectural design.
131. *Ibid.*, p. 443.
132. *Ibid.*, p. 443.

CHAPTER 5
From City Hall to Government House

1. Fanny Chadwick Grayson Smith, unpublished Daily Journal for 1901 (Archives of Ontario, F 1072), p. 33.
2. Simcoe's original town of York became the city of Toronto on March 6, 1834.
3. The Parliament buildings at Front and Simcoe streets (1829–1892) represented the third of four provincial government complexes built in Toronto. The first, which opened in June 1797, was located south of Front Street between Berkeley Street and Parliament Street, overlooking the Bay and was torched by victorious invading American soldiers in 1813. For about a decade, parliamentarians met in such non-government buildings as Jordan's Hotel, which was located across the street from the charred parliamentary ruins, and Chief Justice Draper's residence at King and Wellington. A new Parliament rose from the ashes of the old, but was only in use from 1820 until 1824, when another (non-military) fire claimed the building, and forced parliamentarians to resume their roaming ways. They took shelter in the York Hospital at King and Simcoe until the new, and longer-standing, third parliamentary complex opened in 1829.

For a concise review of the peripatetic Parliament, see Eric Arthur, *Toronto No Mean City*. 3rd ed. (Toronto: University of Toronto Press, 1964; and revised by Stephen A. Otto, 1986) pp. 27–30. For a more leisurely trip through Toronto's parliamentary history, see Eric Arthur, *From Front Street to Queen's Park: The Story of Ontario's Parliament Buildings* (Toronto: McClelland & Stewart, 1979), and Roger Hall, *A Century to Celebrate 1893–1993: The Ontario Legislative Building* (Toronto: Dundurn Press, 1993).

4. In March 1834, York's Town Hall at King and Jarvis became the first of Toronto's four City Halls. After the Great Fire of 1849, St. Lawrence Hall and Market was built on this site. By that time, City Hall had moved south to Front and Jarvis, where Councillors met until their new (now the old) City Hall opened in September 1899.
5. Upper Canada's and then, after Confederation, Ontario's Lieutenant-Governors lived in a variety of privately built mansions, including Elmsley House on the King and Simcoe site where the first *real* Government House was built in 1870. (Before there were houses and mansions, there was, of course, a tent: Captain Cook's tent, which Upper Canada's first Lieutenant-Governor, John Graves Simcoe, pitched not on the shores of Botany Bay, but the shores of Toronto Bay, in 1792.)

6. The Victorians regarded January 1, 1901, not January 1, 1900, as the beginning of the Twentieth Century. Fittingly, perhaps, the consummate nineteenth-century monarch, Queen Victoria, died only weeks into the new century, on January 22, 1901, on the Isle of Wight.
7. Marilyn M. Litvak, *Edward James Lennox: "Builder of Toronto"* (Toronto: Dundurn Press, 1995), p. 24. Others would name the Great Library at Osgoode Hall (1857), the Great Stairway at Queen's Park (1892), and the Great Hall at Union Station (1918), as rivals for this particular architectural award.
8. Despite their masculinist bias and sombre rendering, Reid's murals were important additions to Lennox's municipal building. For nearly a decade, Reid had tried without success to get City fathers to sponsor a mural program at City Hall, both to celebrate the City and to stimulate interest in public art. Inspired by the decoration of the Paris City Hall in the late 1880s and the display of a major work destined for the Boston Public Library, at the 1893 Chicago World's Fair, Reid got together with other major artists of his day to plan a joint work for Lennox's Council Chamber. Three times they approached City Council, and three times City Council refused to provide the paltry funds necessary to implement their program. Finally, Reid

offered to *donate* murals for the Main Hall ... an offer that Council could not refuse. Working on his own, Reid created the two major panels that still flank the main Queen Street entrance: *The Arrival of the Pioneers*, to the left (or east), and *Staking a Pioneer Farm* to the right (or west). Muriel Miller, *George Reid: A Biography* (Toronto: Summerhill Press reissue, 1987), pp. 68–75, 82–83.

9. "Address Delivered by His Worship the Mayor, John Shaw, Esq., Upon the Occasion of the Opening of the New City Buildings, September 18th, 1899," *City of Toronto Council Minutes 1899*, Appendix C, p. 507.

10. *City Council Minutes 1880*, Minute No. 90, p. 27, moved by Ald. Denison, seconded by Ald. Close, January 31, 1880.

11. According to Lennox's report to Council in December 1900, after the building had been opened, but not all the accounts had been settled, about 12,000,000 bricks were used in the new building. *City Council Minutes 1900, Appendix A*, p. 1266. And according to an advertisement in *Construction*, November 1912, some of the bricks had also been made at the Don Valley Brick Works, now home to one of Toronto's regenerated parklands.

12. Not all were content, however: *Picturesque Canada*, published in 1882, called City Hall "a blot upon the city's public buildings, being no less unsightly and dingy than ill-ventilated and unwholesome." *Picturesque Canada*, p. 419. For concise discussions of Toronto's second City Hall see William Dendy, *Lost Toronto* (Toronto: Oxford University Press, 1978), pp. 48–52; and Eric Arthur *No Mean City.*, *op.cit.*, p. 87. While the exterior of the building and the areas devoted to market activities changed dramatically, the interior arrangements of City Hall "remained

largely unchanged," according to Dendy, p. 51.

13. According to John Ross Robertson, the City's Parks Commissioner and Medical Officer were located on the once-grand, second floor of St. Lawrence Hall in 1898. John Ross Robertson, *Landmarks of Toronto* (Toronto; J. Ross Robertson, 1898), vol. 3, p. 81.

14. Fleming, who had been mayor in 1892–93, as well as 1896–97, resigned his post of mayor in August 1897 in order to become Assessment Commissioner. Perhaps he preferred the security of a civic appointment to the insecurity of yearly municipal elections. John Shaw was elected by Council to fill out his term and Council voted to give Fleming "his" mayoral chair. Fleming followed his municipal career by becoming general manager of the Street Railway Company and several utility companies. See Victor L. Russell, *Mayors of Toronto* (Toronto: Boston Mills Press, 1982), pp. 120–124.

15. The City of Toronto was created on March 6, 1834, so March 6, 1884 was its 50th Anniversary. The City was in an ebullient and celebratory mood, which perhaps encouraged it to forge ahead, slowly, with a major public work like the Court House. Civic distraction may also explain why the competition — first suggested in 1883 — was so slow to start.

16. Under the heading "New City Hall," newly elected Mayor Boswell suggested to his colleagues, "I do think the time has arrived when a City Hall, more central in location, more extensive in accommodation, and more healthful in its character, should be erected in Toronto. The assessment of the City today is a little over $65,000,000. Suppose the new City Buildings would cost, over and above what would be received for the present site $300,000. The interest and sinking fund required to pay this amount in thirty years would be

$14,250 ... less than a quarter of a mill." Mayor's Inaugural Address, *City Council Minutes, 1884*, Appendix (No. 1), January 1884, p. 5.

17. June 27, 1884, City Council passed a by-law to this effect, thus authorizing the first of many expenditures on a building that would ultimately cost about $2.5 million. John Ross Robertson published a drawing of a Queen Street Block in 1888 that shows some of the buildings expropriated to create the new City Hall. See, John Ross Robertson, *Landmarks of Toronto*, (Toronto, 1894), vol. 1, between pages 22 and 23.

18. The City held a competition for the Front Street City Hall in 1844 and would hold an International Competition for the new City Hall in the mid-1960s. These competitions apparently went more smoothly than either the City's or the Province's competitions for new homes in the 1880s.

19. Among the requirements established by Storm were "that the main feature of the building should be opposite the centre of [Bay] street, and should also mark the principal entrance"; and that "the total cost of the building ... must not exceed two hundred thousand dollars." His hope that the building would be "erected in Canadian material" was overridden by a Council worried about costs. Even so, the City's early cost-estimate proved to be wildly inaccurate. *City of Toronto. Erection of New Court House. Circular to Architects*, dated March 4th, 1885.

20. For a biography of Alexander Manning as a contractor, see Eric Arthur, *No Mean City.*, *op. cit.*, p. 267. According to Arthur, at the time of his death in 1903, Manning's individual property taxes were the largest in Toronto. He was obviously a major player in local development circles.

21. Matthew Sheard designed the 1885 College of Pharmacy on Gerrard East; and Thomas Fuller would be the architect for the 1891 University Avenue

Armouries. Eric Arthur, *No Mean City.*, *op. cit.*, pp. 258 and 247.

22. City of Toronto, *Circular to Architects: Report of Experts* [Matthew Sheard, Thos. Fuller, Alex. Manning] *Appointed to Examine Plans for Proposed New Court House*, dated August 21, 1885.

23. Litvak, *op. cit.*, p. xiii. For a contemporary biography, see "E. J. Lennox, Esq., Architect of the New Court House" in *The Investigator*, vol. XXVI (April 1898), pp. 3–4.

24. See, for example, "Western Elevation — Teraulay [now Bay] Street," *Evening Telegram*, May 15, 1886. Even before taking his famous multi-city tour in 1887, Lennox had decided on the approach that he adopted for the final complex: a Richardsonian Romanesque building with its dominant tower at the head of Bay Street.

25. E. J. Lennox, "Report [to the Court House Committee] of my inspection throughout some of the principle Cities of the Eastern States," June 13, 1887. Lennox's remarks were made in the middle of the controversy over the Province's selection of a non-Canadian architect who had slagged the plans of Canadian architects for their inadequate layout and ventilation systems. Lennox, according to Litvak, was replying to such criticism. The only building deemed worthy of positive comment was Henry Hobson Richardson's court house in Pittsburgh, which had already obviously exerted a strong influence on Lennox's design.

26. Court House Committee, 1889, *Toronto Municipal and County Buildings*, [p. 7].

27. "Laying the Stone: Important Ceremony at the New Civic Building." *Mail*, November 23, 1891, reprinted in *Big Ben: Official Organ of the City Hall Employees' Association*, vol. 1, no. 7 (December 1924), pp. 2–3.

28. "Address Delivered by Ald. W. H. Gibbs ....," *City Council Minutes 1891*, Appendix (No. 27), pp. 505–506.

29. Other objects buried in the cornerstone include: coins and documentary fragments transferred from the cornerstone of the 1844 City Hall on Front Street, a vellum scroll naming all the VIPs at the ceremony, copies of 1891 newspapers, an 1891 City Directory, a copy of the 1884 Semi-Centennial memorial volume written by Scadding and Worts, and contemporary currency. See Clarke's Address, *op. cit.*; "In the Spotlight," *Toronto Telegram*, February 12, 1948; and Donald Jones, "Historical Toronto," *Toronto Star*, March 2, 1974.

30. "Architect Lennox Steps In," *News*, September 9, 1892. Not surprisingly, Lennox's bold action caused the contractor to launch legal action, which ultimately failed.

31. "An Exalted Ceremony: Finishing Stones in City Hall Tower Laid," *Globe*, July 15, 1898. The bold aldermen who joined the Mayor's bucket party included: Hallam, Hubbard, Burns and Leslie.

32. "Now, New City Hall Open for Business," September 19, 1899.

33. Mayor John Shaw, "Address delivered ... upon the occasion of the opening of the new city buildings, September 18th, 1899," *City Council Minutes 1899*, Appendix C, p. 507.

34. Grayson Smith, *op. cit.*, p. 33.

35. According to Mayor Shaw's September 18, 1899 address, the City had gone to the people to ratify expenditures on the building in January and April 1887, and in May 1889. Additional money was raised in other ways, including Provincial legislation.

36. G. R. Geary, "Mayor's Message, January 9, 1911," *City Council Minutes 1911*, Appendix C, pp. 16–17. See also *Globe*, January 3, 1911, and January 19, 1911.

37. Constance E. Hamilton (1862–1945) was the first woman elected "alderman" in the City of Toronto. She was elected twice, in 1920 and 1921, and was joined in 1921 by the second female councillor, Ethel Small. Prior to her election to Council, Ms Hamilton had been a prominent suffragist, President of the Equal Franchise League of Toronto, and a long-time member of the National Council of Women of Canada (founded with the help of proto-feminist, Lady Aberdeen). The City of Toronto established the Constance E. Hamilton Award, given to people who have worked to secure equitable treatment for Toronto women. (City of Toronto Archives: Biographical File on Constance E. Hamilton.) In an interview just after her Inaugural Meeting, she expounded on her view of "democracy," stating firmly, "In my opinion, there are just as good brains in the man and woman who lives in the cottage as in the man or woman who lives in the palace...." Quoted in *Globe*, January 3, 1920.

38. Mrs. John Clover, *Diary: 1892–1893* (Toronto: Archives of Ontario, unpublished manuscript, F 830), p. 15. On a visit to Canada from England, Mrs. Clover stayed in Toronto for nearly a year, mostly at 74 McCaul Street, and left a lively account of life in the little city.

39. Prominent architect and architectural historian, Eric Arthur, for example, fulminated against the Province, especially Public Works Commissioner Fraser, in his 1979 investigation of Toronto's parliament buildings. Eric Arthur, *From Front Street to Queen's Park, op. cit.*

40. C. Pelham Mulvany, *Toronto Past and Present* (Toronto: W. E. Caiger, Publisher, 1884), p. 47. Being an historian, Mulvany was particularly sensitive to the value of the scarce tracts, old newspapers, and land records so inadequately stored there.

"That a safe receptacle should at once be provided for these is a matter of the first importance to every landowner in Ontario, as the destruction of these all-important documents would destroy all evidence not only of ownership but of the limits and boundaries of each man's property." It was only in 1903 that the Archives of Ontario was created to look after the Province's documentary heritage. Unlike Mulvany, who decried the buildings' "homely exterior," William Dendy took a more favourable view, commenting that "Chewett's design was the grandest of the city's public buildings to date, even though the intended portico over the main entrance was never built." Dendy, *Lost Toronto, op. cit.*, p. 31.

41. Roger Hall, *op. cit.*, p. 24. For detailed discussions of both the flawed design-process and the building of the new Parliament, see both Roger Hall and Eric Arthur, *op. cit.*, pp. 49–63.

42. For example, Hall points out, Fraser's "thick booklet of instructions [required] in painstaking detail, such stipulations as the precise number and nature of bricks to be used in a section of the building, or the absolute sizes of pipes for steam supply, or the precise square footage needed for certain ministerial duties. Now, that was restrictive in itself but the reward for all the exacting labour was absurd: the prize-winner would receive a scant $2,000, the runner-up $1,000, and the third-place winner a paltry $500." Even worse, Hall contends, "Once the plans were presented, the specifications and designs were sent out to tender ... and only if the contract prices returned by the bidders were below the sum of $500,000 would the architect receive his fees and charges...." Hall, *op. cit.*, pp. 28–29.

43. Roger Hall, for example, comments:

There now began extraordinary and quite inappropriate consultations between one of the judges, R. A. Waite, and the minister. Waite, it seems, was a friend to many in the Ontario cabinet and much admired by our old friend Kivas Tully. Waite's task was evidently to advise how far the plans of the first- and second-place winners "would be suitable." The other jury members were not consulted.

Hall, *op. cit.*, p. 29.

Eric Arthur, for his part, summarizes:

The evidence throughout this chapter on the International Competition would indicate that the trio of the Honourable Minister, Mr. C. F. Fraser, Mr. Kivas Tully, and Mr. R. A. Waite, were responsible for torpedoing the competition and eliminating the Toronto firm of Darling & Curry who had been judged first. Mr. Waite surfaced in the muddy waters that were created and became architect for the Parliament Buildings of Ontario.

Arthur, *op. cit.*, p. 60.

44. Fraser, 1886 speech to the House, quoted by Eric Arthur, *op. cit.*, p. 55.

45. Even before Waite's Parliament was completed, it was "formally" (but not yet "officially") opened on September 17, 1892, to celebrate the hundredth anniversary of the opening of the first Parliament in Upper Canada. Politicians and dignitaries paraded from the old Parliament on Front Street up stately-but-unpaved University Avenue to Queen's Park. Lieutenant-Governor Kirkpatrick loftily exclaimed that "this stately pile of buildings ... marks, by its large and massive proportions, by its beauty and symmetry, the great progress which has taken place in the public situation of this Province during the last hundred years." Other notables, including the historically-omnipresent Dr. Henry Scadding, shared their thoughts with the audience. The bands played. The crowds sang "The Maple Leaf Forever." The Public Works Minister, Christopher Findlay Fraser, "formally" declared the buildings open; and ordinary citizens poured into the unfinished buildings. Hall, *op. cit.*, pp. 36–38.

46. Front page, *The Empire*, April 5, 1893.

47. *Saturday Night*, April 8, 1893, p. 13. Gustav Hahn was one of Canada's finest practitioners of this newly fashionable style. His murals, therefore, would soon decorate some of Toronto's finest interiors, including the Chester Massey House on Jarvis Street and the Sir Joseph Flavelle House just up Queen's Park Crescent from the new Parliament.

48. The professional journal *did* admit that the "general scheme seems proper ...," and that "there has been a judicious expenditure of space which makes the inside of the building fine, and is worthy of all praise." Quoted by Eric Arthur, *op. cit.*, p. 125. Arthur, himself, described the building as "dull", but nevertheless found much to praise about its internal layout and superior craftsmanship, especially in the stone and wood carvings that enhance the whole. He reserved his harshest criticism for E. J. Lennox's Edwardian rebuilding of the West Wing after the great fire of 1909. According to Arthur, Lennox's solution not only failed to match the beauty of the Victorian original, but knocked the balance of the exterior off-kilter.

49. Frank Yeigh, "Ontario's Capitol: The Great New Building in the Park: The Noble Pile in which Ontario's Legislators are now in Session," in *The Saturday Globe*, April 15, 1893.

50. Given the subservient role of cities, it is perhaps fitting that their arms cannot be readily identified.

51. Liberal Premier Mowat acknowledged in his own speech that the building had cost an uncool $1.25 million, far more than the originally hoped-for $500,000 or the originally budgeted $750,000. Roger Hall estimates that the building cost "at least $1.4 million, with more tacked on for fittings and furnishings." Hall, *op. cit.*, p. 52.

52. Quotation by Eric Arthur from *The Empire*, *op. cit.*

53. "Sir Oliver Mowat's speech at the Grand Opening," in Eric Arthur, *op. cit.*, pp. 155.

54. In January 1903, newly elected Robert Gamey (PC, Manitoulin) rose in the House to announce that he was changing Parties, much to the astonishment of Liberal Premier George Ross and the consternation of Conservative Leader of the Opposition, James P. Whitney. According to *Globe* reporter, M. O. Hammond, who observed it all from the Press Gallery above the Speaker's Chair, and who was drawn into the tangled affair by Gamey, "few people thought the more of Gamey" for his switch. More was to come, however. Just after Parliament reopened for the spring session, Gamey rose and precipitated "the most sensational political event in Canada for many years," by announcing that he had been offered $500 by the Liberals to cross the floor and support them, and he had strung the accused bribers along for a couple of months in order to gather evidence. He then walked across the floor and handed the supposed evidence to a flabbergasted Whitney.

   "The speech caused the most profound sensation," Hammond confided to his *Journal* for March 11th. In fact, according to another journalist then in the Press Gallery, *Mail* editor Hector Charlesworth, "reporters knocked one another over to get to the telephones" and, a few minutes later, "hundreds and hundreds of people were running towards the Parliament Buildings. The news had spread magically and everyone wished to be on the scene." The Gamey Affair consumed politicians, reporters, and ordinary citizens for weeks. Ultimately, a Royal Commission exonerated the accused, but demonstrated that "influence peddling and backroom politicking were at the very centre of Ontario political life." Whitney and the Conservatives won the next general election. Sources: M. O. Hammond, Archives of Ontario, F1075-5; and Hall, *op. cit.*, pp. 69–70.

55. Frank Yeigh, "Ontario's New Parliament Buildings," in *The Canadian Magazine of Politics, Science, Art and Literature*, vol. 1, no. 1 (March 1893), p. 107. Edited by J. Gordon Mowat, the new general-interest magazine was distinctively and self-avowedly "Canadian" in focus and perspective.

56. Hall, *op. cit.*, pp. 75–76. In the 1990s, however, scorch marks were found near the entrance to the Legislative Chamber, indicating that the fire was much closer to destroying the entire building than previously realized. "Restoration reveals secrets of Queen's Park," *Star*, September 2, 1999.

57. Frank Yeigh, quoted by Eric Arthur, *op. cit.*, p. 120. According to Hall, Yeigh was a government publicist.

58. Litvak, *op. cit.*, pp. 81–82. Whereas Litvak regards Lennox's solution as "cheerful and majestic," Eric Arthur dismisses it as an architectural abomination, "an affair of cold grey marble" that destroyed the feel of the interior, and the original symmetry of the exterior. Arthur, *op. cit.*, p. 111.

59. Mrs. Forsyth Grant, "Memories of Government House: Passing of a Famous Social Shrine," *The Globe*, Saturday, April 27, 1912. Mrs. Forsyth Grant was the daughter of Lieutenant-Governor Sir John Beverley Robinson. This article was illustrated with photographs of the gubernatorial mansion.

60. Before calling a General Election, the federal Prime Minister or provincial Premier must first ask the Governor-General or Lieutenant-Governor to formally dissolve Parliament.

61. Education for Upper Canada College located at the northwest corner until 1891; Damnation for the taverns at the northeast corner; Legislation for Government House at the southwest corner; and Salvation for St. Andrew's Presbyterian [now United] Church at the southeast corner after 1875.

62. In 1884, C. Pelham Mulvany admired the beauty of the house and the gardens, but decried the fact that ordinary people, who paid for the whole thing with their taxes, were not even allowed to see, let alone visit the grounds. Mulvany, *op. cit.*, pp. 51–52.

   On balance, he suggested, it might all be turned into a "People's Palace" or "public library and industrial museum," with the grounds thrown open as a public park.

63. *Landmarks of Canada … a guide to the J. Ross Robertson Historical Collection in the Public Reference Library* (Toronto: J. Ross Robertson, December 1917), p. 71.

64. After his retirement in the early 1930s, Lymer's apartment in the Beaches area of Toronto was filled with photographs, mementos, and gifts from the many aristocratic visitors — including his personal favourite, HRH Prince of Wales — whom he had coddled and served. See Lucy Doyle, "He Has Served Eleven Governors," *The Toronto Star Weekly*, Saturday, January 30, 1932, p. 3.

65. Quoted in *Ibid.*, p. 3.

66. Lymer papers, Archives of Ontario, F 1035.

67. Quoted in Doyle, *op. cit.*, p. 3.

68. Thomas Lymer's papers include a copy of this blue-tasselled menu. Archives of Ontario, F 1035, Thomas Lymer fonds, File 7.

69. First elected in 1888, James Pliny Whitney finally won power in 1905 and held onto the premiership until his death in September 1914, just after the outbreak of war. His tenure was notable for, among other things, establishing a public hydro-electric system and enacting ground-breaking workmen's compensation legislation.

70. Gage offered to sell his own fine estate, near Wychwood Park at Davenport and Bathurst, for $120,000 — the same price as the North Rosedale property B but to use that sum to purchase the race track (now TTC yards) immediately to the south, for a public botanical garden. This, of course, would have given the Province a more centrally located Government House, in an already fashionable area, where the Eatons, Austins, Pellatts and other members of the Toronto elite already lived. City Council apparently liked the idea enough to offer to purchase the Chorley Park site, overlooking the Don Valley, as a public park. But no deal. See William Dendy, *Lost Toronto, op. cit.*, p. 177.

71. Heakes advised the Minister of Public Works that none of the earlier submissions was suitable and all were too expensive, so the Minister instructed him to prepare a new design. Heakes's exterior design was more or less lifted from the winning competitor, G. W. King, and his overall plan relied heavily on John Lyle's fine, rejected, submission. Despite Heakes's apparent concern for the public purse, his building cost over a million dollars, nearly five times the originally budgeted $215,000. Dendy, *Lost Toronto, op. cit.*, p. 177.

72. "Ontario's New Government House: Chorley Park, Rosedale, Toronto, The Site of the Lieutenant-Governor's Palatial Residence," *Construction*, February 1916, p. 39.

73. *Ibid*, p. 37.

74. Although Chorley Park ceased to be the Lieutenant-Governor's residence, it did continue on for a time as a military hospital. Eventually, in the late 1950s, it was demolished. Today, only the driveway from Roxborough Drive survives as a reminder of the grandeur that once was.

75. *Construction, op. cit.*, p. 41.

76. *Doyle, op. cit.*, p. 3.

CHAPTER 6
From Farmer's Market to Carriage Trade

1. In 1884, James Ritty invented the first successful mechanical cash register, soon known as the "Incorruptible Cashier." Almost immediately, John H. Patterson launched the National Cash Register Company (NCR) in Dayton, Ohio, and, within a few years, the National Cash Register Company of Canada was established north of the border. Success was immediate and astounding. By early 1890, NCR had manufactured 10,000 registers, and in 1911, the American company manufactured its 1,000,000th machine. It went international in 1886, and before long it was operating in 121 countries. Sources: Web sites for The Brass Cash Register Shoppe and the National Cash Register Company.

2. Along with NCR's high-minded Art Nouveau, Renaissance, and Ionic designs, was their American rival, Hallwood's famous "girlie machine," with curvaceous nudes embossed on the sides of the machine case, which was probably too racy for sober Toronto merchants. The NCR Empire case was entirely suitable, and in American production from 1898 until 1915. Source: http://www.Brasscash registers.com/page4b.html, December 2000.

3. See Keith Walden, *Becoming Modern in Toronto: The Industrial Exhibition and the Shaping of a Late Victorian Culture* (Toronto: University of Toronto Press, 1997), *passim*, for a discussion of the operation and the meaning of the proto-CNE.

4. C. Pelham Mulvany, *Toronto: Past and Present* (Toronto: W. E. Caiger, Publisher, 1884), p. 144.

5. Saturday, November 5, 1803 became Toronto's first, formally proclaimed Market Day near the site of what is now St. Lawrence Hall. Proclamation published in York, *Upper Canada Gazette*, November 5, 1803, reproduced in Edith Firth, *The Town of York, 1793–1815* (Toronto: University of Toronto Press for the Champlain Society, 1962), p. 128.

6. John Ross Robertson, *Landmarks of Toronto* (Toronto: J. Ross Robertson, 1908), vol. 5, p. 144.

7. The location of John Mallon's 1895 butcher stalls is confirmed by an engraving looking north from Front Street through the North Market, around the time the South Market opened in 1902. A shop just inside the entrance to the west bears a sign saying that the Davies Co. had moved to the "New Market." John Ross Robertson, *Landmarks, vol. 5, op. cit.*, p. 147.

8. For information about John Mallon, see G. Mercer Adam, *Toronto Old and New* (Toronto: The Mail Printing Company, 1891. Coles Canadian Collection facsimile reproduction, 1974), pp. 177–178; and Mary Mallon, *John Mallon of Brockton and Toronto (1836–1913)* (Toronto: Pro Familia Publishing, 1990), *passim*. The butcher business was kind to the Mallons: they occupied two large houses in the west end of Toronto, Mallon Hall at 1716 Dundas Street West and Avondale (named after Irish nationalist, Charles Stewart Parnell's birthplace) at

316 Landsdowne Avenue. For readers interested in the details of the butcher's trade ca. 1897, Ms Mallon lists the equipment necessary for Mallon to operate his business, on pages 14–15.

9. In its report of the opening of the new market on November 15, 1902, the *Mail and Empire* summarized the situation:

> There was a time when but few men were bold enough to maintain that any good could come out of the new market. Now it is regarded as one of the brightest jewels into Toronto's crown. Aldermen, who less than a year ago, were out with their hammers rudely knocking what they were then pleased to term "the white elephant," now find that they always had an abiding faith in the future of the new market. Now in their minds-eye they can see radial railways converging at the new building, which is destined to become the centre of a great and growing trade.

Although the converging radials never materialized and the city's trade patterns were not revolutionized, the Market was a commercial success and a worthy use of municipal monies.

10. *Mail and Empire*, November 17, 1902.
11. For an architectural history of the St. Lawrence Market, see William Dendy, *Lost Toronto* (Toronto: Oxford University Press, 1978), pp. 48–51, and William Dendy and William Kilbourn, *Toronto Observed: Its Architecture, Patrons, and History* (Toronto: Oxford University Press, 1986), pp. 43–45. For a discussion of St. Lawrence Hall and Market, see Glenn McArthur and Annie Szamosi, *William Thomas: Architect* (Ottawa: Archives of Canadian Art, Carleton University Press, 1996),

pp. 47–51. For a social history of St. Lawrence Market, see Linda Biesenthal, *To Market, To Market: The Public Market Tradition in Canada* (Toronto: PMA, 1980), pp. 86–98. See also Information file at the City of Toronto Archives, Research Hall, and Alderman Daniel Lamb's Scrapbook, City of Toronto Archives, Fonds 1246.

12. By 1905, Robertson listed the following retail occupants of the South Market: 23 butchers, 10 fruiterers, 8 florists, 6 poultry dealers, 4 confectionery and fruit dealers, and 1 fish salesman. A restaurant operated in the northeastern portion. The Basement contained 4 large cold storage rooms used by large fruit dealers during the fruit season, and 16 other storage rooms that were rented out. The old, abandoned Council Chamber contained a printing office that employed at least 25 people. Robertson, *Landmarks of Toronto, vol. 5, op. cit.*, p. 149.

13. Various newspaper reports from *Lamb Scrapbook, op. cit.*, pp. 70–71, 98–99.

14. Coatsworth quoted in an unidentified clipping dated February 26, 1902, in *Lamb Scrapbook, op. cit.* The St. Lawrence Market went online in 2000 when it launched its first website at http://www.stlawrencemarket.com.

15. Robertson, *Landmarks of Toronto, vol. 5, op. cit.*, p. 149.

16. For example, on Saturday, January 21, 1905, 26 farmers and 15 wholesale butchers were open for business at the North Market, whereas on Tuesday, January 24, only 3 farmers and 6 butchers were open. Robertson, *Landmarks of Toronto, vol. 5, op. cit.*, p. 149.

17. J. V. McAree, *Cabbagetown Store* (Toronto: Ryerson Press, 1953), p. 16. Born around 1875, McAree joined the family store at 283 Parliament Street after his mother died and his father went on the

road, so his observations of retail (and other) life cover mostly the 1880s and '90s. Thomas Lipton pioneered the first packaged tea in 1888, which provides a benchmark for the changes described by McAree.

18. In 1897, seven houses dominated the wholesale grocery trade, doing an estimated $5,000,000 of business. George W. Engelhardt, *Toronto Canada: The Book of its Board of Trade* (Toronto: Toronto Board of Trade, 1897–98), pp. 128–129.

19. Figures were compiled by the Board of Trade, *op. cit.*, pp. 104–105. At the very least, the relative, if not the exact, importance of the food trade is illustrated by these figures.

20. *Ibid.*, pp. 128–130.

21. "In an age before supermarkets, the Ward seemed to have a variety or grocery store on every corner. Soon the local manufacture of foods competed with the importers and provisions," commented Harney and Troper on the evolution of the food trades in immigrant areas of Toronto. Meanwhile, "Italians, Macedonians, Greeks and Syrians trudged many miles through unfamiliar parts of the city to sell peanuts, popcorn and homemade confection," not to mention bananas. By 1897, the Italians dominated the banana trade, pushing and pulling over a 100 banana wagons around the city. Robert F. Harney and Harold Troper, *Immigrants: A Portrait of the Urban Experience, 1890–1930* (Toronto: Van Nostrand Reinhold Ltd., 1975), p. 56.

22. *Ibid.*, p. 16

23. *Ibid.*, pp. 17–18.

24. One of the first Coca-Cola girls was Metropolitan Opera star Lilian Nordica, who probably never sang the company's new slogan, "Drink Coca-Cola Delicious and Refreshing." Juliann Sivulka, *Soap, Sex, and Cigarettes: A Cultural History of American Advertising* (Belmont, CA: Wadsworth Publishing

Company, 1996), pp. 74–77. For the history of North American advertising, see Roland Marchand, *Advertising the American Dream: Making Way for Modernity 1920–1940* (Berkeley, CA: University of California Press, 1985). See also Thomas J. Schlereth, *Victorian America: Transformation in Everyday Life 1876–1915* (New York: Harper-Perennial, 1991), pp. 141–167.

25. Board of Trade, 1897, *op. cit.*, p. 108.

26. Even the denizens of Cabbagetown occasionally visited Michie's, where they appreciated not only the wide selection of "blended teas with exotic names," but also the "coin boxes carrying change [that] whirred overhead," and, before Prohibition, the "large stock" of wines and liquors. George Rust-D'Eye, *Cabbagetown Remembered* (Toronto: Boston Mills Press, 1984), p. 41.

27. "1 & 5 King Street West — Residential Condominium Development," Report to Toronto Preservation Board, October 9, 2000, p. 3. This report assesses a proposal for a major condominium development on the site of the former Michie Building (1894–5) and the former Dominion Bank Building of 1914, which were located on the southwest corner of King and Yonge.

28. See Schlereth, *Victorian America, op. cit.*, p. 152, and Sivulka, op. cit., pp. 95–96, and 145–146. By the late 1920s, A&P operated more than 15,000 stores, and Piggly Wiggly operated over 3,000.

29. According to the 1910 City Directory, William Davies Company had about a dozen branches in Toronto. For additional images, see *William Davies Store, ca. 1910* in Chapter 4, and the following photographs of various Davies outlets in the City of Toronto Archives: Fonds 1244, Items 337A, 338A and 338B; and Fonds 1177, Item 3.

30. Johnston's store was located near the intersection of Wellesley and Church Streets just about where Novack's Rexall drugstore was still operating in 2005. This store gives nice physical evidence of the shift, from small independents (Johnston) to large franchises (Rexall) that characterized North American retail evolution during the twentieth century; and emphasizes the tenacity of some retail uses (in this case, pharmacy) for certain locations (in this case the intersection of Church and Wellesley). Other nice examples are provided by the association of fashionable photography with 31 King Street East, and hotels with 100 Front Street West. These are discussed in the section on the cariage trade.

31. Even the apothecary at Colonial Williamsburg stocked tobacco and clay pipes. The link between drugstores and tobacco is a very old one. It's also distressingly close, for example, in the case of drugstore magnate, Louis K. Liggett's association with the Liggett & Myers tobacco company, which distributed *L&M* cigarettes, among other brands.

32. The link between selling books and selling patent medicines is also very old. William Lyon Mackenzie, for example, ran a store in Dundas, Upper Canada during the early 1820s that featured patent medicines, stationary, and books. Similar combinations were often found in England, Scotland and other old countries, where the distribution systems used to disseminate patent medicines, proved to be useful for the distribution of books and stationary supplies, as well.

33. Schlereth, *Victorian America, op. cit.*, p. 153.

34. Harney and Troper, *op. cit.*

35. The Koken company name is entwined in the metal footrest. Ernest Koken of St. Louis patented his first barber chair in 1881. From 1922–1927, Koken was the leader in barber-chair production and sales in the United States. William Stage, "Force Behind the Throne," http://www.riverfronttimes.com (December 8, 2000).

36. Board of Trade, 1897, *op. cit.*, p. 85. George McKibbon (spelt with an "o") lived in a large, Romanesque Revival house at 37 Spadina Road, in the heart of the newly opening Annex area.

37. For a contemporary, and well-illustrated, late-nineteenth-century American view of the department store phenomenon, see Samuel Hopkins Adams, "The Department Store," *Scribner's Magazine*, vol. 21 (1897), pp. 4–27.

38. In November 1887, under questioning by carpenter Samuel Heakes of the Labour Commission, Timothy Eaton admitted that his saleswomen were "required to stand on their feet the whole time they [were] engaged in the store," from 8 a.m. opening until 6 p.m. closing. Samuel Heakes, quoted in Greg Kealey, *Canada Investigates Industrialism* (Toronto: University of Toronto Press, 1973), p. 90.

39. "A Merchant in a Market Town," *Eaton's Golden Jubilee 1869–1919* (Toronto: T. Eaton Company, 1919), pp. 29–49. For example: "The appearance of the modern tank waddling over trenches and shell holes was scarcely more surprising than the introduction fifty years ago [in 1869] of this idea of selling only for cash at fixed prices." *Ibid.*, p. 36. According to McAree, one way the small, corner store could compete with the big department store was by extending credit, as they always had. (Of course, many little stores went out of business, while Eaton's sailed smoothly onward ... until the late 1990s.)

40. Another dry-goods merchant, by the name of Robert Simpson, moved into 178 Yonge Street when Eaton moved on. Between them, Eaton and Simpson made the corner of Yonge and Queen the new retail centre of the city, when Edwardian office buildings were transforming the city's first retail centre along King Street into a financial centre. See, for example,

Gunter Gad and Deryck W. Holdsworth, "The Emergence of Corporate Toronto," in Donald Kerr and Deryck W. Holdsworth (eds.), *Historical Atlas of Canada: Addressing the Twentieth Century* (Toronto: University of Toronto Press, 1990), Plate 15.

41. Eaton's Methodism was mixed in with a good dollop of Benthamite utilitarianism. This philosophical stance was reflected in one of the founder's favourite sayings, "The Greatest Good to the Greatest Number," by which he may have meant "the Greatest Goods to the Greatest Number," since the singular motto decorated more than one mail order catalogue. See cover to the *T. Eaton Company Catalogue No. 36*, Fall — Winter 1896/7.

42. Simpson's success continued on into the Edwardian era, hand-in-hand and cheek-by-jowl with its rival on the north side of Queen Street. For a pro-Simpson's perspective, see Norman Patterson, "Evolution of a Departmental Store," in *Canadian Magazine*, 1906, pp. 425–435.

43. "Canada's Greatest Store!" *T. Eaton Company Catalogue No. 36*, Fall — Winter 1896/7.

44. Commentary on the back of each stereographic card offers management's story of the Big Store, and makes fascinating reading, both for the facts and the perspective presented. See City of Toronto Archives, SC 125.

45. In the early years, and arguably still, advertising tended to be divided into the "plain talk" or "reason why" school versus the "peppy jingles" or "atmosphere advertising" school. See Schlereth, *Victorian America, op. cit.*, pp. 158–159.

46. *A Visit to the T. Eaton Company*, 1896, which was illustrated by sketches of the recently expanded store, which had gained 2 1/4 acres of new floor space in a single year.

47. "Canada's Greatest Store!", *T. Eaton Company Catalogue No. 36*, Fall — Winter 1896/7.

48. Wayne Kelly, *Downright Upright: A History of the Canadian Piano Industry* (Toronto: Natural Heritage, 1991), p. 45. The name of the company changed over time. Founded in 1864, the Bell Company became the Bell Organ & Piano Company in 1888, and the Bell Piano & Organ Company in 1907.

49. Small, neighbourhood stores survived especially well in working-class and/or ethnic areas, where language, trust, and need for credit reinforced consumer loyalty, long after chain stores and department stores swept across the retail landscape. For an intriguing study of Chicago, see Lizabeth Cohen, "Encountering Mass Culture at the Grassroots: The Experience of Chicago Workers in the 1920s," American Quarterly, vol. 41, no. 1 (March 1989), online at: http://www. jstor.org.

50. Commentary on the back of Eaton's "Stoves and Hardware" stereograph, 1910, City of Toronto Archives, SC 125, Item 14.

51. *Golden Jubilee, op. cit.*, p. 161.

52. *Golden Jubilee, op. cit.*, pp. 204–205.

53. Webb continued to expand. On June 5, 1889, he opened a Restaurant and Dining Room at 66 and 68 Yonge Street, where he fed "the elite of Toronto's professional and commercial circles." He must have fed many of Toronto's non-elite as well, since his daily average was around a thousand customers. The new building also contained "a ballroom, assembly hall, smoking and dressing-rooms, &c., and all the fittings and decorations [were] on the most superb scale." The *Dominion Illustrated*, 1892, *op. cit.*, p. 45. In December 1897, Webb catered that decade's most extravagant social event, the Victorian Era Ball.

54. Describing the activities of local soft drink creator, Charles Wilson of 519 Sherbourne Street, the 1892 *Dominion Illustrated* commented, "During the hot months of summer nothing is more refreshing, nor indeed, can there be anything more acceptable than a draught of some sweet, cooling beverage [like Wilson's celebrated 'none such' ginger ale]. Unlike intoxicants, the result is wholly beneficial, consequently the manufacture of such goods merits universal recognition." *Dominion Illustrated, op. cit.*, p. 63. By 1891, Wilson was producing 12,000 bottles of soda per day.

55. Robert Green was so proud of his creamy confection that his will specified that "Originator of the Ice Cream Soda" be engraved as his epitaph. Schlereth, *Victorian America, op. cit.*, p. 229.

56. According to Schlereth, "The sundae originated in the 1890s and the ice cream cone first appeared at the 1904 St. Louis Exposition." Schlereth, *Victorian America, op. cit.*, p. 230.

57. The Fletcher Manufacturing Company, established in 1882, manufactured all manner of items related to baking, candy and ice-cream making, and was operating ice cream parlours and related businesses. By 1912, it had factories in Toronto and Glencoe, and a new showroom at 29–41 Hayter Street. Its product line ranged from cookie cutters to candy-pulling machines, from soda fountains to furnaces, and its 1915 catalogue declared "Onyx Fixtures our specialty" under a small photograph of a soda fountain. Founder Edgar S. Fletcher was also something of an inventor: he developed the spiral design of straws, which replaced earlier models that had used a straight glued seam. *Fletcher Manufacturing Co. fonds*. City of Toronto Archives, Fonds 44.

58. See also City of Toronto Archives: Fonds 1525, Item 8, for another Diana Sweet location, which was dominated by candy counters and a long soda fountain, but displayed the same design accents as the location illustrated here.

59. Board of Trade, op. cit., p. 147.

60. C. S. Clark, *Of Toronto the Good: The Queen City of Canada as it is* (Montreal: The Toronto Publishing Company, 1898, in Coles facsimile reproduction, 1990), *passim*.

61. Around the same time that this photograph was taken, the Grand Central Oyster Bar opened in New York's famous railway station. Unlike this Toronto bar, the Grand Central Oyster Bar was still operating over 80 years after its founding.

62. G. Adam Mercer, *op. cit.*, p. 53.

63. Gunter Gad, William Code, Neil Quigley, "Financial Institutions," in Donald Kerr and Deryck W. Holdsworth (eds.) *Historical Atlas of Canada: Addressing the Twentieth Century* (Toronto: University of Toronto Press, 1990), Plate 9.

64. Board of Trade, *op. cit.*, p. 71.

65. Board of Trade, *op. cit.*, pp. 69–76.

66. Gunter Gad and Deryck W. Holdsworth, *op. cit.*, Plate 15.

67. *Construction* magazine for December 1914 devoted two long articles to Darling & Pearson's Edwardian marvel, one to the banking and office areas, and one to the vaults and mechanical services headquartered in the basement.

68. The vault actually broke the pavement of King Street when it was dragged into place. Because it is so huge and heavy, modern condominium redevelopers decided to leave it in situ, and transform it into "the world's smallest condominiums" ... suitable for storing stock certificates, expensive jewellery, and precious digital data disks ... or perhaps the most secure sports bar in the Dominion.

69. Manager, Historical Preservation Services, *Report on 1 & 5 King Street West to Toronto Preservation Board*, October 9, 2000.

70. Board of Trade, *op. cit.*, p. 72.

71. *Dominion Illustrated* 1892, *op. cit.*, p. 85.

72. Mulvany, *op. cit.*, p. 41. For more details on specific businesses located along King Street in the mid-1880s, see *Industries of Canada: Historical and Commercial Sketches of Toronto* (Toronto, 1886), *passim*. For an elegant engraving of fashionable King Street around this period, see "King Street, The Great Thoroughfare of Toronto, from a photograph by Notman & Fraser," in *Canadian Illustrated News*, 1880.

73. After Notman & Fraser (1870–1883) came Josiah Bruce (1884–1885), then Millman & Company (1886–1887), and then Herbert E. Simpson (1888–1925).

74. Board of Trade, *op. cit.*, p. 159.

75. See Board of Trade, *op. cit.*, p. 122 for photographs of both the Ryrie Brothers jewellery store at the corner of Yonge and Adelaide (later the site of a Holt Renfrew store), and the City's golden present, which bore an image of Lennox's rising-but-still-not-complete City Hall, with a queenly crown on top.

76. Ryrie Brothers were among the first retail jewellers in Toronto to have Edison's incandescent electric lights introduced into their stores in 1890.

77. The Queen's Hotel itself evolved out of mid-century Sword's Hotel. During its heyday, the Queen's Hotel accommodated English and European royalty (Princess Louise and Russian Grand Duke Alexis), theatrical royalty (Ellen Terry and Sarah Bernhardt), and Canadian political royalty (Sir John A. Macdonald). According to some reports, Sir John A. "ran the country from the red parlor quite as much as from Parliament Hill or Ernescliffe Ottawa," between 1878 and 1891. In 1927 the Queen's Hotel was demolished to make way for the Royal York Hotel, which was not only fashionable, but also very big. When it opened in 1929, it was the largest hotel in the British Empire. (See "Stately Old 'Red Parlor' to be Reproduced Intact: will not be permitted to become just a memory when Queen's Hotel is razed to make room for the big hostelry of the C.P.R.." In A. R. Hassard's scrapbook, City of Toronto Archives, Fonds 1087, pp. 234–235.

78. *Industries of Canada*, 1886, *op. cit.*, p. 95.

79. Ruth Cathcart, *Jacques & Hay: 19th Century Toronto Furniture Makers* (Toronto: Boston Mills Press, 1986), pp. 18–21. When the hotel was being demolished in 1927, among the furniture sold at auction were 126 wardrobes (in various woods), 217 bureaus with mirrors, 36 walnut chairs with leather seats, and the celebrated Jacques & Hay "Great Sideboard" which had won the Jacques & Hay a place of honour at the 1860 Philadelphia Exposition. Spadina House in Toronto has Jacques & Hay furniture on permanent display, which gives some idea of the splendour of the old hotel.

80. See the series of post-1904 fire photographs by W. J. Wittingham, City of Toronto Archives, Fonds 1408, especially Item 8.

CHAPTER 7
Inner Sancta

1. Poor men had precious little access to large, private studies, libraries, or socially elite clubs, but some did have access to such bastions of maleness as union power-structures, mechanics institutes, and less-elite clubs and societies. Some also argue that the saloon, or local pub, functioned as the working-man's club.

2. See Goss's photograph, *Crowded Kitchen, 1913*, in Chapter 3.

3. When — like the Klu Klux Klan — secret societies have been racist, sexist, Anti-semitic, or otherwise socially harmful, they move way beyond the "silly" to the socially unacceptable.

4. See Stephen A. Kent, "Freemasonry," in *The Canadian Encyclopedia*, CD-ROM, 1996; and the website maintained by the Grand Lodge of Canada in the Province of Ontario. Masonic ritual is built around mythic links to the stone masons who built the cathedrals and great buildings of medieval Europe. Their symbols include plumb rules and levels, their costumes include craft aprons, and their monotheistic references are to The Great Architect. See: The Grand Lodge of Ancient Free & Accepted Masons of Canada in the Province of Ontario, *Regulations for Organizing a Lodge* (Toronto: Grand Lodge, 1909), *passim*.

5. Henry Scadding, edited by Frederick H. Armstrong, *Toronto of Old* (Toronto: Dundurn Press, 1987), p. 64

6. C. Pelham Mulvany, *Toronto Past and Present* (Toronto: W. E. Caiger, 1884), pp. 129–136. Mulvany, who was obviously a Mason, describes not only the Toronto Street hall, but also gives information about the other Masonic lodges then meeting in Toronto.

7. This marvellous, now-razed, building was erected by another, quasi-secret society, the International Order of Forresters.

8. Mulvany, *op. cit.*, pp. 119–120.

9. An unrepentant booster and serious snob, C. Pelham Mulvany began his chapter on *Social Life* in Toronto as follows:

> The society of Toronto, even from the first settlement of Governor Simcoe's dozen houses, was never other than metropolitan. It had no shoddy stage to pass through.... Little York, although it consisted but of a cluster of log-houses, whose "mud" clings to its memory, was from the first the abode of the most cultured and aristocratic society of the new Province. It was, from its first rude beginnings, distinctly metropolitan. The leaders of its society were fine ladies and distinguished gentlemen, whom Governor Simcoe's wife could make welcome at her log-built Government House, "Castle Frank," and whom an exiled noble of one of the noblest houses of France could regard as socially his equals.
>
> C. PELHAM MULVANY, *op. cit.*, p. 116.

10. Ronald G. Haycock, "Sir Samuel Hughes," *Canadian Encyclopedia* CD-ROM, 1996.

11. Sir John A. joined the Club shortly after it was founded in 1883, and was a member until his death in June 1891. The link between Macdonald and the Club was so strong that less than an hour after the Prime Minister died on June 6, 1891, the Club received a telegram saying, "Our old chieftain passed away quietly at 10:30." Albany Club Archives, 91 King Street East.

12. Quoted by Joe Martin, "Club Feat," *The Beaver* (August–September 1998), p. 41.

13. C. Pelham Mulvany, *Toronto: Past and Present* (Toronto: W. E.. Caiger, 1884), p. 120. The social prominence of the Toronto Club continued. For example, according to the City Directory of 1910, the Club's secretary was Agar Adamson — the well-connected husband of Mabel Cawthra, a Rideau Hall chronicled by Ottawa social columnist, "Amaryllis," and cherished character recreated by Sandra Gwyn, *op. cit.*, *passim*.

14. Historian J. M. S. Careless described George Albertus Cox as "the canny leader of Toronto corporate finance, power behind the Bank of Commerce, Canada Life, and other investment enterprises in or far beyond the city." J. M. S. Careless, *Toronto to 1918: An Illustrated History* (Toronto: James Lorimer & Company, Publishers, 1984), p. 151. The 1913 *Grain Growers' Guide*, suggests that Cox was the best-connected "plutocrat" in Toronto, with multiple links to most other members of the Edwardian power elite. "Toronto 'Plutocrats'," reproduced by Gunther Gad and Deryck W. Holdsworth, "The Emergence of Corporate Toronto," in Donald Kerr and Deryck W. Holdsworth *Historical Atlas of Canada: Addressing the Twentieth Century* (Toronto: University of Toronto Press, 1990), Plate 15. Based on newspaper coverage of this 1912 banquet, Cox may have been well-connected and even much-respected, but he was also long-winded, and not very witty.

15. Eric Arthur, *Toronto No Mean City* (Toronto: University of Toronto Press, 2nd ed., 1974), p. 218. Of the Club's 1888 design, Arthur commented, "In a way it is the history of architecture from Jacobean to Georgian times — all held together by the skill of the architect." The architect was Frank Darling.

16. Women artists needed places to display, discuss, and create their art. Unlike their male counterparts, they had few opportunities to exhibit their

creations, and none devoted to the handicrafts. In 1886, socially prominent artist Mary E. Dingman invited a group of women artists to her studio in the Yonge Street Arcade, where other artists (such as George and Mary Hiester Reid) also had studios. Before long, the women had established a Women's Sketch Club that met in the Canada Life Building at 40–46 King West. With the patronage of proto-feminist Lady Aberdeen, who was instrumental in the establishment of the Victorian Order of Nurses and the National Council of Women, Dingman and company founded the Women's Art Association of Canada in 1896 — with groups established across the country — to stimulate and raise public awareness about women's contributions to the arts. Among their projects were exhibitions of handicrafts at fashionable 594 Jarvis Street, and the creation of an exquisite Canadian Historical Dinner Service, which was presented to Lady Aberdeen when she and her Governor-General husband returned to Scotland in 1898. (The WAAC's nationalist creation unfortunately still resides in a special cabinet at Haddo House, Aberdeenshire, Scotland.) Such prominent artists as Emily Carr on the West Coast and both Frances Loring and and Florence Wylie in Toronto became active members. In 1916, the WAAC purchased the old Yorkville house at 23 Prince Arthur Avenue, which became a hub of women's art and is still spreading the word.

17. The Heliconian Club was founded in 1909, at about the same time as the male Arts and Letters Club and along the same lines, i.e., drawing its membership from people active in art, music, and literature (later adding dance, drama, and the humanities). At the founding meeting, called by Toronto Music Conservatory teacher Mary Hewitt Smart, on January 20, 1909, the 59 founding members also decided to adopt classicist Goldwin Smith's suggestion that their name be based on Mt. Helicon, where the mythical Muses were said to live. In 1923, the Heliconian Club bought the 1875 "Carpenter's Gothic" church at 35 Hazelton Avenue, where the Club still meets and exhibits. Prior to that, members gathered in tea rooms around the city.

18. The 1921 list of members, published in *The Torontonian Society Blue Book*, indicates that the membership was drawn heavily from The Annex, Rosedale, Forest Hill, and other wealthy parts of Toronto. The ladies were, of course, listed according to their husbands' names — e.g., Mrs. William H. Gooderham of 8 Bedford Road (in the Annex), Mrs. Britton Osler of 67 Binscarth Road (in Rosedale), and Mrs. David Henderson of 69 Forest Hill Road (in the more-recently developed Forest Hill) — unless they were actually Ladies — e.g., Lady Hearst of 80 Glen Road (in Rosedale).

19. Victor L. Russell, *Mayors of Toronto* (Erin, Ontario: Boston Mills Press, 1982), pp. 120–124. According to J. V. McAree, author and occupant of the "Cabbagetown Store," R. J. Fleming was one of the relatives who made good. J. V. McAree, *Cabbagetown Store* (Toronto: The Ryerson Press, 1953).

20. *Toronto Municipal and County Buildings*, 1889, floor plan and description. (City of Toronto Archives: Information files on Toronto City Hall, 1899–1965.)

21. According to an obituary published on February 2, 1950, much of Tommy Church's popularity was directly linked to his actions during the Great War. "Forces leaving, forces returning — T. L. Church was always there. And the public never forgot it." After leaving municipal politics, Church served as a Conservative (but *not* a *Progressive* Conserva-tive) MP, from 1921 until his death in 1950, with only two interruptions — electoral defeats in 1924 (when he tried to come back as mayor) and 1930. Biography File, City of Toronto Archives.

22. Roger Hall, *A Century to Celebrate 1893–1983* (Toronto: Dundurn Press, 1993), pp. 96–97.

23. "Ontario's Capitol: The Great New Building in the Park: the Noble Pile in which Ontario's Legislators are now in Session," *The Saturday Globe*, April 15, 1893.

24. See "The Ontario Cabinet, 1893" in, *Frank Yeigh, Ontario's Parliament Buildings* (Toronto: The Williamson Book Company Ltd., 1893), p. 122.

25. Eric Arthur, *From Front Street to Queen's Park: The Story of Ontario's Parliament Buildings*, (Toronto: McClelland & Stewart, 1979) p. 117.

26. J. M. S. Careless, *Toronto to 1918: An Illustrated History* (Toronto: James Lorimer & Company, 1984), pp. 172–173.

27. The Dominion Bank used images of its head office boardroom in ads at least until the 1950s. See, for example, Dominion Bank advertisement in *Toronto Calling: The Monthly Magazine of Toronto Life*, June 1950.

28. *Construction*, December 1914, pp. 443–444. The chandeliers in the 1914 photograph were later replaced by even larger and flashier brass chandeliers.

29. Women's creative spaces are so rare that they are seldom mentioned, let alone photographed. Often, women "tucked" their writing in around other household activities, and did their composing in kitchens or parlours or other shared spaces.

30. Carlie Oreskovich, *Sir Henry Pellatt: The King of Casa Loma* (Toronto: McGraw-Hill Ryerson, 1982), p. 149.

31. Oreskovich, *op. cit.*, p. 154

32. The other two were Sidney Strickland Tully and a Mrs. McGillivray Knowles. The City of Toronto

Archives has most, but not all, of these photographs by William James.

33. For contemporary "Canadian Art Icon," Betty Goodwin, the studio "where she meditates and creates" is also her Ainner sanctum." Deirdre Hanna, "Betty Goodwin," *NOW* (November 12–18, 1998), p. 47.

34. Another lifelong Liberal then living in Toronto, Goldwin Smith, was also an advocate of the free trade, laissez-faire, "invisible hand" model of economics (and society) fashioned by Enlightenment Scotsman, Adam Smith. Goldwin Smith probably had a copy of Adam Smith's masterwork in his library at The Grange.

35. Russell, *op. cit.*, pp. 112–115.

36. The Victorians considered January 1, 1901 the beginning of the twentieth century, not January 1, 1900.

37. O. A. Howland, "Mayor's Inaugural Address," Appendix "C." *City of Toronto Council Minutes, 1901*, pp. 1–2. Howland did not necessarily mean constitutional change. A century later, some Torontonians were still promoting a variation on this provincial theme; especially after the final Ontario Government of the twentieth century, led by arch Conservative Premier Mike Harris, imposed amalgamation on the seven municipal governments that had made up the Metropolitan Toronto area in 1997, against the direct, expressed will of the electorate. Although 76% of those voting in local referenda on amalgamation voted *against* the idea in March 1997, the Harris Government went ahead with enforced municipal restructuring in January 1998, ensuring that many Torontonians continued thinking about provincial status, or at least a "new deal" for the city. Other topics mentioned by Mayor Howland also strike a responsive chord a century later: waterfront development and inequalities in municipal tax assessment.

38. "Announcement by His Worship the Mayor of the Death of Her Most Gracious Majesty Queen Victoria," Appendix "C." *City of Toronto Council Minutes, 1901*, p. 9. Queen Victoria died on January 22, 1901.

39. In 1897, O. A. Howland was Vice-President of the Canadian Bar Association and Chairman of the Canadian Deep Waterways Commission.

40. Ramsay Cook, "Smith, Goldwin," *Dictionary of Canadian Biography* (Toronto: University of Toronto Press, 1994), vol. XIII, p. 968.

41. Born Harriet Elizabeth Mann Dixon, the new Mrs. Goldwin Smith was the widow of prominent Toronto Tory, William Henry Boulton, and the owner of the Boulton mansion, The Grange. After the death of both Harriet and Goldwin Smith, The Grange became the home of the Toronto Art Gallery, which is now the Art Gallery of Ontario. Perhaps surprisingly, given both the political and personality differences between William Henry Boulton and Goldwin Smith, the Boulton-Smith marriage seems to have been a very successful one for both partners.

42. *Ibid.*, p. 971.

43. V. I. Dickens, "Woods in City's Heart Seen by William Chinn," [1934] in *Scrapbook*, compiled by F. Rogers. City of Toronto Archives, Fonds 70.

44. See William James's photograph of mourners converging on The Grange to view Smith's lying-in-library-state. City of Toronto Archives: Fonds 1244.

45. Cook, *op. cit.*, p. 970. Smith, like Richard Cobden and John Bright of the Manchester School of Economics, was a strong advocate of laissez-faire capitalism.

CHAPTER 8
From Late Victorian to Proto-Modern

1. Oscar Wilde arrived in Toronto on the Queen's Birthday, May 24, 1882, as part of his ten-month tour of North America. Not only did he (incongruously) attend the lacrosse match, where he made this comment to inquisitive reporters from the *Globe*, but he also gave two lectures, visited the University and an art exhibition, stayed at the Queen's Hotel, and annoyed John Ross Robertson's *Telegram* staff so much that it lampooned "Miss Wilde" and her impractical, aesthetic judgments. His aesthetic judgment on Toronto's "white brick" was undoubtedly influenced by seeing such buildings as St. James Cathedral and Jarvis Street mansions — like Edward Blake's and Hart Massey's — along the route to the lacrosse grounds at Jarvis and Wellesley streets. His judgments on domestic interior design, spelled out in "The House Beautiful" and "Art Decoration," could hardly have been more at odds with the heavy, dark, cluttered taste seen in the homes of Robertson and his late-Victorian neighbours. As for the "war of the bricks" in late-nineteenth-century Toronto, red was about to overtake white as the brick colour of choice, but this triumph had little or nothing to do with Wilde. See "Oscar Wilde: Arrival of the Apostle of "estheticism in Toronto," *Globe*, May 25, 1882; "Oscar in the Sanctum: Miss Wilde Visits The Telegram Office," *Telegram*, May 27, 1882; *San Francisco Daily Chronicle*, March 30, 1882 (reprinted at http://www.sfmuseum.org/hist5/wilde.html); and "The White and the Red," *The William Morris*

Society of Canada Newsletter (winter 1992–93).

2. *Construction*, May 1929, p. 139.

3. Acceptable walking distance has varied dramatically over time. Richard Harris, for example, has written that Toronto's blue-collar residents were willing to walk as far as four miles to work in the early part of the twentieth century. Richard Harris, *Unplanned Suburbs: Toronto's American Tragedy 1900 to 1950* (Baltimore: John's Hopkins University Press, 1996), p. 277. In the 1880s, Rosedale was a suburb, Parkdale was a far-distant suburb, and the City's boundaries were from Dufferin Street to the Don River, Bloor Street to the Lake. Suffice it to say, that in 1881, Toronto was more compact and Torontonians more willing to walk.

4. According to one family member by marriage, "Aunt Lil" Robertson:

> ... between the years 1880 and about 1910, John Ross Robertson was the Tsar of Toronto. He choose (sic) who would be Mayor, who would be elected to the city council, and what they would do after elected.

Lilian Westgarth Grant (formerly Robertson), "[H]istory of the John Robertson family of Toronto," p. 18. Unpublished manuscript, January 1974. Archives of Ontario, F 1174, MU 7422, File 11, "Genealogy." Robertson's influence was certainly not limited to this period. Shortly after Robertson died on May 31, 1918, Mayor Tommy Church described him as "Toronto's most distinguished citizen." Quoted in "John Ross Robertson is Dead: Noted Publisher and Benefactor," *The Globe*, June 1, 1918. For a more detailed and balanced assessment, see Minko Sotiron, "John Ross Robertson," in *Dictionary of Canadian Biography*, 1911–1920 (Toronto: University of Toronto Press, 1998), vol. XIV, pp. 876–881.

5. See James Lemon, *Toronto Since 1918: An Illustrated History* (Toronto: James Lorimer & Company, 1985); and Randall White, *Too Good to be True: Toronto in the 1920s* (Toronto: Dundurn Press, 1993).

6. Toronto remained astonishingly "British" throughout this period. By 1931, the population was still over 80% British, and the largest "ethnic" group was "Jewish" (mostly Eastern European) which had grown to about 7%. All other groups remained tiny by comparison. See "Table VII, Birthplace of Toronto's Foreign-born Population, 1911–81 (%)," in Lemon, *op.cit.*, p. 196.

7. Architectural education at the University of Toronto combined elements of the traditional and the modern. For example, a 1933 examination on "Elements of Architectural Form", set by Professor Eric Arthur, asked students "Of what importance is the muntin bar in a Georgian window?" and a staff-set examination on "Architectural Design" in 1935 asked students to design "A Georgian Music Room." Other examinations set by Arthur and his colleagues asked for solutions to such modern design problems as "A Terminal Station for a Radial Street Car Line" (in 1931) and "A Bus Station" (in 1932, soon after the TTC's new, Art Deco bus station opened on Bay Street). Eric Arthur himself was an interesting blend of modern designer (e.g., the 1937 Erichsen-Brown House and the 1959 Women's Athletic Building at the University of Toronto) and historic preservationist. These, and other examinations, from the 1930s are found in the City of Toronto Archives, Series 600, Subseries 4, File 64.

8. For a succinct discussion of these themes, see the reissue of the 1987 Bureau of Architecture and Urbanism (BAU), *Toronto Modern: The Exhibition Revisited* (Toronto: Coach House Press with

Association for Preservation Technology International, 2002), with a new introduction by Michael McClelland and Mark Fram.

9. "John Ross Robertson is Dead: Noted Publisher and Benefactor," *The Globe*, June 1, 1918.

10. See "John Ross Robertson," in Jesse Edgar Middleton, *The Municipality of Toronto: A History* (Toronto: The Dominion Publishing Company, 1923), vol. 2, p. 57.

11. Archives of Ontario, F 1174, *J. Ross Robertson family fonds*, Box MU 7422, *Scrapbook* of ephemera, including the heather collected by "Aunt Charlotte, Aunt Jessie, Jack and I" in September 1872.

12. The hallstand was a Victorian invention. Usually composed of four functional elements — umbrella stand, hat hooks, mirror, and sometimes a small table with narrow drawer — the hallstand reached its peak of decorative importance in the 1870s, and had passed out of style by 1920. Rarely found in lower-class homes, the it was a distinctly middle- to upper-middle-class artifact, a mark of some social standing. Robertson's was big and elaborate, suiting his social status as a prominent Torontonian. Kenneth L. Amers, "Meaning in Artifacts: Hall Furnishing in Victorian America," in Thomas J. Schlereth, (ed.), *Material Culture Studies in America* (Nashville: American Association for State and Local History, 1981), pp. 206–221.

13. Lilian Westgarth Grant, *op. cit.*, p. 13.

14. Although no plans have survived, both building permits and assessment records suggest that Robertson made substantial alterations to his home between late 1903 and mid-1904. In the fall of 1903, Robertson obtained two building permits: #1845, for an additional storey and alterations in brick, valued at $3,000; and #2103, issued on December 9, 1903 to architect [S.] G. Curry, for a two-storey verandah in brick and timber, valued at $700.

Meanwhile, the assessed value for buildings at 291 Sherbourne Street rose from $7,000 in June 1903, to $10,000 in June 1904, and the frontage increased from 70 to 78 feet. (The earlier assessment had remained constant for many years; and adjoining properties remained relatively unchanged in 1904.)

15. An earlier exterior photograph of Culloden House clearly shows the Sherbourne frontage with only one bay window, as well as the slender Victorian verandah, shown in the late-1880s photograph reproduced here. See "The Residence of Mr. J. Ross Robertson, 291 Sherbourne, 1882: 'Culloden'," Toronto Public Library, T 11459.

16. John Ross Robertson, *Landmarks of Toronto*, 6 volumes (Toronto: *Evening Telegram*, 1894 to 1914). Robertson's magnum opus, *Landmarks*, is based on articles that first appeared in the *Evening Telegram*. There is no way to determine which articles Robertson himself wrote, although the provincial archivist noted how often he encountered Robertson digging through the archives. But he was certainly responsible for the publication of the series. *Landmarks* is not always accurate, but it is a good place for local historians to start their research.

17. The Toronto Public Library has a photograph of this unusual object, T 11463. This artifact reflects both Robertson's collecting prowess and his connections with City Hall.

18. John Ross Robertson's death on May 31, 1918 received saturation coverage. See: "Death of J. Ross Robertson After Illness of Two Weeks," *Evening Telegram*, May 31, 1918; "John Ross Robertson is Dead: Noted Publisher and Benefactor," *The Globe*, June 1, 1918; and "Duke Sends Message to Robertson Home," *Daily Star*, June 1, 1916. The "private" funeral was also covered. See "Many Honored J. R. Robertson," *The Globe*, June 4, 1918.

19. Although the toilet is discreetly hidden from view in the photograph, it is now available for inspection through the City of Toronto, which preserved it, along with a pedestal sink and some fragments of marble, when the house was undergoing renovations in the late-twentieth century (Acc. X.3406). By 1890, substantial homes were designed with bathrooms, such as one featured in *Canadian Architect and Builder*, vol. 3, no. 1 (January 1890).

20. A similar — probably the same — statue can be seen on the great Jacques & Hay sideboard in the dining room.

21. "Death of J. Ross Robertson After Illness of Two Weeks," *Evening Telegram*, Friday, May 31, 1918, p. 15.

22. "John Ross Robertson is Dead: Noted Publisher and Benefactor," *The Globe*, June 1, 1918.

23. Quoted in Sotiron, *op. cit.*, p. 877. In the early days, Robertson frequently turned down advertisements if the desired ratio of ads-to-copy would be exceeded. See *Evening Telegram*, April 19, 1926.

24. According to Robertson, Goldwin Smith invited him to dinner at The Grange, asked how much it would cost to found an "independent daily evening newspaper," and said Robertson could "draw on me for $10,000. And pay me back when convenient." Robertson used about $6,000 of the offered $10,000 and repaid it all within 2 years. Letter to Professor W. T. Hewett, Cornell University, June 4, 1912. Archives of Ontario, F 1174, File 1, Box MU 7584. See also the account quoted in the *Evening Telegram*'s 50th anniversary issue, April 19, 1926, which quoted the paper's founder, saying, "I called at the Grange and was ushered into the great library, where he was standing in front of the blazing grate fire." (See Chapter 7 for a photograph of Smith's great library.)

25. Sotiron, *op. cit.*, p. 878. See also *Evening Telegram*, April 19, 1926 for a description of the founding and early success of the paper.

26. Robertson's scrapbook at the Archives of Ontario includes a certificate for *Toronto Typo. Union No. 91*, dated July 1, 1867, that lists J. R. Robertson as one of its "Honorary Members." This certificate for Toronto's oldest union also provides the names of the Officers and Members in Good Standing. Archives of Ontario, F 1174, *J. Ross Robertson family fonds*, Box MU 7422, *Scrapbook*.

27. See Sotiron, *op. cit.*, p. 878, and Gregory S. Kealey, *Toronto Workers Respond to Industrial Capitalism, 1867–1892* (Toronto: University of Toronto Press, 1978), p. 91. According to Sotiron:

In 1882 the *Telegram* became the first target among the Toronto dailies of a boycott organized by the International Typographical Union with the support of the Toronto Trades and Labor Council. The boycott failed in 1884 and the paper remained defiantly non-union until 1891.... The unionization of the *Telegram*'s printers was significant in that it completed the unionization of all Toronto newspapers and hastened the acceptance of trade unions as a legitimate part of industrial organization.

28. "Aunt Lil", *op. cit.*, p. 10. Upon his death in 1918, Robertson's estate was worth about $1.75 million. Sotiron, *op. cit.*, p. 881.

29. Sotiron, *op. cit.*, p. 881.

30. After inspecting newspaper offices in other cities, Robertson had an "imposing and attractive building" constructed at King and Bay streets. Telford drew illustrations of the following new rooms: the counting room (which was also photographed in the late 1880s), the manager's room (or Robertson's private office), the editor's room, the composing room, the press room, a reporter's room, news

editor's room, and library. For a description of the Telegram's early quarters, see *Evening Telegram*, April 19, 1926.

31. "A Handsome Business Office," in *The Canadian Architect and Builder*, vol. 1, no. 1 (January 1888), p. 10. Online from McGill University, http://digital.library.mcgill.ca/cab.

32. *Ibid*. The engraving of the room clarifies areas of the room that are overexposed in the photograph. For example, the Venus de Milo seen from the Counting Room can be seen on Robertson's desk. On the other hand, the photograph reveals details that are not evident in the illustration, such as the name of the book on the pedestal in the foreground.

33. "Founding of The Telegram," *Evening Telegram*, April 19, 1926, p. 28.

34. According to the City Directory for 1905, a Miss Mary Dawson was a telephone operator at the *Telegram* and lived at 1921 George Street. No telephone is evident in this photograph, so Miss Dawson's true occupation may have embraced more than routing phone traffic. By 1926, on the 50th anniversary of the newspaper, the editorial staff of the paper numbered 83, of whom 11 were women. "Story of Constant Growth To The Telegram of Today," *The Evening Telegram*, April 19, 1926, p. 26.

35. The growth in daily journalism between 1900 and 1930 is nicely illustrated by comparing this small reporters' room with the 1930 *Toronto Star* newsroom documented by William James. By then, telephones, typewriters, cigarettes and more women had made their way into the Star's much larger room, although many of the reporters remained ink-stained wretches, pushing pens rather than banging on keyboards to create their copy. See City of Toronto Archives, Fonds 1244, Item 2054.

36. See Gregory S. Kealey, "Printers and mechanization," in Gregory S. Kealey, *Toronto Workers Respond to Industrial Capitalism, 1867–1892* (Toronto: University of Toronto Press, 1978), pp. 83–97.

37. See, for example, Jesse Edgar Middleton, "John Ross Robertson," in *The Municipality of Toronto: A History* (Toronto: The Dominion Publishing Company, 1923), vol. 2., p. 57.

38. Kealey, *op. cit.*, pp. 95–97. Kealey quotes American Federation of Labor (AFL) president Samuel Gompers as follows:

> The printers have had a most remarkable history, particularly within the last five years. The machine ... was introduced, and it is one of the cases where a new machine, revolutionizing a whole trade, was introduced that did not involve a wholesale disaster even for a time; and it is due to the fact that the I.T.U. has grown to be an organized factor and recognized by those employing printers as a factor to be considered.

Some of the printers who went on strike in 1892 founded the *Evening Star* with the blessing of the local labour movement. See Randall White, *op. cit.*, p. 74.

39. The Linotype machine enabled a single compositor to set an entire line of type mechanically. The operator sat in front of a keyboard, typed out the copy, which was then formed into a single line of type from molten metal. For a good description of printing processes — including composing, stereotyping, and actual printing — see "Story of Constant Growth To The Telegram of Today," *Evening Telegram*, April 19, 1926, pp. 26–27.

40. According to Robertson's own *Landmarks*, he carried the Orange colours in 1896 when he defeated another Conservative Orangeman, Emerson Coatsworth, Jr., for the Conservative nomination in East Toronto and ultimately won the election. "It was with a feeling of duty well done that the brethren celebrated the Orangemen's New Year Day that year," Robertson commented. John Ross Robertson, *Landmarks of Toronto* (Toronto: *Evening Telegram*, 1914), vol. 6, p. 173.

41. After Sir John A. Macdonald's death in 1891, Robertson was appointed to succeed Macdonald as grand representative of the Grand Lodge of England in Canada; and in 1902, to commemorate the coronation of Edward VII, which he attended, Robertson received the honourary rank of Past Grand Warden of England. The overlapping social and political circles are obvious. See Jesse Edgar Middleton, "John Ross Robertson," in *The Municipality of Toronto: A History* (Toronto: The Dominion Publishing Company, 1923), vol. 2, p. 57–58.

42. Grace E. Denison, "Toronto Society in 1904," *Toronto Christmas Magazine*, December 1904.

43. Robertson had started pushing for a Canadian copyright act in the late 1880s when he helped found the Canadian Copyright Association. After becoming president of the association in 1889, he met with the British Minister of Justice to demand a "national policy" for the Canadian book trade. Canada did not achieve autonomy in copyright matters until 1911. See Sotiron, *op. cit.*, p. 879.

44. Quoted in "Reminiscences of John Ross Robertson," *Toronto Daily Star*, June 1, 1918. This article was accompanied by photographs of 291 Sherbourne Street; Robertson in masonic attire; and lines of nurses from the Nurses Residence he built in honour of his first wife, Marie Louisa Gilbee, who had died in 1886.

45. Sotiron, *op. cit.*, p. 880.

46. Quoted in "Reminiscences," *op. cit.*

47. "Reminiscences," *op. cit.* Robertson also gave paintings to the City of Toronto, most notably a

series of large oil paintings by Owen Staples showing historical recreations of York/Toronto in 1794, 1820, 1824, 1828, 1834, 1842, 1850, 1854, and 1897, and a contemporary view of Toronto in 1908. The City still owns these paintings, which are on display in various civic locations.

48. Letter from the Public Library of Toronto to the Commissioner of Parks, January 25, 1912. City of Toronto Archives, RG 12, Series A, File 4.

49. Apartment-building grew dramatically during the 1920s, from 1.4% of all building in 1922 to 14.3% of all building, and 42% of all residential building, in the peak year of 1928. By 1932, however, the apartment boom had evaporated: no permits were issued for new buildings. Even with the addition of these apartments, Toronto's housing stock was overwhelmingly single-family housing. See Richard Dennis, "Apartment Housing in Canadian Cities, 1900–1940," in *Urban History Review/Revue d'histoire urbaine*, vol. XXVI, No. 2 (March 1998), pp. 18–19 .

50. "A. D. Gorrie Sales and Service Building, Toronto," in *Construction* (September 1928), p. 309. See also T. A. Russell, President Willys-Overland, Limited, "Automobile Manufacturing in Toronto: A Growing Industry," in A. C. Curry (compiler), *Toronto Year Book: Story of a City* (Toronto: Municipal Intelligence Bureau, 1929), pp. 125–136.

51. See, for example, S. G. Curry, "Toronto's Traffic Problem: With Suggestions for Its Solution," *Construction* (May 1928), pp. 156–166.

52. "Bay-Adelaide Garage, Toronto" in *Construction* (April 1928), p. 141.

53. "Sociological and Economic Advantages of the Apartment House," *Construction*, vol. 1, no. 1 (November 1907), p. 44. *Construction* magazine, a Canadian architectural magazine, was distinctly pro-apartment houses. This initial article looked at

a range of apartments then available in Toronto, from Wineberg's working-class building in The Ward — which bordered on being a tenement, despite the glowing tributes — to Traders' Bank Apartments, and Madison Apartments which fell toward the luxury end of the spectrum. In fact, few working-class buildings were ever built.

54. Dennis, 1989, *op. cit.*, pp. 13–14. St. George Mansions cost $100,000 to build.

55. For discussions of the meaning and evolution of apartment housing in Toronto, see the following publications by Richard Dennis: *Toronto's First Apartment-House Boom: An Historical Geography, 1900–1920* (University of Toronto, Institute for Urban and Community Studies, 1989); "Interpreting the apartment house: modernity and metropolitanism in Toronto, 1900–1930," *Journal of Historical Geography*, vol. 20, no. 3 (1994), pp. 305–322; and "Apartment Housing in Canadian Cities, 1900–1930," *Urban History Review/Revue d'histoire urbaine*, vol. XXVI, no. 2 (March 1998), pp. 17–31.

56. According to assessment information collected on June 15, 1899, eight people lived at 291 Jarvis Street. Since Robertson's family included a wife and two children, this entry suggests that there were four resident servants. This would not include day staff, and perhaps missed stable boys. City of Toronto Archives, 1900 Assessment Roll, Ward 2, Division 1, p. 37.

57. The second boom crashed precipitously with the onset of the Great Depression: in 1930, only 10 permits were issued, and in 1932, no permits at all were issued for apartment buildings. All statistics are from Dennis, 1998, *op. cit.*, p. 19.

58. *Construction*, November 1907, p. 49.

59. Having stores and services on the ground floor was a common, and often laudable, feature of even

luxurious apartments in this era.

60. On April 18, 1907, Building Permit No. 7051 was issued to Harry Wineberg of 71 Bay Street to erect a three-storey brick building, with stores and apartments at the northeast corner of Agnes and Elizabeth Streets). J. H. Herbert was the architect and R. Chalkley & Son, the builder. According to the Assessment records, the ownership of this property varied from year to year (with Wineberg only appearing on the roll compiled in July 1909); many suites remained vacant (although this could be related to inadequate record-keeping, rather than actual vacancy); the average household size ranged from 5 to 6, with as many as 10 being crammed into small units; and the ethnic composition of the residents — but not the owners — changed significantly by the end of the Great War. Nearly all the Chinese residents were adult males, who looked for cheap accommodation so they could send money to families back in China. For discussions of the Toronto Chinese community, see: Valerie A. May, "An In depth Look at Toronto's Early Chinatown 1913–1933," (University of Toronto, Unpublished paper, August 1977), City of Toronto Archives, Fonds 92, Item 388; and Dora Nipp, "The Chinese in Toronto," in Robert F. Harney (editor), *Gathering Place: Peoples and Neighbourhoods of Toronto, 1834–1945* (Toronto: Multicultural History Society of Ontario, 1985), pp. 147–175.

61. *Construction*, November 1907, *op. cit.*, p. 55.

62. Dennis, 1998, *op. cit.*, p. 24. Unfortunately, as discussed in Chapter 2, another early-twentieth-century experiment in housing the working poor, Spruce Court and Riverdale Courts, failed. The Toronto Housing Company provided excellent apartments, but at too great an expense for the intended audience. Twenty-first century Toronto

continues its struggle with housing its most vulnerable citizens.

63. After 1912, when Toronto City Council passed a bylaw limiting apartment-building construction to commercial streets in order to keep them out of residential areas — especially *wealthy* ones — most buildings were located on commercial streets (like Queen Street), and many were located on corner sites (like Stewart Manor). Corner sites were prized, both because lighting was better for the apartments than would be the case in the middle of blocks, and because corner locations provided a toehold onto adjacent "residential" (i.e., business- and apartment-free) streets. Future builders could — and did — argue that they should be allowed to build additional apartment buildings since there was already one on the street. See Richard Dennis, *op. cit.*

64. The "living room" name for this room was written on Micklethwaite's original negative.

65. Richard Dennis discusses the intense opposition that arose in Toronto as apartment buildings became more frequent. Although Toronto never built true "tenements" — of the sort that plagued New York and other large American cities — opposition to constructing any multiple-occupancy buildings was intense. Dr. Charles Hastings — who should have known better — decried "apartments" as "tenements," as did Mayor Tommy Church, who characterized them as "chicken coops." This led to the ban in 1912 of apartment buildings on residential streets.

66. The original photographer's numbers suggest that the rooms were in the same apartment: the bedroom has #424 in the lower left corner, while the parlour has #422 in the lower left corner.

67. According to assessment-roll data recorded in April 1928, Kathleen Vaughan was the owner of the building and resident in Suite 16. According to the City Directory for the previous year, 1927, the only Kathleen Vaughan in Toronto was a school-teacher living at 374 Berkeley Street. Whether this is the same person is unclear. What is clear is that this building, like many apartment houses built in the early twentieth-century, was owned by a person, not a company. The pattern shifted, as Dennis points out, so that as corporate financing became available, buildings became bigger, and vice versa into the future.

68. According to the Tax Assessment Roll for 1929 (compiled in April 1928), the first residents of Stewart Manor included a photographer, baker, two widows, radio merchant, dining-car waiter for the CPR, store supervisor, auditor, chauffeur, mechanic, shoe-store manager, clerk, builder, Bell Telephone construction engineer, and the unmarried owner of the building.

69. Only two households had four occupants: 42-year old Hector L. Clayton, a dining-car waiter with the CPR, occupied Suite 5 with three other, unidentified people; and Blackford's shoe-store manager, 54-year old Harry C. Knowlton occupied Suite 6 with three other, also unidentified people.

70. In 1907, the City Directory for Toronto started listing the names of "apartment houses" in its business section. During the 1920s, these listings doubled, from about 300 in 1920 to about 600 in 1930. These listings probably missed a lot of apartment buildings, especially at the lower end of the market, but nevertheless provide a useful measure of the new housing form.

71. Richard Dennis, *op. cit.* In November 1907, *Construction* magazine, for example, lauded the luxurious new Traders Bank apartments at Yonge and Bloor. The six-storey French Renaissance Traders Bank contained a new bank branch and sundry convenience stores on the ground floor, and 19 spacious apartments on four upper floors. Among the many conveniences for the mostly businessman clientele was a large café on the top floor. *Construction, op. cit.*, pp. 45–46. About 20 years later, in January 1928, *Construction* was still singing the praises of luxury apartments, like *The Claridge*, which offered tenants "all the ultra-modern refinements found in the finest homes, clubs and hotels" such as a restaurant and a "handsomely appointed" private dining room. *Construction*, January 1928, p. 24.

72. According to Richard Dennis, the Alexandra Palace on University Avenue was the second, and even grander, apartment building to open in Toronto. Dennis, 1989, *op. cit.*, p. 14. The seven-storey, brick and stone building contained 72 suites — with an average household size of 2.6 — and separate dining rooms. Among its residents were Chief Justice Hon. Sir William R. Meredith (1909) and Professor James Mavor (1915).

73. Advertisement in *The Torontonian Society Blue Book and Club Membership Register for 1933* (Toronto: The Torontonian Society Blue Book, 1933). The Alexandra Palace advertised in the *Blue Books* at least until the 1940s.

74. "The Clarendon Apartments, Toronto," *Construction*, January 1928, p. 23. As it turned out, the elitist writer of this article was not too far off the mark with his prediction that by the late 1950s, single-family house building would be a thing of the past in urban centres like Toronto (though not on the periphery). And the trend sweeps on in the form of luxury condos and high-end rental buildings.

75. William Dendy and William Kilbourn, *Toronto Observed: Its Architecture, Patrons, and History* (Toronto: Oxford University Press, 1986), p. 239.

76. *Ibid.*

77. See *Construction* in March 1929 and the *Journal of the Royal Architectural Institute of Canada* in September 1931.

78. W. F. Moore, "Architectural Photography," in *Construction* (April 1932), p. 87.

79. *Construction*, March 1929, p. 93.

80. One of the complaints against apartment living, lodged by uptight Torontonians, was that close proximity, and the mixing of "public" and "private" spaces would lead to immodest, even sinful behaviour: visitors in the parlour might be able to see into an adjacent bedroom; and guests for dinner might have to pass by bedrooms located between a parlour at the front and a dining room at the back. Dennis, "Interpreting the apartment house..." *op. cit.*

81. The concrete in The Claridge, was laid by John V. Gray, a specialist in reinforced concrete building. Gray compiled a set of Moore and Nixon-James photographs to document his company's work, not only at The Claridge, but also at other prominent buildings of the time. See City of Toronto Archives, Fonds 1639.

82. See Florence Waterworth, *The Smiths of Fisherman's Island*, unpublished manuscript, City of Toronto Archives, which contains a family history and associated newspaper clippings.

83. Loblaw's straightforward motto, "We Sell For Less," can be seen in a full-page advertisement featuring the new Toronto warehouse and head office, as well as properties in Chicago and Buffalo, in A. C. Curry (editor), *Toronto Year Book 1929* (Toronto: Municipal Intelligence Bureau), p. 202.

84. City of Toronto, *By-Law No. 52-2001, To designate the property at 500 Lake Shore Boulevard West (Loblaw Groceteria Company building) as being of architectural and historical value or interest, Heritage Property Report, Schedule*, enacted by Council, February 1, 2001. See also Donald M. Ross, "The Loblaw Warehouse, Toronto," in *Construction*, June 1928, pp. 209–210, and photographs on 203 and 205.

85. *Construction*, June 1928, p. 209

86. Toronto was part of a larger, national trend. By December 1928, when Eaton's revealed its plans for College Street, *Construction* magazine declared that Canada's department-store giants were building "new stores on a scale largely surpassing their old ones, at the same time increasing the variety of conveniences and social services offered to their customers." And doing so across the country, in Montreal, Toronto, Saskatoon, Calgary and elsewhere. See "Department Store Growth in Canada," *Construction* (December 1928), pp. 400–412 and 423.

87. E. Boyde Beck, *Art in Architecture: Toronto Landmarks 1920–1940*, p.36. See also John Blumenson, *Ontario Architecture: A Guide to Styles and Building Terms 1784 to the Present* (Toronto: Fitzhenry & Whiteside, 1990); and Tim Morawetz, *Defining Art Deco Architecture*, definitions handed out during an architectural walk on August 2002; and The Art Deco Society of Toronto website, www.art decotoronto.com.

88. Sinaiticus, "The Addition to Robert Simpson Store, Toronto," in *Construction*, March 1929, p. 73.

89. *Ibid.*, p. 75.

90. *Ibid.*, pp. 76–77.

91. Sinaiticus, "Eaton's College Street Store, Toronto," *Construction*, November 1930, p. 352. Sinaiticus did not mention the auditorium, which only opened ca. 1931, but he did pay tribute to the adjacent Art Deco restaurant, The Round Room.

92. For example, see Harold Kalman, *A History of Canadian Architecture* (Don Mills, Ontario: Oxford University Press, 1995), vol. 2, pp. 768–770; and Christopher Hume, "Elegant Eaton treasure revived in restoration," *Toronto Star*, September 5, 2002, p. B4. Finally, after years of neglect and decline, the lovingly restored Eaton Auditorium and Round Room were reopened, as The Carlu, in May 2003. Architect Carlu also worked on New York City's Rockefeller Plaza and hailed from Paris, the city at the centre of the Art Deco movement and host of the 1925 Exposition des Arts Décoratifs et Industriels.

93. Sinaiticus, *Construction* (November 1930), p. 358.

94. E. Boyde Beck, *op. cit.*, p. 24.

95. Jim Wilkes, "Gladstone gets new lease on life," *Toronto Star*, October 14, 2002.

96. Designated "Mrs. N. Robinson" in the 1889 City Directory, Susanna Robinson was probably a widow and certainly the owner of the 4-storey hotel that was under construction at 1206–1208 Queen Street West in September 1890. Other family members — probably her sons, William, Robert and Harry — also worked in the family business, as hotel clerks, managers, and bartenders. (See Assessment Rolls recorded in September 1890, 1891, and 1893.) The assessed value of the hotel remained around $35,000 throughout the period of growth, 1890 to 1911 when the photographs were taken. The adjoining drug and tobacco stores had a combined value of about $10,000.

97. "Hotel Gladstone," advertised in the 1909 City Directory. According to this ad, the hotel had been "Re-Fitted and Re-Furnished Throughout" and it was probably this interior that was photographed for the 1911 publication. At the time, the Gladstone was owned by the widow Agnes Smith and her son, George F., who operated it.

98. In late September 1927, the CPR held a three-day auction to sell off the contents of the old Queen's Hotel before demolition began. On November 3rd,

the last bricks were hauled off and nothing but memories remained of Toronto's first, great hotel. Adam Mayers, "An era goes on the block: The Queen's Hotel was the haunt of Toronto's who's who until it gave way to the Royal York," *Toronto Star*, July 2, 1997.

99. A. C. Curry (compiler), *Toronto Year Book: 1929* (Toronto: Municipal Intelligence Bureau, 1929), p. 238.

100. "The New C.P.R. Hotel, Toronto," in *Construction* (March 1928), p. 102. The hotel lost its title a couple of years later when the 34-storey Canadian Bank of Commerce Building (1929–1931) opened at King and Bay. A photograph of the pre-Bank of Commerce waterfront appears in Sinaiticus, "The Royal York Hotel, Toronto," *Construction* (July 1929), p. 221.

101. The dominance of the Royal York Hotel and its near neighbour, the 34-storey Canadian Bank of Commerce that opened in 1931, is especially evident in photographs taken from the north. Their dominance lasted until the 56-storey Toronto Dominion Centre rose in the mid-1960s.

102. This transition from personal to corporate financing affected many aspects of city-building from this period forward. For example, Richard Dennis, *op.cit.*, discusses the change in the apartment-house sector that occurred.

103. Postcards are notoriously hard to date and, therefore, must be used with great care in historical research. Is the "right" date the date when the photograph was originally taken, which may be long before the date the card was created or sent; or the date when the postcard itself was designed and printed; or the date when the postcard was actually sent, as indicated by a postmark? In fact, each date can be important and, indeed, "correct," depending on the nature of the research and how

the information is used. This photograph was taken around the time the Royal York Hotel opened, but could have been sent (and therefore postmarked) for many years afterwards.

104. Sinaiticus, "The Royal York Hotel, Toronto," *Construction* (July 1929), pp. 208–222 and 227–236.

105. See *Toronto Year Book: 1929*, *op. cit.*, p. 239.

106. Detlef Mertins, "Mountain of Lights," in Bureau of Architecture and Urbanism (BAU), *Toronto Modern: The Exhibition Revisited* (Toronto: Coach House Press with Association for Preservation Technology International, 2002), p. 10. This edition is a reissue of the 1987 exhibition catalogue with a new introductory essay by Michael McClelland and Mark Fram.

107. For a discussion of the evolution of the Canadian office building and skyscraper see, for example, Kalman, *op. cit.*, pp.570–574. The first tall structure in Toronto — and Canada — to be built with a self-supporting steel frame structure was Horwood and Burke's Robert Simpson store of 1895 (discussed Chapter 6). See also Angela Carr, *Toronto Architect Edmund Burke* (Montreal & Kingston: McGill-Queen's University Press, 1995), pp. 99–125. According to Kalman, this put Horwood and Toronto at the forefront of the new architecture in North America. Kalman *Canadian Architecture*, vol. 2, *op. cit.*, p. 574.

108. The stepped — or "wedding cake" — profile emerged from regulations established by New York City in 1916 that established, among other things, the setting back of exterior walls above a specified height to allow light to reach the street. "Sky-scrapers," in Kenneth T. Jackson (editor), *The Encyclopedia of New York City* (New York and New Haven: Yale University Press and New York Historical Society, 1995), pp. 1073–1075.

109. As discussed in *Toronto Modern*, *op. cit.*, one of

the dominant characteristics of Modern and/or International School architecture was a desire to sweep the slate clean, replace older and fussier architecture with the new "rational," "form follows function" architecture. Now, with Post-Modernism and other forms having replaced or augmented Modernism, Toronto Modern itself has become an "historic" style and, ironically, worthy of preservation on that basis. In fact, according to an active group of heritage preservationists known as DOCO-MOMO (which stands for DOcumentation and COnservation of the MOdern MOvement), "The architectural heritage of the Modern Movement in architecture is today more at risk than that of any other period, due to its age, its often innovative technology, the functions it was designed to perform, and the present cultural climate." Docomomo was founded in 1990 and now has branches around the world, including in Canada. Quoted in *docomomo canada-ontario news* (March 2003), online at: http://www.heritageontario.org/DOCO/ doco0303.html.

110. Patricia McHugh, *Toronto Architecture: A City Guide*, 2nd ed. (Toronto: McClelland and Stewart, 1989), p. 83.

111. The Dominion Bank at 1 King West is also discussed in Chapters 4 and 6.

112. The 9/11 attack on New York City's World Trade Centre may have temporarily tamed corporate notions that "higher" equals "more important." By 2005, however, Toronto was once again reaching for the sky with ever-taller buildings. See for example, John Bentley Mays, "Spirit of Ingenuity in the Sky," *Globe and Mail*, January 7, 2005 and Kenneth Kidd, "Urban Tall: Harry Stinson and the race to build Toronto's newest skyscraper," *Toronto Star*, March 13, 2005.

113. Shortly after moving into its new building at 80 King Street West, the *Star* finally surpassed its arch

rival, the *Telegram*, in total circulation, with a daily sale of 37,077 copies compared to the *Telegram*'s 31,884. For another 27 years, however, the *Telegram* still out-sold the *Star* within the city itself. Ross Harkness, *J. E. Atkinson of the Star* (Toronto: University of Toronto Press, 1963), p. 66.

114. Despite a fierce battle waged by heritage preservation activists (see citations below), Toronto City Council voted in mid-May 2002 to give up on preserving the Concourse Building as an authentic, integral whole. Council voted, instead, to authorize a major redevelopment that would demolish the building and preserve only fragments of facades and a few decorative highlights. One of the unsuccessful activists, and the first Chair of the post-amalgamation Toronto Preservation Board, architect Cathy Nasmith, later summarized the dire circumstances facing heritage preservationists in the newly amalgamated City of Toronto. Lacking adequate funding, an integrated heritage preservation and urban planning system, and, most significantly, the legislated power to prevent (rather than simply delay) demolition, Nasmith observed, "there is nowhere in Ontario where heritage preservation reaches internationally accepted practice...." Based on her experience, Nasmith commented,

> What has evolved in the city is what I call the culture of compromise — those [civic officials] negotiating for heritage assume that the development industry must be accommodated and that of course heritage protection will have to suffer. The most dramatic recent example was the fragmenting of the Concourse Building, perhaps the best we could get given the current legislation but sadly below international standards.

See Cathy Nasmith, "Remarks to the Save Union Station Meeting, September 30, 2002, posted on the *Save Union Station* website, http://www.saveunionstation.ca/background7.cfm; and also Catherine Nasmith, "Rewriting history. Do the Tories still have time to pass a new preservation law?"*eye* (February 20, 2003), http://www.eye.net/eye/issue/issue_02.20.03/news/heritage.html. Finally, on April 19, 2005, Dalton McGuinty's Liberal government passed legislation granting municipalities the power to refuse to issue demolition permits for heritage buildings. This will dramatically alter the balance of power between preservationists and developers, but not in time to save the Concourse Building from radical alteration. See Christopher Hume, "New muscle for Heritage Act," *Toronto Star*, April 21, 2005, p. B2.

For an international perspective on heritage preservation, and the basic requirements for success, see Anthony M. Tung, *Preserving the World's Great Cities: The Destruction and Renewal of the Historic Metropolis* (New York: Clarkson Potter, 2001). Tung visited Toronto in 2002 and advised preservationists to "get a law," i.e., the power to prevent, not just delay, demolition of heritage buildings.

For local commentary on the Concourse battle, see: Lisa Rochon, "Trees? Moraine? Historic building? Oh, spare us," *Globe and Mail*, May 17, 2000; Natalie Southworth, "Go-ahead given to demolish Art Deco site," *Globe and Mail*, May 3, 2000; Karen Palmer, "Edifice complex: Treasure or tower?" *Toronto Star*, May 8, 2000; Robert Fulford, "An unfortunate sacrifice," *National Post*, May 8, 2000; Christopher Hume, "There's no future in destroying our past," *Toronto Star*, May 18, 2000; Robert Benzie, "Council approves skyscraper to

replace historic building," *National Post*, May 11, 2000; Natalie Southworth, "Owner rejects bid to save Art Deco skyscraper," *Globe and Mail*, March 23, 2000. See also *By-laws* re: Official Plan Amendment and Rezoning re: Concourse Building and related sites, passed by City Council on May 9, 10, and 11, 2000; and the later Heritage Easement, on file at the City of Toronto Archives, along with photographs of the building.

115. On May 9, 2000, City of Toronto Council authorized the radical redevelopment of the Concourse Building site, allowing the construction of a 41-storey office tower and the demolition of most of the original 16-storey Concourse Building, in return for certain public benefits (such as a daycare centre); and a commitment both to retain the existing facades on the first three floors facing Adelaide Street, and to display on-site "exterior art work" not relocated onto the new building facade, as well as "significant art work located in the lobby." *City of Toronto Toronto Community Council Report No. 8* for City of Toronto Council Consideration on May 9, 2000, Item 24. The developer's plans were available online at http://www.oxfordproperties.com/100Adelaide/images/100Adelaide.pdf

116. J. E. H. Macdonald, quoted in *Construction*, May 1929, p. 141.

117. The completion of the Victory Building was delayed until 1931 and the building stood empty until 1938. Dendy & Kilbourn, *op. cit.*, p. 219.

118. Macdonald, *op. cit.*, p. 141.

119. *Construction* magazine quotes, with approval, the (occasionally grandiose) sentiments expressed by such Canadian poets as Bliss Carman, Duncan Campbell Scott, and Archibald Lampman.

Bibliography

See also notes to each chapter for additional references

Adam, G. Mercer. *Toronto Old and New*. Toronto: The Mail Printing Company, 1891. Coles Canadian Collection facsimile reproduction, 1974.

Adams, Annmarie. "Eden Smith and the Canadian Domestic Revival." *Urban History Review/Revue d'histoire urbaine* vol. 21, no. 2 (March 1993): 104–115.

Adams, Annmarie, and Peter Gossage. "Chez Fadette: Girlhood, Family, and Private Space in Late-Nineteenth-Century Saint-Hyacinthe." *Urban History Review/Revue d'histoire urbaine* vol. 26, no. 2 (March 1998): 56–68.

Adams, Samuel Hopkins. "The Department Store." *Scribner's Magazine* vol. 21 (1897): 4–27.

Alland Sr., Alexander. *Jacob A. Riis: Photographer & Citizen*. Millerton, NY: Aperture, Inc., 1974.

Ames, Kenneth L. "Meaning in Artifacts: Hall Furnishings in Victorian America." *Material Culture Studies in America*. Ed. Thomas J. Schlereth. Nashville: American Association for State and Local History, 1981. 206–221.

Annual Reports of the Chief Constable of the City of Toronto for the Years 1880–1929.

Armstrong, Christopher, and H. V. Nelles. *The Revenge of the Methodist Bicycle Company: Sunday Streetcars and Municipal Reform in Toronto, 1888–1897*. Toronto: Peter Martin Associates Limited, 1977.

Arthur, Eric. *From Front Street to Queen's Park: The Story of Ontario's Parliament Buildings*. Toronto: McClelland & Stewart, 1979.

——. *Toronto No Mean City*. 2nd ed. Toronto: University of Toronto Press, 1974.

——. *Toronto No Mean City*. 3rd ed. Toronto: University of Toronto Press, 1974; and revised by Stephen A. Otto, 1986.

Backhouse, Constance B. *Petticoats and Prejudice: Women and Law in Nineteenth-Century Canada*. Toronto: The Osgoode Society, 1991.

——. "Nineteenth-Century Canadian Prostitution Law: Reflection of a Discriminatory Society." *Histoire sociale — Social History* vol. XVIII, no. 36 (November 1985): 387–423.

Baker, G. Blaine. "Legal Education in Upper Canada 1785–1889." *Essays in the History of Canadian Law*, vol. II. Ed. David H. Flaherty. Toronto: The Osgoode Society, 1981. 49–142.

Baldwin, T. Stith. *Picture Making for Pleasure and Profit: A Complete Illustrated Hand-Book on the Modern Practices of Photography in All its Various Branches*. Chicago: Frederick J. Drake & Co., 1903.

Ball, Helen. "Tea in the Parlor on Mother's day at home." *The Villager*, January 1978. City of Toronto Archives: *Helen Ball Scrapbooks* (on microfilm), SC 228.

Baskerville, Peter and Eric W. Sager. *Unwilling Idlers: The Urban Unemployed and Their Families in Late Victorian Canada*. Toronto: University of Toronto Press, 1998.

Bébout, Richard, ed. *The Open Gate: Toronto Union Station*. Toronto: Peter Martin Associates Limited, 1972.

Beck, Boyde. *Art in Architecture: Toronto Landmarks 1920–1940*. Toronto: The Market Gallery of the City of Toronto Archives, 1988.

Berkovits, Joseph Gondor. "Prisoners for Profit: Convict Labour in the Ontario Central Prison, 1874–1915." *Crime and Criminal Justice*. Ed. Jim Phillips, Tina Loo, and Susan Lewthwaite. Toronto: University of Toronto Press for the Osgoode Society for Canadian Legal History, 1994. 478–515.

Boles, Derek. "The Canadian Pacific Railway's North

Toronto Station." *Canadian Rail Passenger Review*, Number 4 (2005/6).

Boritch, Helen. *The Making of Toronto the Good: The Organization of Policing and Production of Arrests, 1859 to 1955*. Toronto: unpublished PhD dissertation, 1985.

Brace, Catherine. "Public Works in the Canadian City: the Provision of Sewers in Toronto 1870–1913." *Urban History Review/Revue d'histoire urbaine* vol. 23, no. 2 (March 1995): 33–43.

Brown, W. Douglas. *Eden Smith: Toronto's Arts and Crafts Architect*. Toronto: W. Douglas Brown, 2003.

Brunet, Elise. "The law office at the turn of the century." *Ontario Lawyers Gazette* May–June 1999: 32–33.

Burant, Jim. "The Visual World in the Victorian Age." *Archivaria* vol. 19 (Winter 1984–85): 110–121.

Bureau of Municipal Research (New York). "Report on Physical Survey." *Report on Survey of the Treasury, Assessment, Works, Fire and Property Departments*, vol. 2. Toronto, 1914.

Bureau of Municipal Research (New York?). *What is "The Ward" Going to Do With Toronto?* 1918.

Byrtus, Nancy, Mark Fram, and Michael McClelland, eds. *East/West: A Guide to Where People Live in Downtown Toronto*. Toronto: Coach House Press for Society for the Study of Architecture in Canada, 2000.

Careless, J. M. S. *Toronto to 1918: An Illustrated History*. Toronto: James Lorimer & Company, 1984.

Carnegie, David. *The History of Munitions Supply in Canada 1914–1918*. London: Longmans, Green and Co., 1925: passim.

Carr, Angela. *Toronto Architect Edmund Burke*. Montreal and Kingston: McGill-Queen's University Press, 1995.

Cathcart, Ruth. *Jacques & Hay: 19th Century Toronto Furniture Makers*. Toronto: Boston Mills Press, 1986.

Chadwick, Marion Fanny. *Daily Journal*. Archives of Ontario: F 1072.

City Directories (Toronto). Various years. City of Toronto Archives: Research Hall.

Clark, C. S. *Of Toronto the Good: The Queen City of Canada as it is*. Montreal: The Toronto Publishing Company, 1898, Coles facsimile reproduction, 1990.

Clover, Mrs. John. *Diary: 1892–1893*. Toronto: Archives of Ontario, unpublished manuscript, F 830.

Cohen, Lizabeth. "Encountering Mass Culture at the Grassroots: The Experience of Chicago Workers in the 1920s." *American Quarterly* vol. 41, no. 1 (March 1989): 6–33.

Cole, Curtis. "McCarthy, Osler, Hoskin, and Creelman, 1882 to 1902: Establishing a Reputation, Building a Practice." *Beyond the Law: Lawyers and Business in Canada, 1830 to 1930*. Ed. Carol Wilton. Toronto: Osgoode Society, 1990. 149–166.

Cook, Ramsay. "Smith, Goldwin." *Dictionary of Canadian Biography*. Toronto: University of Toronto Press, Vol. XIII, 1994. 968–974.

Craven, Paul. "Law and Ideology: The Toronto Police Court 1850–80." *Essays in the History of Canadian Law*, vol. II. Ed. David H. Flaherty. Toronto: The Osgoode Society, 1981. 248–307.

Crawford, Pleasance. "The Roots of the Toronto Horticultural Society." *Ontario History* vol. LXXXIX, no. 2 (June 1997): 125–139.

Cumming, Carman. *Sketches from a Young Country: The Images of Grip Magazine*. Toronto: University of Toronto Press, 1997.

Davies, Stephen. "'Reckless Walking Must be Discouraged': The Automobile Revolution and the Shaping of Modern Urban Canada to 1930." *Urban History Review/Revue d'histoire urbaine* vol. XVIII, no. 2 (October 1989): 123–138.

Dendy, William. *Lost Toronto*. Toronto: Oxford University Press, 1978.

Dendy, William, and Kilbourn, William. *Toronto Observed: Its Architecture, Patrons, and History*. Toronto: Oxford University Press, 1986.

Denison, George Taylor. *Recollections of a Police Magistrate*. Toronto: The Musson Book Company Ltd., 1920.

Denison, Grace E. "Toronto Society in 1904." *Toronto Christmas Magazine* December 1904. City of Toronto Archives, Larry Becker Collection.

Denison, Merrill. *CCM: The Story of the First Fifty Years*. Toronto: CCM, [1946].

Dennis, Richard. *Toronto's First Apartment-House Boom: An Historical Geography, 1900–1920*. Toronto: University of Toronto, Institute for Urban and Community Studies, 1989.

——. "Interpreting the apartment house: modernity and metropolitanism in Toronto, 1900–1930." *Journal of Historical Geography* vol. 20, no. 3 (1994): 305–322.

——. "Private Landlords and Redevelopment: The 'Ward' in Toronto 1890–1920." *Urban History Review/Revue d'histoire urbaine* vol. XXIV, no. 1 (October 1995): 21–35.

——. "Apartment Housing in Canadian Cities, 1900–1930." *Urban History Review/Revue d'histoire urbaine* vol. XXVI, no. 2 (March 1998): 17–31.

"Dominion Bank Building, Toronto." *Construction* vol. 7, no. 12 (December 1914): 427–455.

Dominion Illustrated: Toronto, The Commercial Metropolis of Ontario. Montreal: Sabiston Litho. & Publishing Company, 1892.

Duffy, Dennis. "Furnishing the Pictures: Arthus S. Goss, Michael Ondaatje and the Imag(in)ing of Toronto." *Journal of Canadian Studies/Revue d'études canadiennes* vol. 36, no. 2 (summer 2001): 106–129.

——. "Money to Burn: Chapter Four of Reservoir Ravine." Unpublished manuscript.

Eastlake, Lady Elizabeth. "Photography." *The Quarterly Review* vol. 101 (April 1857): 441–468.

Eaton, Flora McCrea. *Memory's Wall: The Autobiography of Flora McCrea Eaton.* Toronto: Clarke, Irwin & Company Ltd., 1956.

Engelhardt, George W. *Toronto Canada: The Book of Its Board of Trade. For General Circulation Through the Business Community.* 1897–98. City of Toronto Archives, rare books collection.

Ennals, Peter and Deryck W. Holdsworth. *Homeplace; The Making of the Canadian Dwelling over Three Centuries.* Toronto: University of Toronto Press, 1998.

Firth, Edith . *Toronto in Art.* Toronto: Fitzhenry & Whiteside, 1984.

Flanders, Judith. *The Victorian House: Domestic Life from Childbirth to Deathbed.* London: Harper Perennial, 2003.

Frager, Ruth. " Class, Ethnicity, and Gender in the Eaton Strikes of 1912 and 1934." *Gender Conflicts: New Essays in Women's History.* Ed. Franca Iacovetta and Mariana Valverde. Toronto: University of Toronto Press, 1992. 316–322.

Friedland, Martin A. *The University of Toronto: A History.* Toronto: University of Toronto Press, 2002.

Frizot, Michel, ed. *A New History of Photography.* Cologne: Könemann, English language edition, 1998.

Garrett, Graham W. "Photography in Canada 1839–1841: A historical and biographical outline." *Photographic Canadiana* vol. 22, no. 1 (May/June 1996): 4–6.

Gentilcore, R. Louis, ed. *Historical Atlas of Canada: Canada in the Nineteenth Century,* vol. 2. Toronto: University of Toronto Press, 1993.

Gernsheim, Alison. *Victorian and Edwardian Fashion: A Photographic Survey.* New York: Dover Publications, Inc., 1963, 1981 reprint.

Gernsheim, Helmut and Alison. *The History of Photography, from the Earliest Use of the Camera Obscura to the Beginning of the Modern Era.* London: Oxford University Press, 1955.

Gibson, Sally. *More Than an Island: A History of the Toronto Island.* Toronto: Irwin Publishing, 1984.

Gibson, Sarah Duane Satterthwaite. *Sense of Place — Defense of Place: A Case Study of the Toronto Island.* Toronto: University of Toronto, Department of Geography, unpublished dissertation, 1981.

Glasbeek, Amanda. "Maternalism Meets the Criminal Law: The Case of the Toronto Women's Court." *Canadian Journal of Women and the Law* vol. 12, no. 2 (1998): 480–502.

Goheen, Peter. *Victorian Toronto 1850 to 1900: Pattern and Process of Growth.* Chicago: Department of Geography Research Paper No. 127, 1970.

Golden Jubilee 1869–1919. Toronto: The T. Eaton Co., 1919.

Gould, Stephen Jay. "Cabinet Museums; Alive, Alive, O!" *Dinosaur in a Haystack: Reflections in Natural History.* Ed. Stephen J. Gould. New York: Crown Publishers, 1995. 238–47.

Graham, Elizabeth. "Schoolmarms and Early Teaching in Ontario." *Women at Work 1850–1930.* Ed. Linda Kealey et al. Toronto: Canadian Women's Educational Press, 1974. 165–209.

Gray, Charlotte. *Mrs. King: The Life & Times of Isabel Mackenzie King.* Toronto: Penguin Books, 1998.

Greenhill, Ralph, and Andrew Birrell. *Canadian Photography 1839–1920.* Toronto: The Coach House Press, 1979.

Groves, Herbert, ed. *Toronto Does Her "Bit."* Toronto: Municipal Intelligence Bureau, March 1918.

Gwyn, Sandra. *The Private Capital: Ambition and Love in the Age of Macdonald and Laurier.* Toronto: McClelland and Stewart, 1984.

Hall, Roger. *A Century to Celebrate 1893–1993: The Ontario Legislative Building.* Toronto: Dundurn Press, 1993.

Hall, Roger, Gordon Dodds, and Stanley Triggs. *The World of William Notman: The Nineteenth Century Through a Master Lens.* Toronto: McClelland & Stewart, 1993.

Harney, Robert F., and Harold Troper. *Immigrants: A Portrait of the Urban Experience, 1890–1930.* Toronto: Van Nostrand Reinhold Ltd., 1975.

Harney, Robert F., ed. *Gathering Place: Peoples and Neighbourhoods of Toronto, 1834–1945.* Toronto: Multicultural History Society of Ontario, 1985.

Harris, Richard. *Unplanned Suburbs: Toronto's American Tragedy 1900 to 1950.* Baltimore: Johns Hopkins Press, 1999.

Hastings, Dr. Charles. *Report of the Medical Health Officer Dealing with the Recent Investigation of Slum Conditions in Toronto, Embodying Recommendations for the Amelioration of the Same.* Toronto: Department of Health, July 1911.

Hiley, Michael. *Seeing Through Photographs.* London: Gordon Fraser, 1983.

Holmes, Oliver Wendell. "The Stereoscope and the Stereograph," *The Atlantic Monthly* vol. 3 (June 1859): 738–748.

Homel, Gene Howard. "Denison's Law: Criminal Justice and the Police Court in Toronto, 1877–1921." *Ontario History* vol. 73 (1981): 171–186.

Honsberger, John D. "E. E. A. DuVernet, KC: Lawyer, Capitalist, 1866 to 1915." *Beyond the Law — Lawyers and Business in Canada, 1830–1930.* Ed. Carol Wilton. Toronto: The Osgoode Society, 1990. 167–200.

Hood, J. William, ed. *Street Railways: Toronto 1861 to 1930.* Toronto: Maps Project, 1999.

Ierley, Merritt. *The Comforts of Home: The American House and the Evolution of Modern Convenience.* New York: Clarkson Potter Publishers, 1999.

Industries of Canada: Historical and Commercial Sketches of Toronto and environs. Toronto: M. G. Bixby & Co., 1886.

Jack Canuck, various years between 1911 and 1918. City of Toronto Archives: Fonds 1125.

Jacobs, Jane. *The Death and Life of the Great American Cities*. New York: Vintage Books, 1961.

Jones, Laura. *Rediscovery: Canadian Women Photographers 1841–1941*. London, Ontario: London Regional Art Gallery, 1983.

Kastner, Nancy. "The Notebooks of His Honour Judge F. M. Morson." *The Law Society Gazette* vol. 15, no. 4 (December 1981): 399–441.

Kealey, Greg, ed. *Canada Investigates Industrialism*. Toronto: University of Toronto Press, 1973.

Kealey, Gregory S. "Printers and mechanization." *Toronto Workers Respond to Industrial Capitalism, 1867–1892*. Ed. Gregory S. Kealey. Toronto: University of Toronto Press, 1978. 83–97.

Kealey, Linda. *Enlisting Women for the Cause: Women, Labour and the Left in Canada, 1890–1920*. Toronto: University of Toronto Press, 1998.

Kelly, Wayne. *Downright Upright: A History of the Canadian Piano Industry*. Toronto: Natural Heritage/Natural History, Inc., 1991.

Kerr, Donald, and Deryck W. Holdsworth, eds. *Historical Atlas of Canada: Addressing the Twentieth Century* vol. 3. Toronto: University of Toronto Press, 1990.

Kilbourn, William. *Toronto Remembered: A Celebration of the City*. Toronto: Stoddart, 1984.

Klein, Alice, and Wayne Roberts. "Besieged Innocence: The 'Problem' and the Problems of Working Women — Toronto 1896–1914." *Women at Work 1850–1930*. Ed. Linda Kealey et al. Toronto: Canadian Women's Educational Press, 1974. 211–259.

Koltun, Lilly. "Pre-Confederation Photography in Toronto." *History of Photography: An International Quarterly* vol. 2, no. 3 (July 1978): 249–263.

Koltun, Lilly, ed. *Private Realms of Light: Amateur Photography in Canada/1839–1940*. Toronto: Fitzhenry & Whiteside, 1984.

Laycock, Margaret and Barbara Myrvold. *Parkdale in Pictures: Its Development to 1889*. Toronto: Toronto Public Library Board, 1991.

Lebr, John C., and H. John Selwood. "The Two-Wheeled Workhorse: The Bicycle as Personal and Commercial Transport in Winnipeg." *Urban History Review / Revue d'histoire urbaine* vol. XXVII, no. 1 (October, 1999): 3–13.

Lemon, James. *Toronto Since 1918: An Illustrated History*. Toronto: James Lorimer & Company, 1985.

Leslie, Genevieve. "Domestic Service in Canada, 1880–1920." *Women at Work 1850–1930*. Ed. Linda Kealey et al. Toronto: Canadian Women's Educational Press, 1974. 71–125.

Litvak, Marilyn M. *Edward James Lennox: "Builder of Toronto."* Toronto: Dundurn Press, 1995.

Lowe, Graham S. "'The Enormous File': The Evolution of the Modern Office in Early Twentieth-Century Canada." *Archivaria* vol. 19 (Winter 1984–85): 137–151.

Lownsbrough, John. The Privileged Few: The Grange & Its People in Nineteenth Century Toronto. Toronto: Art Gallery of Ontario, 1980.

Lundell, Liz. *The Estates of Old Toronto*. Toronto: Boston Mills Press, 1998.

Maciejewski, Andrzej. *After/D'Après Notman*. Toronto: Firefly Books, 2003.

McAree, J. V. *Cabbagetown Store*. Toronto: The Ryerson Press, 1953.

McArthur, Glenn, and Annie Szamosi. *William Thomas: Architect*. Ottawa: Archives of Canadian Art, Carleton University Press, 1996.

McCourt, Bill. *Outline of History of Roads in Toronto*. City of Toronto Archives: Papers & Theses Collection, Box 10, File 4, ca. 1975.

McHugh, Patricia. *Toronto Architecture: A City Guide*. 2nd ed. Toronto: McClelland and Stewart, 1989.

McMurry, Sally. "City Parlor, Country Sitting Room: Rural Vernacular Design and the American Parlor." *Winterthur Portfolio* vol. 20, no. 4 (Winter 1985): 261–280.

McShane, Clay. *Down the Asphalt Path: The Automobile and the American City*. New York City: Columbia University Press, 1994.

Martyn, Lucy Booth. *Aristocratic Toronto: 19th Century Grandeur*. Toronto: Gage Publishing, 1980.

Massey, Raymond. *When I was Young*. Toronto: McClelland and Stewart, 1976.

Middleton, Jesse Edgar. *The Municipality of Toronto: A History*. Toronto: The Dominion Publishing Company, 1923: *passim*.

Mitchell, William J. *The Reconfigured Eye: Visual Truth in the Post-Photographic Era*. Cambridge, Mass.: MIT Press, 1992.

Moore, Christopher. *The Law Society of Upper Canada and Ontario's Lawyers, 1797–1997*. Toronto: University of Toronto Press, 1997: 135–185.

Moore, W. F. "Architectural Photography." *Construction* April 1932: 87–90.

Morrow, Lillian I. *Memories*. City of Toronto Archives: SC 467.

Morton, Desmond. *Mayor Howland: The Citizens' Candidate*. Toronto: Hakkert, 1973.

Mulvany, C. Pelham. *Toronto: Past and Present, A Handbook of the City*. Toronto: W. E. Caiger, Publisher, 1884.

New York Bureau of Municipal Research. "Property Department." *Report on Survey of the Treasury, Assessment, Works, Fire and Property Departments* part 2 of 2, 1913. City of Toronto Archives.

Newhall, Beaumont. *The History of Photography from 1839 to the present day*. New York: Museum of Modern Art, 1964.

Oliver, Andrew. *The Toronto Camera Club: The First Hundred Years*. Toronto: Toronto Camera Club, 1988.

Oliver, Peter. *"Terror to Evil-Doers": Prisons and Punishments in Nineteenth-Century Ontario.* Toronto: University of Toronto Press for The Osgoode Society for Canadian Legal History, 1998: *passim.*

____. "'A Terror to Evil-Doers': The Central Prison and the 'Criminal Class' in Late Nineteenth-Century Ontario." *Patterns of the Past: Interpreting Ontario's History.* Ed. Roger Hall et al. Toronto: Dundurn Press, 1988. 206–237.

Partridge, Larry. *Mind the Doors, Please!: The Story of Toronto and Its Streetcars.* Toronto: Boston Mills Press, 1983.

Patterson, Norman. "Evolution of a Departmental Store." *The Canadian Magazine* 1906: 425–436.

Petroff, Lillian. *Sojourners and Settlers: The Macedonian Community in Toronto to 1940.* Toronto: Multicultural History Society of Ontario, 1995.

Phillips, Sandra S., Mark Haworth-Booth, and Carol Squiers. *Police Pictures: The Photograph as Evidence.* San Francisco Museum of Modern Art, 1997.

Piva, Michael J. *The Condition of the Working Class in Toronto — 1900–1921.* Ottawa: University of Ottawa Press, 1979.

Plumptre, George. "Strange Tale of the Kentia Palm: Exotic Origins of the Ubiquitous Houseplant." *Architectural Digest* October 1995: 90–96.

Pursley, Louis H. *Street Railways of Toronto: 1861–1921.* Los Angeles: Electric Railway Publications, 1958.

Rawling, Bill. *"Technology and Innovation in the Toronto Police Force, 1875–1925."* Ontario History vol. LXXX, no. 1 (March 1988): 53–71.

Report of the Commission of Enquiry. Central Prison Investigation. 1885. Ontario Sessional Papers (No. 26), 1886.

Report of the Commissioners Appointed to Enquire into the Prison and Reformatory System of Ontario, 1891. Toronto: Warwick & Sons, 1891: *passim.*

Richardson, Douglas. *A Not Unsightly Building: University College and Its History.* Toronto: Mosaic Press for University College, 1990.

Richardson, Douglas, and Stephen Otto. *Meeting Places: Toronto's City Halls.* Toronto: The Market Gallery, City of Toronto Archives, 1986.

Riddell, John. *The Railways of Toronto: The First Hundred Years.* Thornhill, Ontario: John Riddell, 1991.

Riis, Jacob. "How the Other Half Lives." *Scribner's Magazine* December 1889: 643–663.

____. *How the Other Half Lives: Studies among the tenements of New York,* with a new preface by Charles A. Madison. New York: Dover Publications, Inc., 1971.

Robertson, John Ross. *Landmarks of Toronto.* 6 volumes. Toronto: Evening Telegram, 1894 to 1914.

Rogers, Nicholas. "Serving Toronto the Good: The Development of the City Police Force 1834–84." *Forging a Consensus: Historical Essays on Toronto.* Ed. Victor L. Russell. Toronto: University of Toronto Press, 1984. 116–40.

Rooney, Frances. *Working Light: The Wandering Life of Photographer Edith S. Watson.* Ottawa: Carleton University Press, 1996.

Rosenblum, Naomi. *A World History of Photography.* 3rd edition. New York: Abbeville Press Publishers, 1997.

Rudofsky, Bernard. *Streets for People: A primer for Americans.* Garden City: Doubleday Anchor Press, 1969.

Russell, Loris S. *A Heritage of Light: Lamps and Lighting in the Early Canadian Home.* Toronto: University of Toronto Press, 1968, reprinted with a new foreword, 2003.

Russell, Victor L. *Mayors of Toronto.* Toronto: Boston Mills Press, 1982.

Rust-D'Eye, George H. *Cabbagetown Remembered.* Toronto: Boston Mills Press, 1984.

Sangster, Joan. "Criminalizing the Colonized: Ontario Native Women Confront the Criminal Justice System, 1920–1960." *The Canadian Historical Review* vol. 80 (March 1999): 32–60.

Sante, Luc. *Evidence.* New York: Farrar, Straus and Giroux, 1992.

Saturday Night, October 12, 1901.

Scadding, Henry. *Toronto of Old: Collections and Recollections.* Toronto: Adam, Stevenson & Company, 1873.

Schlereth, Thomas J. "The World and Workers of the Paper Empire." *Cultural History & Material Culture: Everyday Life, Landscapes, Museums.* Charlottesville: University Press of Virginia, 1992. 145–178.

____. *Victorian America: Transformation in Everyday Life.* New York: Harper Perennial, 1992.

Schwartz, Joan M. "'Records of Simple Truth and Precision': Photography, Archives, and the Illusion of Control." *Archivaria* vol. 50 (Fall 2001): 1–40.

Sekula, Allan. "Photography Between Labour and Capital." *Mining Photographs and Other Pictures 1948–1968: A Selection from the Negative Archives of Shedden Studio, Glace Bay, Cape Breton.* Ed. Benjamin H. D. Buchloh and Robert Wilkie. Halifax: The Press of the Nova Scotia College of Art and Design and The University College of Cape Breton Press, 1983. 193–268.

Severa, Joan. *Dressed for the Photographer: Ordinary Americans and Fashion, 1840–1900.* Kent, Ohio: The Kent State University Press, 1995.

Sewell, John. *Doors Open Toronto: Illuminating the City's Great Spaces.* Toronto: Alfred A. Knopf Canada, 2002.

Sherk, Bill. *The Way We Drove: Toronto's love affair with the automobile in stories and photographs.* Toronto: Boston Mills Press, 1993.

Simmins, Geoffrey. *Fred Cumberland: Building the Victorian Dream*. Toronto: University of Toronto Press, 1997.

Sinclair, Magnus. "'It Was a Long and Bitter Fight....'" Reprinted in *ATU Local 112 1899–1999: 100th Anniversary*. Toronto: ATU, 1999: 18–19 (excerpted from *Motorman & Conductor*, May 1939).

Social Survey Commission of Toronto. Report. September 29, 1915. City of Toronto Archives, Reports Collection, Box 4, Folder 2.

Solomon-Godeau, Abigail. *Photography at the Dock: Essays on Photographic History, Institutions, and Practices*. Minneapolis: University of Minnesota Press, 1991.

Sontag, Susan. *On Photography*. New York: Doubleday Anchor Books, 1977.

———. "The Photographs Are Us: Regarding the Torture of Others." *The New York Times Magazine* 23 May 2004: 24–29, 42.

Sotiron, Minko. "Robertson, John Ross." *Dictionary of Canadian Biography, Vol. XIV 1911–1920*. Toronto: University of Toronto Press, 1998. 876–881.

Speisman, Stephen A. "Fox, Rivka (Rebecca) (Landsberg)." *Dictionary of Canadian Biography, Vol. XIV 1911–1920*. Toronto: University of Toronto Press, 1998. 375.

Stacey, Robert. *The Canadian Poster Book: 100 Years of the Poster in Canada*. Toronto: Methuen, 1979.

Stamp, Robert M. *Bright Lights, Big City: The History of Electricity in Toronto*. Toronto: The Market Gallery of the City of Toronto Archives, 1991.

Strange, Carolyn. *Toronto's Girl Problem: The Perils and Pleasures of the City, 1880–1930*. Toronto: University of Toronto Press, 1995.

———. *Imposing Goodness: Crime and Justice in "Toronto the Good" 1793–1953*. Toronto: The Law Society of Upper Canada and The Market Gallery of the City of Toronto Archives, 1992.

Sufrin, Eileen. *The Eaton Drive: The Campaign to Organize Canada's Largest Department Store 1948 to 1952*. Toronto: Fitzhenry & Whiteside, 1982. 17–32.

Stieglitz, Alfred. "Pictorial Photography." *Scribner's Magazine* vol. 26 (1899): 528–537.

Tagg, John. The Burden of Representation: Essays on *Photographies and Histories*. Minneapolis: University of Minnesota Press, 1993.

T. Eaton Co. Limited. *The 1901 Editions of the T. Eaton Co. Limited Catalogues for Spring & Summer, Fall & Winter*. Toronto: Stoddart, 1970.

Thomas, Alan. *The Expanding Eye: Photography and the Nineteenth-Century Mind*. London: Croom Helm, 1978.

Thompson, Austin Seton. *Jarvis Street: A Story of Triumph and Tragedy*. Toronto: Personal Library Publishers, 1980.

———. *Spadina: A Story of Old Toronto*. Toronto: Pagurian Press, 1975.

Thompson, Octavius. *Toronto in the Camera*. Toronto: O. Thompson, Photographic Publisher, 1868.

Tippett, Maria. *By a Lady: Celebrating Three Centuries of Art by Canadian Women*. Toronto: Penguin Books, 1992.

Toronto Housing Company. *Cottage Flats At Riverdale Courts*. Spring 1915. City of Toronto Archives, Fonds 1018.

Trachtenberg, Alan. *Reading American Photographs: Images as History Mathew Brady to Walker Evans.*

New York: Hill and Wang, Division of Farrar, Straus and Giroux, 1989.

Tung, Anthony M. *Preserving the World's Great Cities: The Destruction and Renewal of the Historic Metropolis*. New York: Clarkson Potter, 2001.

Victorian Era Ball. Toronto: 1898. City of Toronto Archives, rare books collection.

Walden, Keith. *Becoming Modern in Toronto: The Industrial Exhibition and the Shaping of a Late Victorian Culture*. Toronto: University of Toronto Press, 1997.

Ward, Peter. *A History of Domestic Space: Privacy and the Canadian Home*. Vancouver: UBC Press, 1999.

Whyte, William H. City: *Rediscovering the Center*. Garden City: Doubleday, 1988.

Wilson, Barbara M., ed. *Ontario and the First World War 1914–1918: A Collection of Documents*. Toronto: Champlain Society for Government of Ontario, University of Toronto Press, 1977.

Wilton, Carol. "Introduction; Beyond the Law — Lawyers and Business in Canada, 1830–1930." *Beyond the Law — Lawyers and Business in Canada, 1830–1930*. Ed. Carol Wilton. Toronto: The Osgoode Society, 1990. 3–44.

Wodson, Harry M. *The Whirlpool: Scenes from Toronto Police Court*. Toronto: University of Toronto Press, 1917.

Wornum, Enid. *Scrapbook of Toronto Society Functions, 1897–1914*. City of Toronto Archives, Fonds 1557.

Yeigh, Frank. "Ontario's New Parliament Buildings." *The Canadian Magazine* vol. 1, no. 1 (March 1893): 102–109.

Index

The body text within this book was typeset using Sabon, designed by Jan Tschichold in 1967.
Known as a Garamond variation, Sabon was loosely created from a 1592 specimen
of a 14 pt. Roman that was attributed to Claude Garamond.

The photo captions were set in News Gothic. The lighter weights were designed by
Morris Fuller Benton in 1908. A powerful san serif whose bold weights were added in 1958.

The large script letters were set in Andantino, a digital revival of an original font
designed in 1953 by Karl Klauss. Reflecting an era of elegance,
it adds an intended grace to a look at the past.